USEFUL RESEARCH

Useful Research

ADVANCING THEORY AND PRACTICE

Susan Albers Mohrman

Edward E. Lawler III
and Associates

Berrett–Koehler Publishers, Inc.
San Francisco
a BK Business book

Berrett-Koehler Publishers, Inc.
235 Montgomery Street, Suite 650
San Francisco, CA 94104-2916
Tel: (415) 288-0260   Fax: (415) 362-2512   www.bkconnection.com

Ordering Information

QUANTITY SALES. Special discounts are available on quantity purchases
by corporations, associations, and others. For details, contact the "Special
Sales Department" at the Berrett-Koehler address above.

INDIVIDUAL SALES. Berrett-Koehler publications are available through
most bookstores. They can also be ordered directly from Berrett-Koehler:
Tel: (800) 929-2929; Fax: (802) 864-7626; www.bkconnection.com

ORDERS FOR COLLEGE TEXTBOOK/COURSE ADOPTION USE. Please
contact Berrett-Koehler: Tel: (800) 929-2929; Fax: (802) 864-7626.

ORDERS BY U.S. TRADE BOOKSTORES AND WHOLESALERS. Please
contact Ingram Publisher Services, Tel: (800) 509-4887; Fax: (800) 838-
1149; E-mail: customer.service@ingrampublisherservices.com; or visit www
.ingrampublisherservices.com/Ordering for details about electronic ordering.

Berrett-Koehler and the BK logo are registered trademarks of Berrett-Koehler Publishers, Inc.

Printed in the United States of America

Berrett-Koehler books are printed on long-lasting acid-free paper. When it is available,
we choose paper that has been manufactured by environmentally responsible processes.
These may include using trees grown in sustainable forests, incorporating recycled paper,
minimizing chlorine in bleaching, or recycling the energy produced at the paper mill.

Library of Congress Cataloging-in-Publication Data
Useful research : advancing theory and practice / [edited by] Susan Albers Mohrman,
Edward E. Lawler III. — 1st ed.
     p.   cm.
  Includes bibliographical references and index.
  ISBN 978-1-60509-600-1 (hardcover : alk. paper)   1. Management—Research.
     2. Organization—Research.   3. Organizational behavior—Research.
     I. Mohrman, Susan Albers.   II. Lawler, Edward E.
     HD30.4.U82   2011
     302.3'5072—dc22

                                                                          2010038066

First Edition
16 15 14 13 12 11   10 9 8 7 6 5 4 3 2 1

BOOK PRODUCED BY: Westchester Book Group
COVER: Irene Morris
COPYEDITOR: Pat Cattani
INDEXER: Ken DellaPenta

Contents

PART V Putting It All Together

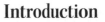

Introduction

SUSAN ALBERS MOHRMAN

AND EDWARD E. LAWLER III

THE PURPOSE OF THIS BOOK is to provide frameworks and evidence-based guidance to scholars interested in doing research that advances both academic knowledge and practice. For us, and for many of the contributors to this book, this topic has been a career-long concern. We believe that the contribution of research to organizational practice is of critical importance in a world where organizations of all kinds are shaping the future and fundamentally impacting the quality of life and the health of societies.

Dual-impact research has been the mission of the Center for Effective Organizations (CEO) at the University of Southern California's (USC's) Marshall School of Business since its founding in 1979. In 1983, we held a workshop of prominent organization and management researchers that resulted in an edited book, *Doing Research That Is Useful for Theory and Practice* (Lawler et al., 1985; reissued with a new foreword and introduction in 1999). Authors wrote chapters, discussed and refined their ideas about useful research at the workshop, and then revised their chapters for the book. Researchers were invited to be part of this project based on their doing research that was useful to theory and practice. The express purpose of that book was to demonstrate the legitimacy and importance of dual-purpose research.

Useful Research: Advancing Theory and Practice revisits the topic of research that is useful for theory and practice. Once again, we assembled prominent researchers, including some authors from the original book. Our purpose was to reexamine this important topic, this time focusing on what has been learned about how to do dual-purpose research. Again, researchers wrote chapters for a workshop, this time held on December 1, 2009. Their chapters were then revised for this book to reflect the exchange that occurred during the workshop.

Today, doing research that addresses theory and practice is *not* the predominant orientation of the fields of management and organizational sciences. If anything, it is less a focus than it was in 1983. There are, however, beacons of hope as a number of leading scholars are intentionally and successfully conducting research that is significantly impacting management and organizations. There have been and continue to be periodic eruptions of voiced concern about the need for research to have a greater impact. Some of these have come from leading scholars such as Sara Rynes, Denise Rousseau, Don Hambrick, and others who have been highly successful in careers based on traditional research. Recently there have been a number of special journal issues and conferences on the topic, and many proposals and initiatives that are intended to bridge the relevance gap between management research and practice have been made. In his 2010 Presidential Address to the Academy of Management, Jim Walsh pointed out that more than half of the last 16 presidents of the Academy have used the occasion of their presidential addresses to emphasize the importance of doing research that contributes to practice, and have decried the lack of impact of prevailing research approaches.

The seemingly low impact of these waves of concern about bridging the gap between research and practice testifies to how deep seated the experienced conflicts are between rigor and relevance, theory and practice, career concerns and societal contribution. A dull murmur in the 1990s about the need for relevance has turned into a more strident advocacy of relevance to practice. Nevertheless, journals remain predominantly oriented toward the status quo, top-level business schools seem unconcerned that their research faculty do not carry out useful research, and entry-level organizational and management researchers continue to publish primarily or exclusively in the traditional research journals. There is a great chasm between the advocates of bridging the gap and the behavior of the many researchers who do not even try to do so and who do not believe it is an important or legitimate issue.

Recounting what is known about the nature of the gap between research and practice is not the major purpose of this book. Others have done so already. Rather, our purpose is to identify and describe research strategies and approaches that simultaneously advance academic and practical knowledge. We believe that research can lead to improvements in practice as well as advances in theoretical understanding. Academic knowledge is advanced when scientific theories, frameworks, and models accurately reflect and lead to greater understanding, explanation, and prediction of individual and organizational behavior. Practical knowledge is advanced when research enables organizations to carry out their purposes more effectively. In our view, the test of whether knowledge is useful to practice is not whether it is "theoretically" impactful—but whether it is actually used and results in improved practice.

The focus of this book is more on the challenge of linking research to practice than on the challenge of linking research to the advancement of theoretical knowledge. This choice should not be taken as a statement that all is well with respect to the latter. Indeed, many advocates of reducing the gap between theory and practice believe that a root cause of the lack of impact of research on practice is that research has not sufficiently advanced theoretical understanding.

Both Andrew Van de Ven (2007) and William Starbuck (2006) have compellingly described the methodological pitfalls of rigorous positivistic research that lead to a false complacency that such research is enhancing the understanding of organizations. They and others (e.g., Daft & Lewin, 2008) have described the tendency for research studies to become increasingly narrow and therefore unable to elucidate complex organizational phenomena. Starbuck has questioned whether our attempts to examine a representative sample to find average relationships through variance-based analyses are in any way informative to organizations that aspire to be excellent. Ongoing debates pit various methodological preferences and perspectives against one another, but these debates among research paradigms are not a major focus of this book. Instead, our focus is on how to do dual-purpose research.

In the opening chapter, we set the stage by discussing the mission of organizational researchers to do research that contributes to theory and practice. We believe that mission stems directly from the societal importance of organizations as well as from the role of professional schools. We examine different perspectives on what this mission means for the practice of and the practitioners of organizational research. We argue that impact can be achieved through a number of research approaches and ways of connecting to practice, and that all are necessary in today's turbulent environment when the very nature of organizations and organizing is experiencing a fundamental change.

The authors in Part I were invited to write chapters because they are carrying out research with the purposes of generating academic knowledge and enabling more effective practice. They describe the choices they make and the tactics they employ in order to accomplish these goals.

Amy C. Edmondson describes her evolving research program at the Harvard Business School's Technology and Operations Unit. She has been looking at the relationship of various team dynamics to outcomes such as medical error rates and quality in health care settings. She stresses the benefits to theory development as well as to practice that come from doing problem-focused research, spending time in the field, and working across boundaries.

Susan Albers Mohrman and Allan M. Mohrman, Jr. describe the longitudinal, collaborative, multicompany research approach that they have used at the Center for Effective Organizations at USC. It starts with an exploratory, grounded approach to understanding a broad problem, such as why companies in the 1990s were reporting that the teaming approaches that worked well in their factories were not working effectively in their engineering and technology units, and what they could do to improve their capacity for cross-functional knowledge work teaming. Using exploratory methodologies in several company sites to formulate a model, they tested the model through a rolling series of multimethod studies, including confirmatory action research.

Lynda Gratton describes a collaborative, multistaged, multimethod research program centered at the London Business School. She and her team started with a general problem that was raised by various companies of how to increase the performance of innovation teams, and moved through several highly participative stages of research to develop and test a model. Both the Mohrman and Gratton chapters describe research programs that include a research stage during which tools and methodologies are developed based on the knowledge that was generated in earlier exploratory and model-building phases of the research.

J. Richard Hackman has done foundational research on behavior in organizations, and the frameworks yielded by his research have had a major impact on practice. In his commentary on Part I, he bemoans the increasing disciplinary nature of scholarship in business schools, its orientation toward narrow, discipline-focused journals, and the distance between research and actual organizational behavior. He extols the advantages of Lewinian action science and calls for inventive ways to conduct fundamental research in context.

In Part II, we hear from four highly respected researchers whose lifeworks have had significant and broad impact on practice. They describe how they approached their careers and research programs in order to have the impact they desire.

Philip Mirvis and Edward E. Lawler describe the latter's transition from very traditional, although field oriented, theory-driven psychology research to the development at the University of Michigan of a multimethod, multidiscipline, longitudinal approach to systematically examining the impact of interventions designed to create high-involvement work systems. They describe their ongoing commitment to research that is able to examine complex organizational problems. For Lawler, this led to his founding and directing the Center for Effective Organizations, which he specifically designed to house useful research.

Shortly before his untimely death, C. K. Prahalad wrote about his research career, in which he spent large amounts of time in the field working with companies and connecting to what he called "the preoccupations" of managers. Through learning about trends and picking up "weak signals," he and his colleagues were able to anticipate, form a point of view, and learn and write about the emerging set of challenges and opportunities to be faced by companies.

Michael Beer describes a career that began in industry but led to the Harvard Business School, where he has worked closely and collaboratively with organizations to apply organizational knowledge that helps them improve their performance. In so doing, he evolved, tested, and published increasingly comprehensive intervention theories and methodologies and a model of high-performance organizations.

In the final chapter of Part II, Michael L. Tushman describes his research career at Columbia University and more recently the Harvard Business School. It is driven by a meta-question that he formulated when he was working as an engineer. The question is how can companies survive fundamental technology transitions. He describes a model that he and his colleagues at several universities have evolved for carrying out action-based executive education programs that are a catalyst to dual-focused research. In these programs, the academics build close relationships with executives that serve as a basis for the identification of important research questions relating to the problems their companies experience. The companies commit to house not only the action projects associated with the executive education programs but also academically oriented research.

Part III explores pathways to practice beyond the standard academic journal publication process that has been the major value stream for academia through time. The first three chapters look at the potential of bridging roles—consultancies, executive PhDs, and organizational development (OD) professionals—bringing academic knowledge to practice. Ruth Wageman recounts the benefits and difficulties of collaborating with consultants from the Hay Group in order to conduct a study of top leadership teams. The goal was to produce knowledge that contributes to academic theory and practitioner-oriented publications that would be a natural conduit to practice. She provides an in-depth account of the collaborative process working across the boundaries of academia and practice.

Ramkrishnan (Ram) V. Tenkasi shares learnings from his experience at Benedictine University teaching in an executive PhD program that equips line managers to become theory-based change agents and researchers in their corporations. He provides a systematic account of the ambidextrous dynamics set up by these scholar practitioners who combine their theoretical and methodological knowledge with the realities and culture of practice in order to address the performance strategies of their companies.

Jean M. Bartunek and Edgar H. Schein discuss the conditions under which OD professionals are conduits of academic knowledge to help organizations achieve their development goals. In their view, their influence does not rely on a diagnostic nor prescriptive presentation of academic knowledge. Rather, such knowledge is infused into the dialogic process by which people in the system, working with the OD professional, think through the issues and take action steps to improve performance. This requires that the OD professional have knowledge of the literature, especially of system dynamics, and is able to learn from the organization as well as enable it to develop.

The importance of cross-boundary relationships for researchers carrying out dual-purpose research and for scholar practitioners bringing academic knowledge to bear on company problems is mentioned in all of the chapters described so far. Generating and applying academic knowledge that is useful for practice requires the development of relationships with practitioners that enable a deep understanding of their world. Wayne F. Cascio describes the active role that professional associations such as the Society for Industrial and Organizational Psychology (SIOP) are playing to build relationships between academics and practitioners and to make academic knowledge accessible to practice. He points out that these relationships provide valuable research opportunities for academics who are willing to invest energy, build relationships, and learn about the world of practice, its interests, and how to communicate with it.

Denise M. Rousseau and John W. Boudreau focus on the need to learn new communication approaches. They suggest that academic knowledge is more accessible to practice if it is communicated using "sticky concepts"—attention grabbing, memorable, and credible—that are useful in enabling practitioners to make better decisions.

George S. Benson takes a look at a particular form of communication—the role of management books. He finds that many of the most popular management books, as measured by sales, do appear to have sticky messages but are not based on systematic research knowledge. He suggests that influential academic researchers impact practice through periodic books that are aimed at particular target audiences and that describe the practical implications of their research streams to date.

In a commentary on Part III, Gary P. Latham reiterates the availability of many ways for academics to better connect their work to practice. Encouraging and rewarding young academics for doing useful research is a key challenge facing the field. He argues that encouragement is the responsibility of senior academic leaders, who must push back on the prevailing norms that have developed in business schools. As he notes, it is the senior academic leaders who hire new faculty and establish tenure expectations and who thus decide what kind of performance is valued.

A panel discussion with practitioners was held at the end of the first day of the workshop, and we present excerpts from it. David Nadler and Ian Ziskin shared their reactions to the preliminary chapters and to the discussion at the workshop, and their own thoughts about relevance to practice. They emphasized the importance of helping practitioners solve problems and of getting beyond jargon and esoteric theory to clearly and efficiently communicate learnings about practice.

Part IV examines the trends in the critical institutions that shape the field—business schools, journals, and the Academy of Management. Thomas G. Cummings recounts the barriers to doing useful research and provides a rather pessimistic view on whether useful research can find a comfortable home in business schools. He sees these schools as being driven by market forces that make them dependent on ratings and prestige that is primarily based on publications in top-level academic outlets.

Sara L. Rynes then counteracts this pessimism by recounting the major forces in the Academy of Management, key management journals, and various academic communities of practice that are encouraging and recognizing the kind of longitudinal, qualitative, problem-oriented research that is advocated in this book. She argues that a high level of prestige and career success is likely to come to academics who do dual-purpose research effectively.

Finally, James O'Toole provides an essay in which he argues that scientific research is not an adequate or even appropriate methodology to use in order to discover useful knowledge for organizations. He believes that business schools should evolve a professional model in which researchers and clinical faculty are equally valued.

Part V takes stock of the themes from the book and the implications for academics who aspire to do research that has an impact on practice and theory. Andrew H. Van de Ven relates the themes of this book to the framework he provided in *Engaged Scholarship* (2007). There he described methodological approaches for conducting multistakeholder collaborations in order to examine important complex problems. He advocates knowledge "arbitrage"—taking advantage of differences in knowledge across participants in order to more fully understand complex problems and to yield theoretical enrichment and advancement. Van de Ven's advice to young scholars is first to practice the basics of sound research with input from stakeholders and then to proceed to more complex, multistakeholder investigations. He is optimistic that following such a course will lead to successful academic careers with impact.

Finally, we lay out two overarching challenges for academics who want to impact practice. The first is to better connect with the complex value stream through which organizations seek useful knowledge. The second is to build the rich personal networks of cross-boundary relationships that are needed to combine knowledge effectively and to ensure the generation of actionable and relevant knowledge. We invited authors to write the chapters for this book based on their ability to address these two challenges. Doing research that has dual purposes requires an expansion of knowledge and capability beyond a solely theoretically driven research program, but it can be done. We believe that young scholars should develop their skills and take advantage of opportunities to broaden their awareness and knowledge of practice, just as the authors of the chapters in this book have done. In this way they will learn to combine their knowledge with knowledge from practice and other disciplines, and to connect effectively to the value stream through which organizational practitioners get knowledge.

REFERENCES

Daft, R. L., & Lewin, A. Y. (2008). Rigor and relevance in organization studies: Idea migration and academic journal evolution. *Organization Science, 19,* 177–183.

Lawler, E., Mohrman, A., Jr., Mohrman, S., Ledford, G., Cummings, T., & Associates. (1999). *Doing research that is useful for theory and practice.* Lanham, MD: Lexington Books. (Original work published 1985)

Starbuck, W. H. (2006). *The production of knowledge: The challenge of social science research.* Oxford: Oxford University Press.

Van de Ven, A. H. (2007). *Engaged scholarship: A guide for organizational and social research.* New York: Oxford University Press.

Walsh, James. (2010). *Embracing the Sacred in our Secular Scholarly World.* Presidential Address to the Academy of Management, August 8, Montreal, Canada.

ONE

Research for Theory and Practice

Framing the Challenge

SUSAN ALBERS MOHRMAN

AND EDWARD E. LAWLER III

ORGANIZATION AND MANAGEMENT researchers have for decades emphasized theory development and testing with little concern for impact on practice.
Why now the increased voicing of concern for relevance? As we look through
the rapidly expanding research literature and listen to the voices that are
advocating change, multiple rationales for closing the gap between research
and practice are apparent. They include instrumental and pragmatic arguments, values-based positions, and methodological and epistemological
arguments. The third rationale is based on the artifactual nature of organizations and the need to understand them in relationship to the purposes
that people have for their organizations. Although these rationales are not
mutually exclusive, each offers a different window on why and how to seek
relevance and make a difference to practice.

In this chapter, we first examine these three rationales for focusing on relevance. We then address their key implication for the conduct of research that
contributes to practice, specifically, the need to bridge multiple communities
of practice. We suggest that relevance depends not only on the content and
focus of the research, but also on how academics position their work in
the broader landscape of actors who generate and develop knowledge to inform organizational practice. Finally, we raise the questions that researchers
need to answer as they build their careers.

Why Relevance?

Instrumental Rationales

Instrumental and pragmatic arguments posit that it is in the self-interest of practitioners and researchers to close the relevance gap, because each will then be better able to accomplish their purposes. For example, evidence-based management—practice that is informed by research-based knowledge—is advocated as leading to greater organizational effectiveness (Rousseau, 2007). Rynes (in press) argues that broad social and economic trends in the environment make it important and advantageous for employers to base their human resources practices on research-based knowledge. As an example, she refers to the legal context that requires organizations to be able to demonstrate the validity of their employment practices. For researchers, there is evidence that closer links to practice provide access to high quality data, and that the amount of researcher time in the field is associated with greater academic citations as well as greater practitioner use of the findings (Rynes, in press).

Society has expectations that professional schools will deliver knowledge that can be used in practice. Funding is increasingly being directed to research involving collaboration with companies and defined in a manner likely to be valuable to practice. Examples include the Advanced Institute of Management initiative (AIM) in the United Kingdom that has funded research expressly designed to be more relevant to policy, competitiveness, and practitioner needs. In the United States, both the National Science Foundation (NSF) and the National Institutes of Health (NIH) have funded university-industry research initiatives with similar purposes. This shaping of research priorities through societal funding mechanisms has been linked to the growing importance of the commercialization of knowledge in today's economy, with a seeming acceptance that knowledge has shifted from a public good to intellectual property and a source of competitive advantage.

This shift in the relationship between science and society also relates to changes in the institutional structures of knowledge generation and application that challenge the privileged position of academic research. The generation of knowledge no longer occurs primarily in universities but rather is happening in a more distributed manner involving many stakeholders (Gibbons et al., 1994). Knowledge is being created in new venues closer to use and application—institutes, temporary consortia, venture companies, and consulting firms, to name a few. Nowotny, Scott, and Gibbons (2003) argue that there is a shift from Mode 1 research—university-based knowledge generation incorporating positivistic epistemologies—to a Mode 2. The latter is characterized by greater institutional and methodological flexibility, co-production among many stakeholders, and greater linkage of knowledge production to application.

Mode 2 knowledge dynamics have become prevalent in the fields of management and organization, where many alternatives to universities—consulting firms, commercial knowledge bundlers, survey researchers, professional societies and consortia—are now providing knowledge that informs practice. Advances in information and communication technology have motivated and enabled a shift to problem-focused research that is no longer defined through the narrow boundaries of disciplines and professions. Practitioners seek information and knowledge relevant to their problems from these many sources and often through new Web-based media that are often disconnected from academia.

One response by university researchers to the changing landscape of organizational knowledge production and consumption is to focus on making their research findings more accessible. The assumption underlying this response is that the work done by academic researchers yields useful knowledge and that the failure is in communication. Researchers are urged to cull through the staggering archives of research and conduct meta-analyses that distill them into clear findings and principles that can be readily shared with practitioners to guide their decisions (Rousseau & McCarthy, 2007; Rousseau, Manning, & Denyer, 2008). Academics are urged to publish practitioner-oriented articles and books and to contribute to Web-based repositories of knowledge that reach practitioners. They are also counseled to write in a compelling and interesting style that captures the minds (through communication based on logos), hearts (through pathos), and consciences (through ethos) of practitioners (Bartunek, 2007, and Van de Ven, 2007, drawing on Aristotle as translated in 1954). As a foundation, academics are urged to have more contact with practitioners to become more aware of their concerns, gain their trust, and establish a relationship with them, so that they will become more capable of crafting research that is useful.

If spending more time with practitioners in the field, learning to write in a compelling manner, and focusing on what we know is useful to practitioners are the keys to doing research that is relevant to practice, then one has to wonder what is keeping academics from doing these things. Pragmatic considerations alone might be expected to motivate academic researchers to close the gap between their research and organizational practice. Yet many who advocate that both academics and practitioners can better achieve their purposes through better connections with practitioners also point to the structural and institutional barriers to such connections. University promotion criteria do not motivate researchers to spend more time in the field, conduct research on relevant topics, and ensure that the knowledge they produce is disseminated to both academic and practitioner users. Journals do not favor the publication of research that can have an impact on practice.

To address an apparent lack of interest by practitioners in most academic research, some advocate measures that would turn management into a profession that depends on and orients itself to a systematic knowledge base. They argue that establishing a professional certification would stimulate greater practitioner attention to research findings, create a greater understanding of research and the principles of management that stem from it, and lead managers to make evidence-based decisions.

Perhaps the most obvious reason for the persistent distance between academic organizational research and organizational practice may be that many academics do not place a value on doing relevant research. The fact that a number of highly respected academics have had very successful careers pursuing dual-purpose research suggests that there are factors beyond institutional barriers that lead to academics not doing useful research. Indeed, those who advocate doing useful research often have a strong values-based argument for doing so.

Values-Based Rationales

Building on personal values, Denise Rousseau, in her 2005 presidential address at the Academy of Management, talked of her early hopes and then disillusionment that the study of organizations would make organizations more fulfilling places to work and eliminate bad management practices (Rousseau, 2006). She argued that academics should develop an evidence-based management infrastructure and build evidence-based management capabilities in order to connect managers with the knowledge they need to become more effective. In Chapter 16, Commentary, Gary P. Latham states that "The narrowing of the scientist-practitioner gap through research that is used by the public warrants attention because we are citizens of this globe first and foremost, and secondarily scientists, practitioners, or scientist-practitioners." He argues that it is unethical for researchers not to communicate to practitioners knowledge that will help organizations become more effective.

Values are also reflected in the choice of topics to be researched. A number of studies demonstrate that even when academia has developed, or thinks it has developed, sound knowledge to guide practice, there is often little connection between this knowledge and the concerns of practice (e.g., Cascio & Aguinis, 2008). Furthermore, it has been pointed out that academia is rarely the source of major organizational innovations (Mol & Birkenshaw, 2009; Pfeffer, 2007). In fact, the advancement of practical knowledge often precedes the generation of associated academic knowledge, putting academics in the position of playing catch-up and not being able to contribute meaningfully to change (Bartunek, 2007; Lawler et al., 1985). Whether this lack of impact on practice is of concern to academics depends on their values, their beliefs about the mission of professional schools, what they feel researchers owe to society, and their personal aspirations for making a difference in the world.

Some researchers argue that since management and organizational studies are applied sciences and are often carried out in professional schools, contribution to practice is inherent in the very definition of good research. In their view, discussions that assume a researcher has to make a choice between doing rigorous research or practice-relevant research are conceptually flawed. Relevance should be a defining characteristic of rigor in the study of organizations (Starkey, Hatcheul, & Tempest, 2009) and should become one of the standards of excellence in the field (Hambrick, 2007; Mohrman et al., 1999).

One of the strongest values-based statements of concern came from Sumantra Ghoshal (2005), who clearly stated that the purpose of researchers in business schools should be to make the world a better place. He pointed out that values are inherent in all theory and research, and he decried not only prevailing methodologies but also the prevailing economics-centric theoretical base underpinning much organizational research. Framing the field in terms of economic models has in his view contributed to a pessimistic view of organizations and people. It also has created a focus on dysfunctions and control, on a self-fulfilling cycle of management behavior based on these pessimistic views, and on research that does not have the potential to make the world a better place. The recent positive organization studies movement tries to set up an alternative to the focus on the sources of dysfunctionality in organizations by conducting research that focuses on positive human dynamics and outcomes. However, it is unclear that this theoretical and empirical focus is associated with a value on the relevance of the research.

Values-based arguments, if internalized, may lead to important changes among academic researchers, including how they spend their time, how they see their responsibility to ensure that knowledge reaches practitioners, and what their criteria are for good research and for the topics they research. Perhaps there may even be changes in the theoretical underpinnings of the field. Our argument in our 1985 book that organizational researchers should be concerned with their impact on theory and practice reflected deep-seated values about the outcomes that define important and good research. How organizations are designed and operate has a fundamental impact on people and society. These values also reflect a belief that organizations are mutable artifacts that can be shaped by knowledge, not simply studied and understood. This perspective has implications for the means—the methodologies and kinds of theories—that should be used to do research.

Organizations as Artifacts Shaped by Practice

Arguments for bridging the gap between research and practice often rest on ontological and epistemological considerations—conceptions of organizations as artifacts that are shaped by practice and associated implications for how organizational knowledge is created and used. According to this view, valuable knowledge can *only* be created when there is a close connection between research and practice. Organizations are not inanimate objects that exist independent of the intentions and understandings of their members. They and their members cannot be studied as subjects in a way that distances the researcher from the context and its participants.

Organizations are socially created and express the purposes of their creators and those who subsequently design and implement their ongoing changes. Organizational and management researchers are not studying stable entities with stable characteristics and dynamics, but rather continually unfolding social systems whose characteristics and dynamics result from the decisions and activities of their members. Practitioners do not respond to "prescriptions" from academic studies as if they are in some sense "right"— but rather in the context of what they are trying to accomplish, the many factors they are considering in the course of carrying out their practice, and the needs of a particular situation (Chia, 2004; Emirbayer & Mische, 1998; Jarzabkowski, 2005).

Starkey, Hatcheul, and Tempest (2009) also point out that methodologies that assume stability are not appropriate for organizations because management is a relatively new practice area that is pre-paradigmatic and new forms of organization are continually being created. In their view, organizational research should focus on new models of organization, since the world we all live in is being shaped by the way businesses decide to operate. Simon (1969) and others (Avenier, 2010; Mohrman, Mohrman, & Tenkasi, 1997; Romme, 2003; Van Aken, 2005) have argued for synthetic rather than analytic approaches to study artifacts and for methods that yield knowledge that contributes to solutions and designs relevant to organizational problems. An organization design orientation requires research to be situated in the organizational context and to apply interdisciplinary knowledge, and multimethod, multilevel approaches that can capture the complexity of the phenomena and the purposes of the various actors. Because these purposes are often in conflict, organizational research necessarily has an ethical element (see also Scherer, 2009; Willmott, 2003). Methodologies must be capable of taking into account the viewpoints, values, and intentionality of the stakeholders.

The adaptive research framework (described more fully in Chapter 6, Rigor and Relevance in Organizational Research) used in the Quality of Worklife

(QWL) research program that was conducted at the University of Michigan in the 1980s (Lawler, Nadler, & Cammann, 1980; Seashore et al., 1983) is an example of an approach that recognized the dynamic and continually changing nature of organizations. It systematically studied organizations that were intentionally changing to become high-involvement systems—work systems designed to yield high performance by providing the workforce with greater knowledge and skills, information, power, and rewards. At the core of these studies was a belief that organizational research should yield knowledge about how organizations can be more effective for their various stakeholders. Interventions to alter the work systems were carefully studied by a team of researchers to test their underlying theories and to determine their effectiveness. The methodology involved tracking changes and their impact, including those that were being introduced through intentional interventions, by longitudinally measuring many aspects of each complex system at multiple levels and using multiple methodologies. This approach aimed at both theory development and practical impact.

The arguments for bridging the gap between research and practice, whether based on pragmatics, values, or epistemology, suggest use of research approaches that differ from the traditional university-centered, discipline-based, positivistic approaches that have constituted the prevailing scientific model. Perhaps the most daunting challenge facing academics who aspire to doing research that impacts organizational practice is to connect with organizational practitioners and other stakeholders who represent different communities of practice. The next section discusses some of the elements of this challenge.

Bridging Multiple Communities of Practice

Core to almost all discussions of the relationship between academic research and organizational practice is that they are two very distinct knowledge and practice communities. The academic community typically develops and publishes theoretically framed generalizable knowledge based on rigorously peer-reviewed research. Organizational practitioners develop and refine knowledge in the course of solving problems and addressing challenges to accomplish their purposes in a particular setting. Each community develops its own language and frameworks of knowledge, its own methodologies for creating and applying knowledge, and its own standards of relevance and rigor. Indeed, the gap between theory and practice—which might be more accurately described as the gap between academic research practitioners and organizational practitioners—stems in part from the different communication systems, ways of knowing, purposes, and criteria for making decisions in the two communities of practice.

At one extreme, academics claim that these two specialized social systems are necessarily self-referential and that the communication elements of one cannot be integrated into the communication system of the other (Kieser & Leiner, 2009). It is therefore impossible for academics, even if they work closely with practitioners, to develop knowledge that is relevant to organizational practice. Other academics, while recognizing that the two communities have different communication systems, believe that each practice-based communication system represents partial knowledge and is incomplete in addressing complex problems. A pluralism is therefore required to investigate complex problems and yield actionable knowledge (Pettigrew, 2005; Van de Ven & Johnson, 2006).

As is pointed out by Van de Ven and Johnson (2006), most discussion of the relationship of theoretically based academic knowledge to practical knowledge concerns how academic knowledge can contribute to practice. Indeed, many advocates of bridging the gap assume that practical knowledge derives from research knowledge, and not the other way around. This perspective seems to ignore the fact that any empirically based theoretical knowledge of organizations stems from studies of the knowledge of organizational practice in action and is inevitably influenced by the current state of practical knowledge.

Many recent discussions of relevance acknowledge that the knowledge loop must go in both directions in order for academic research to have an impact (e.g., Bartunek, 2007; Pfeffer, 2007; Weick, 1995). Even those who view the movement of knowledge as following a linear path from rigorous academic knowledge generation to practice often recommend that researchers learn enough about practice to contribute to approaches that help introduce such knowledge into practitioner decision making. They view this as critical to dissemination and adoption. For academic knowledge to influence organizational practice, it must be appropriated by organizational settings that also have their own legitimate and pragmatically tested knowledge (e.g., Rousseau, 2006).

Organizational practitioners act on the basis of empirically developed, even if not systematically rigorous, local theories. Organizational practices also have developed their own systematic, local-knowledge creation mechanisms, such as variance and root cause analysis, cost-benefit analysis, and other local research activities. Rousseau posits that the ideal would be for organizational practitioners to make decisions based both on what she refers to as "E" (evidence from generalizable organizational research findings) and as "e" (evidence from local analysis). This suggests that researchers generate evidence that can be combined with local knowledge.

The view that generating actionable knowledge about complex phenomena requires combining the knowledge from different knowledge communities rather than a linear view that academic research knowledge should inform practice sets a high hurdle for bridging the gap. Awareness and familiarity that allow researchers to better transfer knowledge to practitioners are not sufficient. Phenomena cannot be fully understood from any one knowledge perspective because each is partial—limited by the narrow framework within which it operates.

Academic disciplines and subdisciplines, in particular, become increasingly narrowly focused through time (e.g., March, 2004)—and perhaps more distant from the phenomena they purport to understand—as they are shaped by journals that reflect the particular interests and theoretical focuses of the community that forms around them (Daft & Lewin, 2008). Organizational practitioners operate with context-specific knowledge, much of which is tacit and intuitive, and not easily accessible to academics. Advancing organizational knowledge that impacts practice occurs at the intersection of different practices—an intersection that has to be carefully built by the participants.

In our 1985 book we posited that contributing to the advancement of both practice and theory requires combining the knowledge of multiple academic disciplines and the knowledge of practice. We advocated for the diversity of understanding and exploration that is provided not only by multiple disciplines but also through the use of multiple methods, examining phenomena at multiple levels of analysis, and studying diverse practice settings. Similarly, Van de Ven and Johnson (2006) point out the value of knowledge arbitrage and the value of variation in the theories, methods, and knowledge brought to bear in learning about important problems.

The challenges of communicating and combining knowledge are present not only between academics and organizational practitioners; they are also present among academics from different disciplines who apply different theories and frameworks to the study of organizations. In the hard sciences the same challenges exist. For example, physicists, chemists, and material scientists working together to examine nano-scale phenomena take two years or more to learn enough about each other's frameworks to be able to combine knowledge (Mohrman & Wagner, 2006). Yet all of these scientists operate from a positivistic epistemology and value the rigor of theoretically driven empirical research. When it comes to organizations, throwing into the mix the tacit and experience-based knowledge from organizational practice adds to the difficulty of knowledge combination.

There is evidence that social familiarity and working relationships provide a foundation for the transfer of existing knowledge and the combination of knowledge to create new knowledge (e.g., Brown & Duguid, 1991). Thus those who advocate increased relevancy prescribe that researchers spend time in the field to develop deep and lasting relationships that continually inform their academic perspectives with the perspectives and knowledge of practice.

Key Questions for Researchers

The first relevance question that organizational researchers must answer is whether they aspire to connect their research to organizational practice. We believe that often this question is not even asked. Young researchers are socialized in PhD programs that do not make this option salient nor encouraged. Some researchers pursue careers in which they believe they are investigating important topics and impacting practices, only to realize eventually that their work has not reached practitioners or is not appreciated by them. Impacting practice demands intentional decisions about one's research practice and the gradual building of the resources and capabilities to do so.

If researchers aspire to impact organizational practice, the key questions they must ask and answer include: How might my research impact organizational practice? What kind of research questions should I ask? How can the knowledge from my research reach and influence practitioners? How should I conduct research if I want it to influence organizational practice? How do I learn to do this kind of research? We briefly visit each of these questions in the following sections and thereby introduce some of the major themes that are further developed in this book.

How Does Research Impact Organizational and Management Practice?

For research to impact practice, it has to provide knowledge useful to practitioners as they try to solve problems at hand and perform effectively in a particular context. They are guided primarily by experience-based knowledge that is shaped by the communities of practice in which they exist. Academics, shaped by their own communities, often conduct research that they believe will solve theoretical problems and lead to high-quality publications. The problems being addressed by practitioners in the organizations they study and write about are often irrelevant to academics.

Even when couching research in terms of results that they assume characterize an organization's purposes—such as performance levels, productivity, and utility—academic researchers may find that their theories and empirical results are not compelling to practitioners. Practitioners respond to an ongoing and equivocal stream of events and make decisions based on a broad set of criteria, including their impact on the organizational social system of which they are a part (Latham & Whyte, 1994; Rynes, in press). Researchers may design a study to discover how particular variables influence profitability, while practitioners may have to worry about how those variables (and many others) also influence other outcomes, such as the well-being and commitment of employees and the company reputation.

Given the complexity of the world of organizational practice, what can researchers contribute to practice? One possibility is that the work of academics can contribute to evidence-based management (Rousseau, 2006). It can help organizational practitioners make decisions that take into account the *evidence:* the "expanding research base on cause-effect principles underlying human behavior and organizational actions" (Rousseau, 2006, p. 256). Similarly, Locke (2002) advocates the transfer to practice of *principles* that are fundamental truths that have been inductively discovered.

Researchers can make practitioners aware of evidence and principles, but there is no certainty that they will act on them. We know that awareness alone does not always change behavior and that practitioners are looking for actionable knowledge that addresses the problems they experience. Addressing what should be taught to students in the classroom, Rousseau (2006, p. 266) suggests that teaching *solutions* should complement the teaching of cause-effect principles in order to have the best chance of leading to application. Formulating solutions is only possible if academics are versed in the problems that practitioners face. Knowledge gleaned from academic research can be transferred to practice in the form of artifacts—*tools, frameworks,* and *decision aides* that embody knowledge from research and connect to the ongoing decisions that practitioners make (Hodgkinson & Rousseau, 2009; Rousseau & Boudreau, Chapter 14, Sticky Findings, this book).

An opposing argument is that academic research is not suited to generate "facts" or "solutions" for organizational practice. In order to transfer knowledge, academics should provide *ways of framing problems* that stimulate practitioners to think about and approach their tasks and decisions differently (Nicolai & Seidl, 2010; March, 2004). This method of impact may face hurdles beyond a straightforward notion of transfer of knowledge. Organizational practitioners have to find the knowledge compelling enough that they are willing and able to step out of the logic of their own practice, reflect on it, and change it.

Members of practice communities deal with "matters at hand" and may even be unaware of the principles that govern them because the logic of their practice is implicit in their actions (Bourdieu, 1977). Efforts, including those of researchers and of the practitioners themselves, to model that logic are likely to change or distort it. The very process of research necessarily results in new representations of the phenomena in question.

Connecting sufficiently to the logic in practice so that research knowledge can contribute to changing it requires active engagement with the practitioners whose practice is being impacted, and who have to develop their own new representations. This nexus is clearly demonstrated in Chapter 8, Making a Difference *and* Contributing Useful Knowledge, by Michael Beer. He describes his approach to creating academic knowledge while bringing academic frameworks to bear on organizational transformation efforts. Managers in the companies he studies are involved in modeling and developing new representations of their system and new approaches to solving its problems. Indeed, the field of organization development, which was once guided primarily by an external diagnostic process that led to the formulation of solutions based on academic knowledge, has changed to become more of a dialogic process in which academic knowledge is only one of the elements of the development work in the organization (see Chapter 12, Organization Development Scholar-Practitioners).

Academic knowledge may achieve the biggest impact when it is relevant to discontinuities that are being experienced by organizations. It is then that they may be most open to new ways of perceiving and acting. The knowledge that is produced can connect to the self-designing activities that occur at such a time. Self-designing is a continual process in organizations as members adjust their activities to address the challenges they face. For the most part these adjustments result only in incremental changes within the overall logic of their practice. Periodically more fundamental shifts are required to address the problems and challenges that an organization faces. In Chapter 7, Can Relevance and Rigor Coexist?, Prahalad described his research career, where he achieved impact by being very close to the problems that organizations were experiencing and by anticipating the big changes that would require new frameworks and knowledge.

Researchers who aspire to careers that influence practice have to develop a perspective on *how* they intend to do so. As is demonstrated in many of this book's chapters, there are a number of approaches to influencing the frameworks, decisions, and actions of practitioners. Actionable knowledge contributes to the ability of organizational actors to redesign the system of practice or their roles within it to accomplish their purposes (Argyris & Schon, 1989; Mohrman, Gibson, & Mohrman, 2001). To be actionable, academic knowledge has to be combined with knowledge of practice and with other knowledge bases that are relevant to understanding the complex problems faced by organizations. They often involve many interacting subsystems and have dynamics far beyond the focus of any particular theory or principle. Achieving relevance requires researchers to consider how they fit into this big picture.

Asking Research Questions That Can Impact Practice

Recent studies have shown that the topics researchers choose to study and the questions they ask are often not well aligned with practitioner concerns. Lack of impact on practice may result as much from what topics are studied as from the failure to make research-based knowledge available, salient, and compelling to practitioners. Research shows that Academy of Management members often miss the opportunity to bridge the gap between research and practice because of the topics that they research (Shapiro, Kirkman, & Courtney, 2007, p. 249).

Most research articles build on the knowledge of previous articles and often simply extend investigations in ways that may more fully develop a theory but do not broaden the understanding of organizations and how they operate. Journal editors' preoccupation with theory, in the eyes of some, precludes the publishing of descriptive work that might form the basis for extending organizational understanding into important new areas (Hambrick, 2007). Current discipline-based positivistic methodologies often constrain the questions that are investigated and limit the value of research. Starbuck (2006), for example, argues that the assumptions of stability and the pursuit of generalizable findings that underpin variance-based research designs lead to the study of uninteresting and commonplace phenomena, and often lead to erroneous findings. He argues that these methodologies are not suitable for understanding the dynamic and complex world of organizations. In his view, researchers should spend more time on predictive research and on research based on intentional change interventions rather than on the naturally occurring flow of events. Starbuck's argument is reminiscent of Lewin's (1948) observation that the best way to understand a social system is to try to change it. Both Starbuck (2006) and McKelvey (2006) argue that current methodologies are generally geared to answering questions about "average" relationships—and that this does not produce information useful to organizations, none of which want to be average. They each propose that we should spend more time studying exceptional organizations to find out what enables them to excel.

Van de Ven (2007) stresses the value of involving practitioners in the selection of research questions. If researchers want the knowledge they create to be relevant to organizational practice, the questions they ask should be formulated in connection to real problems that are being experienced in practice. He focuses especially on "big problems" and argues that today's complex problems cannot be addressed by narrow disciplines. As a consequence, he argues for including perspectives from practice and different academic disciplines in the problem definition phase and in the formulation of research questions.

Contributions to practice might be more likely if researchers think of the impact they would like to have with a program of research rather than focusing on a single study (Mohrman et al., 2007; Van de Ven, 2007). Through a series of related studies, researchers can collaborate with a variety of organizations and researchers from other disciplines, apply multiple theories, and home in on the best understanding of the complex problems and phenomena in question. The QWL studies in Michigan operated in this manner, drawing on the knowledge of dynamic teams of interventionists and researchers who were conducting related studies in multiple organizations, each of which wanted to put in place more effective work systems. These studies brought to bear current academic knowledge from several fields and looked at each organizational context in detail using multiple methods of data collection and different levels of analysis. The research team, working with the interventionists, managers, and union representatives, incorporated learning from each organization in the questions it asked as it proceeded to the next. Together they generated and tested a remarkably robust framework for designing high-involvement work systems that has been used by many organizations over the years (Seashore et al., 1983).

The chapters in this book by Edmondson (Chapter 2, Crossing Boundaries to Investigate Problems in the Field), Mohrman and Mohrman (Chapter 3, Collaborative Organization Design Research at the Center for Effective Organizations), and Gratton (Chapter 4, A Ten-Year Journey of Cooperation) offer examples of research programs that proceed through phases. The studies in each phase yield knowledge but also make the researchers aware of other questions that have to be answered in order to develop a fuller understanding and ability to address important organizational problems.

Pathways to Practice

Asking questions that are relevant to organizational problems does not ensure impact on practice. Research knowledge still has to be made accessible through pathways that lead to awareness, interpretation, and assimilation by practitioners. For knowledge to be used, it must be interpreted and contextualized by the various actors in a network of practice. Change in organizations rarely occurs as the result of the activities of a single person or team. In most cases, it occurs through complex networks of people, knowledge flow, and activities that are internal and external to the organization (Mohrman, Tenkasi, & Mohrman, 2003). Thus, in order to impact practice, academics must find their place in a broad network of influence.

Academic research may have a direct impact on practice in those organizations that participate in a study. These organizations typically receive feedback. In the process, they may engage in dialogue to interpret the findings and may learn by designing new approaches to take advantage of the knowledge from the study (Mohrman, Gibson, & Mohrman, 2001). This stage in the process might be considered the first test of whether knowledge is actionable. But a broader impact on practice occurs only when knowledge pathways that make the knowledge more widely accessible are built. One can conceptualize the pathways to practice as an expanded linear flow of knowledge to practice or as movement and exchange of knowledge among stakeholders in a complex multidirectional network. These are briefly described below:

An expanded linear value stream for organizational knowledge. Figure 1.1 depicts the linear knowledge stream that implicitly underlies many discussions of bridging the gap between academic research and practice. The assumption is that knowledge emanates from the different disciplines of academia. This depiction departs from the assumptions of many organizational researchers in that organizational and management research is regarded as practice and application oriented and as building on basic research knowledge from different social science disciplines. This view fits with Simon's (1969) notion that the organizational research that occurs in professional schools should aim at utilizing the abstract knowledge of basic discipline research to inform designing and managing organizations. It is also consistent with the notion from medical schools of differentiating between basic and clinical researchers. A similar differentiation was suggested for business schools by Jim O'Toole and Warren Bennis (Bennis & O'Toole, 2005; O'Toole, 2009; also described in James O'Toole, Chapter 20, On the Verge of Extinction, this book). They decry the fact that the extreme discipline orientation of business schools results in research that does not reflect the systemic character of organizations. Differentiating between those doing basic discipline research and those doing research aimed at practice is controversial. This assumption is not necessary to the core notion introduced in Figure 1.1 that there is an increasingly diverse value stream between academic research and organizations.

It should be pointed out that researchers interested in organizations can position themselves at any of the stages of this value stream and at more than one position. Researchers should consider how close to practice they want to be—and this should be congruent with the amount of influence they want to have on practice.

Most commentators on the gap between academia and organizational practice agree that practitioners are not likely to read academic journal articles. These articles are the primary way that academic communities of practice formalize and share their knowledge, but they are not a pathway to influence practice. To be useful, academic knowledge must be embodied in

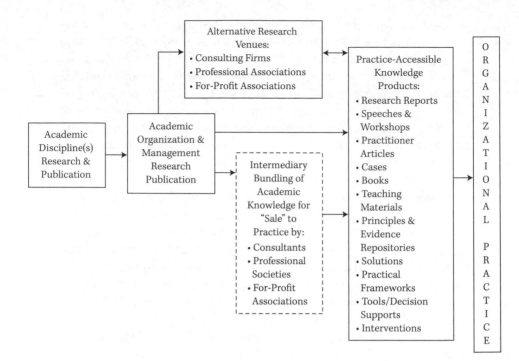

FIGURE 1.1 Linear View of the Knowledge Stream

practice-accessible forms. Some of the forms listed on Figure 1.1, such as the dissemination of research reports and the creation of teaching materials and cases, are consistent with the traditional role of academics, although the extent to which the viewpoints and knowledge of organizational practice are taken into account in preparing these varies greatly. Ironically, teaching materials and cases often do not even focus on research-based knowledge (Rousseau, 2006).

Most researchers do not package their knowledge in forms that are practice accessible. They do not create tools and solutions, planned interventions in organizations, or practitioner-oriented articles, workshops, and speeches. Practice-accessible packaging of research knowledge does not take place in part because these activities are time consuming and difficult, require awareness well beyond the confines of theory and empirical research, and are not rewarded by many universities.

We should not underestimate the extent to which the activities involved in making research knowledge practice-accessible require a transformation of the knowledge. As an example, Bartunek (2007) has noted that academics study how change occurs, whereas practitioners are interested in how they can change an organization. For knowledge gathered to answer the academic question to be useful to practice, it has to be reframed in terms of what practitioners can do that promotes desired change.

In a 1998 presentation at the Academy of Management meeting, Kathleen Eisenhart, an academic that has influenced both theory and practice, described the differences in how she cast the results from her study of decision making in high-velocity environments for an academic article in *Administrative Science Quarterly* and for a practitioner article in the *Harvard Business Review*. In the former, she aggregated her cases to test and advance theory through the use of rigorous research methods. In the latter, she described particular cases and practices and presented action recommendations.

Transforming academic knowledge so that it is accessible to practitioners is time consuming. It requires substantial contact with the organizational practice community in order to gain insight into the way knowledge is created in practice and how practitioners respond to and incorporate academic knowledge. Academics may choose not to get engaged in these activities and hope that their knowledge will be transformed and disseminated by others in a way that can impact practice. In some rare instances, this transformation does occur. The middle box in Figure 1.1 shows intermediate "bundling" of knowledge by consultants, professional societies, and for-profit membership organizations. These translaters are presumably knowledgeable about the world of practice and may be knowledgeable enough about the results of academic research to turn them into practice-accessible products and services.

Both the direct pathway from academic research to practice-accessible knowledge and the indirect pathway through translaters require that the academic knowledge has the potential to be described in a way that is perceived as relevant and useful to organizational practitioners who are trying to improve practice. One piece of evidence that academic research may not be perceived that way is that increasingly practitioners are going to other sources for external knowledge. Consistent with the notion of Mode 2 knowledge production, alternatives for knowledge creation are springing up. Often they are much closer to practice, investigate problems of high interest and import, and rapidly provide knowledge that practitioners feel is actionable. Groups that started as intermediaries between academic knowledge and practice—consulting firms, professional societies, and for-profit organizations—are increasingly positioning themselves as conducting research and providing research services. Often, their research would not be viewed by academics as rigorous and theoretically driven, but it is viewed by many practitioners as accessible and actionable.

In some cases, consulting firms team with academics to do dual-purpose research. The consulting firms support rigorous research that will be published by the academics in research journals while intending to turn the knowledge into intellectual property and consulting products. Consortia of companies are also partnering with academics to investigate problem areas in which they share an interest. Wayne F. Cascio, in Chapter 13, Professional Associations, describes several practitioner and practitioner/academic professional societies that play active roles in shaping and supporting research projects with input and participation from both groups. They also are spearheading the creation of practitioner-friendly articles and tools embodying academic knowledge. Even when partnering with these downstream stakeholders, academics must be sufficiently knowledgeable about organizational practice to generate knowledge in areas relevant to organizational problems—and to know how the knowledge they generate relates to other participants' knowledge.

The complex multidirectional network of knowledge creation. As consortia, consulting firms, professional associations, organizations, and knowledge services groups become involved in doing research and applying research knowledge, the knowledge value stream is best conceptualized as a network of diverse knowledge-related activities with knowledge exchange occurring in all directions. Figure 1.2 provides a less linear (and more idealized) view of a network of connections between academic research and practice. It shows the knowledge of different stakeholders being combined during multistakeholder problem-oriented research and along the value stream to yield and disseminate knowledge. This combinatorial knowledge network fits with the notions of engaged scholarship and adaptive research, and with the characterization of organizational and management research as design sciences. The knowledge of organizational practice is incorporated into the organization and management research process, which is now framed as a combinatorial process focused on problems of mutual interest to academia and practice.

Ideally this network of organizational knowledge results in research that identifies problems, asks questions, uses credible methodologies and yields knowledge relevant to understanding an issue from the viewpoint of organizational practice. As research programs unfold over time, the knowledge of each community of practice increases and altered practice and academic knowledge inform the ongoing investigation of the problem area. Theories are enriched and advanced because they more aptly connect to the evolving nature of practice in complex, dynamic organizations. Even the nature of the problems changes as practice is informed by the knowledge that is developed and as new solutions and designs are put into place. A research program may lead to new designs that incorporate the knowledge from multiple practices and that enrich each practice's knowledge base in an iterative manner.

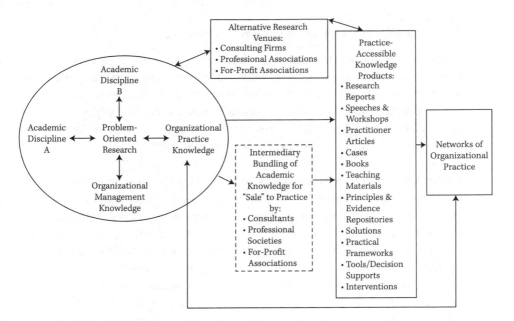

FIGURE 1.2 The Knowledge Network

Broad dissemination is a challenge even within this network view. Many organizations do not actively participate in research programs and do not have the opportunity to learn experientially from them. Practice-accessible knowledge products and services that can reach a more general organizational audience are still required. Figure 1.2 depicts the diverse pathways and actors that reflect today's world of organizational knowledge production and dissemination. It includes alternative research venues such as consulting firms that do research and create knowledge close to practice. These Mode 2 knowledge producers may well continue to hone their research skills and build an increased capacity to provide knowledge that is valid in the context of practice.

Academics interested in having an impact on practice might consider establishing partnerships and involving consultants and other professional service providers in the multistakeholder problem-oriented research process. Engaging with these intermediaries can bring important knowledge to the research process because their business practices often involve close connections to organizational practice and deep expertise in bringing external knowledge to organizations and creating accessible knowledge products.

Methodologies for Connecting Research to Practice

It is beyond the scope of this chapter to deal in depth with methodologies for carrying out research in a manner that involves connection to practice and for operating further along the value stream to create knowledge products that enable organizational practitioners to transform that knowledge into applications. We will briefly mention some recurring themes from the literature, in order to give the reader a sense of what is required.

Participation and collaboration. A great deal of the literature about bridging the gap calls for academic researchers to develop deeper relationships with practitioners and for active practitioner involvement in research. Van de Ven does an excellent and insightful job of describing four approaches to engaged scholarship, which he defines as participative research "for obtaining the different perspectives of key stakeholders (researchers, users, clients, sponsors and practitioners) in studying complex problems" (2007, p. 9). The four approaches are (1) basic research that is informed by knowledge from other stakeholders; (2) collaborative research (also called co-production in other current discussions of research and practice); (3) design/evaluation research that entails eliciting and studying new designs and practices; and (4) action/intervention research that is concerned with applying and generating knowledge in the process of solving the problem of a particular client. There is a literature about each of these approaches. Van de Ven delves into the various methodological approaches for conducting engaged research, including engaged approaches to formulate problems, develop theory, design studies, and communicate research results.

Knowledge combination. The importance of combining knowledge effectively in the course of a research project is a second major theme. Van de Ven refers to the process of knowledge arbitrage—benefiting from the differences in perspective and knowledge of different participants — when trying to understand a complex problem. Combining theoretical knowledge from different disciplines with knowledge from practice is required to guide research and yield research findings that apply to complex, dynamic, artifactual phenomena such as organizations. Knowledge combination requires familiarity with each other's knowledge and building conceptual bridges such as prototypes or other boundary objects to link the knowledge bases.

Studying problems in context. The need to bring context into organizational research is a common theme. Whereas academics tend to ignore or to control for contextual information that is viewed as irrelevant to the theory and variables of interest, practitioners have to understand and reinterpret abstract knowledge in context in order to act. Organizational members look for contextual similarity in determining whether knowledge from research can be applied in their setting. Rich case descriptions, for example, may provide the detail needed by organizational practitioners to evaluate whether and how otherwise abstract academic knowledge may be applied to their situation.

More prediction, less retrospection. Because organizations are shaped by members' actions and decisions taken to achieve their desired outcomes, research may be most useful if it points to new ways of organizing that can change the dynamics of the organization and its outcomes. Researchers often employ cross-sectional methodologies to find out what patterns of relationships currently exist, rather than what would happen if the organization changed the way it operated. The best understanding and most rigorous test of theory often comes from changing the organization while predicting and then studying the impact of the change, and organizations are most likely to be open to new frameworks and practices during times when they are faced with transitions. New organizing approaches and designs may result, along with the contextual understanding of when they are appropriate.

Implications and the Flow of This Book

Those concerned with bridging the gap between academic research and practice differ in the extent to which they feel that to do so will require fundamental change. Some believe it can be done within the prevailing positivistic paradigm, whereas others argue for a fundamentally different way of doing research. The former advocate greater researcher awareness of the interests and needs of organizational practitioners and more effective communication of research findings to practitioners. They also advocate the professionalization of management so that managers will pay attention to research-based evidence. At the other end of the continuum are those who advocate a more constructivist way of doing research—one that brings practitioners into the research process more fully, combines the knowledge of both communities in pursuing new knowledge, and solves problems and discovers new ways of organizing.

Both these views call for new research skills, spending time differently, and conducting research differently. In either case, a key question remains: How do researchers who have been trained by faculty who are unconcerned with bridging the gap and who are in institutions that do not reward or value doing so learn to carry out more connected research? How will they come to feel that this is a legitimate route to take?

Some claim that connected research must happen in institutional settings that exist expressly for this purpose and where there are role models, mentors, and rewards for creating knowledge that is useful and used in practice. Others argue that universities should change their performance criteria and explicitly place value on doing research that is useful. Another suggestion is for researchers' careers and research programs to be "full-cycle" (Chatman, 2005)—to alternate between observation-based and manipulation-based research thus bridging the gap by going back and forth across it (Tranfield & Starkey, 1998).

This book has been crafted by the editors and authors as a resource to academics aspiring to do dual-purpose research. The chapters in Part I, Exemplars of Useful Research, and Part II, Bodies of Work That Have Influenced Theory and Practice, provide examples of research programs and research careers that are characterized by dual-purpose research. These concrete examples provide a sense for the different strategies that a researcher can adopt to have a research career that impacts practice. Part III, Pathways, illuminates a number of possible pathways through which academic knowledge can connect to practice and provides scholars with a sense of how they might use these various pathways. The chapters in Part IV, Barriers and Enablers, describe some of the institutional factors that provide a context for choices about crafting research. Part V, Putting It All Together, provides overview frameworks that should be useful to young scholars as they consider how to position themselves with respect to organizational and management knowledge creation.

REFERENCES

Argyris, C., & Schon, D. A. (1989). Participatory action research and action science compared: A commentary. *American Behavioral Scientist, 32*(5), 612–623.

Aristotle. (1954). *Rhetoric* (W. R. Roberts, Trans.) New York: Modern Library.

Avenier, M-J. (2010). Construction and use of generic knowledge in organization science viewed as a science of the artificial. *Organization Studies, 31,* 1229–1255.

Bartunek, J. M. (2007). Academic-practitioner collaboration need not require joint or relevant research: Toward a relational scholarship of integration. *Academy of Management Journal, 50*(6), 1325.

Bennis, W. G, & O'Toole, J. (2005). How business schools lost their way. *Harvard Business Review,* 96–104.

Bourdieu, P. (1977). *Outline of a theory of practice.* Cambridge: Cambridge University Press.

Brown, J. S., & Duguid, P. (1991). Organizational learning and communities of practice: Toward a unified view of working, learning, and innovation. *Organization Science, 2*(1), 40–57.

Cascio, W. F., & Aguinis, H. (2008). Research in industrial and organizational psychology from 1963 to 2007: Changes, choices, and trends. *Journal of Applied Psychology, 93*(5), 1062.

Chatman, J. (2005). Full-cycle micro-organizational behavior research. *Organization Science, 16*(4), 434–447.

Chia, R. (2004). Strategy-as-practice: Reflections on the research agenda. *European Management Review, 1*, 29–34.

Daft, R. L., & Lewin, A. Y. (2008). Perspective: Rigor and relevance in organization studies: Idea migration and academic journal evolution. *Organization Science, 19*(1), 177–183.

Eisenhardt, K. M. (1998). *Powerful theory.* Paper presented at the annual meeting of the Academy of Management, San Diego, CA.

Emirbayer, M., & Mische, A. (1998). What is agency? *American Journal of Sociology 103*(4), 962–1023.

Ghoshal, S. (2005). Bad management theories are destroying good management practices. *Academy of Management Learning and Education, 4*, 75–91.

Gibbons, M., Limoges, C., Nowotny, H., Schwartzman, S., Scott, P., & Trow, M. (1994). *The new production of knowledge: The dynamics of science and research in contemporary sciences.* Thousand Oaks, CA: Sage.

Hambrick, D. C. (2007). The field of management's devotion to theory: Too much of a good thing? *Academy of Management Journal, 50*, 1346–1352.

Hodgkinson, G. P., & Rousseau, D. M. (2009). Bridging the rigour-relevance gap in management research: It's already happening! *Journal of Management Studies, 46*(3), 534–546.

Jarzabkowski, P. (2005). *Strategy as practice: An activity-based approach.* London: Sage.

Kieser, A., & Leiner, L. (2009). Why the rigour-relevance gap in management research is unbridgeable. *Journal of Management Studies, 46*, 516–533.

Latham, G. P., & Whyte, G. (1994). The futility of utility analysis. *Personnel Psychology, 47*(1), 31–46.

Lawler, E., Mohrman, A., Mohrman, S., Cummings, T., & Ledford, G. (Eds.). (1985). *Doing research that is useful for theory and practice.* San Francisco: Jossey-Bass.

Lawler, E., Nadler, D., & Cammann, C. (1980). *Organizational assessment: Perspectives on the measurement of organizational behavior and the quality of work life.* New York: Wiley.

Lewin, K. (1948). *Resolving social conflicts.* New York: HarperCollins.

Locke, E. A. (2002). The epistemological side of teaching management: Teaching through principles. *Academy of Management Learning and Education, 1*, 195–205.

March, J. G. (2004). Parochialism in the evolution of a research community: The case of organization studies. *Management and Organization Review, 1*, 5–22.

McKelvey, Bill. (2006). Comment on Van De Ven and Johnson's "engaged scholarship": Nice try, but . . . . *Academy of Management Review, 31*, 822–829.

Mohrman, S. A., Gibson, C. B., & Mohrman, A. M. (2001). Doing research that is useful to practice: A model and empirical exploration. *Academy of Management Journal, 44*(2), 357–375.

Mohrman, S., Mohrman A. M., Jr., Cohen, S., & Winby, S. (2007). The collaborative learning cycle: Advancing theory and building practical design frameworks through collaboration. In A. B. Shani, S. A. Mohrman, W. A. Pasmore, B. Stymne,

& N. Adler (Eds.), *Handbook of collaborative management research* (pp. 509–530). Thousand Oaks, CA: Sage.

Mohrman, A. M., Jr., Mohrman, S. A., Lawler, E. E., III, & Ledford, G. E. (1999). Introduction. In E. E. Lawler III, A. M. Mohrman, Jr., S. A. Mohrman, G. E. Ledford, T. G. Cummings, & Associates (Eds.), *Doing research that is useful for theory and practice* (pp. ix–xlix). Lanham, MD: Lexington Press.

Mohrman, S. A., Mohrman, A. M., Jr., & R. V. Tenkasi. (1997). The discipline of organization design. In C. L. Cooper & S. E. Jackson (Eds.), *Creating tomorrow's organizations* (pp. 191–206). Chichester, UK: Wiley.

Mohrman, S. A., Tenkasi, R. V., & Mohrman, A. M., Jr. (2003). The role of networks in fundamental organizational change: A grounded analysis. *Journal of Applied Behavioral Science, 39*(3), 301–323.

Mohrman, S., & Wagner, C. (2006). *The dynamics of knowledge creation: A baseline for the assessment of the role and contribution of the department of energy's nanoscale science research centers.* Submitted to the U.S. Department of Energy/Office of Science through Contract No. DE-AC02-04ER30321, July 2006.

Mol, M. J., & Birkenshaw, J. (2009). The sources of management innovation: When firms introduce new management practices. *Journal of Business Research, 26*(12), 1269–1280.

Nicolai, A., & Seidl, D. (2010). That's relevant! Towards a taxonomy of practical relevance. *Organization Studies, 31,* 1257–1285.

Nowoty, H., Scott, P., & Gibbons, M. (2003). Introduction "Mode 2" revisited: The new production of knowledge. *Minerva, 41*(3), 179–194.

O'Toole, J. (2009). The pluralistic future of management education. In S. Armstrong and C. Fukami (Eds.), *The SAGE handbook of management learning, education, and development* (pp. 547–558). Thousand Oaks, CA: Sage.

Pettigrew, A. M. (2005). The character and significance of management research on the public services. *Academy of Management Journal, 48,* 973–977.

Pfeffer, J. (2007). A modest proposal: How we might change the process and product of managerial research. *Academy of Management Journal, 50*(6), 1334.

Romme, A.G.L. (2003). Making a difference: Organization as design. *Organization Science, 14,* 559–573.

Rousseau, D. M. (2006). 2005 presidential address: Is there such a thing as "evidence-based management"? *Academy of Management Review, 31*(2), 256–269.

Rousseau, D. M. (2007). A sticky, leveraging, and scalable strategy for high-quality connections between organizational practice and science. *Academy of Management Journal, 50,* 1037–1042.

Rousseau, D. M., Manning, J., & Denyer, D. (2008). Evidence in management and organizational science: Assembling the field's full weight of scientific knowledge through syntheses. *Academy of Management Annals, 2,* 475–515.

Rousseau, D. M., & McCarthy, S. (2007). Educating managers from an evidence-based perspective. *Academy of Management Learning and Education, 6,* 84–101.

Rynes, S. L. (in press). The research-practice gap in industrial-organizational psychology and related fields: Challenges and potential solutions. Oxford Handbook of Industrial and Organizational Psychology. Oxford: Oxford University Press.

Scherer, A. G. (2009). Critical theory and its contribution to critical management studies. In M. Alvesson, H. Willmott, & T. Bridgman (Eds.), *The Oxford handbook of critical management studies* (pp. 29–51). Oxford: Oxford University Press.

Seashore, S., Lawler, E., III, Mirvis, P., & Cammann, C. (1983). *Assessing organizational change: A guide to methods, measures, and practices.* New York: Wiley.

Shapiro, D. L., Kirkman, B. L., & Courtney, H. G. (2007). Perceived causes and solutions of the translation problem in management research. *Academy of Management Journal, 50*(2), 249–266.

Simon, H. A. (1969). *The sciences of the artificial.* Cambridge, MA: The MIT Press.

Starbuck, W. H. (2006). *The production of knowledge: The challenge of social science research.* Oxford: Oxford University Press.

Starkey, K., Hatcheul, A., & Tempest, S. (2009). Management research and the new logics of discovery and engagement. *Journal of Management Studies, 46*(3), 22–238.

Tranfield, D., & Starkey, K. (1998). The nature, social organization, and promotion of management research: Towards policy. *British Journal of Management, 9*(4), 341–353.

van Aken, J. E. (2005). Management research as a design science: Articulating the research products of Mode 2 knowledge production in management. *British Journal of Management, 16,* 19–36.

Van de Ven, A. H. (2007). *Engaged scholarship: A guide for organizational and social research.* New York: Oxford University Press.

Van de Ven, A. H., & Johnson, P. E. (2006). Knowledge for theory and practice. *Academy of Management Review, 31,* 802–821.

Weick, K. (1995). What theory is not, theorizing is. *Administrative Science Quarterly, 40,* 385–390.

Willmott, H. (2003). Organization theory as a critical science? Forms of analysis and "new organizational forms." In H. Tsoukas & C. Knudsen (Eds.), *The Oxford handbook of organization theory: Meta-theoretical perspectives* (pp. 88–112). New York: Oxford University Press.

PART I

Exemplars of Useful Research

TWO

Crossing Boundaries to Investigate Problems in the Field

An Approach to Useful Research

AMY C. EDMONDSON

FOR MOST SCHOLARS in organizational behavior, the importance of advancing theory is obvious. In a field that arose in response to management challenges (Miner, 2002), one might argue that research advancing practice should be highly valued as well. Indeed, the need for strategies to manage the challenges faced by the organizations that inspire and fund our work creates an obvious imperative for research that helps those who manage and work in them.

We are told that the norms and demands of academic careers limit our ability to be useful (e.g., Fox, 2003). As the scholars in this book illustrate, however, the hurdles are far from insurmountable. Perhaps the dichotomy between theory and practice need not be so pronounced. Indeed, many of us draw inspiration from Kurt Lewin (1945, p. 129), who argued, over a half century ago, "Nothing is as practical as a good theory." In this well-known statement, Lewin was not claiming that theory, by its very existence, is practical and should be respected as such, but rather that a good theory is one that can demonstrate its claim. As Lewin's student Chris Argyris (e.g., 1980, 1982, 1993) has argued tirelessly, this is a tall order, but one that management researchers must embrace if we are to make a difference in the world. Though few journals appear to seek out or publish work with a practical component, the tradition of action research has remained vital and inspiring over the intervening decades (e.g., Argyris, Putnam, & Smith, 1988; Clark, 1980; Fox, 2003; Schein, 1987; Schwarz, 1994).

What drew me to the field of organizational behavior twenty years ago was exactly this opportunity—to engage in research and teaching aimed at understanding and informing practice. Yet those just starting research careers might be well advised not to read on. The approach I describe in this chapter—starting with problems, going out into the field, and reaching across boundaries of several kinds—is almost certain to slow you down and may even harm your career. (Of course, I hope not, and I don't believe it to be true. But many do, and so I offer this reluctant caveat as an invitation to help challenge it.)

This chapter presents experiential reflections rather than systematic analyses. I did not conduct a literature search to identify and analyze useful studies so as to determine what they have in common, but instead reflected on my own research activities over the past two decades to consider what factors have been most instrumental in tying me to practice. I did not need to be convinced to pursue practical knowledge. This aim was embedded in my long-standing sense of purpose. Coming from a family of inventors and engineers, I began the study of organizational behavior in the early 1990s with a deep bias toward the pursuit of the practical. A decade earlier, in my first job after college, I worked as an engineer for Buckminster Fuller, designing and building geodesic domes for uses ranging from food production to emergency shelter. Fuller—a college dropout from the Harvard class of 1917 and at the time an internationally known inventor, architect, and author— was the perfect mentor to reinforce my bias against further academic endeavors. Drawing from these family and early career influences, I had been certain that making a difference in the world did not involve time out for graduate school. Furthermore, at that time, I was not yet aware of the field of organizational behavior.

What happened to change my course from applied engineering to organizational research? To begin, while working with Fuller, I led the occasional team in the construction of full-scale geodesic prototypes, sparking an initial, but still largely dormant, interest in organizational dynamics that affect collaborative work. After Fuller's death in 1983, I wrote a book about his mathematical concepts (Edmondson, 1987) but remained mute on his efforts to inspire and engage people in work that made a difference in the world— ideas well captured by others (e.g., Baldwin, 1996; Kenner, 1973). It was not until a few years later, working for a small consulting firm that helped managers implement change programs in companies, that I became aware of the need for better knowledge about the design and management of organizations. In that job, I spent many hours interviewing and observing in large companies as varied as General Motors and Apple, obtaining the beginnings of an education in organizational behavior. I decided to apply to graduate school at the point when I realized that my ignorance in psychology, management, and business was limiting my usefulness in these settings.

As a doctoral student, however, I soon found that usefulness was not at the top of the list of criteria with which scholars evaluated research in organizational behavior. Discovering the predecessor to this book, *Doing Research That Is Useful for Theory and Practice* (1985), thus had been profoundly reassuring. The essays and dialogue among so many of the field's leading researchers—Chris Argyris, Paul Goodman, Richard Hackman, Ed Lawler, Dick Walton—made it clear to me that an aspiration to develop practical knowledge in organization studies was consistent with the purpose of the field.

Reflecting on how this quest has played out in the past two decades in my own work, I identified three attributes of my approach to conducting research that may increase the chances of the research being useful: starting with an important problem, getting into the field (early and often), and not being afraid to collaborate across disciplinary and organizational boundaries. Although of dubious merit as a theory of relevance, these elements are likely to increase the chances of stumbling into useful knowledge and almost certainly make the research journey more interesting.

Three Elements of Useful Research

Start with Problems

Problems provide a natural connection with practice. Studying a compelling problem, researchers are motivated to care about action. Problems matter! They matter to actors in the field coping with them, of course, and those reading one's work are likely to find them interesting as well (Fox, 2003). As compelling as publishing articles for scholarly colleagues may be, research that might help solve a problem in the world is usually that much more so.

The problem with problems is, of course, their apparently low status as "applied" research (Fox, 2003; Greenwood & Levin, 1998). And, problem-driven research brings additional risks to scholars. First, the work might turn out to be mundane if it merely addresses a problem that seems important to practitioners but uninspiring to other scholars. Second, problem-driven research risks rediscovering the obvious or generating pragmatic but situation-specific recommendations. Theory-driven research, in comparison, is awarded higher status and is believed to be more general and enduring (Fox, 2003). I nonetheless argue that problems open doors to new ideas and new theory. Starting with an important problem does not mean one must solve it single-handedly but rather that one can use it as a lens with which to investigate an organizational phenomenon that has importance for practices as well as for theory. Starting with a problem does, I believe, call for at least interest in solutions, as well as for empathy for those who face the problem.

One obvious reason that research motivated by problems might increase its usefulness is that efforts to understand a problem are likely to trigger ideas about how to solve it. Occasionally, solutions to problems can be investigated, tested, or refined, whether in the same or in subsequent research projects (Clark, 1980). More subtly, problems may facilitate the production of useful research because real problems in organizations are complex and multifaceted, provoking consideration of issues beyond those that motivated the study in the first place. In contrast to theory-driven research, which often remains tightly focused—adhering to a specific research framework and design—problem-driven research may sometimes follow the trail of problems where it leads. Lateral thinking about issues related to the initial problem then may trigger ideas for practice as well as new ideas for theory. Perhaps most important, developing knowledge about a problem builds the depth of understanding that makes the solutions researchers or their organizational partners might design more likely to work.

A study of errors. To illustrate, medication error in hospitals is an example of a real world problem. Motivated by research interests in both organizational learning and workplace safety, in the early 1990s I joined a team of nurses and physicians in an in-depth study of medication errors in hospitals. The team was organized to collect data to measure error rates in a dozen or so hospital units (work groups that provide patient care) in two hospitals with attention to potential organizational causes of error. I thus joined the team with a narrow research question: Did better teams make fewer errors? My design would predict the team-level error rate (being assessed by data on medication errors to be collected by clinicians over a six-month period) with data on team design, team process, and leader behavior, collected during the first month of the study. I used a modified version of Richard Hackman's team diagnostic survey to measure team properties (Wageman, Hackman, & Lehman, 2005). From a practice perspective, if my main hypothesis was supported, efforts to build stronger unit-based teams might help reduce errors.

The reality of drug errors was more complex than my initial design had considered. Reflecting a risk for problem-driven research in general, the process of digging into the problem of drug errors uncovered a new, related problem. This came to light when my analysis of the painstakingly collected quantitative data produced findings that appeared to be the exact opposite of what I had predicted: Well-led teams with good relationships among members were apparently making *more* mistakes related to medications, not fewer. There was a significant correlation between teamwork and error rates in what I initially considered "the wrong direction." This was a surprise—and of course, a puzzle. Did better-led teams *really* make more mistakes? With what I had learned of the phenomenon already at that point—the many handoffs across caregivers, the need for communication, coordination, help-seeking, and double-checking to achieve safe, error-free care—I did not think it made sense that good teamwork would increase the chance of errors. The opportunity to get into the field, described in the section titled "Strategies for Building Understanding in the Field," was essential to getting to the bottom of this unexpected result.

Other problem-inspired studies. Although medication errors present a particularly tangible example, organizational problems come in many forms and can motivate a variety of research projects. Other examples from my own work include action research with a senior management team in a midsized U.S. manufacturing company facing declining revenues and profits after a half century of growth (Edmondson & Smith, 2006), a study of the difficulties of changing surgical team behaviors to accommodate a new technology (Edmondson, Bohmer, & Pisano, 2001a), an investigation of inconsistent use of best practices across neonatal intensive care units (NICUs) in North American hospitals (Tucker, Nembhard, & Edmondson, 2007), and a study of speaking up failures in a multinational company (Detert & Edmondson, 2010).

All of these studies were motivated by problems and management challenges that were important to people working in the involved organizations. At the same time, I entered each of them hoping to be able to contribute knowledge to organizational learning research as well. Further, none of these studies produced the findings or theoretical contributions I expected or hoped for at the outset. Although I believe the actual contributions were more interesting than those planned, I am not an objective judge. In any case, the time spent studying the issues that started the projects invariably led to new questions, new insights, and some unexpected contributions to the literature.

For example, at the beginning of our study of a new surgical technology, my colleague, Gary Pisano, wanted to study learning curves in a service setting. As an economist with expertise in manufacturing—particularly in the process innovations involved in the manufacture of complex pharmaceuticals (see Pisano, 1996)—Pisano saw cardiac surgery as a novel setting for investigating learning curves. With a well-developed network in health care businesses, he soon identified a device maker launching an innovative technology for minimally invasive surgery and requested its help collecting data on surgical time for consecutive operations from several of the adopting hospitals. Both the company and the hospitals participated willingly, hoping to learn from the research.

Unexpectedly, in his early conversations, salespeople in close contact with the clinicians repeatedly told Pisano that success with the new technology was all about "the team" and its "teamwork." These comments made Pisano understandably nervous; as an economist, teamwork was not something he had been prepared to consider, let alone measure. But, my office was next door to his, and soon he had me as a new collaborator. (Richard Bohmer, a physician, also joined the team, a crucial addition, as noted in the section titled "Disciplinary boundaries.") Together, we shifted gears to include extensive interviews with all members of the operating room teams and others close to the technology implementation efforts in 16 hospitals. Having been led by the sales representatives to study the "problem" of needing a new kind of teamwork to succeed with minimally invasive surgery, we had a new focus to our collaborative research. Indeed, fewer than half of the 16 adopting cardiac surgery departments we studied successfully implemented the technology (that is, they continued to offer the procedure after an initial learning period). Others abandoned the effort, leaving future patients without the option of a less invasive operation and a quicker recovery. As our qualitative data revealed, operating room teams had to figure out new ways of working together to accommodate the new technology, and this proved far from easy.

Similarly, the problem of a weak strategy and deteriorating business results that initiated our action research with the senior management team in the manufacturing company also unveiled a new, different problem for us to study: how to manage emotion-laden interpersonal conflicts in a decision-making group (Edmondson & Smith, 2006). This new problem was of great interest to us as scholars, and the challenge it presented captured the attention of our executive colleagues as well.

Back in the hospital context, when my colleagues and I set out to study best practice implementation teams in the NICU, the perceived problem according to the two physicians who first contacted me was to speed up team learning. But, along the way, a new problem emerged: the state of medical knowledge (the "evidence") supporting the practices being implemented by the unit-based teams varied widely. With less research evidence of medical efficacy, teams had more difficulty implementing the required changes in their organizations (Tucker, Nembhard, & Edmondson, 2007).

Summary. In each of these projects, problems were helpful for focusing and motivating the research activities. Problems spawned research questions, generated insights and solutions, and most of all, facilitated access to field sites. Without problems, our field-based collaborators would have been far less likely to welcome us into their world, offering us access to data. And, in each case, the initial problem did not tell the whole story of the phenomenon. Field-based research allowed the problems and plots to shift and to thicken.

Go Out into the Field

Unless you have an unusual office location, sitting at your desk is unlikely to be the most conducive situation for gaining insight into the kinds of organizational phenomena previously described. Although one can learn about an industry or company from written materials, fuller understanding and new ideas are more likely when meeting and observing people who work in that setting. Deciding to pursue field-based research also has its risks. One can negotiate access to a site only to have it fall through, or have it not offer the kind of data needed for answering a research question. Moreover, understanding a situation well requires multiple observations, and some interviews or visits do not yield anything useful. Further, as noted in the prior section titled "Start with Problems," the research question one asks may evolve as understanding of the setting deepens, posing challenges for consistency. In short, the research process can be inefficient, fraught with logistical hurdles and unexpected events (see Edmondson & McManus, 2007). Nonetheless, getting into the field is essential for building understanding of a context and of the variables that matter therein.

Strategies for building understanding in the field. I have engaged in two basic types of field research. The first involves open-ended exploration of a phenomenon or a research possibility without extensive structure, careful sampling, or highly structured interview protocols. In this type of research, one spends time in the field to get up to speed in understanding a setting—learning relevant terminology and discovering issues that matter. The second type is more focused and involves more systematic techniques of collecting data to develop, support, and sometimes test a theoretical proposition. Generally, the first kind of research experience precedes the second, although exploratory forays do not lead inexorably to subsequent, more structured phases.

For example, the time I spent in the field to investigate medication errors occurred in two distinct phases. In the first phase, I participated in bi-weekly research meetings at one of the hospitals for most of a year, reviewing many of the detected errors and conducting interviews to gain insight into what had happened leading up to, during, and after many of the errors. These experiences helped me to develop survey items that were meaningful in the hospital context, as well as to build confidence in my understanding of health care delivery and its many challenges, including its highly specialized terms and jargon. In the second phase of fieldwork, I asked a research assistant (Andy Molinsky, now a professor of organizational behavior at Brandeis University) to observe and interview members of the hospital units to better understand any organizational differences they might have. At that point, I was hoping to shed light on the unexpected correlation between error rates and teamwork, and it was important that the research assistant remain blind to the error data, the survey data, and to the new idea I had about what might explain the significant correlation between them. From Molinsky's perspective, the data collection was highly unstructured, by design. From my perspective, I knew the relationship I wanted to explain, and I hoped that he would find evidence of unit-based differences in error-reporting behavior.

Why might stronger teams have higher error rates? As I thought further about this question, it occurred to me that well-led teams, compared to teams with poor relationships among colleagues or with punitive leaders, might have a climate of openness that made it easier to report and discuss error. The good teams, I reasoned, do not *make* more mistakes, they *report* more. When I suggested this to the study's principal investigators, they were skeptical. This interpretation suggested that we might not be finding the definitive error rate—a primary goal of the larger study—and that errors might be systematically underreported in some units due to retaliatory interpersonal climates. The physicians' skepticism led me to conduct further analyses and to collect additional data to test this new proposition.

I ran additional analyses with the error and survey data and waited while Molinsky—still blind to both sets of measures and unaware of my new hypothesis—conducted open-ended interviews and observations in the hospital units over several weeks to gain insight into these small workplaces (see Edmondson, 1996, for more detail). These new data strongly suggested that there were palpable differences in interpersonal climate across units. It was particularly noteworthy that people's reported levels of willingness to speak up about errors appeared to vary widely. Furthermore, these differences—the independent ratings of unit openness—were highly correlated with the detected error rates. This observation, gleaned from the field interviews, gave rise to a new stream of inquiry on psychological safety (e.g., Edmondson, 1999, 2002, 2003b).

Working in this new stream, my next field study showed that psychological safety varies significantly across groups and predicts team learning and performance (Edmondson, 1999). This project also involved two distinct phases of qualitative data collection in the field, one more open ended and one more focused. The earlier phase developed understanding of the context (a midsized manufacturing company serving corporate customers) and investigated team processes for evidence of the construct of team psychological safety and to inform survey construction. The later phase, following survey administration and analysis, was a targeted examination of the phenomenon of team learning, comparing high- and low-learning teams. This intensive field-based research greatly enhanced the study by illuminating the phenomenon of team learning and making relationships between constructs far more compelling and convincing than they would have been with the survey data alone (see Edmondson, 1999; Edmondson & McManus, 2007).

Shifting questions, insights, and implications. Although very few studies produce statistically significant results that are the opposite of those predicted, field-based research rarely fails to yield some surprises along the way. As already noted, all of the problem-driven research projects previously discussed experienced important shifts in emphasis as a result of the time spent in the field. For example, our action research on the senior management team revealed a team stuck in persistent conflicts. These executives seemed unable to resolve deeply held conflicting views about firm strategy. The team debated crucial decisions about product position and price for months, making little progress, as we observed and recorded their conversations. Spending time in the field with the team was essential for understanding why it was making so little progress. Diana Smith and I observed and recorded full-day meetings and conducted interviews with individuals. Our analysis of the transcript data focused on the conversations featuring disagreements that continued over time, from meeting to meeting.

Reading the literature on team conflict while analyzing these data, Smith and I took note of prominent theories that task conflict promotes, while relationship conflict harms, team effectiveness (e.g., Amason, 1996; Jehn, 1997). Although both the claim of distinct conflict constructs and the theoretical argument about differential effects were logical and intuitively appealing, our data suggested a different perspective. Analyzing transcript after transcript, supplemented by private interviews with team members, we began to notice that certain types of task conflict in this team naturally triggered relationship conflict. Specifically, when team conflicts encompassed opposing value systems—deeply held opinions or organizational values—relationship conflicts were virtually inevitable. We argued that this fusion occurred because in the process of arguing one or another side of a debate, participants could not help making negative interpersonal attributions about those arguing a view that opposed their own. These attributions—whether essentially about others' incompetence or stubbornness—were readily revealed to us in interviews.

We further suspected that the executives' intention to remain on the business topics and avoid interpersonal issues made it difficult for them to make progress in their strategic decision-making task (Edmondson & Smith, 2006). The relationship tensions under the surface were off limits— "undiscussables" (Argyris, 1980)—and the mutual pretense that only business-based discussion was occurring added to, rather than lessened, the team's challenge. We thus used the data—on both the problem and on the interventions and their effects—to propose (and test in several settings) a new approach to managing relationship conflict in management teams.

When Jim Detert and I started the study of speaking-up failures previously mentioned, we wondered what made psychological safety for voice low in the knowledge-intensive company we called HiCo. We were not thinking about or looking for implicit theories of voice until our analysis of reams of interview data, which encompassed over 170 specific episodes of speaking up (or not speaking up) at work, suggested some common (and surprising) features of how people thought about speaking up. In this way, we identified a set of implicit theories about when and where speaking up is unsafe or inappropriate in corporate hierarchies. These implicit theories function, we argued, as cognitive programs leading people to choose silence over voice, even with content that is not inherently threatening. That is, even with good ideas rather than bad news, people may frequently hold back on voice, much to the detriment of the organization, and in the long run, to themselves.

In this study, it was deeper investigation of the intrapersonal sense making that underlies specific voice decisions—in the context of real organizational situations—that led us to revisit the literature on implicit theories and then to formulate what we hope is a novel contribution to the voice literature. What we found especially satisfying about the implicit theories perspective was its potential to develop actionable communication strategies for managers who wish to better engage employee voice (Detert & Edmondson, 2011).

New variables emerge. Extensive fieldwork was also crucial to developing insight into the nature of the behavioral changes required to successfully implement the new cardiac surgical technology. For instance, many of the usual variables associated with differences in innovation success, such as top management support, level of resources, or status of the project leader, provided no explanatory value in this setting. As we learned in the field, cardiac surgeons had enormous status and generated considerable resources for hospitals and so were less vulnerable to the need for support from senior management. However, many underestimated the need for behavioral changes in the operating room, by themselves and by other members of the team. The surgeons who framed the implementation process as a team-learning journey—fewer than half of those studied—oversaw successful implementations (Edmondson, 2003b).

Similarly, to understand the problem faced by the NICU improvement teams and the setting in which they worked, my colleagues and I visited four hospitals to do extensive interviews. We used these visits to develop brief case studies on ten improvement projects occurring in the four hospitals, projects that ranged in focus from hand hygiene to intergroup relations between the maternity/delivery and NICU units. The case studies, in turn, informed the development of a survey instrument and helped us to understand what made quality improvement challenging in hospitals. But a crucial variable that differentiated these improvement projects, which we had not been aware of when we started the research, was the level of evidence supporting a given practice being implemented. The fieldwork allowed us to add this variable to our quantitative data collection efforts that followed.

Summary. Research questions and problems are likely to shift during field research, building greater understanding and pointing to additional theoretical and practical possibilities. At the same time, field researchers must be prepared to accept that every foray into the field will not lead to an article in a top scholarly journal. Field research is replete with false starts and dead ends, as noted earlier. Yet, field visits—even those that do not end up as full-blown research sites—can provide data for illustrating insights and mechanisms in papers or talks, or for developing case studies for teaching. The opportunity to gain firsthand knowledge in a field site is thus valuable for personal learning and for improving the ability to communicate ideas and findings to others. Field-based case studies serve as data points that build understanding and generate ideas. Moreover, prior field experience triggers a virtuous cycle of access to future field experience, building credibility for future, more promising research sites.

Collaborate across Knowledge Boundaries

In most field research sites, it takes time to understand both the organization and the industry. Collaborators who bring different perspectives and expertise can accelerate the learning needed to get up to speed and offer novel insights. For me to understand drug errors in hospitals, for example, would have been extremely difficult without working closely with the physicians and nurses in the larger research project. Similarly, working with scholars in other disciplines allows a fuller picture of the phenomenon under study to take shape, compared to working alone or working with similarly trained colleagues. This fuller picture, I believe, increases the chances of producing actionable knowledge. In our cardiac surgery study, for example, my two colleagues and I looked at what was happening in these teams from very different perspectives, which we were able to integrate to ultimately develop papers for both researchers and practitioners. In sum, there are two kinds of knowledge boundaries worth crossing in problem-focused, field-based research: organizational and disciplinary. Some collaborations cross both, but one is likely to be more salient than the other in a given project.

Organizational boundaries. Clearly, working closely with practitioners—managers, clinicians, engineers, other professionals—encourages attention to practical issues. For example, clinician collaborators in the drug error study brought disciplinary knowledge that I lacked, but as actors in the organizations under study, they brought practitioner perspectives that were especially valuable to my understanding the interdependence of how drugs are delivered in these complex organizations. This insight suggested that interpersonal climate might be an important variable in predicting error rates.

These findings had clear implications for practice. They helped to generate productive discussion of the problem of fear in medicine, both behind closed doors in physician residency programs and publicly. In particular, they began to introduce into the larger health care dialogue consideration of how reluctance to speak up about errors or to ask for help was making patients less safe than they would otherwise be (e.g., Edmondson, 2004; Leape, 1999, 2007; Shortell & Singer, 2008). Since that time, many hospitals have pursued blameless reporting policies to increase the chances of detecting, correcting, and preventing future error (see Edmondson, Roberto, & Tucker, 2002). The study also had implications for theory, in that the discovery of the role of psychological safety influenced my own and others' subsequent theory and research on learning and teams (Baer & Frese, 2003; Edmondson, 1999, 2002, 2003b; Levin & Cross, 2004). Additionally, the relationships with health care insiders in this work led to additional research opportunities in other hospitals (e.g., Tucker, Nembhard, & Edmondson, 2007; Nembhard & Edmondson, 2006).

Although in a less technically complex setting, my study of 51 teams in a low-tech manufacturing company ("ODI") would not have been possible without the active participation of a manager I called Dave Kane (Edmondson, 1996). Kane's request for help assessing the teams at ODI allowed me to gather data to test a theoretical model of team learning (Edmondson, 1999). Kane and his colleagues' engagement in the research as it unfolded allowed me to build understanding of the teams' work, to obtain superb response rates, and to help push my thinking about psychological safety and team learning.

More recently, I have investigated organizational learning failures through case study research in a variety of settings. Although few of these projects led to scholarly papers, they fostered the development of practical knowledge on how to lead change in highly uncertain contexts (Edmondson, Roberto, & Tucker, 2002); how to anticipate and respond to ambiguous threats (Edmondson et al., 2005); and how to build psychological safety in a large organization (Edmondson & Hajim, 2003), communicated in book chapters, managerial articles, teaching notes, and the occasional research paper. I have found such case studies, focused initially on pedagogical aims, to be helpful in generating future research ideas (e.g., Edmondson et al., 2005; Hackman & Edmondson, 2007). In most of these studies, organization members have been crucial partners. Their involvement helped to focus each investigation, bringing together well selected interviewees, and to identify managerially relevant decisions and tensions, which was especially important for furthering knowledge about practice in reasonably complex organizational settings.

Disciplinary boundaries. The other kind of collaboration involves crossing boundaries between academic disciplines. Colleagues in other fields may have experience in an industry or perspectives on a phenomenon that complement those from behavioral and organizational sciences. In the study of cardiac surgery teams, Pisano, an economist, brought expertise in operations and learning curve analysis and Bohmer, a physician, demystified the surgical task while I helped them to better understand the research on teams. The journey was both engaging and challenging; we had many discussions in which taken-for-granted assumptions within our different disciplines— especially economics and organizational behavior—clashed. For example, economics had little history with the kinds of qualitative data I proposed to use to assess differences across sites. Such differences led to interesting discussions in both scholarly (Pisano, Bohmer, & Edmondson, 2001; Edmondson, Bohmer, & Pisano, 2001a) and managerial (Edmondson, Bohmer, & Pisano, 2001b) articles. Our first publication, describing the heterogeneity of learning curves in the service context, would not have been possible without Bohmer's help conversing with surgeons to identify the right control variables (Pisano, Bohmer, & Edmondson, 2001). Our final paper described what we had discovered about fast-learning teams to a managerial audience (Edmondson, Bohmer, & Pisano, 2001b).

Similarly, in our later study of NICUs, collaborating with scholars with deep expertise in operations management (Anita Tucker) and health care management (Ingrid Nembhard) allowed the development of a survey instrument that included significant predictors of implementation success taken from our three different respective literatures.

My collaboration with Diana Smith crossed another type of boundary between researchers: action research in a consulting setting versus normal science research in an academic setting. Although both trained in organizational behavior, Diana and I differ in our skills and methods. She is an extraordinarily skillful action researcher who intervenes in management contexts to improve practice and build new knowledge (Smith, 2008), while I have largely developed and tested conceptual models. Working together helped us both push our thinking about the phenomenon of conflict in management teams— with mutual intellectual benefits and considerable fun along the way.

Summary. Communicating across knowledge boundaries is challenging. People within a field learn specific, technical language and concepts that they take for granted, making it hard to communicate effectively across fields (e.g., Dougherty, 1992); and the same has been found for membership in a given organization or site (Sole & Edmondson, 2002). Overcoming these hurdles offers the potential to enrich individual perspectives on both sides of any knowledge divide, whether between disciplines or organizations. Moreover, collaborative research lends itself to conversations about practice because it is the phenomena under study collaborators have in common.

Discussion

This chapter presents an approach to conducting research that informs theory and practice—an approach characterized by collaborating across boundaries to study problems in field settings. Although this approach has been presented as separate choices, the interrelatedness among them is undeniable. Researchers motivated by an important problem are enabled in their efforts to understand it by time spent in the field. Fieldwork puts problems in rich, complex contexts, revealing their multiple facets and facilitating fortuitous connections that may give rise to new theories and new ideas for practice. And, time spent in the field and with practitioners reveals new, interesting problems that are difficult to detect by reading the literature alone. Likewise, real problems in organizations are unlikely to be explained adequately by analysis within a single discipline; different disciplines, bringing the attention of actors with different perspectives, working together often provide new insights into existing problems. Finally, collaborating across academic boundaries sometimes reveals problems that might go unnoticed by researchers in one field—the problem of differences in error reporting across hospital units surfaced by importing a social psychological lens into the medication error study. Figure 2.1 thus depicts these three elements with mutually reinforcing relationships.

Despite the interrelatedness shown in Figure 2.1, every project need not emphasize all three elements equally. The level of collaboration may be higher or lower, the degree to which a problem takes center stage in motivating the work, and the extent of time spent in the field all may vary across projects depending on the question and the context. My argument is merely that these elements help tie researchers to practice in different ways.

Using the Literature

The literature—that is, prior research that informs and shapes the research question—plays a crucial role in helping to keep these elements working together for research purposes. The literature is an integrating force, helping to shape research to make its best contribution. Familiarity with what has come before in a given field that relates to your research question makes sure prior findings are integrated, elaborated, or refuted in the current work. More specifically, with respect to understanding a problem, finding out what others have done to understand that problem lowers the risk of reinventing the wheel.

Prior research in a field of inquiry informs and shapes one's research question; this statement is just as applicable for researchers who aspire to inform practice as for those who consider advancing theory their sole aim. Field re-

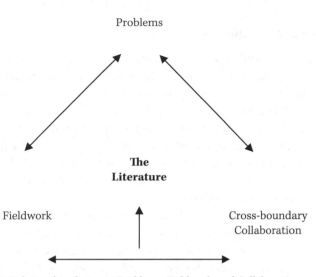

Problems

The
Literature

Fieldwork

Cross-boundary
Collaboration

FIGURE 2.1 Relationships between Problems, Fieldwork, and Collaboration

search that produces novel contributions to the literature requires careful thought about methods that fit the current state of knowledge. For instance, new areas of research require qualitative data to explore and identify dimensions of interest and possible relationships among them, while more mature streams benefit from quantitative data and careful tests of hypotheses. In either case, the literature is crucial for shaping methodological and scope decisions, and hybrid approaches allow researchers to test associations between variables with quantitative data and to explain and illuminate novel constructs and relationships with qualitative data (Edmondson & McManus, 2007).

When collaborating across academic disciplines, it is important to identify the literature one hopes to advance. The insights from different fields are likely to enrich one's thinking, as previously noted, but then they must be tamed and focused. The literature provides a force to focus and sharpen what one has found, before communicating it to others. Focusing on the state of the literature helps to avoid the trap of the overly broad or superficial observation in favor of offering precise statements on the advance that has been made.

In this discussion of the role of the literature, it is not my intention to take a step away from the practical. To the contrary, understanding what has been discovered previously is an essential step toward useful research because it allows the best use of limited time and resources. Thus, the inclusion of the literature in the center of Figure 2.1 is meant to highlight its important role in doing research that informs theory and practice.

Rewards and Limitations

Problem-focused, field-based interdisciplinary research projects, by their very nature, present learning opportunities. Pursuing this approach makes it virtually impossible not to learn something new and interesting about work or about organizations. Moreover, if, as I have argued, it increases the chances of developing findings with implications for practice, the process thus provides an additional source of satisfaction. By getting to know the people for whom one's ideas matter, one is both more able and more likely to generate implications for practice. By working across knowledge boundaries, one may develop a broader audience for one's work.

There are, of course, important limitations to this approach. First, while organizational behavior lends itself to the study of real problems in the field and tolerates a certain level of boundary spanning, this approach may be more challenging in other, even closely related, disciplines such as social psychology, in which norms and methods are more orthodox. Second, data collected in naturalistic settings are almost always limited in important ways, including the nonrandom nature of the sample and the extent and timing of data collection (Edmondson & McManus, 2007). Working in the field can mean that a carefully planned time frame suffers due to constraints outside your control. Third, there is a risk that research following this strategy may be labeled as "too applied." Critics may view the work as mere application of theory rather than as a theoretical contribution. Fourth, and perhaps most important to guard against while building a scholarly career, it may be easy to chase too varied an agenda, developing superficial rather than deep expertise.

Conclusion

The studies discussed in this chapter were conducted with the aspiration to produce useful knowledge. Barriers remain, however. More must be done to communicate and work with practitioners to facilitate translation from research findings to actionable practice. These findings, for the most part, have presented starting points for further experimentation and adjustment rather than concrete recommendations for action. To illustrate, I showed that psychological safety is measurable, varies systematically across groups, and affects speaking up and learning (Edmondson, 1996, 1999), and that people in leadership positions affect the psychological safety of others (Edmondson, 2003b; Nembhard & Edmondson, 2006). Good managers may understand this intuitively, but methods for helping others understand and act on this knowledge remain undeveloped. Similar arguments can be made for our findings that clinical practices that have a stronger evidence base are more likely to be successfully implemented (Tucker, Nembhard, & Edmondson, 2007) or that leaders who frame a change process in ways that take group dynamics into account increase the chances that disruptive new technologies will be accepted in the organization (Edmondson, 2003a). For our findings showing that people in hierarchies think about speaking up in counterproductive ways, Jim Detert and I have only begun to consider what managers might do to ameliorate these effects (Detert & Edmondson, 2011). Finally, as discussed, Diana Smith and I found that simmering relationship conflicts in a team that are not addressed impede progress on the task—and that addressing them effectively is both desirable and feasible (Edmondson & Smith, 2006). However, it may take an interventionist with the extraordinary skill that Smith brings—after decades of practice—to put this knowledge into action.

In conclusion, many paths may lead scholars toward useful research. The approach and the work discussed in this chapter are by no means the only or the best route to take. The work, the journey, has been engaging and satisfying, especially in terms of the people I have had the chance to work with, the ideas we have had the privilege to explore, and the potential—that occasionally feels within reach—for making a difference in organizations that operate in and affect the world in smaller and larger ways.

REFERENCES

Amason, A. (1996). Distinguishing the effects of functional and dysfunctional conflict on strategic decision making: Resolving a paradox for top management teams. *Academy of Management Journal, 39*(1), 123–148.

Argyris, C. (1980). Making the undiscussable and its undiscussability discussable. *Public Administration Review, 40*(3), 205–213.

Argyris, C. (1982). *Reasoning, learning, and action: Individual and organizational.* San Francisco: Jossey-Bass.

Argyris, C. (1993). *Knowledge for action: A guide to overcoming barriers to organizational change.* San Francisco: Jossey-Bass.

Argyris, C., Putnam, R., & Smith, D. (1988). *Action science.* San Francisco: Jossey-Bass.

Baer, M., & Frese, M. (2003). Innovation is not enough: Climates for initiative and psychological safety, process innovations, and firm performance. *Journal of Organizational Behavior, 24*(1), 45–68.

Baldwin, J. (1996). *BuckyWorks: Buckminster Fuller's ideas for today.* New York: Wiley.

Clark, A. (1980). Action research: Theory, practice, and values. *Journal of Occupational Behavior, 1,* 151–157.

Detert, J., & Edmondson, A. (2011). Implicit theories of voice: Taken-for-granted rules of self-censorship at work. *Academy of Management Journal* (forthcoming).

Dougherty, D. (1992). Interpretive barriers to successful product innovation in large firms. *Organization Science, 3*(2), 179–202.

Edmondson, A. (1987). *A Fuller explanation*. Boston: Birkhauser.

Edmondson, A. (1996). Learning from mistakes is easier said than done: Group and organizational influences on the detection and correction of human error. *Journal of Applied Behavioral Science, 32*(1), 5–28.

Edmondson, A. (1999). Psychological safety and learning behavior in work teams. *Administrative Science Quarterly, 44*(4), 350–383.

Edmondson, A. (2002). The local and variegated nature of learning in organizations: A group-level perspective. *Organization Science, 13*(2), 128–146.

Edmondson, A. (2003a). Framing for learning: Lessons in successful technology implementation. *California Management Review, 45*(2), 34–54.

Edmondson, A. (2003b). Speaking up in the operating room: How team leaders promote learning in interdisciplinary action teams. *Journal of Management Studies, 40*(6), 1419–1452.

Edmondson, A. C. (2004). Learning from failure in health care: Frequent opportunities, pervasive barriers. *Quality and Safety in Health Care, 13*(6), 3–9.

Edmondson, A., Bohmer, R., & Pisano, G. (2001a). Disrupted routines: Team learning and new technology adaptation. *Administrative Science Quarterly, 46*(4), 685–716.

Edmondson, A., Bohmer, R., & Pisano, G. (2001b). Speeding up team learning. *Harvard Business Review, 79*(9), 125–134.

Edmondson, A., & Hajim, C. (2003). Safe to say at Prudential Financial. Harvard Business School case #9-603-093.

Edmondson, A., & McManus, S. E. (2007). Methodological fit in management field research. *Academy of Management Review, 32*(4), 1155–1179.

Edmondson, A., Roberto, M., Bohmer, R., Ferlins, E., & Feldman L. (2005). The recovery window: Organizational learning following ambiguous threats. In M. Farjoun & W. Starbuck (Eds.), *Organization at the limits: NASA and the Columbia disaster* (pp. 220–245). London: Blackwell.

Edmondson, A., Roberto, M., & Tucker, A. (2002). Children's Hospital and Clinics. Harvard Business School case #9-302-050.

Edmondson, A., & Smith, D. M. (2006). Too hot to handle? How to manage relationship conflict. *California Management Review, 49*(1), 6–31.

Fox, N. (2003). Practice-based evidence: Towards collaborative and transgressive research. *Sociology, 37*(1), 81–102.

Greenwood, D., & Levin, M. (1998). Action research, science, and the co-optation of social research. *Studies in Cultures, Organizations, and Societies, 4*, 237–261.

Hackman, R., & Edmondson, A. (2007). Groups as agents of change. *Handbook of organizational development*. Thousand Oaks, CA: Sage.

Jehn, K. (1997). A qualitative analysis of conflict types and dimensions in organizational groups. *Administrative Science Quarterly, 42*(3), 530–557.

Kenner, H. (1973). *Bucky: A guided tour of Buckminster Fuller.* New York: William Morrow.

Leape, L. (1999, January 12). Faulty systems, not faulty people. *The Boston Globe.*

Leape, L. (2007, August 23). Why pay for mistakes? *The Boston Globe.*

Levin, D., & Cross, R. (2004). The strength of weak ties you can trust: The mediating role of trust in effective knowledge transfer. *Management Science 50*(11), 1477–1490.

Lewin, K. (1945). The Research Center for Group Dynamics at Massachusetts Institute of Technology. *Sociometry, 8*(2), 126–136.

Miner, J. (2002). *Organizational behavior: Foundations, theories, and analyses.* Oxford: Oxford University Press.

Nembhard, I., & Edmondson, A. (2006). Making it safe: The effects of leader inclusiveness and professional status on psychological safety and improvement efforts in health care teams. *Journal of Organizational Behavior, 27*(7), 941–966.

Pisano, G. (1996). *The development factory: Unlocking the potential of process innovation.* Boston: Harvard Business School Press.

Pisano, G., Bohmer, R., & Edmondson, A. (2001). Organizational differences in rates of learning: Evidence from the adoption of minimally invasive cardiac surgery. *Management Science, 47*(6), 752–768.

Schein, E. (1987). *Process consultation.* Reading, MA: Addison-Wesley.

Schwarz, R. (1994). *The skilled facilitator: Practical wisdom for developing effective groups.* San Francisco: Jossey-Bass.

Shortell, S., & Singer, S. (2008). Improving patient safety by taking systems seriously. *Journal of the American Medical Association, 299*(4), 445–447.

Smith, D. M. (2008). *Divide or conquer: How great teams turn conflict into strength.* New York: Portfolio.

Sole, D., & Edmondson, A. (2002). Situated knowledge and learning in dispersed teams. *British Journal of Management, 13*, S17–S34.

Tucker, A. L., Nembhard, I., & Edmondson, A. C. (2007). Implementing new practices: An empirical study of organizational learning in hospital intensive care units. *Management Science, 53*(6), 894–907.

Wageman, R., Hackman, R., & Lehman, E. (2005). The team diagnostic survey: Development of an instrument. *Journal of Applied Behavioral Science, 41*(4), 373–398.

ABOUT THE AUTHOR

Amy C. Edmondson, Novartis Professor of Leadership and Management at Harvard Business School, studies leadership, teams, and organizational learning. Her recent publications include "Methodological Fit in Management Field Research" (*Academy of Management Review, 2007*). She received her PhD in organizational behavior from Harvard University in 1996. Before her academic career, Edmondson was Director of Research at Pecos River Learning Centers, where she worked on organizational change programs in a variety of Fortune 100 companies. In the early 1980s, she was Chief Engineer for architect-inventor Buckminster Fuller, and her book *A Fuller Explanation* clarifies Fuller's mathematical contributions for a nontechnical audience.

THREE

Collaborative Organization Design Research at the Center for Effective Organizations

SUSAN ALBERS MOHRMAN
AND ALLAN M. MOHRMAN, JR.

WE DESCRIBE A RANGE of collaborative research approaches used over several decades in research programs at the Center for Effective Organizations (CEO) in the Marshall School of Business at the University of Southern California. These programs have focused on generating knowledge that is theoretically and practically useful about an unfolding set of organizational effectiveness and design challenges that have confronted companies through time. These programs and their constituent studies have been recursive: The knowledge gained in each project has informed ensuing research. We describe our foundational assumptions about design and design research that have guided our choices of research topics and methodologies, and we discuss the nature and importance of programmatic research approaches to address complex problems. We develop our view that collaboration is critical to organizational design research and describe some key elements of one particularly fruitful collaboration. Finally, we suggest a network collaboration approach that we are using in a current research program to increase relevance and speed of knowledge generation to better address the dynamic issues and innovative designs that characterize today's organizational landscape.

CEO: The Institutional Base for the Research

The Center for Effective Organizations was founded in 1978 by Edward E. Lawler, who designed it to embody the principles of collaborative, adaptive research, and to focus on key issues of organizational effectiveness. CEO's mission is to conduct research that generates new knowledge that is (1) useful to and used by the participating organizations as well as useful and accessible to the broader organizational community, and (2) academically

57

useful and valued. Our publication strategy is to report the results of our research in both practitioner and academic outlets. This dual focus combines a collaborative approach (Shani et al., 2007) and rigorous research methodologies that build on existing knowledge. The following pillars support the mission:

1. Building on past knowledge by bringing knowledge of theory and practice to the collaboration.

2. Relating the research to the problems and contextual realities of the participating organizations.

3. Building a collaborative research team with study participants, to incorporate the interests and purposes of all parties to the collaboration.

4. Carrying out related studies in multiple organizational settings in order to discover what knowledge can be generalized and the boundary conditions for its applicability, as well as to elucidate and investigate new theoretically and practically important aspects of the problem.

5. Addressing multiple stakeholder interests by attending to organization, manager, customer, and employee outcomes.

6. Using multimethod research designs that meet the standards of diverse communities of practice regarding legitimacy, validity, and usefulness of the findings; methods that match the problem being studied and that are agreed to by our collaborators.

We have a twofold strategy to access knowledge of practice and to identify research collaborators. First, CEO has built a network of companies who sponsor our mission of carrying out academic research and contributing to practice. These companies provide base funding through membership fees. We learn about the trends in these companies and the issues they are dealing with through regular interaction with their representatives. Second, as theoretically relevant organizational problem areas emerge, we build collaborative research projects with sponsor organizations and other interested collaborators. Research projects are funded by various sources: the participating organizations, government, foundations, or other research partners.

Many of CEO's studies focus on how organizations and new organizational capabilities can be created or changed by design in order to address problems and opportunities and to increase effectiveness. These research projects focus on new and emerging organizational directions. Our collaborators are often early adopters with whom we can learn about and assess new approaches and contribute to the knowledge required for organizations to use them effectively. The approach is based on the perspective that organizations are social artifacts (Simon, 1969), built and changed by people to accomplish their purposes. The study of organizations is thus the multilevel study of how people as individuals and collectives go about organizing to accomplish their purposes.

Although conceptualizing organizations as dynamic phenomena that are continually being changed and redesigned, we generally employ established analytical social science methods whenever possible. We develop theory grounded in the phenomena of interest, carry out the description and measurement of phenomena in terms of the constructs and their relationships contained in the theory, and systematically assess the impact on outcomes. In that sense our methodology is similar to the University of Michigan Quality of Worklife (QWL) studies described by Mirvis and Lawler in Chapter 6, Rigor and Relevance in Organizational Research. In order to impact the application of research knowledge and to test its validity in practice, we also take a synthetic approach, often working with participating companies to develop and test in situ organizational design methods and tools based on the research knowledge

Research that takes a design perspective is inherently collaborative. Full understanding of designs and design processes involves the combination of different kinds of knowledge. New designs are socially constructed by the participants in the setting, using many sources of knowledge. These sometimes include knowledge from organizational research and always include knowledge from the local communities of practice. Methodologies for applying and testing the design and implementation of new organizational forms include action research (Elden & Chisholm, 1993; Eden & Huxham, 1996; Reason & Bradbury, 2001), and evaluation research (Campbell & Stanley, 1963). Research teams investigating the generation of new practices and designs necessarily include members who have deep knowledge of organizational design principles and processes and who bring theory-based frameworks to complement the knowledge in practice (Galbraith, 1994; Mohrman & Cummings, 1989; Romme, 2003; Romme & Endenburg, 2006; van Aken, 2004, 2005).

Design Research

Several premises underlie our approach to design research. The first is that the field of organization research is a "science of the artificial" (Simon, 1969), similar to engineering and medical sciences. Organizations are purposefully created by people; they are continually re-created through the self-designing activities of people in the organization (Weick, 2003) as they work together and encounter performance challenges or as their purposes change. They are also deliberately designed and redesigned by managers in order to align structure, processes, rewards, and people in support of the organization's strategy (Galbraith, 1994), and to allow coordination, boundary mainte-nance, and goal-oriented behavior that links the organization to the external environment.

A second premise is that because organizations and the contexts in which they operate regularly change, organizational practice often precedes academic knowledge. Research methodologies are required that are suited to study organizations as dynamic rather than as fixed entities with endur-ing features (Huber & Glick, 1993; Lawler et al., 1985). We agree with Kurt Lewin (1951) that the best way to understand organizations is to study them when they are changing. This is true not only because many organizational dynamics are exposed during a period of change, but also because this is the best time to generate knowledge that can contribute to organizational change.

A third premise of design research is that a full understanding of organi-zations requires three focuses: (1) on the structures and processes that com-prise the organization; (2) on the cognitive understandings and behaviors of the human beings whose aspirations and worldviews influence organiza-tional behavior; and (3) on the design processes, formal and informal, that organizations and the people who occupy them use to change organizational structures to better carry out their purposes in a changing environment (Mohrman, Mohrman, & Tenkasi, 1997). These focuses drive us to ask many associated questions, be informed by multiple theories, including theories from practice, and apply an array of research approaches suited to the vari-ous questions. Such multifaceted research programs have also been de-scribed and advocated by others (e.g., Lawler, 1999; Seashore et al., 1983; Van de Ven, 2007).

Collaboration in Design Research

During the design of a complex system, knowledge, preferences, and purposes from various sources are combined. For example, in designing an airplane, the knowledge of structures, combustion, aerodynamics and materials, soft-ware, and information technology, to name a few, are combined along with the aesthetic and instrumental preferences of the designers. In the design process, these specialized knowledge bases are used in the context of the goals for the system being designed and of the other knowledge elements. The same is true in the design of an organization, where design occurs in a system that has a context including goals and strategies and where the knowledge bases, purposes, preferences, values, and aesthetics of various in-dividuals and communities of practice come together. The design process includes the knowledge and preferences of the various disciplines of academic researchers, who are no less than organizational practitioners shaped by their communities of practice and guided by their own purposes (see Chapter 1, Research for Theory and Practice).

We highlight the importance of who participates in the research process for two reasons. First, because the knowledge represented in the research planning and in the designing process will be reflected in how the problem to be investigated is defined and approached. Second, because all design is a political process and allocates value in an organization. The determination of what questions to research, how to frame them theoretically, and how to design the study are all values-based decisions (Ghoshal, 2005). Those who participate have the chance to get their purposes and their knowledge considered and those who do not are at best represented by others.

Organizational designs are evaluated as to whether they foster the accomplishment of the criteria to which they were designed—criteria determined by design participants. Similarly, knowledge created by research is evaluated in terms of the study's objectives, as formulated by the research participants. If there is no interaction among practitioners and academics about the important questions to examine and the contexts being studied, practitioner knowledge and concerns are ignored and study criteria are misaligned with practice. It is no wonder that such research is neither viewed as relevant nor used. It is equally suspect theoretically when researchers study organizations with little knowledge about the problems practitioners face or their purposes.

Problem-Focused Research

A problem-focused approach has guided much of the research at CEO. Our topics have roots in our own experience-based and theoretical interests in organization, but they emerge and are shaped in close interaction with practitioners. Problem-focused research provides a natural home for and evokes a need for collaboration that brings together multiple perspectives, including those of theory and practice. The most important problems are often not readily resolvable within any current community of practice. They call for the combination of knowledge from multiple perspectives, expertises, and disciplines (Mohrman, Galbraith, & Monge, 2006; Mohrman et al., 1999; Stokes, 1997; Van de Ven, 2007).

Problems create a context in which practitioners are more likely to be open to influence from research. Problems represent anomalies and present a need to step outside the daily reality that is driven by implicit theories and ready-to-hand solutions, and to try to achieve a detachment that enables the search for new understandings that can guide action (Argyris, 1996; Schön, 1983; Weick, 2003). "It is in these moments of interruption that theory relates most clearly to practice and practice most readily accommodates the abstract categories of theory" (Weick, 2003, p. 469).

Programmatic Research

Conducting problem-focused research that yields information useful to organizations in designing solutions to the problems they face most likely requires a program of research rather than a single study. One study does not adequately address a complex problem area, such as how to design a performance management (PM) system that effectively contributes to the achievement of strategy and performance objectives and to future-oriented capability development. Such a system was the focus of one of CEO's early research programs. We worked with multiple companies through different stages and modes of investigation that included exploratory, descriptive, and action research. These companies were interested in redesigning their performance management systems to be forward-looking business tools not just backward-looking appraisals. The studies examined the individual level, but also manager/subordinate dyads, and larger performance units—always with the purpose of contributing to design knowledge. Participating organizations engaged in the research to learn how to redesign PM to be more effective Business tools (Mohrman et al., 1989). The study in each company exposed the researchers to new aspects of the dynamics of performance management that were evoked by a particular system in its context and the experiential learning that had occurred as part of it. Each study setting thus brought questions to be studied, and in the process of answering them, raised new ones, pertinent to and answerable in another setting with another study.

Figure 3.1 shows the sequence of studies that constituted this research program. It began with a study at General Electric. GE's PM practices had proliferated, resulting in over a hundred different appraisal forms and practices company-wide. GE wanted to determine which approaches best contribute to capability development and business performance. Our CEO research team worked closely with a GE corporate project manager and a steering committee of human resources (HR) executives representing each of GE's business units. Their input was crucial in defining and planning the study, constructing interviews and questionnaires, and responding to findings.

A government grant enabled us to expand the study into seven very different corporations, each with multiple business units. We consistently found across all eight companies that development of capabilities and business

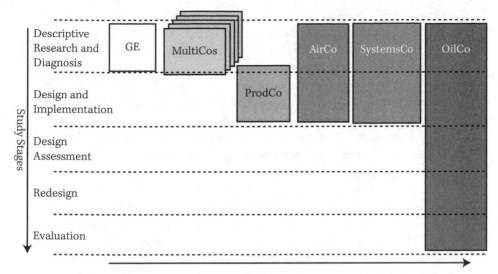

FIGURE 3.1 CEO's Program of Collaborative Performance Management Studies

performance are related to: (1) the extent to which the performance management process involves a two-way exchange between the appraisee and appraiser; and (2) the extent of alignment of individual objectives and performance criteria with the unit's business goals. Particulars of the form used and numbers of rating categories had no impact on the effectiveness of the system. These findings among others provided clear direction for redesign of the systems. For example, focus a system on guiding the processes and not on finding the most accurate measurement instruments.

From these initial primarily descriptive and hypothesis-testing studies, we began to test our knowledge in three separate action research projects in which we worked with corporate teams to assess needs and then design and implement new PM systems. This sequence of studies culminated in a longitudinal multiyear study with four large business units of an oil company ("OilCo") that wanted to design a performance management system to catalyze and accelerate work system change. This study included a baseline, multimethod, and multilevel component to test and extend theory in this increasingly team-based organization. The next phase was to test the knowledge through action in the form of design, implementation, and assessment of new PM systems. A third phase consisted of using the learnings from the assessment in a highly participative iterative redesign, implementation, and evaluation process (Mohrman & Mohrman, 2003).

We believe that multifaceted programmatic research such as this—with many related studies building on one another cumulatively and recursively—at least partially addresses a number of issues that plague management research. The knowledge from early studies provides an enticement to other companies to participate in research and extend knowledge. The research can in this way eventually involve enough cases with sufficient variation to learn about the many features and dynamics of complex, dynamic human systems and the boundary conditions of the knowledge. Such a program of research is not possible without strong collaborations that include people with diverse discipline backgrounds and from diverse communities of practice (see Chapter 1, Research for Theory and Practice, Figure 1.2).

In each program of research, new questions surface for theory and practice that lead to the next program of research. Over the course of the 30 years during which we have used this approach, our research focuses have evolved along with the increase of complexity and connectedness of the global economy and the associated changes in the corporate landscape.

Through the previously mentioned collaboration with OilCo, we developed an appreciation for and theory about the central role that PM can play, either as a key element of change or alternatively as a stubborn barrier to change in a complex organizational system. We became acutely aware of the tight connection between the design of the work system and the design of the performance management system (Mohrman & Mohrman, 1998; Tenkasi, Mohrman, & Mohrman, 1998). OilCo was changing their work systems in fundamental ways as they moved to a more lateral way of operating characterized by cross-functional teams in almost all aspects of their business. They had encountered a problem that they could not solve given current hierarchical conceptualizations of performance management, and they knew they needed to develop new understandings and practices. For OilCo, the knowledge generated in the research contributed to the fundamental redesign of PM.

These final performance management studies and our ongoing interactions with our general sponsor base made us aware of a new problem that companies were facing and for which there was inadequate organizational theory and academic understanding. Companies were struggling with the wide-scale adoption of cross-functional teaming approaches to rapidly solve problems, make improvements, develop innovative products, and meet customer needs. They were finding that the guidance they took from the sociotechnically based teams paradigm being used in factories was insufficient to help them effectively design teams for knowledge work settings. They were also finding, like OilCo, that their organizational systems and processes worked against effective teaming. We began to study the design of team-based organizations in knowledge settings—focusing on the entire organization and all processes, including PM (Mohrman, Cohen, & Mohrman, 1995).

Figure 3.2 shows a stream of CEO's team research programs. Each research program was a series of related studies building on each other to

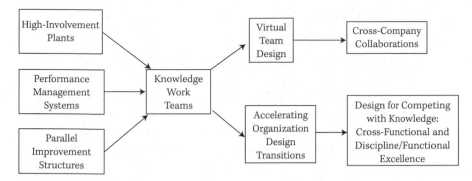

FIGURE 3.2 A Recursive Sequence of Programs in the Organization Design Research at CEO

more fully understand the organizational dynamics and design choices for particular problems. Each program built on the knowledge generated and the new issues that became salient in the previous program. The close collaborations and extensive contact with organizational members that were inherent in our work made us aware of some of the core problems that they were facing. The knowledge work teams (KWT) research built on our earlier work that studied design for high-involvement, organizational improvement systems and high-performance factory systems, and on our performance management and change research. Those KWT studies, in turn, exposed us to theoretical and practical issues that stimulated subsequent research programs, such as one that looked at the problem of how to organize for virtual teaming and another that looked at the learning processes entailed in a shift from hierarchical to lateral work processes.

The next section examines our knowledge work teams research program with special attention to the research collaborations that composed it and how collaboration was built. We then take a deeper dive examining the elements of one highly successful collaboration.

Collaboration in a Knowledge Work Teams Research Program

The KWT research program lasted for five years, and its purpose was to gain knowledge useful to the design of effective team-based work systems in knowledge work settings. Our initial step was to convene a "special interest group workshop" of companies interested in talking about their experiences with knowledge work teams and creating a research agenda. That meeting led first to a ten-month collaboration with the

Hewlett-Packard Corporation (HP) and to subsequent collaborations with nine other companies.

1. The HP research project was collaborative. The research team consisted of four academics from CEO and four members of the Strategic Change Services (SCS) group at HP. Our HP collaborators were focused on learning how to design effective new product development teams to speed time to market. The use of cross-functional teams for this purpose was new to the company. It was proving more difficult than anticipated to become effective at this work design in the research and development (R&D) part of the company, despite the company's impressive success using team designs in factories.

   This study used a grounded research approach to understand teaming in knowledge-work settings (Glaser & Strauss, 1967). We took into account existing theories of teams that had been developed mostly in production and back office settings, although we knew from our special interest group meeting that companies were having trouble applying these theories effectively. We also built on theories of work design and technology. We conducted structured interviews with approximately 15 managers, team leaders, and members in a succession of ten HP product divisions. After each set of division-specific interviews, two members of the research team coded the themes; then the entire research team met to interpret the findings and make refinements to our working models as we became aware of salient elements in each setting. Through the succession of ten cases, the design team generated theory and a foundational design model for highly interdependent knowledge work.

   One test of this model was through action research in the participating HP divisions. The HP collaborators turned the learnings from the study into an intervention tool, worked with the redesign processes in many HP divisions, systematically assessed the impact of changes, and developed a dissemination strategy so that divisions across HP became aware of and started to use the design model.

Through the collaboration with HP it had become clear that the difficulty companies were having building effective knowledge work teams stemmed from the ambiguity of authority in these cross-functional structures, the dynamic contexts in which they operated, and the extreme interdependence in these settings. They needed features to deal with each of these contextual realities. Subsequent collaborations with other companies built on, tested, and extended this understanding and contributed to more generalizable theory and to enriched models of knowledge-work teaming. These collaborations, illustrated in Figure 3.3, included the following:

2. The replication of the exploratory HP study in a corporation that had a very different business model and employed different technologies. There we studied teams designing large electronic and information technology (IT) systems. We enlarged our focus to deal with the integration between multiple interdependent teams involving as many as hundreds of engineers, scientists, technicians, and analysts. Through this second collaborative study we further elaborated our theory and models and started conceptualizing the design features of business units (such as electronics programs) that operated with a cross-functional team-based work design.

3. A third collaboration included developing a survey instrument to measure the theoretical constructs and field testing it in a corporation that employed cross-functional teams to research and develop innovative consumer foods products. The line management sponsors in this setting wanted to understand how to increase the effectiveness of these cross-functional teams. They were interested in a diagnostic tool that would help them determine causes of team dysfunctions and underperformance.

4. Seven other companies collaborated to improve and validate the survey and the theory-based team model in companies with different kinds of teams and technologies. Their agenda was to learn a new framework, but also to gain a tool— a diagnostic survey.

5. Two of the seven companies in step 4 continued on with a formal redesign of their team-based work systems based on the findings from the diagnostic surveys. We worked with them to carry out systematic assessment and iterative design, thereby developing a more nuanced understanding of how theoretical concepts worked in practice.

During the three years of these studies, periodic conferences were held for the participating companies, in which current results were shared and discussed. Companies and academics shared perspectives and interpretations of study findings and of what the companies were changing and learning in their companies about how to make their teams more effective. The systematic findings from the research were only one input into wide-ranging discussions that focused primarily on the knowledge and experience of practice. These sessions were important for the CEO researchers in understanding the contexts in which the research is used (or not) and in further understanding the actual challenges of practice.

Various academic- and practitioner-oriented articles, chapters, and presentations were generated along the way. At the end of the program of the collaborations, when we felt confident in the overall model that had been

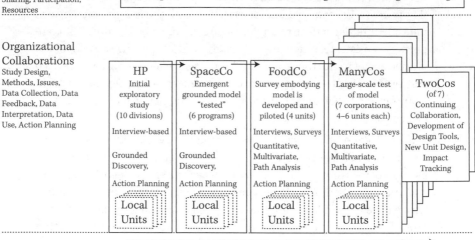

Multiorganizational Collaboration
Program Design, Knowledge Sharing, Participation, Resources

Special Interest Group Meeting: Problem Definition
Participant Conferences: Results Sharing and Knowledge Exchange

Organizational Collaborations
Study Design, Methods, Issues, Data Collection, Data Feedback, Data Interpretation, Data Use, Action Planning

HP	SpaceCo	FoodCo	ManyCos	TwoCos
Initial exploratory study (10 divisions)	Emergent grounded model "tested" (6 programs)	Survey embodying model is developed and piloted (4 units)	Large-scale test of model (7 corporations, 4–6 units each)	(of 7) Continuing Collaboration, Development of Design Tools, New Unit Design, Impact Tracking
Interview-based	Interview-based	Interviews, Surveys	Interviews, Surveys	
		Quantitative, Multivariate, Path Analysis	Quantitative, Multivariate, Path Analysis	
Grounded Discovery,	Grounded Discovery,			
Action Planning	Action Planning	Action Planning	Action Planning	
Local Units	Local Units	Local Units	Local Units	

FIGURE 3.3 Multilevel Collaboration in the Recursive Knowledge Work Team Program Studies

generated, the cumulative results of the research program were published in a book (Mohrman, Cohen, & Mohrman, 1995) aimed at a mixed audience of academics and practitioners. We quickly received feedback from some of our company collaborators that a 389-page book was not viewed by many practitioners as a particularly useful product. These collaborators had found participation in the study and the study findings useful in helping them to make changes in the design of their knowledge work teams that contributed to more effective performance. Yet we still faced the challenge of how to "package" learnings from this study to make them broadly accessible and compelling to the managers in their organizations. This need led to an additional collaboration:

6. Two of the participating companies collaborated in the creation of a design workbook that placed the findings from the research study into a practical design tool (Mohrman & Mohrman, 1997). Representatives of these companies worked with us to think through the parameters that should characterize a useful design tool. Ideally they wanted a tool that could be used by line managers independently once they understood the model. To help do this, an instructional designer was brought into the team. This person brought graphic design ideas and was an expert in the visualization of complex information—skills none of the academic research team

possessed. Both collaborating companies provided several beta sites—units that were redesigning or being formed anew. The unit managers used a draft of the workbook with the design team and provided feedback on how to change and improve the tool.

The HP Collaboration—The Knowledge Combination Process

The first study (with HP) in the KWT research program illustrates some key elements of a highly successful collaboration from the perspective of the different involved stakeholders. This collaboration is described in greater detail elsewhere (Mohrman et al., 2007). In this chapter, we will focus on the knowledge contributions and roles of members of the different communities of practice in the research, alignment and differentiation of purpose and interests, and the unfolding of the collaborative relationship through time.

The four members of HP's SCS group who were our direct collaborators were experienced internal organizational effectiveness consultants. Several had specialized in the design and implementation of high-involvement factory work systems. Thus, although representing two different communities of practice (academic researchers and company-based organizational consultants), there was considerable overlap in knowledge bases, and purposes were readily aligned. Both were concerned with extending existing knowledge to contribute to the design of innovative organizational approaches to address important organizational problems. The groups shared common values on business, technical, and social features and outcomes that were inherent in the sociotechnical systems models that had underpinned the practical work at HP and had been the focus on some of the previous CEO research.

The head of this group, Stu Winby, saw the collaboration with USC as the first test of a new way of operating for his group. His vision was that SCS would partner with academic researchers to yield knowledge that would become embodied in the capabilities of HP through the SCS's development of models, frameworks, and tools to help HP achieve a competitive advantage (Kaplan, 2000; Kaplan & Winby, 1999). In Stu's words, "In many ways the SCS mission was similar to the USC-CEO mission. We had action research as the core and base of all our operations. Sharing a similar mission from external and internal perspectives made the outcomes all the more robust" (Mohrman et al., 2007).

The study team exchanged and iterated articles and working documents and had several teleconferences in which the members described our goals for the study and shared ideas about how these might be accomplished. We then spent a day together, agreeing on purpose and on a high-level research design. The purposes were to learn from the nascent product development teaming efforts in the corporation about the following areas:

- the nature of knowledge work teaming
- how knowledge work teaming differs from factory floor teaming
- what design features influence the effectiveness of knowledge teams in accomplishing business, customer, and employee outcomes
- how existing models of team systems and existing intervention models need to change to reflect the knowledge that is developed

Nested within the overall CEO/HP collaboration were a series of local collaborations that brought in a third community of practice: the managers and team leaders who were trying to use cross-functional new product development teams as a business tool. A study team was set up in each participating division to help shape the micro design of the study at the local level and articulate local goals and questions for the study. This local team also interpreted the data patterns that emerged from the study and identified action implications. The study teams at the local level minimally included the general manager, key functional managers, and several team leaders.

The common problem aligned the interests of the divisional leaders with the research. They were interested in understanding and redesigning their new product development teams to be more effective. Their focus on action aligned with our belief that the test of the knowledge in practice happens through a design process in which the new design is socially constructed by the participants.

CEO members saw this collaboration as a first step in creating a robust theory and a model of knowledge teams that could become part of the academic and practitioner literatures, and a design model for knowledge teams that could be employed by many organizations. The goal for the HP's SCS members was to create a grounded, substantive model to guide team transitions and redesigns at HP, to test the model through their various consulting interventions, and to "productize" the model and the design intervention process so that it could more easily diffuse throughout the organization (Kaplan & Winby, 1999). HP's intervention models and the working model for knowledge teams that the CEO researchers wrote up and carried forward into next studies were variants of the same knowledge base that was created through the collaboration and in particular through collaborative interpretation of the data patterns. Both understood the results through the lens of their roles, values, and goals, and encoded the resulting knowledge in formats that fit their communities of practice and contributed to the intended trajectory of their professional activities.

CEO's knowledge work teams research program further developed the programmatic approach that we had used with the earlier performance management studies. With interested companies we identified a broad problem and moved through a series of studies and addressed the various stages of knowledge creation. This process started with the identification of a problem and moved from exploratory research to theory generation and testing, model creation, and the testing of the knowledge through action research. In both the performance management program and the knowledge work teams program, the initial grounded work was enabled through collaboration with a large corporation with internal organizational effectiveness units comfortable with research and interested in the opportunity to work with academic researchers to generate knowledge. These initial collaborations yielded a baseline theory and design model that attracted additional companies to replicate, extend, and then test the model through systematic evaluation research. Throughout the process, we published the incremental knowledge for both communities, in both cases finally "packaging" the combined knowledge in books aimed at the dual communities of research and practice (Mohrman, Cohen, & Mohrman, 1995; Mohrman et al., 1989).

HP would collaborate with CEO in two more research studies during the next decade—one focusing on the acceleration of fundamental changes in organization designs and the other on the design features for effective virtual teaming. Many companies in CEO's network of sponsors and collaborators were experiencing problems in these areas—a fact that led CEO to initiate multicompany research programs. Both communities of practice were attending to the same unfolding environmental, organizational, and competitive dynamics that were reshaping organizations. Organizational practitioners in companies around the world were, through experience and design, developing knowledge and approaches to deal with these forces. Academic knowledge was also being generated in universities and research groups globally. These were the knowledge bases we brought together in collaborative problem-oriented research.

Recursive Research Programs

By 1995, CEO's KWT research team had worked intensely together for six years. Through our experiences studying the ten companies, we subsequently became interested, collectively and individually, in related problems that emerged from the team study. We pursued these questions in subsequent collaborative research programs (see Figure 3.2). Susan Cohen teamed with Cris Gibson to conduct longitudinal, multicompany, collaborative studies of the features and dynamics of virtual teams, which were becoming more and more prevalent and added layers of complexity to the challenge of designing effective teams (Gibson & Cohen, 2003). This was followed by a series of studies of virtual teaming across company boundaries (Mankin & Cohen, 2004).

Mohrman and Mohrman sequentially pursued two multistudy, multicompany research programs that stemmed directly from the theoretical and practical challenges encountered during the knowledge work teams program. The first included academic colleague Ram Tenkasi and ten companies to explore the change and learning challenges companies were confronting as they moved from the functional, hierarchical designs to cross-functional, lateral organizations (Tenkasi, Mohrman, & Mohrman, 1998). The purpose of the participating companies was to learn how to accelerate such changes. The second research program was a collaboration with academic colleagues David Finegold and Jan Klein and nine companies to examine design approaches to address the competing tensions faced by technical firms as they try to maintain cutting-edge technical capability while using cross-functional teaming to meet performance pressures (Mohrman, Klein, & Finegold, 2003; Mohrman, Mohrman, & Finegold, 2003). The purpose of the companies was to understand how to operate cross-functionally yet continually extend their discipline and functional capabilities. The purpose of the academic researchers was to understand how organizations build the capacity to manage these multiple focuses that establish apparently conflicting interests in the organization.

Both these multiple company studies were longitudinal in nature, allowing us to examine the dynamics and impacts of change over time. Because we often did not have the good fortune to work with internal researcher-consultants as we had in the HP example, we developed a permutation of our approach; in some companies, a member of the academic research team worked closely as a participant collaborator in the company's action research process, while the others focused on the systematic longitudinal data gathering and analysis.

Studying Our Collaborative Research Process: The Importance of Relating to Internal Design Processes

To gain insight into whether and how collaborative research is useful to organizations, Chris Gibson, who was then a newly arrived researcher at CEO, teamed with us to craft a retrospective study of the ten companies that had participated in the research program aimed at generating knowledge about how to accelerate organization design transitions. The study was based on previous theory about how different communities are able to incorporate each other's knowledge to yield changes in the way they practice (Boland & Tenkasi, 1995; Tenkasi & Mohrman, 1999). The data were gathered using a structured interview methodology, coded and analyzed, and interpreted by two researchers who had not been involved in the original research nor in any of the previous CEO collaborative research programs.

This investigation (Mohrman, Gibson, & Mohrman, 2001) in our view confirmed the suitability of collaborative research with a design perspective to yield useful knowledge. Whether these companies viewed the research as having been useful related to whether they actually used the findings. Did they incorporate the findings into their internal sense-making and organizational design processes? Did they make changes to their organization taking the findings into account? Usefulness also related to whether the company participants experienced the researchers as having incorporated the perspective of practice into the research and to whether time had been spent mutually interpreting the data patterns. Interestingly, usefulness was not related to practitioner involvement in the design and conduct of the research. This finding suggests that the usefulness of research knowledge does not depend on turning practitioners into researchers. It depends on bridging the meaning gap and generating knowledge that can be contextualized by the organization to inform changes in the way they operate.

The onus of usefulness is not only on the academic researcher. Usefulness depends on the members of the company engaging in the hard and intentional work of applying the knowledge to make changes in how they function. In the HP example, the SCS group's role was to create tools and interventions to make this possible. It produced models that were disseminated and became widely available to guide line managers and organizational effectiveness professionals leading and working with many HP units moving toward team-based designs. According to their leader, Stu Winby:

> What we discovered about ways of organizing and the artifacts we developed were helpful to people in conceptualizing what they were about. Years later I saw the models out on managers' desks. People don't understand the impact because it's all tacit. We formalized all that into a model that could be used in consulting, not just by our group, but by many others in the organization. (Winby in Mohrman et al., 2007, p. 523)

The SCS group used the project with CEO to hone its approach to contribute value to HP, including finding ways to disseminate the learnings from the project more broadly. The group was aware from experience that successful design innovations do not diffuse easily. They sponsored a series of Work Innovation Network (WIN) meetings, where line managers and various other groups came together to hear about the experience of HP units that had used the models to redesign. The sessions were used to talk with each other about what is required and what would lead to improvements in the model and to have participants leave with both contacts and awareness of how they could utilize this knowledge locally. Winby reflects on the role of the WIN meetings:

> We all read Dick Walton's work that pointed out that you often do a new plant start up that is highly successful but never diffuses anywhere else in the company. We hired a person who started working on diffusion approaches and we developed a model for diffusing work innovations. The principle was to develop a pull system rather than rely on pushing the innovation out. Get the line managers to present their results at our Work Innovation Meeting, which became the distribution and marketing arm of the model. We would do the work with the customer and measure the results and even if it was a failure it was presented at the WIN meeting—the General Manager and another manager from the division and one of our group would stand up and present what happened. It was videotaped and shared beyond even the attendees. People from other businesses would come up and say, "Can I do that? Can I send someone to your business to learn?" This often provided next generation projects so that the learning could be extended to new areas. (Winby in Mohrman et al., 2007, p. 523)

This example illustrates the challenge and extent of multistakeholder involvement required for knowledge to be turned into changed practice. Conversely, it illustrates how easy it would be for even the most collaborative of research to lead to no change, if the companies do not put in place the processes for learning and change.

Challenges and Future Approaches in Design Research

Organization sciences face major hurdles in meeting the demands of rigorous science. In following the tenets of rigorous positivistic science, these disciplines also face major barriers to relevance to organizations. In our view, the hurdles of science and relevance converge. We believe that a programmatic collaborative organizational design research approach, while not solving these problems completely, addresses some of these challenges.

One science challenge is examining enough instances of a phenomenon to be able to draw inferences that seem valid and reliable from instance to instance—the challenge of generalizability. Practitioners sense this same shortcoming and feel a lack of confidence that the patterns of academic findings are relevant to them in their context facing their particular set of performance challenges. Collaboratively examining issues with multiple companies, methodologies, and from multiple perspectives helps address the problems of generalizability and contextual variability.

Another science challenge is executing longitudinal and predictive research designs to increase confidence in the value of the knowledge to people and organizations to help address their problems and become more effective. Alternating descriptive and predictive research (Chatman, 2005) helps deal with the need for rigorous knowledge and predictive power and begins to bridge the gap between the theory-driven world of academia and the context and results-driven world of organizational practice.

The complexity of organizational systems, in terms of both the number of elements, actors, and relationships and their dynamic nature, poses a challenge for researchers, whose methodologies have only slowly evolved to be able to deal with complex systems. There is a mismatch between methodologies and the reality of complex organizational contexts; the former demand control and can only handle a narrow range of variables, and the latter does not afford practitioners the luxury of analytically separating out its parts when making decisions about how to operate. Practitioners look for tools and interventions that make a difference in solving problems—actionable approaches that do not come couched in terms of variables and causal relationships abstracted from practice. Research programs that include action components by necessity place knowledge squarely into the complex world of practice.

Collaborative, programmatic, design research approaches only partially deal with these challenges. We know from our own research that even the participants in such studies only sometimes apply the knowledge that is generated. Furthermore, many of the companies in our CEO network and beyond are increasingly resistant to time-consuming research to solve problems that they are struggling with right now. They seek the holy grail of tested "best practices" believed to be effective in other companies viewed as successful and able to be quickly and readily implemented.

Yet the need for research is evident. Organizations face no shortage of challenges and pressures to change their practices to be successful in areas that are poorly understood. Today's fast-paced environment is characterized by unprecedented levels of global interdependence and the ongoing reconfiguration of players, strategies, capabilities, and resources. The problems companies confront are increasingly complex and urgent. If the organizational sciences are to be useful in such an environment, then there must be increased speed, greater incorporation into research processes of the problems of organizational practice, and the ability to deal with increased complexity through greater multidisciplinarity in our research approaches.

We feel confident that collaborative design research is an approach that promotes usefulness. Yet we know that this potential will not be achieved if we do not enhance our capabilities to conduct research more quickly and in a way that addresses the changing realities faced by organizations. At CEO we are working on ways to create parallelism in erstwhile time-consuming, sequential research processes. We are creating broader and more diverse networks of collaborators loosely configured to simultaneously bring multiple methods and theories together to focus on a common problem. One such problem that we are addressing is how to elevate contribution to societal and ecological sustainability to be core organizational focuses and primary outcomes. We are building a collaborative research network with diverse stakeholders including the knowledge bases needed to accelerate the conduct of research and the sharing of ideas and findings. In this way we hope to break down the sometimes competitive silos between researchers and to combine the knowledge of multidisciplinary research and organizational practice. Such a network of collaborators ideally will collectively and quickly detect, examine, catalyze, and study changes in organizing practices.

This goal is lofty and the challenges are immense. These include the complexity of the substantive challenges being investigated—of organizing for new purposes and in new ways. Perhaps most challenging, however, are the process elements of building the research network in new ways. Only by innovating our organizational research practices can we hope that research knowledge will be relevant to the organizations we study and with whom we collaborate—and to the immense organizing challenges in today's world.

We at CEO are definitely not alone in advocating the need for such changes in how we operate. The proposed tenets of "engaged research," beautifully developed by Van de Ven (2007), are similar to our approach. Engaged research is also aimed at collaborating to solve important problems. In effect, organizational researchers are facing the very same challenges faced by the organizations we study in this dynamic and complex environment. We have to change the way we operate to reflect and address the changing context in which we are trying to add value.

REFERENCES

Argyris, C. (1996). Actionable knowledge: Design causality in the service of consequential theory. *Journal of Applied Behavioral Science, 32*, 390–406.

Boland, R. J., & Tenkasi, R. V. (1995). Perspective making and perspective taking in communities of knowing. *Organization Science, 6*(4), 350–437.

Campbell, D. T., & Stanley, J. C. (1963). *Experimental and quasi-experimental designs for research.* Chicago: Rand McNally & Co.

Chatman, J. (2005). Full-cycle micro-organizational behavior research. *Organization Science. 16*(4), 434–447.

Eden, C., & Huxham, C. (1996). Action research for the study of organizations. In S. Clegg, C. Hardy, & W. R. Nords (Eds.), *Handbook of organizational studies* (pp. 526–542). Thousand Oaks, CA: Sage.

Elden, M., & Chisholm, R. F. (1993). Features of emerging action research. *Human Relations, 46*(2), 121–142.

Galbraith, J. R. (1994). *Competing with the lateral, flexible, organization.* Reading, MA: Addison-Wesley.

Ghoshal, S. (2005). Bad management theories are destroying good management practices. *Academy of Management Learning & Education, 4*(1), 75–91.

Gibson, C., & Cohen, S. (2003). *Virtual teams that work: Creating conditions for virtual team effectiveness.* San Francisco: Jossey-Bass.

Glaser, B. G., & Strauss, A. L. (1967). *The discovery of grounded theory.* Hawthorne, NY: Aldine.

Huber, G. P., & Glick, W. H. (Eds). (1993). *Organizational change and redesign: Ideas and insights for improving performance.* New York: Oxford Press.

Kaplan, S. (2000). Innovating professional services. *Consulting to management, 11*(1), 30–34.

Kaplan, S., & Winby, S. (1999). *Knowledge asset innovation at Hewlett Packard.* Hewlett Packard Internal Working Paper.

Lawler, E. (1999). Challenging traditional research assumptions. In E. E. Lawler III, A. M. Mohrman Jr., S. A. Mohrman, G. E. Ledford, T. G. Cummings, & Associates (Eds.), *Doing research that is useful for theory and practice* (pp. 1–17). Lanham, MD: Lexington Books.

Lawler, E., Mohrman, A., Mohrman, S., Cummings, T., & Ledford, G. (Eds.). (1985). *Doing research that is useful for theory and practice.* San Francisco: Jossey-Bass.

Lewin, K. (1951). *Field theory in the social sciences.* New York: Harper & Row.

Mankin, D., & Cohen, S. G. (2004). *Business without boundaries: An action framework for collaborating across time, distance, organization and culture.* San Francisco: Jossey-Bass.

Mohrman, A. M., Jr., & Mohrman, S. A. (1998). Catalyzing organizational change and learning: The role of performance management. In S. A. Mohrman, J. R. Galbraith, E. E. Lawler III, & Associates (Eds.), *Tomorrow's organization: Crafting winning capabilities in a dynamic world* (pp. 362–393). San Francisco: Jossey-Bass.

Mohrman, A. M., Jr., & Mohrman, S. A. (2003). Self-designing a performance management system. In N. Adler, A. Shani, & A. Styhre (Eds.), *Collaborative research in organizations: Leveraging academy-industry partnerships* (pp. 313–333). Thousand Oaks, CA: Sage.

Mohrman, A. M., Jr., Mohrman, S. A., Lawler, E. E., & Ledford, G. E. (1999). Introduction. In E. E. Lawler III, A. M. Mohrman, Jr., S. A. Mohrman, G. E. Ledford, T. G. Cummings, & Associates (Eds.), *Doing research that is useful for theory and practice* (pp. ix–xlix). Lanham, MD: Lexington Books.

Mohrman, A. M., Jr., Resnick West, S., & Lawler, E. E. (1989). *Designing performance appraisal systems.* San Francisco: Jossey-Bass.

Mohrman, S. A., Cohen, S. G., & Mohrman, A. M., Jr. (1995). *Designing team-based organizations: New applications for knowledge work.* San Francisco: Jossey-Bass.

Mohrman, S. A., & Cummings, T. G. (1989*). Self-designing organizations: Learning how to create high performance.* Reading, MA: Addison-Wesley.

Mohrman, S. A., Galbraith, J. R., & Monge, P. (2006). Network attributes impacting the generation and flow of knowledge within and from the basic science community. In J. Hage and M. Meeus (Eds.), *Innovation, science and industrial change: The handbook of research* (pp. 196–216). London: Oxford University Press.

Mohrman, S. A., Gibson, C. B., & Mohrman, A. M., Jr. (2001). Doing research that is useful to practice. *Academy of Management Journal, 44*(2), 347–375.

Mohrman, S. A., Klein, J. A., & Finegold, D. (2003). Managing the global new product development network: A sense-making perspective. In C. Gibson & S. Cohen, (Eds.), *Virtual teams that work: Creating conditions for virtual team effectiveness* (pp. 37–58). San Francisco: Jossey-Bass.

Mohrman, S. A., & Mohrman, A. M., Jr. (1997). *Designing and leading team-based organizations: A workbook for organizational self-design.* San Francisco: Jossey-Bass.

Mohrman, S. A., Mohrman A. M., Jr., Cohen, S., & Winby, S. (2007). The collaborative learning cycle: Advancing theory and building practical design frameworks through collaboration. In A. B. Shani, S. A. Mohrman, W. A. Pasmore, B. Stymne, & N. Adler (Eds.), *Handbook of collaborative management research* (pp. 509–530). Thousand Oaks, CA: Sage.

Mohrman, S. A., Mohrman, A. M., Jr., & Finegold, D. (2003). An empirical model of the organization knowledge system in new product development firms. *Journal of Engineering and Technology Management, 20*(1–2), 7–38.

Mohrman, S. A., Mohrman, A. M., Jr., & Tenkasi, R. (1997). The discipline of organization design. In C. L. Cooper & S. E. Jackson (Eds.), *Creating tomorrow's organizations: A handbook for future research in organizational behavior* (pp. 191–205). West Sussex, UK: Wiley.

Reason, P., & Bradbury, H. (2001). *Handbook of action research: Participative inquiry and practice.* London: Sage.

Romme, A.G.L. (2003). Making a difference: Organization as design. *Organization Science, 14,* 559–573.

Romme, A.G.L., & Endenburg, G. (2006). Construction principles and design rules in the case of circular design. *Organization Science, 17,* 287–297.

Schön, D. A. (1983). *The reflective practitioner: How professionals think in action.* San Francisco: Jossey-Bass.

Seashore, S. L., Lawler, E. E., Mirvis, P. H., & Cammann, C. (Eds.). (1983). *Assessing organizational change: A guide to methods, measures, and practices.* New York: WileyInterscience.

Shani, A. B., Mohrman, S. A., Pasmore, W. A., Stymne, B., & Adler, N. (Eds.). (2007). *Handbook of collaborative management research.* Thousand Oaks, CA: Sage.

Simon, H. A. (1969). *The sciences of the artificial.* Cambridge, MA: The MIT Press.

Stokes, D. E. (1997). *Pasteur's quadrant: Basic science and technological innovation.* Washington, DC: Brookings Institution Press.

Tenkasi, R. V., & Mohrman, S. A. (1999). Global change as contextual collaborative knowledge creation. In D. L. Cooperrider & J. E. Dutton (Eds.), *Organizational dimensions of global change: No limits to cooperation (Human dimensions of global change)* (pp. 114–136). Thousand Oaks, CA: Corwin.

Tenkasi, R. V., Mohrman S. A., & Mohrman, A. M., Jr. (1998). Accelerating learning during transition. In S. A. Mohrman, J. R. Galbraith, E. E. Lawler III, & Associates (Eds.), *Tomorrow's organization: Crafting winning capabilities in a dynamic world* (pp. 330–361). San Francisco: Jossey-Bass.

van Aken, J. E. (2004). Management research based on the paradigm of the design sciences: The quest for field-tested and grounded technological rules. *Journal of Management Studies, 41,* 219–246.

van Aken, J. E. (2005). Management research as a design science: Articulating the research products of mode 2 knowledge production in management. *British Journal of Management, 16,* 19–36.

Van de Ven, A. H. (2007). *Engaged scholarship: A guide for organizational and social research.* New York: Oxford University Press.

Weick, K. (2003). Theory and practice in the real world. In H. Tsoukas & C. Knudsen (Eds.), *The Oxford handbook of organization theory: Meta-theoretical perspective* (pp. 453–475). New York: Oxford University Press.

ABOUT THE AUTHORS

Susan Albers Mohrman is senior research scientist at the Center for Effective Organizations (CEO) in the Marshall School of Business at the University of Southern California. Her research and publications focus on organizational design for lateral integration and flexibility, networks in basic science, design for sustainable effectiveness, organizational change and implementation, and research methodologies for bridging theory and practice. She is cofounder and a faculty director of CEO's certificate program in organization design. In the area of useful research, she is an editor and author of the *Handbook of Collaborative Management Research* (2007).

Allan M. Mohrman Jr. is a founding member of the Center for Effective Organizations (CEO) in the Marshall School of Business at the University of Southern California. His research and publications focus on performance management, organization design, team-based organizations, and research methodologies that bridge theory and practice.

FOUR

A Ten-Year Journey of Cooperation

LYNDA GRATTON*

PREPARING THIS CHAPTER has provided a marvelous opportunity to consider the way in which my own research agenda has evolved and how engaged scholarship and action-based research (Van de Ven & Johnson, 2006) has been so central to my working life. Looking back, I see a long and continuous process of questioning where I have learned and continue to learn about a number of topics that are profoundly important to me.

One of the emerging themes in this book has been the extent to which the personal interests and experience of this group of scholars have shaped their research. I am no exception to this. Having spent the first ten years of my postdoctoral career in both a major company and a consulting practice before returning to a full-time post in academia, it is no surprise that my interest is in active collaboration with practicing managers. Like many of the scholars in this book, my initial training was as an industrial/organizational psychologist. My research preference is a combination of case writing, to build a deep understanding, and of diagnostics/instrumentation, to work at a broader canvas and discern the emerging themes. I like to use multiple methods to triangulate on the truth, and like Michael Beer, I am definitely a groundhog focusing on one or two domains of practice. So although I was trained as a psychologist to examine the individual, increasingly I have found myself intrigued by the complexities of large companies, particularly those that operate on a global scale. I find their scale fascinating, and I believe, like my colleagues Sumantra Ghoshal and Peter Moran (2005), that they can play an important and valuable part in the everyday lives of people across the world.

---

* Although I am the author of this chapter, as will become clear this research was very much a team endeavor. It began with the work of Sumantra Ghoshal and I, and the cases I refer to are all co-written by both of us. Next, Janine Nahapiet worked with me on the development of the early cooperative model and the general theory building. She was joined by Andreas Voigt, who remained a close colleague on this project for the next eight years and, in fact, managed the research supported by the Singapore Ministry of Manpower.

There are many phenomena and challenges that are being played out in large global companies right now. The area that I have chosen to focus on is innovative capacity and particularly the way in which knowledge-based task forces, project teams, and other collaborative work forms such as communities or partnerships are being developed to bring flexibility and potential innovation (Gibson & Cohen, 2003; Mankin & Cohen, 2004). For example, at the telecoms company Nokia, I have studied how a team has been tasked with considering how to bring innovations to customers in China. At the global bank Standard Chartered, the challenge was rather different—to integrate a new information technology (IT) system in the back office of four countries. Over the last ten years, I and my colleagues have studied many of these teams. What is interesting is that while the specific challenges they face may be unique, the solutions are often remarkably similar—to bring people together either virtually or in person, often from different parts of the company to work on the common task that requires the effective use of networks and "ecosystems" both within and outside the organization.

The formulation of the problem began in two rather different ways. Back in 1995, I ran a series of strategy sessions along the lines I had described in an early book, *Living Strategy* (Gratton, 2000). I ran these strategy sessions with many companies around the world and on the human resources (HR) program I have directed at London Business School for more than 20 years. This involved my working with teams of executives to create a "risk matrix"—a means by which they could identify the areas of risk they believed they would encounter in meeting their long-term business strategy. After analyzing more than 20 of these workshop outcomes, what was striking was the extent to which the capacity to support team working and to actively share knowledge across boundaries and to make the connections was seen as the most common area of risk (Gratton, 1996).

At around the same time I designed, with my colleague Sumantra Ghoshal, a senior executive program at London Business School. In it we took six teams of executives from six companies on a three-module program lasting for one year. It was clear that forging links across businesses was a crucial issue. We went on to explore this more in a paper published in *Sloan Management Review* in 2003 that went on to win the Richard Beckhart best paper award—another point to convince us we were on the right track (Ghoshal & Gratton, 2003). As Mike Tushman and Charles O'Reilly report (2007), we found that these executives programs provided a marvelous opportunity to link research to practice. Again I heard how executives struggled with working within and across teams and actively communicating with each other.

Listening to these various executives and analyzing the data convinced me that this issue was worthy of further development—while also providing the initial energy boost that kept my colleagues and I working on this complex topic for what turned out to be over a decade. Like Amy Edmondson, I was intrigued by the organizational dynamics that affect collaborative research, and it is interesting to see the similarities and differences our journeys took from a similar starting point.

I have described the evolution of this decade of research in two ways—as the actual journey with its various stakeholders and their involvement and later as a series of evolving research themes. Looking back on this decade I am struck by four themes of what we might call action research, themes which will form the backbone to the description in this chapter.

1. *Connection Forming.* I am struck by how much this decade of research has involved forming a wide range of connections with a whole host of people, companies, and governments. What these connections have in common is an interest in the topic and a willingness to engage in the collection of data and conversation about the outcomes. I am particularly interested in taking a multidisciplinary focus on a single topic. So over time I networked with many different types of people to gain their insight on the topic.

2. *Legitimacy and Company Interest.* Although engaging with executives at a superficial level is relatively easy, I have discovered that to do so on a deeper, more time-consuming level requires the development of a program of research that they believe is capable of adding value to their company in a number of different ways. This necessity means that in the design of a research program one has to acknowledge and understand a much wider range of stakeholder interests. In the case on Singapore Ministry of Manpower (MOM) described later, I show clearly the extent of energy required to get buy-in to action research.

3. *Surprising Twists.* As Amy Edmondson described in her chapter, I am always surprised by the findings and theoretical contribution and the unplanned nature of some of these. One can certainly design a closely argued research project—but sometimes it does not go as you expect. As I will show later, our research with both the Singapore government and Nokia took some unexpected twists. Perhaps the most surprising was the Nokia twist that, as a result of time and cost pressure, we had to shift our whole approach into a community portal (Gratton & Casse, 2010). This was a technique I had no prior knowledge of and would not have been persuaded to use under normal circumstances. However, the result of this unexpected twist is that my research team and I are now very knowledgeable about community portals—so much so that the Future of Work research program I have recently launched is mediated exclusively on a community portal.

4. *Combination, Synthesis, and Transformation.* What has also been striking is the real value that can be gained by combining knowledge from the

academic research with the knowledge of practice. My bias is towards synthesis rather than analysis when studying such complex phenomena. It is in the process of combination and synthesis that occasions deeper, richer, and more useful insights. However, this combination cannot be successfully made without the transformation of ideas as the combination occurs. In my case, for example, I have put a great deal of energy into transforming my own and other academic ideas into a form which is useful, relevant, and exciting to practitioners. This transformation is not simply about rephrasing—although this is indeed important. It is also about thinking carefully about presentation and design. It is interesting to note that the last person to join my research team is not an academic but a talented graphics designer who is tasked with ensuring that the models, tools, and ideas we communicate to managers are visually exciting.

This transformation in bridging across boundaries can also result in self-transformation in the sense of becoming a chameleon (Kilduff & Tsai, 2003). I am aware for myself that in jumping across the boundaries between academia and practice I have to transform the way I speak, the words and concepts I use, and even the clothes I wear. I agree with Michael Beer—being a boundary spanner is definitely a challenge, and like him I find myself being marginal in each of these communities. But frankly, I would have it no other way. As I hope I can show you through my ten-year research journey—being a boundary spanner can be the most exciting, energizing, and innovative place to be.

The Phases of the Research Agenda

Over the decade, the research agenda co-evolved from research insights, the interests and feedback from the companies, and responses to the broader academic developments in related fields. The research agenda has progressed through these three phases as shown in Figure 4.1.

Phase 1: Understanding the Nature of Cooperation

At the beginning of the AIM research initiative, Sumantra Ghoshal and I were both chosen as AIM scholars. We decided to work together to take a closer look at an aspect of integration and coordination that we both found fascinating—that of cooperation. With the aid of a major research grant from the United Kingdom's Advanced Institute of Management, we were able to explore this issue in greater depth. This government grant was crucial to the research. At a time when there had been a steady decline in public financial support

1999 The UK's Advanced Institute of Management (AIM) awards Senior Fellowship for a three-year period, which supports research buy-out and research assistance — the focus is on cooperation.

2000 A literature search results in a number of hypotheses and models.

2001 The Cooperative Advantage Research Consortium is launched with involvement from 15 company members in partnership with a U.S. research/consulting practice The Concours Group.

2002 Cases on cooperation in Nokia, Goldman Sachs, and BP.

2003 Researchers study cooperation in over 20 teams. Prepare articles for *Harvard Business Review* (Gratton & Erickson) and *Sloan Management Review* (Gratton, Voigt & Erickson), Articles in the *Financial Times* and the *Wall Street Journal* increase the practitioner visibility of the research.

2004 The Hot Spot model is developed and the book *Hot Spots — Why Some Organisations and Teams Buzz with Energy and Others Don't*—is prepared (Gratton, 2007).

2005 *Hot Spots* is published and the Hot Spots Movement launched with an initial website http://www.hotspotsmovement.com to encourage broader participation.

2006 Work begins on creating a computerized team-based diagnostic and report capable of benchmarking and commenting on the elements of the Hot Spot model.

2007 The diagnostic in many teams, including 100 teams in Nokia, and further benchmarked data, created. The key developmental team issues are identified and a "60-day learning journey" is designed to address these issues.

2008 The Singapore Ministry of Manpower (MOM) identifies the research and supports an initial 30 teams in Singapore to participate in the Hot Spot diagnostic and team development. We benchmark the Singapore teams and also shift the focus to teams and their capacity to learn.

2009 The findings are presented at the *MOM Human Capital Summit* and the sample size is extended to 60 teams. Work begins on analyzing the team and development data in more detail. The individual level book *Glow: Why Some People Glow with Energy and Others Don't* is published (Gratton, 2009).

2010 Membership of the Hot Spot community reaches 3,500. The second research consortium, The Future of Work and the Adoption of Innovative Practice, is launched with membership from 23 companies, many of whom are from the earlier Cooperative Advantage Research Consortium. A weekly blog updates the community: http://www.lyndagrattonfutureofwork.com.

FIGURE 4.1 The Research Timeline

(Sonnenberg, 2004), the U.K. initiative was an important boost to scholarship in the United Kingdom. Also, it is notable that much of the third phase of the work was underwritten by a grant from the Singapore government.

At that time we asked a deceptively simple question: What is the current understanding of how and why cooperation occurs, particularly with regard to knowledge sharing and innovation, and what are the key variables? This was a topic of particular interest to Sumantra, who had argued forcibly (Ghoshal & Moran, 1996) that a focus on opportunistic behavior favored at that time by economists had negated the role cooperation and trust could play. Between 2002 and 2004, Sumantra and I wrote case studies on Nokia (Gratton, Ghoshal, & Donaldson, 2004), BP (Gratton & Ghoshal, 2002), the Royal Bank of Scotland (RBS) (Gratton & Ghoshal, 2004), and Goldman Sachs (unpublished case). Together these brought a deeper awareness of how cooperation and integration was being played out in complex companies.

After Sumantra passed away in March 2004, I continued the research with our colleague Janine Nahapiet, who had already thought deeply about the role cooperation could play in creating organizational advantage. Janine and I began by developing a theoretical model of cooperation and knowledge that became the basis for the team study (Nahapiet, Gratton, & Rocha, 2005). We thought about the impact of cooperation and knowledge sharing at the level of the individual, the team, and the context of the organization (Gratton, 2005). This multilevel way of thinking about the problem was to become the cornerstone of much of what was to follow.

Phase 2: Focusing on Contemporary Teams and Innovation

At this stage, I was joined by a research assistant, Andreas Voigt. We entered the second phase of the research determined to increase our understanding of teams and the relationships between the aspects of the model shown in Figure 4.2 through large-scale team surveys. However, we faced a number of real challenges. The most obvious challenge was that whereas the first phase had been underwritten by a major grant from the AIM, this more practical and action-based phase did not receive a research grant—so participating companies had to make a financial contribution. As a consequence, this second phase of the research became closer to the CEO model of a corporate membership organization. To help us create this organization, we partnered with a consulting practice (The Concours Group) headed by a great friend, Tamara Erickson. The Concours Group had an extensive database of companies engaged with the idea of cooperation and had run contracted research in the past.

The next challenge with this phase was that the extent and depth of the analysis we required meant that the survey we had developed—even in its

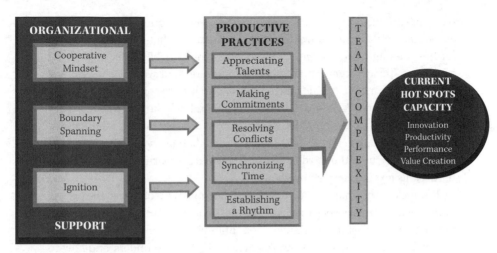

FIGURE 4.2 The Cooperative Working Model

computerized form—took participants 45 minutes and stakeholders 10 minutes to complete. As we will see later in the MOM study, this was to be a major challenge to creating buy-in to the research.

Finally, we began to learn that for many companies the unit of value and analysis was still the individual and not the team. Although understanding that teams were important to many executives, we observed that for most companies there was no natural conduit for action-based research on the performance of innovative, complex teams. I believe this is a problem for any action research that attempts to observe phenomena that lie across the boundaries of a company.

Despite these challenges, we were able to move to the second phase, where we took a broad view of how cooperation worked inside teams and the impact on the actions and performance of the teams—in particular the impact on innovation. The research question evolved to this: To what extent do these variables impact the performance and innovation of the team? And in what way is this impact moderated, and under what circumstances are cooperation and knowledge sharing enhanced? To understand this, we developed a performance instrument that we used with the stakeholders of the teams, such as suppliers and customers. This instrumentation became the basis of both the research with the Singapore Ministry of Manpower and the large-scale Nokia study we undertook.

Phase 3: Making It Actionable—Teams and Learning

As Michael Beer writes in Chapter 8, Making a Difference *and* Contributing Useful Knowledge, "Knowing about relationships between managerially relevant variables does not, however, ensure effective action." He believes the emphasis should be on knowledge that is actionable "that provides guidance for how managers should go about solving problems." By this third phase of the research, we knew what the problems were—but what we had not yet done was to work with managers to understand how to solve them. The book about the research *Hot Spots* (Gratton, 2007) had, of course, provided some answers, but I was keen that we become more actively involved. Like Rousseau (2006), I was interested in "evidence-based management." This approach became the focus of the third phase and required the learning of a whole new set of skills around supporting change.

It was clear that once we had developed the model and observed the performance of the teams we began to see, as others had, that some teams achieved much higher performance (Edmondson, Bohmer, & Pisano, 2001). The companies we had partnered with were particularly keen to understand how to increase the performance of teams, and we became interested in team learning. So the final question was the following: Under what circumstances are teams able to learn and increase their performance? To understand this, we had to begin to actively build, pilot, and test tools that we believed would increase the performance of teams using the ideas and theories we had developed.

The challenge I set for myself and the team was to create a set of tools and techniques that could be used by virtual teams as well as colocated teams. As Ram Tenkasi describes in Chapter 11, Integrating Theory to Inform Practice, this third phase required us to create "mastery of the techniques of getting things done in the organization." Over the period of a year, we did indeed achieve mastery by working with a multidisciplinary team of learning specialists, web designers, graphic designers, and community software experts to create a series of development interventions that could be administered virtually.

The online diagnostic profile completed by team members, team leaders, and importantly, the stakeholders of the team (their customers and suppliers) enabled us to collect baseline performance data on the team. The "temperature check" administered after 60 days allowed us to monitor performance changes. During the 60-day learning journey, teams were coached and presented with a series of learning modules made up of videos, podcasts, articles, and tasks around the model we had developed.

Rather than build another corporate membership organization, I decided in this phase to work with a smaller number of organizations who were prepared to work in a more experimental way. In particular, Singapore's Ministry of Manpower and Nokia became deeply involved with piloting the learning journey. My thinking was that we did not, as in Phase 2, need to collect a great deal of data; instead, we needed to form a strong learning relationship with a small number of organizations prepared to take the risks with us. These two cases and the learnings from them are described later in the chapter and, as you will see, we were very fortunate in our partnership.

Findings and Reflections: The Nature of Cooperation

The first phase of the research began with a literature search and the development of a set of ideas that became the model of cooperation and knowledge sharing in subsequent research. During this first phase, the case writing on BP, Nokia, and Goldman Sachs enabled us to observe cooperation and knowledge sharing as it is naturally embedded in the day-to-day activities of employees. From the case observations and the analysis of the literature came two sets of ideas that formed the basis of all the subsequent studies: the first was the multistranded nature of cooperation, and the second the embedded nature of cooperation.

The Multistranded nature of cooperation. Our first perspective was that to understand why and how people cooperate and share knowledge, we had to look at a number of overlapping fields of research to create an integrated, multistranded perspective. Specifically, we came to believe that four areas were important to individuals and the teams that they inhabited (Gratton, 2007). (1) However motivated to cooperate an individual may be, the actual act of cooperation is more likely to occur when they and others are engaged with a task, a question, or a vision that excites and motivates them and forms what we called the "ignition." (2) Although this point of ignition could potentially pull people together, the opportunity for them to be innovative also depends on the extent and breadth of networks held at both the level of the individual and at the level of the group. We called this "boundary spanning," and it has its roots in the work of the network analysts. (3) The ability to then actively exchange ideas and contacts within these ignited networks depends on the habits and attitudes of individuals with regard to cooperation. We called this "cooperative mindset," and its roots are within the literature on cooperation. (4) Underlying these networks and habits of cooperation are a series of what we called "productive practices" that ensure and enable the ideas and creativity of the team to actual translate into performance and innovation. In particular, we focused on the competencies of conflict resolution, commitment making, and creating opportunities for reflection.

The embedded nature of cooperation. At the same time as developing the model for how innovative cooperation could take place in teams and communities, we also examined cross-boundary cooperation in three companies. We wrote cases on what was called the process of "peer assist" at BP, on the modular structure of Nokia, and on the complex cooperative people practices at Goldman Sachs. In each company, we interviewed around 20 people and took a close look at the organizational structures and practices. What was very clear from these case studies was that the capacity and motivation to work with others in a cooperative manner was embedded in the whole context of the organization. Like Susan Mohrman and her work at CEO (Mohrman, Mohrman, & Tenkasi, 1977), we came to the conclusion that a full understanding of organizations required three levels of focus, which was, in turn, particularly crucial to an understanding of cooperation and boundary spanning.

The first level was the individual. It was clear, for example at Goldman Sachs, that much of the elaborate selection process with its multiple interviews was solely focused on shielding the company from highly competitive and self-orientated individuals. This finding was corroborated with the personal psychology literature, which had drawn attention to the cooperative personality that is more "other centered" than "self-centered." However, we also observed in these cases that when individuals at Goldman Sachs or BP came together, the teams they created also had cooperative norms of their own. This second level was the team. Our observations had shown clearly that the norms and expectations of the team influenced the cooperative attitudes of new joiners and of those who had been in the team for some time. The research on teams had made the same point, and so we realized that any model we created would have to have a team element. The third level we observed was that of the organization. As we studied these three companies, it became clear that for an individual's natural propensity to be cooperative, if indeed it existed, to become an activity of acting cooperatively depended a great deal on the signals they received from the organization. We heard many people tell us, for example, that the individual reward structure reduced their capacity or willingness to cooperate. We also heard how positively influenced they were by the role models from senior executives.

These two observations of the multistranded and embedded nature of cooperation led us to create the working model shown in Figure 4.2. Although this model has been refined and understood further, it has remained the touchstone for all subsequent research.

Findings and Reflections: A Closer Look at the Model

Over the next year we were able to examine the model more closely in the Cooperative Advantage Research Consortium, which was launched with involvement from 15 company members in partnership with a U.S. research/consulting practice, The Concours Group, directed by Tamara Erickson. What we had in this research was data from over 20 teams based on the perceptions of the team leader and the team members. Crucially in a process of measurement, reflection, and conversation, we went back to each company to discuss their perceptions. We found this activity to be immensely important. For example, in the case of Nokia we held a workshop in Finland attended by 25 senior executives involved in knowledge and innovation. Over the period of one day we were able to show the data and gain their perceptions about what was happening and why it was important. These practices of co-creation often lead to new insights for both the executives and the research team. Looking back on this phase of the research, I perceive three insights that have stood the test of time.

1. *The Antecedents to Cooperation.* We had seen in the development of the model that to truly understand cooperation we had to bring in the individuals, the team, and the organization. We became fascinated by the antecedents of cooperation. Analysis of the data allowed us to observe the factors we had included in the model, whereas the cases broadened our understanding. The article about the antecedents of cooperation was published in the *Harvard Business Review* and became an important way of describing to executives what it was we believed in (Gratton & Erickson, 2007).

2. *The Development of Fault Lines.* Often in our conversations with members of these complex teams, team members described how frustrated they often felt about the lack of knowledge transfer across subgroups. We realized the transfer of knowledge was a particularly pressing challenge for the diverse teams many companies were constructing. At the same time, the literature on fault lines provided some useful insights into why knowledge transfer failed to occur. So we began to analyze the team data on the basis of the diversity of the team members and the extent to which fault lines had emerged. We found that, indeed, under certain conditions fault lines did emerge but also that a certain sequence of leadership styles reduced the negative effect of this condition. Again, publishing rapidly in the *Sloan Management Journal* created a broader conversation (Gratton & Voigt, 2007). At around the same time, I wrote an article that appeared in the *Wall Street Journal* about managing virtual teams that created a series of long conversations with people all over the world.

3. *The Nature of Organization Cooperative Signatures.* As Sumantra and I wrote the cases in the earlier phase of the research and talked to the wider group of executives about cooperation, we began to see that there was no "one size fits all" with regard to how cooperative teams were put together (Gratton & Ghoshal, 2005). For example, Nokia teams had a complex social architecture that enabled them to cooperate across boundaries, whereas RBS had invested considerable sums in offices that encouraged

people from different functions and businesses to meet and exchange ideas. From this observation evolved the idea of a "signature process." We showed that when considering a concept such as cooperation, an executive team had both to bring in good practice from outside and simultaneously create and shield a set of practices or processes that were unique to it and difficult for others to imitate (Erickson & Gratton, 2007).

Findings and Reflections: On Learning and Performance Boosting

In the third phase of the research, our interest was in developing tools that would actually increase the performance of teams. During 2009, we were able to work with over 30 teams to pilot these ideas. The data from the teams in Singapore were positive. After the 60-day learning period, the temperature check showed that 40 percent of the teams had been observed by stakeholders to significantly increase their performance, while 30 percent were observed to moderately increase their performance. We were able to analyze the conditions and experiences of those teams who increased their performance most significantly, and of those teams that had failed. We found four aspects that impacted their capacity to learn and increase their performance:

1. *The Power of Healthy Teams.* We found that those teams that learned the most did so from a foundation of team health. When a team entered the learning journey with strong cooperation and a capacity to resolve conflicts, they were more likely to increase their performance in the eyes of the stakeholders.

2. *Involvement of Stakeholders.* Those teams that learnt the most actively engaged their stakeholders in their development activities. This is an interesting aspect since most traditional developmental activities in organizations do not actively bring in stakeholders.

3. *Real Tasks.* Those teams that learned the most typically focused on real developmental tasks during the 60-day learning period. This aspect suggests that it is wise to select tasks that the whole team can engage with and which link outwards to the stakeholders.

4. *Create a Virtual Learning "Signature."* The far-flung nature of many of the teams made it difficult for them to come together, so there was much emphasis on virtual learning. We found that there was not "one size fits all" in terms of what works best. Instead, teams that boosted their performance developed their own "signature" based on their technological sophistication, their preferred way of learning, and the technological norms

of the company (for example, whether the company had a shared learning portal).

During 2008–2009, two major projects changed the nature of our research as we engaged with two "early adopters." One was Nokia, where we were able to work with over 100 teams in a very short period of time; the second was Singapore's Ministry of Manpower, which became a significant supporter of the research.

Case No. 1: A Government-Led Initiative—The Singapore Ministry of Manpower

In early 2008, I was approached by a number of civil servants from Singapore's MOM to engage with them on teams and innovation. At this time, the concept of innovation was becoming a major government theme. The following is how Leo Yip, the Permanent Secretary of the MOM, described it:

> Singapore itself has built up a store of experience in human capital development and management over the years. Developing its human capital as its sustainable competitive advantage is a key national priority. In the development of new thinking on Asian human capital strategies, more research needs to be done to generate new knowledge on what works, and how effective approaches can be contextualised for application by companies operating in Asia. This is an area in which Singapore is keen to contribute. (*Ethos,* 2008: Issue 5, Foreword)

It is interesting to note how these civil servants found me. As I was to learn, from 2007 onwards MOM had sent out groups of civil servants around the world to look for innovative practice around human capital. These government officials had embarked on a rigorous analysis of the key ideas in the field of human capital and had attended most of the major human capital conferences in Asia, Europe, and the United States. In 2007 the book *Hot Spots* (Gratton, 2007) had been published, and later that year I was the keynote speaker at the Human Resource Planning Society (HRPS) conference in Las Vegas. As a consequence, I was asked by the Singapore government to visit the country as a senior visiting fellow to the civil service. This position had a defined role created to bridge the gap between academia and practice in the field of human capital.

During the week I spent in Singapore, the Ministry arranged a series of breakfasts and a workshop with chief executive officer's and heads of HR from Singapore companies and other companies based in the region. Following the visit, I was asked to submit a proposal for the engagement with the ideas of cooperation and complex teams I had described in the book *Hot Spots.* As Leo Yip described it:

Singapore's Ministry of Manpower is working with Professor Lynda Gratton from the London Business School on a research programme to develop innovation Hot Spots for Singapore-based companies. The findings will be shared at the next Summit in 2009. (*Ethos,* 2008: Issue 5, Foreword)

The research team then wrote a proposal to engage with teams, to understand the drivers of innovation, and to determine whether there were indeed differences between the data for the Singapore teams and that which we had collected for teams outside Singapore. By accepting the proposal, MOM agreed to financially support the piloting of the team process to 30 teams in Singapore with the assumption that these teams would be drawn from 10 companies, to actively engage with the research team to encourage these companies to join the pilot phase, and to ensure that MOM also participated. In the proposal, we agreed to prepare a report on the findings of the diagnostics in the 30 teams and to present these findings at the 2009 Human Capital Conference in Singapore.

From September 2008, MOM began to approach companies to participate. The process of adoption of this innovative practice was initially planned to take September and October. In reality, engaging companies to sign up to the diagnostic and the 60-day learning journey we had designed was still taking place in January 2009. In total, MOM team approached around 25 companies to participate. By January 2009, seven companies had confirmed their participation. Those that participated wanted to create or deepen relationships with MOM, valued the opportunity to network with other local organizations in Singapore as part of the program, believed that collaborative forms of working or innovation in general were key priorities on their strategic agenda, or valued the opportunity to trial comprehensive team development program tools at low cost compared to market rates because of MOM sponsorship.

However, even with a financial incentive, many companies chose not to participate. Generally their reasons were they had no bandwidth with regard to time and resources to market the initiative internally and find participating teams. At the same time, the economic downturn in the region resulted in resources being focused away from longer-term challenges to the more urgent short-term issues, while worries about the time commitment played a part. Finally, since this program was a pilot, there were concerns about the lack of client references or case studies that would illustrate how increasing team performance had been successfully implemented in other companies.

Despite these concerns, by February 2009 MOM had increased the number of participating teams to 28. They had achieved this level of participation through assiduous marketing of the work, a dedicated team within MOM, and inclusion of four of their own teams in the practice.

The Singapore data, combined with the data from the Nokia teams, enabled us to refine the original model and create a more insightful and contextual view of why and how people within and across teams would be prepared to cooperate, to share knowledge, and ultimately to innovate.

Case No. 2: Large-Scale Single Company Adoption—Nokia

In December 2008, we were approached by executives to work with Nokia on the rollout of project-based structure and learning in one of Nokia's key businesses. This was part of a long-term research relationship with Nokia that had developed over more than a decade. Nokia had been associated with our research from the beginning. They had been members of the initial Cooperative Advantage Research Consortium and had allowed us to write a case on their innovative organizational strategy. In part, the partnership developed through the resonance of ideas. In his review of the *Hot Spots* book, Hallstein Moerk, Executive Vice President, Global HR, had this to say:

> The capacity of teams to work cooperatively across functions, countries and with partners is important to the success of every company, and crucial to a company like Nokia. We have collaborated with Professor Gratton on researching how the potential energy from teams can become the basis of our competitive advantage.

Both Nokia and MOM perceive themselves as innovators and so are well framed when it comes to thinking about innovative practice. This "innovator" mindset also means that both organizations are well networked outside the corporate boundaries by actively engaging in communities of practice where they come across new ideas. One possible reason for this mindset is that these "boundary spanning" capabilities and values have been developed in other parts of the business or organization. For example, the technologists of Nokia are encouraged to work closely with university teams. Similarly, the Singapore government has made many commitments to outreach. As a consequence, "organizational muscle" has developed around scanning the environment for innovative practice. Both Nokia and MOM approached us, whereas we approached most other companies.

In autumn 2008, the corporate learning group at Nokia was putting together a "booster program" designed to increase the performance of their teams in one of the Markets businesses. The program was ambitious. It had to cover all 5,000 employees of the Markets business unit, encourage cross-functional and cross-hierarchical working, and be ready to roll out across the world in the space of three months with a relatively low budget.

The design team recognized that the traditional form of initiating top-down change would be too slow and would ignore the capacity of emerging technologies to allow employees to be part of the solution. The social network technologies that are rapidly emerging on the back of Enterprise 2.0 tools created the environment for Nokia's long-term commitment to employee involvement to play out in a faster, more paced manner.

On the basis of this, the learning group decided on a blended solution with three main streams of activities: the team diagnostic would be made available to 100 of the teams; following this, all team leaders would attend a two-day face-to-face workshop with team leaders; finally, the 60-day learning journey was morphed into an online social network community. The two-day workshops were run in locations across the world (including Beijing, White Plains in the United States, Helsinki, London, and Dubai) with about 100 potential change leaders in each. Having completed the workshop, the 700 participants then returned to their teams to engage them in the ongoing process. At this point, the online community came to the fore. Working with specialist partners we designed an intranet site accessible to workshop participants and all employees of the Markets business. The online community was designed to provide information on team performance; but importantly, it was no longer a one-way communication channel. Instead, it was also capable of hosting conversations and communications with senior managers and exchanging information and ideas with content experts and community members.

This innovation to our 60-day learning journey proved very successful. All 5,000 members of the business participated in an open dialogue between community members, frontline employees, and senior managers about the real challenges, concrete ideas, and required support (Gratton & Casse, 2010). The online community created real opportunities for anyone in the business to be active and to make the company agenda their agenda. We found that many people elected to steer discussions that interested them, post content they thought others would find useful, create groups of like-minded people around specific topics, or raise igniting questions or issues. At the same time, others preferred to react to the ideas in the community or even to remain silent users, preferring to read and take in information. The online community also ignited a whole host of unintended actions. For example, one team in Germany took the initiative to invite 100 colleagues to an empty hangar where they shared material from the booster community and facilitated a question-and-answer session.

The senior team at Nokia has always espoused cooperation as a means to tap into the wealth of knowledge and experience of employees. What's changed in the last five years is the way that community-based technologies can facilitate and speed this process. The booster online community enabled senior managers and content experts to frame the initial comments and set the tone. It was then possible for the community of employees to decide how best to implement these ideas. Indeed, we found that employee discussion threads quickly moved from commenting on the direction to more practical ideas on how to make the changes. After six months, over 3,000 discussion threads had been posted. Many discussion threads were in the form of questions or described the context under which employees saw the changes possible or difficult to achieve. These discussion threads reduced repetition and meant that the conversation always moved forward across boundaries.

Reflections on Nokia and MOM

In my work with both MOM and Nokia, a clear action-orientated research base has been grounded in a collaborative partnership. In both cases, we were able to meet many of the criteria Tom Cummings describes in Chapter 18, How Business Schools Shape (Misshape) Management Research, which is on action-orientated research; both sides were involved in all stages of the research, and there was a high degree of openness, mutual trust, and respect. However, these two studies progressed in rather different ways, and in the following two sections I illustrate these differences and what we learned from them.

MOM: The Challenge of Active Company Involvement

One of the most crucial challenges of this type of action-based research is engaging companies, and as we have seen throughout this collection of chapters, it requires the development of strong social bonds to create high-quality relationships. The research with MOM illustrates this very clearly.

The case of MOM is a good example of the sheer energy that is required for this type of research to get off the ground. It took over six months of dedicated follow-up from the research team and our MOM partners to make this work. The companies who joined the research had various reasons for doing so. Some simply saw it as an opportunity to create or deepen relationships with MOM; others valued the opportunity to network with other local organizations in Singapore as part of the program; whereas some saw collaboration and innovation as key strategic key priorities and valued the opportunity to trial the methodology at a relatively low cost. However, even with these incentives, many companies still chose not to participate, through lack of time, the need to focus on more short-term issues, or concern about joining a pilot.

Nokia: The Power of Co-Creation

In the case of Nokia, the buy-in came rapidly because the concepts we had developed could be used as part of a planned intervention. However, unlike at MOM, where we were able to run each team in the way we had designed, at Nokia we could not. We had to make immediate adjustments to the study. These took a number of forms. First, we had to substantially increase the computerization of the process; next, we had to develop a volunteer process because we had the resources to diagnose only 100 of the potential 700 teams; and finally, we had to strip out much of the coaching aspects of the 60-day learning journey and transfer the modules to the community portal.

However, from these rapid adjustments we learned some important lessons. The development of the community portal encouraged us to work with a host of specialist partners to design the intranet site, thereby learning skills that we took with us to our current study on the future of work. We also discovered a great deal about the interface between research and communities, and I began to realize that online communities could provide an important tool to the research community. We were fortunate that in working with Nokia we partnered with a team who understood this impact of online communities and could work closely with us to develop our own skills—this was truly co-creation in practice.

The Research Journey Continues . . .

The research journey continues in terms of the community, in the companies involved in the work, and in the development of new ideas. By late 2009, we were engaged with the following areas of research:

- *Singapore.* MOM has agreed to increase the numbers of teams involved in the 60-day learning journey to 60 over the next six months. In many cases, these are companies that are now working with clusters of companies. At the same time, the findings from the initial Singapore research have created a case study that has enabled a number of companies to begin to work actively with teams in a developmental process.

- *Nokia and the Broader Community.* Our co-creation with Nokia and the Finnish portal designers became an important part of the development of the 60-day learning. What we learned from Nokia was the importance of pulling together a broader community of individuals and teams to really boost performance. We also saw firsthand the importance of using an "igniting question" to act as the catalyst for development across the community. As a consequence, in October 2009 we were able to build both a learning community in Singapore for all the teams and also a community for ten teams in British Sky Broadcasting (BSkyB). At this point, we are monitoring the community aspects in both Singapore and the United Kingdom.

- *More Sophisticated Analysis.* With data from more than 100 teams from Nokia, we are in a position to start using more sophisticated mathematical modeling on the data set. Our colleagues at London Business School are beginning to work on this data set.

- *The Future of Work Consortium.* Supported by the MOM, we launched in November 2009 a worldwide conversation about the future of work, which in a sense was a natural development of the work on cooperation. Twenty-four companies (including Nokia) have entered in the debate, with over 200 executives from China, Singapore, India, South America, the United States, and Europe. We are partnering with our Finnish portal designers again and expect this to be a very exciting research journey.

Reflecting on what I have learned over the ten years of this research journey, I am struck by the importance of finding something that truly interests, energizes, and engages you. Without that, the whole piece can became a real drudge. I would also highlight the importance of boundary spanning between academia and practice. It is not an easy boundary to span—and you certainly have to be something of a chameleon. But the combination of academic rigor and theory building combined with the real life challenges and insights from executives can be truly wonderful. These broadenings of networks also can bring marvelous combinations.

Reflecting on this journey leads me to absolutely agree with Tom Cummings's argument (Chapter 18, How Business Schools Shape [Misshape] Management Research), that business schools have the opportunity to be places where different forms of inquiry prosper and productively interact. As a professor of management practice at London Business School, I have a wonderful opportunity to participate in action research and yet still be seen as a fully paid-up member of the academic community. The benefits of interaction are clear. For example, the data we are creating from our action research are currently being analyzed by my colleagues at the school using statistical analyses that are not within my competence domain. It is this opportunity for diversity and collaboration that I believe holds the key to the future of action research.

REFERENCES

Edmondson, A., Bohmer, R., & Pisano, G. (2001). Speeding up team learning. *Harvard Business Review 79*(9), 125–134.

Erickson, T. J., & Gratton, L. (2007, March). What it means to work here. *Harvard Business Review, 85*(3), 104–111.

Ghoshal, S., & Gratton, L. (2003). Integrating the enterprise. *Sloan Management Review, 44*(1), 31–38.

Ghoshal, S., & Moran, P. (1996, January). Bad for practice: A critique of the transaction cost theory. *Academy of Management Review, 21*(1), 13–47.

Ghoshal, S., & Moran, P. (2005). Towards a good theory of management. In J. Birkenshaw & G. Piramel (Eds.), *Sumantra Ghoshal on management: A force for good.* 1–27 London: Financial Times Prentice Hall.

Gibson, C., & Cohen, S. (2003). *Virtual teams that work: Creating conditions for virtual team effectiveness.* San Francisco: Jossey-Bass.

Gratton, L. (1996). Implementing a strategic vision: Key factors for success. *Long Range Planning, 29*(3), 290–303.

Gratton, L. (2000). *Living strategy: Putting people at the heart of corporate purpose.* London: Financial Times Prentice Hall.

Gratton, L. (2005). Managing integration through cooperation. *Human Resource Management, 44*(2), 151–158.

Gratton, L. (2007). *Hot spots: Why some teams, workplaces and organizations buzz with energy—and others don't.* San Francisco: Berrett-Koehler.

Gratton, L. (2009). *Glow: Creating energy and innovation in your work.* San Francisco: Berrett-Koehler.

Gratton, L., & Casse, J. (2010, Spring). Boosting strategy with an online community. *Business Strategy Review, 21*(1), 40–45.

Gratton, L., & Erickson, T. J. (2007, November). Eight ways to build collaborative teams. *Harvard Business Review, 85*(11), 100–109.

Gratton, L., & Ghoshal, S. (2002). *BP: Organisational transformation.* ECCH. Case – Ref: 302-033-1 *London Business School Case – LBS-CS02-002.*

Gratton, L., & Ghoshal, S. (2004). *Royal Bank of Scotland: The strategy of not having a strategy.* ECCH. *London Business School Case.*

Gratton, L., & Ghoshal, S. (2005). Beyond best practice. *Sloan Management Review, 46*(3), 49–57.

Gratton, L., Ghoshal, S., & Donaldson, A. (2004). *Nokia: The challenge of continuous renewal.* ECCH. *London Business School Case.*

Gratton, L., & Voigt, A. (2007). Bridging faultlines in diverse teams. *Sloan Management Review, 48*(4).

Kilduff, M., & Tsai, W. (2003). *Social networks and organizations.* Thousand Oaks, CA: Sage.

Mankin, D., & Cohen, S. G. (2004). *Business without boundaries: An action framework for collaborating across time, distance, organization and culture.* San Francisco: Jossey-Bass.

Mohrman, S. A., Mohrman, A. M., Jr., & Tenkasi, R. (1997). The discipline of organizational design. In C. L. Cooper & S. E. Jackson (Eds.), *Creating tomorrow's organizations: A handbook for future research in organizational behaviour* (pp. 191–205). West Sussex, UK: Wiley.

Nahapiet, J., Gratton, L., & Rocha, H. (2005). Knowledge and cooperative relationship: When cooperation is the norm. *European Management Review, 2*, 3–14.

Rousseau, D. (2006). 2005 Presidential address: Is there such a thing as "evidence based management"? *Academy of Management Review, 31*(2), 256–269.

Sonnenberg, W. (2004). *Federal support for education: Fiscal years 1980–2003*. Washington, DC: U.S. Department of Education, National Center for Education Statistics, NCES 2004-026.

Tushman, M., & O'Reilly, C. (2007). Research and relevance: Implications of Pasteur's quadrant for doctoral programs and faculty development. *Academy of Management Journal, 50*(4), 769–774.

Van de Ven, A., & Johnson, P. (2006). Knowledge for theory and practice. *Academy of Management Review, 31*(4), 802–821.

ABOUT THE AUTHOR

Lynda Gratton is Professor of Management Practice at London Business School where she directs the school's Human Resources strategy program. She is the founder of the Hot Spots Movement (www.hotspotsmovement .com), a worldwide community dedicated to bringing energy and innovation to organizations. Lynda is the author of 6 books and over 10 articles and was rated by the *Times* as one of the top 20 business thinkers in the world. Lynda's current research interest is the Future of Work, on which she is directing a worldwide research consortium in a co-creation process involving more than 30 companies and she is blogging about her experience at www.lynda grattonfutureofwork.com.

FIVE

Commentary

Walking on Three Legs

J. RICHARD HACKMAN

HERB KELMAN, one of the most distinguished social psychologists of his generation and now an emeritus professor at Harvard, has devoted the last several decades to developing and testing strategies for ameliorating intergroup conflict. He has not been shy about taking on the hardest problems— the Mideast and Northern Ireland, for example—and he has learned a lot about what it takes to reverse, or at least to contain, the escalation of such conflicts. As much as anyone I know, Herb works productively right at the intersection of theory and practice. So it brings a smile when one reads what he has posted on the door of his William James Hall office:

> Theory is when you know everything but nothing works.
> Practice is when everything works but no one knows why.
> In this room, theory and practice come together:
> Nothing works and no one knows why.

That tongue-in-the-cheek lament poses the challenge. How have we done at surmounting it in the 25 years since the first edition of this book was published? Has there been discernable progress in developing research strategies that enable theory and practice to inform one another? What now commands the attention of scholars who seek to develop knowledge that is both conceptually sound and of practical use? What obstacles and opportunities are most likely to occupy our attention in the years to come? This commentary addresses those questions, fueled by the provocative essays by Susan Albers Mohrman and Allan Mohrman, Amy Edmondson, and Lynda Gratton.

Where We Have Been

There was real excitement at the previous University of Southern California workshop on this topic, a sense that we were on the cusp of something very important. Some of the intellectual leaders in the field of organizational behavior—people like Chris Argyris, Paul Goodman, Ian Mitroff, Andrew Pettigrew, Stan Seashore, and Dick Walton—vigorously engaged with one another to figure out what was required to conduct research that really would be useful for both theory and practice.

A number of provocative ideas about research directions emerged from that workshop. Although there was a lot of variation around the edges, particularly regarding differences in what is needed for actionable research on organizational design versus individual and group behavior within organizations, there also was real progress in identifying the kinds of research that could help us move forward. For me, the main message of the workshop was that the eventual usefulness of our research would depend jointly on how we frame the *problems* we address and on what types of *products* we generate.

Some research problems are paradigm-driven whereas others are explicitly problem-driven. Paradigm-driven problems may indeed add bricks to the wall of scientific understanding, but the knowledge obtained rarely generates conceptual models that are useful as guides for managerial or organizational practice. Problem-driven research, by contrast, risks becoming so focused on the specifics of a particular situation that, even if the presenting problem is solved, the findings add little to general knowledge about how people and organizations operate. The right place to be, I concluded, was somewhere around the middle of the paradigm-problem continuum.

The kinds of research products we disseminate also fall on a continuum, this one ranging from articles that report trustworthy but practice-irrelevant findings to what could be called tasty nostrums for managers. And, once again, the middle of the continuum seemed a good place to be—bulletproof conclusions that are irrelevant to practice are just as unhelpful as catchy concepts that are supported tenuously, if at all, by empirical research. What we needed, I concluded, were neither validated contingency models so complex that no mere mortal could use them to guide behavior in real time nor injunctions such as "create a culture of trusting, entrepreneurial leadership" that leave practitioners scratching their heads about what they should actually *do* to achieve that high-sounding state of affairs.

I came away from the previous workshop with a renewed commitment to be wary of both ends of those two continua. I realized that merely being in the middle provided no guarantee that a piece of research would contribute simultaneously to theory and practice. Still, the middle regions of those continua did seem to provide a good platform from which to develop the strategies and tactics of actionable research. By the new millennium, I thought, we had a reasonably good chance of demonstrating in our work both parts of Kurt Lewin's oft-cited dictum—that there is nothing so practical as a good theory, but also that there is no better way to inform theory than through a careful analysis of practice. Even better, others at the workshop appeared to share my optimism. It was a heady time.

Where We Are Now

The promise of the previous book has not been fulfilled. Indeed, there are some signs that we may actually be moving in the opposite direction, and I find myself having to marshal my emotional resources to keep from getting depressed about future prospects for actionable research in organizational behavior. Here are three developments that worry me:

1. There is as much variation in research approaches as ever—indeed, probably more—but alternative approaches are less in contention with one another than before.

The field of organizational behavior has prospered in recent decades, with increasing numbers of researchers conducting studies on an ever-expanding set of questions. It probably was inevitable, therefore, that subgroups of researchers would form whose members rely on similar methodological strategies and refer mainly to one another. Although some scholars do identify with multiple subgroups, there is less variation within subgroups than between them—a development that would generate a respectable intra-class correlation but that also attenuates how much the various stripes of organizational researchers learn from one another.

We have, for example, the *JPSP* crowd. We have other researchers whose fondest dream is to land an *ASQ* article. And there are still others for whom a piece in *HBR* would be the ultimate achievement. It is not so much that members of these subgroups disparage one another (although that occasionally does happen), it is more that they *ignore* one another. Because the informal subgroups that have emerged in our growing field provide ample opportunities for social comparison, peer recognition, and the development of methodological advances, there is little need for members of any one subgroup to engage with scholars from other groups who prefer different research strategies.

For what I am calling the *JPSP* crowd, for example, collegial exchanges are likely to focus mainly on ways to refine and improve strategies for experimentally testing social psychological theories in controlled laboratory settings. There is no particular need to examine the phenomena being studied as it exists in the wild or to debate methodological approaches with those who carry out their research in field settings. Field researchers, for their part, do need to manage relations with other groups, but those interactions more often are with gatekeepers and managers in the organizations where the research is conducted than with researchers in other subgroups who rely on different methodological strategies. And those whose main audience is practicing managers may interact mainly with the editors of practitioner-oriented books, journals, and magazines in figuring out how to make their work as accessible, engaging, and informative as possible for those readers whose behavior they hope to influence.

Yes, in describing these three subgroups I have caricatured them a bit. And yes, many researchers, including those present at this workshop (and assuredly the authors of the papers about which I am supposed to be commenting), strive mightily to transcend the boundaries of their "home" subgroups. But I stand by my main points—that organizational researchers increasingly are sorting themselves into moderately homogenous subgroups defined by preferred research strategy, that these subgroups are not in intellectual contention with one another, and that those two developments portend poorly for the development of fresh paradigms for the design and conduct of research that contributes simultaneously to theory and practice.

2. The real players in management research and education are not here—they are playing other games on different fields.

The action these days is not in what I will call old-style organizational behavior, which sought to identify the factors that most strongly affect individual and group behavior in organizational contexts and to analyze the forces that shape the dynamics and development of whole organizations. These days, the real action is in fields such as social cognition, judgment and decision making, behavioral economics, and social network analysis. Those who work in these areas know that they are onto something significant, and their optimism and excitement is just as palpable as it was a quarter century ago for old-style organizational behavior researchers (a group with which, in case there is any doubt, I identify myself).

That's not the problem. Research topics and paradigms come and go, and anyone who resists will be left behind and should be. Scientific understanding moves forward in a slow, amoeba-like way: As the world changes and new issues become fashionable, one pseudopod expands, another one atrophies, and only relics keep on with what they've always done. The real problem is this: Concomitant with the changes in fashion has come a migration of the researcher population. Back when the predecessor of this workshop was held, organizational behavior was firmly situated in management schools, with strong two-way links to psychology departments (especially social psychologists) and sociology departments (especially organizational sociologists). Both organizational and discipline-focused scholars had to contend with the views of colleagues whose skills and perspectives differed, sometimes in fundamental ways, from their own.

No more. My colleagues in sociology tell me that the center of gravity for research on "macro" organizational issues is now in management schools. And I know from personal observation that the same is true for "micro" organizational behavior: No psychology department of which I am aware has an active research program in organizational psychology. Moreover, many management schools are recruiting young faculty who identify mainly with the disciplines in which they were trained and who seek most of all to publish in first-rank disciplinary journals. Indeed, more than a few universities are creating what is, in effect, a second social psychology faculty (and, perhaps less frequently, a second sociology faculty) in their professional schools—especially in management but sometimes also in education or government.[1]

So once again we see movement toward increasingly homogeneous groups whose members need not be in intellectual contention with other groups about conceptual and methodological problems and paradigms. Even more worrisome is the assumption by some discipline-oriented scholars in management schools that first-rate scholarship can be done without either personal immersion in the phenomena under study or explicit attention to the organizational contexts within which those phenomena unfold. For organizational research that aspires to guide practice, that assumption can be fatal. Scholars who are members of organizational behavior groups in professional schools surely ought to know at least a little about organizations, a little about behavior, and perhaps even a little something about what it takes to conduct research that can contribute simultaneously to theory and practice.

3. The siren song of "applied behavioral science" is getting louder, and many organizational scholars are finding it hard to resist.

"Applied" is one of my least favorite words—especially when it is used to modify the word "psychologist," and most of all when those two words are joined to describe me. I object because the connotation is that over there is basic science, over here is the real world, and applied psychologists (merely) bring the former constructively to bear on the latter. My aspiration, consistent with the theme of this book, is to generate fundamental knowledge about social phenomena that is directly useful to those who lead or serve in groups and organizations. I don't want to be just a knowledge carrier.

But my one-person battle against "applied" is not going well, and it is starting to look as if dignified surrender may be my only realistic option. Perversely, it is the constructive efforts of some of my most admired colleagues

---

1. These developments follow the historical lead of a number of universities in creating secondary economics departments, one in the faculty of arts and sciences and another in the institution's business school.

that are doing me in. Taking their lead from the field of medicine, a number of intellectual leaders in organizational behavior are making a strong and persuasive case for "evidence-based management." What we should do, the argument goes, is to identify those basic research findings about management practice that are most robust and reliable, compile and package them in a way that makes clear their implications for practice, and then disseminate them widely throughout the management community. That is what is being done in the medical sciences, and evidence-based medicine apparently does help physicians make good treatment decisions—and, most important, it can steer them away from choices that may seem right but that actually are unsupported by empirical research.

The problem, of course, is that it is quite a distance from the laboratory bench to the physician's consultation room, and neither the laboratory researcher nor the clinical practitioner is likely to have the time or inclination to bridge that gap. So a new medical field, called "translational medicine," has developed, with the specific objective of making trustworthy findings from medical research available to, and accessible by, practicing clinicians.

Can this also be done for management research? It is an attractive possibility. Basic researchers can proceed with their work without having to worry about its possible usefulness. Practitioners can do their jobs without wondering if there is anything in the scholarly journals that they need to know. And the translators will bridge those communities—extracting, aggregating, and disseminating the most trustworthy and high-leverage research findings.

What is wrong with this picture? What is wrong is that evidence-based management, by abstracting scholarly work from both the contexts where it is conducted and the settings where the findings will be used, takes us one additional step away from the Lewinian ideal of action science. There are so many advantages to action science that I am going to defer my surrender for as long as I can. And, from their chapters, I'm guessing that Susan and Allan, Amy, and Lynda will join me in what may be—but I hope will not be—a last stand against the offense being mounted by the Division of Labor in organizational research.

Where We Should Be Going

This commentary has been mainly about those aspects of contemporary organizational research that make it hard to conduct research that contributes both to basic knowledge and to managerial practice. The difficulties—but also the opportunities—are evident in the chapters in this section of the book. Susan and Allan reflect insightfully on their struggles to overcome the epistemological and collaborative challenges they faced in working with organization-based colleagues to properly design problem-focused research, to conduct it efficiently, and then to report the findings in a way that would be useful to all. Collaboration also is a central theme in Amy's chapter, especially as scholars cross organizational and disciplinary boundaries to triage research possibilities and then pursue those that show the greatest promise of generating learning for all parties. And Lynda recounts a multiyear, multiorganization program of consultation that started with a relatively straightforward analysis of what it takes to foster cooperation in organizations, but then evolved in ways that could not possibly have been anticipated or planned for in advance. All three chapters demonstrate convincingly that problem-focused research in organizations takes on a life of its own and therefore requires an unusual measure of initiative, flexibility, and creativity by those brave enough to plunge in without knowing for sure where they will wind up.

Even so, it may be that some minimum conditions must be met if organizational research is to have a reasonable chance of both solving real problems and contributing to basic knowledge. Consider the triangle shown below. Its vertices are (1) the phenomena of interest, (2) theory about those phenomena, and (3) empirical research on those same phenomena. I propose that research of the kind we have been discussing must include work on *all three* of the legs that connect those vertices.

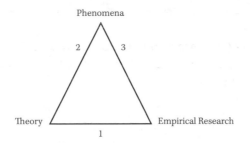

Some scholars, including some discipline-oriented social psychologists (the "JPSP crowd" mentioned earlier), emphasize in their work the first leg of the triangle, the one linking theory and empirical research. Others, such as some business school faculty, emphasize the second leg, inductively developing theory based solely (or mainly) on deep immersion in the phenomena. And still others, such as some "applied" researchers, emphasize the third leg, bringing empirical data to bear on specific problems without worrying too much about conceptual issues.

It is probably asking too much to expect that any one researcher, or even any one research group, will be able to work all three legs of the triangle. The chapters in this section strongly suggest that the development of basic-but-actionable knowledge requires multiple researchers, multiple projects, and no small measure of calendar time. It also will require overcoming, or at least circumventing, several self-imposed barriers that historically have slowed our progress. We will need to quit acting as if writing about the lessons we personally learn from case studies or consulting assignments is, by itself, scholarly work. We will need to quit pretending that the context of behavior is irrelevant to understanding what is happening—let alone to changing it. We will need to become more inventive in developing research strategies that are uniquely suited to our research settings. And then maybe, just maybe, we will no longer find ourselves characterizing our scholarly work as merely "applied" research.

ABOUT THE AUTHOR

J. Richard Hackman is Edgar Pierce Professor of Social and Organizational Psychology. He received his bachelor's degree in mathematics from Mac-Murray College and his doctorate in social psychology from the University of Illinois. He taught at Yale for twenty years and then moved to his present position at Harvard. Hackman teaches and conducts research on a variety of topics in social and organizational psychology, including team performance, leadership effectiveness, and the design of self-managing teams and organizations. His most recent books are *Senior Leadership Teams: What It Takes to Make Them Great* (with Ruth Wageman, Debra Nunes, and James Burruss) and *Collaborative Intelligence: Using Terms to Solve Hard Problems*. He serves on the U.S. Intelligence Science Board and on the Board of Trustees of the Orpheus Chamber Orchestra.

PART II

Bodies of Work That Have Influenced Theory and Practice

SIX

Rigor and Relevance in Organizational Research

Experiences, Reflections, and a Look Ahead

PHILIP MIRVIS

AND EDWARD E. LAWLER III

"THERE IS NOTHING so practical as a good theory." "You cannot understand a system until you try to change it." These are the practical dictums about the relevance of knowledge and its rigorous development offered by Kurt Lewin, the father of social psychology. They represent what we believe and do: in the case of Lawler, as an "applied scholar," and Mirvis, his onetime grad student and longtime friend, as a "scholarly practitioner." Our understandings and pursuit of Lewin's twin precepts about knowledge gathering and use have evolved during a combined 70-plus years studying individuals and organizations.

In this chapter we reflect on matters of rigor and relevance in our scholarship and research programs. The first part is autobiographical as we contend that a scholar's interest in and skills for producing useful knowledge are to some extent a product of self-selection, socialization, and identity formation, all in turn shaped by career stages, twists, and turns. One theme is that the dynamic "fit" between who researchers are and what they study influences (and can transform) their stance on rigor versus relevance over time. Our personal interests and career paths have led us to construct research programs that increasingly stress relevance and that take us deeply into the workings of organizations and management practices.

A related theme is that the fit between a scholar's research program and the environment also informs research opportunities and methodological choices pertaining to rigor versus relevance. Much has been said about how current academic incentives and promotional standards have driven out practical scholarship from the research programs of most business school professors. Rather than examine the reasons for this, we focus instead on what it takes to create practical scholarship that stands up to scientific scrutiny. Our respective choices of content and methods as well as our interpretations and presentations of findings have surely been influenced by where we have worked, what subjects we have investigated, and what was occurring in the organizations we have researched and in the economy/society. Our niche has been largely defined by the study of complex and dynamic phenomena, by the interests of those who have funded and hosted our research, and by our research mission to both humanize and improve organizational behavior.

Moving beyond our personal stories, the second part of this chapter focuses on how to identify and frame interesting and actionable subjects and on what types of research are best suited to building theory and improving practice. It presents a mix of ideas on ways that rigorously relevant research can be designed and executed to pass muster in today's academic *and* organizational environments.

Two Careers

Few academics learn how to "manage" a useful research program in graduate school. We are not exceptions; hence our respective missteps and mastery in crafting research efforts conducive to our interests evolved through on-the-job training. In our careers, we both have sought out new or underexplored subject matter and aimed to promote innovations in organization practice and behavior. In this area, too, we had scant training in market scouting and creative problem finding. Instead, we learned about these things from engaging with innovative organizations and practitioners.

Career Stage 1: The Student Years

We will begin our exploration of what shapes a researcher's bent with Lawler who, as an undergraduate at Brown University, majored in psychology, studied learning theory, and ran lab rats, but had no particular faculty mentor or calling to academia. Nearing graduation, he sought a human resources (HR) job, but interviews at AT&T and IBM did not pan out. He was told that to be an HR executive, he should earn a master's degree. This advice along with his interest in psychology led to multiple applications to graduate programs in industrial and organizational (I/O) psychology that yielded two hits: one was an acceptance to Wayne State (based on his application being rejected by and then forwarded from the University of Michigan!); the other one led him to University of California, Berkeley.

Arriving at Berkeley in 1960, he discovered that they did not have a master's program; rather master's degrees were awarded to those individuals that did not make it in the PhD program. Not wanting a consolation prize, he decided to pursue a PhD. At this point, he certainly was not the scholarly type and did not see himself in a faculty job. He simply wanted to get a degree and a good job in business.

At Berkeley, lacking financial aid, he officiated volleyball and basketball games and graded papers in a course on child psychology taught by Professor Richard Alper, who partnered with Timothy Leary in LSD experiments, studied with spiritual teachers in India, and became known as Baba Ram Dass. Neither the mysticism nor the psychedelics figured into Lawler's scholarly or life explorations. However, meeting up with Lyman Porter, a young assistant professor at the time, opened up new academic vistas.

Porter had launched a large study of managerial attitudes, which Lawler joined. To this point, most studies of workplace attitudes had focused on clerical or blue-collar workers. Porter's work examined managers' outlooks on the job and investigated the effects of organization size, management level, and such on managers' job satisfaction and motivation. Porter was a classically trained researcher and meticulous when it came to research: Are you sure of the data? Are you going too far with that conclusion? This cautious and questioning attitude was drummed into his student by Porter.

Lawler's PhD dissertation on the relationship between attitudes and performance was the basis for his book with Porter on motivation and satisfaction (Porter & Lawler, 1968). His dissertation study involved fieldwork. He talked with managers about the whys and wherefores of the study to solicit their participation and had discussions (e.g., debriefings) with them about what the findings might mean in practice. But this was not a foray into "participatory research," nor was the intent to change the work situations of managers in the study. On the contrary, Lawler's prime attention was to theoretical framing, hypothesis testing, methodological rigor, and of course, to not overstating the implications.

Lawler, like many of his contemporaries, was schooled and socialized in traditional social science research methods. Although that might seem rigid and limiting, there is something to be said for apprenticing in this way. Visual artists, for example, first learn to draw shapes and the human form before embarking on more abstract or multimedia creations. So, too, we would argue that those that choose to step away from traditional research methods are well served by first mastering them, internalizing what they do and do not offer in producing valid and useful knowledge, and then carrying that with them as they explore other methods.

Career Stage 2: Professoring at Yale

Nearing completion of his studies, Lawler was offered a job by Yale University in their Department of Industrial Administration, later called Administrative

Sciences. No interview, no visits, just a job offer that he accepted. He spent his first years focused on teaching, writing scholarly articles for the *Journal of Applied Psychology* (*JAP*) and *Organizational Behavior and Human Performance OBHP* and his motivation book with Porter. Suffice it to say, he was following what was the traditional academic career model at the time.

The Ad Sci Department in the 1960s was led by Chris Argyris and housed a remarkably polyglot group of faculty, some of whom saw themselves developing a new paradigm for organizational research, identified later as action science (Argyris, Putnam, & Smith, 1985). In that camp with Argyris were Clay Alderfer, Fritz Steele, Roger Harrison, and others who kept up the Lewinian tradition and studied T-groups and participatory change processes. They were self-titled, to use Argyis's language, as the "interpersonally competents" and did action research and consulting.

A second group of faculty that included Lawler, J. Richard Hackman, Gerrit Wolfe, Tim Hall, and Ben Schneider were less "touchy-feely" in their choice of subject matters, less apt to be involved in consulting and change work, and more inclined to conduct survey-based and quasi-experimental research. The department divided informally into IPC (ipcee) and IPI (ipee) clusters—the interpersonally competent and the interpersonally incompetent. Lawler was in the latter group.

Although the differences between the two groups could have driven an acrimonious wedge through the faculty (and students), Argyris managed to prevent it from happening by hosting productive discussions of methods and epistemology. The two camps vigorously debated the merits of their different research models. The IPCs advocated Lewin's idea that changing a system was the best way to understand it; the IPIs wondered whether you could do "good science" as a change agent—for example, could you be objective about the results of any interventions you make?

For our purposes, two points about the configuration and operation of Yale's Ad Sci group are significant—as career influencers and as teachable points in the management of researchers. First, the Yale case illustrates how researchers with particular theoretical, methodological, and epistemological preferences tend to self-identify and clan together (aided by the presence of an "out-group"!). Second, it demonstrates the value of peer debate and pluralism within a scholarly community. Whereas the former reinforces scholars' prevailing beliefs and sentiments, the latter can open eyes and minds to alternative views and create respect for diversity.

During his years at Yale, Lawler undertook fieldwork that focused on the interface between person and organization. He studied the effects of organizational structures and practices, including pay, and wrote about the implications of his findings for practice. He and Hackman collected data to test their theory of the impact of job design on motivation (Hackman & Lawler,

1971). He also collected company data for his book on management develop-ment (Campbell et al., 1970). All of this research registers in the "relevance" column. At the same time, his self-questioning, his strong belief in the sepa-ration of research and intervention roles, and his conservatism in choosing methods and framing conclusions kept him solidly in the camp of the IPIs.

Lawler's career at Yale ended when he was denied promotion by econo-mists guarding scarce social science tenure slots. He was contacted by the Institute for Social Research (ISR) and the psychology department at the University of Michigan and asked, "Have you ever raised research money be-fore?" His answer: "No." "Have you ever managed multiple research projects and researchers?" "No." Undaunted, ISR offered him a job in 1972 and he took it. He saw it as a risky move to unfamiliar terrain but also as a chance to do large-scale field research and to learn from the "masters" how to do funded research.

Mirvis, mentored by Lawler through his PhD years in organizational psy-chology at the University of Michigan, got bitten by the organizational change bug as a Yale undergrad in the late 60s, where he was a psychology/ad sci ma-jor. He took a reading course under Hackman, did a traditional field study under Schneider, and met others in the IPI camp. He also participated in T-groups—three courses—to get some IPC credentials. He knew of but never met Lawler on the campus. His college years were marked by campus protest over the Vietnam War and civil rights issues. Many classes pointed out how scholars were part of the establishment; others highlighted their liberating potential. All of this presaged his personal and a larger institutional inquiry into the limitations of positivistic social science and its role in serving the in-terests of "power-elites" (Gouldner, 1962; Guskin & Chelser, 1973).

Career Stage 3: The Institute for Social Research

ISR was founded just after World War II to, appropriately enough, apply be-havioral and social science knowledge to society's conflicts and ills. In the 1970s, it housed research groups concerned with group dynamics, the pub-lic's economic and social behavior, and a coterie of organizational scholars including Rensis Likert, Dave Bowers, Dan Katz, Bob Kahn, Stan Seashore, and others who had advanced theories of organizational behavior and stud-ied them in the field, often through survey research.

Lawler was hired as a program director in the survey research center with the expectation that he would continue his studies of motivation, pay, job design, and organization design. He was also expected to obtain research funding, launch field studies, and support younger research faculty and doctoral students in the organizational psychology program, which Mirvis joined in 1973.

This new career stage presented Lawler with new challenges with respect to the rigor versus relevance dimensions of scholarly work. The teaching and university service dimensions of faculty life shrunk for Lawler, but his role expanded in three areas: (1) theorizing about human behavior in organizations; (2) devising multiple methods to study human behavior at work during and after planned changes; and (3) managing a program of change research involving a complex mix of institutions and actors. The options and choices made in each area revealed complexities within and trade-offs between traditional scientific rigor and relevance.

QWL program. There wasn't a Quality of Worklife (QWL) program at Michigan when Lawler arrived. There was the Quality of Employment interview study and a body of research conceptualizing and studying organizations as social systems. Seashore joined Lawler to co-lead the QWL program group.

The need for a more encompassing and practice-oriented theory of QWL was urgent in the early 1970s. The U.S. Department of Health, Education, and Welfare had issued a report on *Work in America* (O'Toole, 1971) that pointed to growing worker alienation in factories ("blue collar blues") and discontent among office staff ("white collar woes"). In turn, costly counter-productive behavior (absenteeism, turnover, and shoddy workmanship) seemed to be on the rise. The quality problems among U.S. automakers and the rise of Japan Inc. exemplified the consequences. Studies such as *"Where have all the robots gone?"* pointed to the mismatch between educated workers and dumber-than-ever jobs (Sheppard & Herrick, 1972).

Various fixes were being offered to aid American industry ranging from Volvo's "team assembly" of automobiles to the participatory team system at the Topeka Dog Food plant of General Foods. Still, the usefulness of these practices was in question as labor unions generally opposed them, and others doubted their effectiveness.

Many researchers had theories of how redesigned work and organizational systems might address the morale and performance problems facing the nation. For instance, Likert (1967) and Bowers (1976) posited how organizations might feature participatory structures and processes that would promote intrinsic motivation and job satisfaction and capitalize on the ideas of workers. The sociotechnical school proposed that semi-autonomous work groups could function better than the hierarchical model. Richard Walton (1972) laid out principles for a better quality of work life and showed how moving organizational systems from control to commitment would reduce alienation.

But these and many other visions of a more humane and productive workplace were not clearly linked, conceptually or empirically, to scholarship on how organization structure, job designs, supervisory practices, and work group dynamics affect employee motivation, job satisfaction, and performance. The conceptual challenge was to pull these threads together into an overarching model of the quality of work life and link it to theorizing on organization effectiveness. The research challenge was to study these linkages and assess the impact of different ways to improve the quality of work life.

Rigorous methods. The research design for the QWL program was to introduce changes in work organizations that would be formulated and implemented by experts in organization development, sociotechnical systems, and labor-management cooperation. The Michigan QWL group would act as an "independent" assessor of the change process and results. This fit the "third party" assessment logic favored in evaluation research and was in keeping with Lawler's belief that a separation of research and intervention roles was the best way to create credible unbiased results when an organizational intervention is studied.

Devising methods to track the impact of different kinds of interventions across multiple locales was mind stretching for the researchers involved. A job redesign, for example, could alter supervisory behavior, group dynamics, the mix of intrinsic and extrinsic motivators, and the overall experience a jobholder might have. Altering authority patterns via participatory management or changing organizational arrangements via information and communication systems might change the full panoply of individual, group, and organizational behavior. To capture the impact of such broad-based and rippling changes in an organization, the QWL group needed multilevel, multidimensional theories, and multiple research methods, measures, and statistics.

A QWL survey covering the full range of organizational characteristics and individual attitudes was developed. In addition, methods for measuring work performance, absenteeism, and turnover in behavioral and financial terms were devised. Further, to capture features of each intervention and the more qualitative aspects of change, a method for workplace observation was developed. Taken together, these tools provided a way of recording and, in some cases, quantifying the impact of change on the quality of work life (Seashore et al., 1983).

Each of the QWL instruments had its own logic and methods. Pulling them into a coherent assessment meant observing the intervention closely, specifying "mini-models" of expected changes in attitudes and behavior, and testing the effects through repeated measures. To deal with all the factors that might impact conclusions about the results of changes in work systems, Lawler proposed the idea of "adaptive experiments" that included multiple methods and measures. Where feasible, a comparison group within the organization under study and on-site observation were used to yield a mosaic of evidence linking work system changes to all of the factors measured, observed, and recorded (Lawler, Nadler, & Cammann, 1980).

Factoring in relevance. In research of such a large scale and scope, there are multiple stakeholders to consider, many of which have interests that are practice oriented. As an example, the QWL studies were funded by the U.S. Departments of Labor and Commerce and by the Ford Foundation. These sponsors were interested in theorizing and research that would identify "levers" for improving QWL in organizations. They also wanted to document what kinds of interventions would produce significant changes in human and organization behavior. Thus, many of the QWL projects were conceived of as "demonstration projects" to show how work redesign could improve employee attitudes and performance.

Many of the projects involved the creation of joint labor-management committees to sponsor and oversee the change programs. Launching a project involved complex negotiations with large firms and national unions to create a "shelter agreement" whereby interventions could be undertaken that did not conform to existing collective bargaining agreements. Naturally, questions were asked about research methods, standards of proof, and practical matters, such as how much time would be taken from production, who would have access to data, how intrusive the measurements would be, matters of confidentiality, and so on. In many instances, management and labor were not in full agreement about proposed changes nor the value of the research effort. Standard protocols needed to be modified in light of their concerns.

Furthermore, there was friction between interventionists and researchers. Who wants to be "evaluated" by an independent group, let alone one applying semi-standardized criteria and research methods to a unique intervention? In some cases, there was not agreement on the validity and relevance of particular measures and methods, nor on their capacity to capture the more nuanced aspects of organization change. There were concerns, too, that organization members might perceive them as "tests" or simply as unwelcome intrusions into organization life. Finally, there were concerns as to whether or not the researchers were biased and prone to fault finding in the guise of academic inquiry.

The diverse interests and concerns of all of the stakeholders challenged even the relaxed criteria of scientific research rigor. There was simply no way to "shelter" these research projects, as one would a laboratory study, from the complex sociopolitical environment that surrounded them. Nor was it desirable to do so: After all, this mix was part and parcel of the change process.

Managing a research program. The QWL research program illustrates how a scholar who is concerned with generating rigorous and relevant findings faces a plethora of conceptual, research, and operational challenges. In essence, a researcher has to learn how to manage a complex research program—soup to nuts. Factors including a research team, leadership, teamwork, planning, performance reviews, publicity, individual and collective learning, fundraising, and so on need attention.

The competencies required go beyond the intellectual and scientific ones needed for theorizing and researching to include negotiation, relationship building, leadership, and communication. Adaptability and resilience are needed along with patience and persistence. The broad point is that scholars who aim to produce useful research through large-scale field research have to have some degree of managerial acumen and be "closet" or maybe academic entrepreneurs.

To manage the QWL program, Lawler created a matrix structure where one axis was the individual project evaluation teams and the other housed methods specialists on QWL surveys, behavioral-economic assessments, observation methods, and so on. These slots were filled by study directors (akin to assistant professors) and graduate students who had their own research interests and project management aptitudes.[1]

To execute the change side of the QWL program, Lawler created a Washington, DC office. It was staffed with a director and several support individuals who were charged with finding receptive companies and unions and creating a match between a change agent and the project that was identified by the union and management. The Washington office only started projects that agreed to be studied by the assessment team at ISR. Ultimately, eight large-scale union-management projects were created and studied.

Mirvis as mentee. Mirvis came into the QWL program as a first-year graduate student in 1973. The year before Mirvis joined a Business and Employment Council in Ohio. At the council, Mirvis worked with Barry Macy to develop measures of the rate and costs of counter-productive behavior in organizations. When the agency folded, they went to Michigan/ISR as a PhD student and study director, respectively. Macy and Mirvis (1976) handled the behavioral-economic research axis and had evaluation responsibilities in one or more projects.

The doctoral student community at Michigan was very talented. Not surprisingly, it also divided into its own camps. One segment was more orthodox

---

1. The QWL program included Cortland Cammann, Barry Macy, Robert Cooke, Jeanne Herman (Brett), Michael Moch, and Denise Rousseau, full-time study directors, as well as graduate students Jack Drexler, Veronica Nieva, David Nadler, Douglas Jenkins, Nina Gupta, David Berg, Dennis Perkins, Mark Fichman, Gerry Ledford, R. J. Bullock, Mark Peterson, and others.

in its outlook on research rigor and roles and more apt to do dissertations based in establish niches of scholarship and methods. The other segment was more exploratory, more inclined toward qualitative studies, and more apt to be involved as interventionists in action research-type projects.

Career Transitions: Identity Shifts

The QWL community at Michigan was involved in a continuous dialogue on our research methods and on our findings. Given its diversity, there was often debate about the merits of "soft" versus "hard" methods and of quantitative versus qualitative measures of the changes introduced in the organizations studied. In many respects these conversations replicated the IPC versus IPI arguments at Yale but covered some new-to-the-field research questions:

- *Reductionism versus Holism.* Many researchers drilled down into the specific variables to locate QWL changes in organizations, whereas others focused more on the big picture and data patterns. Whose conclusions were more valid?

- *Generalizability of Findings.* Many of the individual projects yielded insights into organizational dynamics, confirmed hypotheses, and testified to the impact of QWL interventions. This sparked debate: Can $n = 1$ studies yield conclusions about the effectiveness of interventions or should caution limit their generalizability? Naturally, the change agents and sponsors had an interest in this debate as well.

- *Attitude Change—What Is Significant?* Several studies found measurable changes ($p > .01$) over time in employee attitudes. Was this an alpha (a change in the attitude measured), beta (a change in the intensity of ratings of an attitude), or gamma change (changes in intensity and the meaning of what is being measured)? And, what if survey data said something different than the "smell of the place"?

The QWL researchers argued about the validity of what we could count (such as physical changes in work arrangements) versus what we could sense (such as psychosocial changes in work relationships); about the role of explicit versus tacit explicit knowledge in interpreting what was going on and drawing conclusions; and naturally, over the use of the "self" as a research instrument. All of these matters were, in turn, framed in larger debates within the social sciences at the time, occasioned by the emergence of symbolic, interpretive, and postmodern theorizing and research methodologies.

We mention these debates for three reasons. First, they reveal the nuances and complexity behind any discussion of rigor versus relevance. The univariate continuum between rigor and relevance exploded into multidimensional space in our research group with traditionalists sometimes allying with action researchers and postpositivists occasionally crying out for more objectivity. Second, although these scrums did not resolve the questions at issue, they evidence the value of dialogue, diversity, and reflective practice. Lawler had experienced this at Yale with Argyris; Mirvis experienced this at Michigan with Lawler and Seashore. Finally, these reflections and the praxis of the QWL program also influenced how we developed as researchers.

Lawler as "action researcher." While studying the QWL projects, Lawler became fascinated with new plant start-ups at TRW, Procter & Gamble, General Foods, Honda, and other corporations. The "greenfield" status of these plants gave companies an opportunity to immediately create a highly participative team-based system without having to go through a change process. This opportunity provided an ideal research setting in which to test his theoretical work concerning motivation, employee involvement, and organizational effectiveness.

Working with the new plants, Lawler fell into the role of being both consultant and researcher. As a result of these projects and his work on gain-sharing plans, he became more interested in creating change in organizations. As much as he "hated" to admit it, he was doing Argyris-type action research. Still, in keeping with his scholarly traditions, he collected survey and performance data over time in these projects.

It may be post hoc justification, but Lawler now feels that he has learned the most about how organizations function and change from projects where he has combined the evaluation and change roles. Among other things, he has learned about the difficulties, challenges, and tough decisions that have to be made when one is trying to guide a change project. Apparently Kurt Lewin was correct on this count!

Mirvis as "reflective practitioner." Mirvis and Lawler also worked on some "one-off" research projects at ISR. One involved an investigation of the financial impact of employee attitudes (Mirvis & Lawler, 1977). By the mid-1970s, Lawler was increasingly interested in more "levers" for effecting change in organizations. He saw the possibility of producing a company integrative report on QWL and making the information known to investors through a firm's annual report. He and Mirvis included a report on QWL in Graphic Controls Corporation for its 1977 Annual Report and, in a subsequent survey of investors, documented its relevance as a new form of social accounting (Lawler & Mirvis, 1981). The work gained some national visibility and earned us the moniker of "meddlers" in business.

Mirvis also became reflective on the research process. He opened up to more "artful" methods of assessment in his dissertation under the guidance of another mentor, Don Michael (Mirvis, 1980). Working with Seashore, he began to think about doing organization research responsibly in a complex social context (Mirvis & Seashore, 1979). This collaboration led to protocols for negotiating research regimens mindful of the interests of and risks to the full range of stakeholders implicated in a study. And, at the urgings of fellow student David Berg, he examined the role of social construction and his own psyche in shaping research findings (Mirvis & Louis, 1985). These reflections, in turn, have shaped his work as an interventionist.

Career Stage 4: Establishing and Managing CEO

Lawler's move to the University of Southern California in 1978 led to the further evolution of Lawler's interest in combining research rigor and relevance. He arrived with the thought that he would take on a regular senior faculty role. He soon realized he had been spoiled by his years at ISR. He was addicted to a setting that was designed to support field research, one that provided data analysts, administrative support, flexible use of time and contacts with research sites and funding sources. When he arrived at USC, none of these existed. Once he realized this, he decided to create a research center that would do the kind of useful research he valued. At this point, we will just briefly discuss CEO as it is covered in Chapter 3.

Running a corporate membership organization. Around the time Lawler moved to USC, the federal government more or less ceased funding in the QWL arena, and private foundations shifted their monies toward social needs. Realizing he could not replicate ISR, he decided to organize CEO as a corporate member research organization where companies would come together to share knowledge about organizational issues and practices and participate in CEO research studies. The corporate members were funders, co-shapers, and consumers of CEO research. Early sponsors included GE, Honeywell, TRW, and Digital. Their influence helped to push Lawler further toward applicable scholarship.

Most scholars and students in the QWL group at ISR were trained in organization psychology. At CEO, Lawler developed a team of scholars trained in multiple disciplines who were oriented toward improving organizational practice. Indeed, the Center has as its purpose improving how effectively organizations are managed. Over the 32 years of the Center's operation, its researchers have had interests and expertise in organization structures and systems, leadership practices, labor economics, business strategy, organization development, and human resource management.[2] With these more "macro" interests and core competencies, theorizing and studies at CEO have tended to focus on how different organizational arrangements impact the financial effectiveness of enterprise as well as the welfare of their employees.

At USC, Lawler's interests increasingly focused on systemic rather than individual or team behavior. Much of his pre-USC research looked at the impact of select organizational attributes, such as compensation systems, on people and organization behavior. At USC he has extended his work to studies of information flows and coordination, the impact of high-involvement management systems, talent management strategies, senior management teaming, and the workings of corporate boards. Scholarship based on theories of human motivation has taken a back seat to studies framed in terms of system functioning. To an extent, this focus can be traced to corporate priorities and funding and to the proclivities of the CEO research team. Generating knowledge about these organizational features, it was reasoned, would give practitioners a better understanding of high-impact management changes and access to bigger levers for organizational improvement.

Finally, as the USC research program unfolded, Lawler shed his preference for separating intervention and research roles. He and the CEO team examine and opine on change management and do studies that combined research and change. In one respect, this is a necessity, as CEO has been self-funded at USC. The team has had to find projects that corporations, the government, and foundations are willing to support. Lawler has found that although there is still some funding for "pure research," there is more interest in research projects that aim to improve organizational effectiveness.

Mirvis's Career Directions

Mirvis left Michigan/ISR in 1980, a newly minted PhD, to look for work as a researcher/study director. He took a hybrid academic appointment at Boston University, teaching in the management school and working at the Center for Applied Social Science alongside psychologists, sociologists, and political scientists, his own mini-ISR. At BU, he modified the QWL survey for use as an employee survey in companies. He also began to study a broad portfolio of levers for change, including the introduction of computer technology in offices and factories, the launch of work-family programs and flextime in companies, and the impact of an acquisition on an enterprise. This latter study

---

2. Allan Mohrman, Susan Albers Mohrman, Gerry Ledford, Jay Conger, Chris Worley, George Benson, Jay Galbraith, Susan Cohen, John Boudreau, Theresa Welbourne, Cris Gibson, Jim O'Toole, Ram Tenkasi, Edy Greenblatt, Alec Levenson, and Gary McMahan are among the researchers who have been part of CEO.

also moved him into an action role when Michael Blumenthal, learning of his work on the human side of acquisitions, asked Mirvis and a former ISR colleague, Mitchell Marks, to assist him in effecting the then-largest takeover in U.S. history (Burroughs and Sperry-Unisys).

When Mirvis lost his tenure case at BU in a political brouhaha, he threw up a shingle and fashioned a career in scholarly practice. The "action" side was emphasized through the 80s and 90s in further mergers and acquisitions (M&A) consultations and involvement with a socially responsible business in building its human organization. His research continued through this period, including a study with Lawler and others on human capital investments in companies. His scholarship became more organic, and his writings featured an anecdotal mix of ideas, case material, and thoughts on practice (cf, Mirvis & Marks, 1991).

Learning and Future Directions

In this part of the chapter, we consider where organizational research is and should be going. We begin the discussion with some observations about what determines the type of research organizational scholars choose to do. Not surprisingly, our observations are very much the product of our career experiences.

Matching the Person and Research (P-R Fit)

One theme emerging from the exploration of our respective scholarly lives is the fit between who we are as people and our research. Although every researcher's journey is unique, a researcher typically changes during his or her career. Lawler's journey matches that of many other senior organizational behavior scholars who "end up" doing useful research. Lawler was socialized early on as a mainstream scientific researcher: exploring core psychological phenomena with traditional methods and tools. His early career experiences at Yale opened him up to other methodological perspectives and the exigencies of running a research shop at Michigan and later USC pulled him to more action-oriented scholarship and research.

Later career writings turned from *JAP* to *HBR* and from books aimed at scholars and students to those aimed at practicing managers. As for person-environment fit, his scholarly identity changed from Yale to Michigan to USC. As for his own motives for turning toward useful research, Lawler, when pressed, explained his outlook, "I get a kick out of doing work that makes people more effective and satisfied. It is rewarding to me. I'd rather do that than solve a crossword puzzle or deal with some statistical issue."

He never has seen himself as a scholar or intellectual. Thus, his progression from *A*-journal research to a focus on useful research expresses his identity as a doer. What has remained constant for Lawler is his focus on gathering data. He began his career with collecting data on rats, and he continues to collect data on topics ranging from corporate board member behavior to the impact of outsourcing HR processes. Data provide the basis for his writing and are key to his focus on doing research that informs theory and practice.

Mirvis opened up to diverse methodologies earlier in his career. Much of his later scholarship involves case studies drawn from his active intervention in organizations, augmented by interviews and shared reflections from organization members. The output of this participatory research is often storytelling. In essence, he, too, has created action-and-research settings congenial to his purposes.

Personal preferences pushed Lawler and Mirvis toward practical ends, but there was also a certain pull to the "job" of doing applied research that has intrinsic appeal. Consider the job design of, say, a traditional versus more practice-oriented researcher. When it comes to "motivating characteristics," both can score well on autonomy, challenge, and even "task completeness." But which type of job offers more variety? And which offers more interaction and deeper social relations? And which scores highest on social significance? On these metrics, at least, more applied research and interaction with practitioners make for more stimulating and enjoyable work (at least for us!).

Matching the Research and Environment (R-E Fit)

Organizational studies are messy. People's attitudes and behaviors may vary for a host of nonintervention and nonwork reasons. And many variables, not necessarily measured or controlled for in a study, may impinge on outcomes like job motivation, satisfaction, and performance. Throw in an intervention and you get Hawthorne effects, plus other unintended and second-order consequences that make it difficult to get a fix on what is theoretically *and* actually happening to the people and organizations that are being studied.

Most organizational researchers who venture into the field try to steer around these complications by conducting pre- and post-intervention surveys that test discrete hypotheses and ignore all the other things that might be going on. In classical positivist tradition, they presume that a "control group" can be found that is somehow unaffected by all of the varied things that go on in organizations. That was Lawler's modus operandi in his early career studies of managerial attitudes, pay, and job design. A more organic, "hands on" research model was used in the adaptive experiments at Michigan.

Lawler's scholarly thrust at ISR and USC has been toward more complex theorizing about organizational dynamics and more intensive measurement of phenomenon in motion. To some extent, this orientation is a function of the "supply side" of research: a combination of scholarly interests and ambitions, the competencies of researchers involved, and the institutional missions and capabilities of university-based research centers. But, the "demand side" also figures in. The study of large-scale organizational activity and change poses complex theoretical, methodological, and operational challenges. To connect to it requires requisite variety in the research gene pool of theoretical know-how and the capacity to theorize in the face of complex change processes.

This shift in one's research focus, process, and organization is, in generic form, a matter of organization-environment fit. Lawler needs a complex research organization to match the complexity of what and whom he is studying. This is essential to meet the demanding standards of his diverse stakeholders for rigor and relevance. It is why he founded and continues to direct CEO, which provides an environment that makes useful research possible.

Obviously a group of very competent colleagues is key to Lawler being able to do useful research. At all three of his job stops (USC, Michigan, and Yale), Lawler has worked with great groups of researchers. Because of them, complex problems could be looked at from multiple points of view, projects got started that he would never have considered, and there was support for larger-scale, longer-term research. This kind of collegiality, we believe, is the most important environmental determinant of research directions and achievement. We also think it is more important in doing useful field studies than in doing most other kinds of organizational research. Useful research requires research teams to embrace multiple research logics and methods; and its success hinges on encouragement, constructive conflict, and lots of social support.

Though not regularly based in a research shop, Mirvis's research arrangements also call for flexibility, adaptability, entrepreneurship, and real-time learning. He, too, undertakes studies involving a shifting team of scholars, from universities and research organizations, often crossing multiple continents. He engages organization members in collecting and analyzing data and in creating learning histories about their change programs, in one case covering a period of ten years (Mirvis, Ayas, & Roth, 2003).

Engaged Scholarship: What Enables Useful Research?

What can researchers do to help assure that their research is useful? Highly beneficial is openly engaging with organizations as co-creators of knowledge. Consider some ways co-creation translates into useful research.

- *Foresight.* In our research, we have sought out new topics and tried to study innovative, often untested organizational practices. Some foresight in spotting emerging managerial and social issues and a willingness to take risks help in this. More important is our exposure to and involvement with fellow researchers who have different interests and points of view. But, the real gold mine has been our engagement with diverse organizations and creative practitioners. In many areas, practice in the best companies is ahead of theorizing. Scouting what they are doing and considering new organization practices can provide a rich roster of interesting and researchable topics.

- *Self-as-instrument.* Close contact with practitioners in field studies, and their active engagement in the research process, often yields a sense of affinity and empathy across the research-practice divide. This more interactive and participatory process thrusts the scholar into the organizational system and, in traditional scientific terms, risks objectivity as the researcher "goes native." At the same time, we find that deep engagement gives scholars a fuller and richer feel for the subject matter and people under study. In the process, the "self" becomes a research instrument that can stimulate insights into what is going on and provoke more grounded theorizing.

- *Managing a research organization.* Another source of connection to practitioners and insights concerning practice comes from reflecting on how we operate our own research organizations. We each manage "mini" research shops, with budgets, employees, deadlines, and the like, and thus experience some of the challenges of management. In his large-scale studies, for instance, Lawler's dealings with multiple funders, organizations, and stakeholders have helped him gain a feel for how to unfreeze and create forward movement in companies—critical for identifying high-impact levers and understanding how change can reverberate through companies. Mirvis has had to learn about multiorganizational dynamics in his consulting and action research with Noel Tichy, the Global Research and Education Network, and others. By comparison, most university professors are well-versed in the literature but are comparatively clueless about how organizations work—see how faculty meetings operate!

- *Adaptive scholarship.* It may seem that we have sacrificed theory-building scholarship and traditional scientific research in service to our respective versions of P-R and R-E fits. But, it happens that our early academic socialization and personal interests in ideas have not faded. On the contrary, we are both animated by theorizing about human and organization behavior and continue to learn about things we think we know a lot about.

- *Finding a balance.* Our simple message is that scholars need to work hard to find the "right balance" among ideals and interests in their research. Most organizations are not particularly sympathetic to cries for rigor when this means intrusive measurement and double-blind experiments. As a result, even the skilled researcher can only press so far when it comes to adding scientific rigor to his or her research agenda. But, in our experience, practitioners are sensitive to the importance of valid data and are open to give-and-take about the design of a credible study. There is no "formula" for finding the right balance between rigor and relevance; much depends on the topic being studied and the history of research in that area. However, we do feel strongly that when doing and evaluating research, if the relevance is high then less rigor should be accepted as a natural trade-off, just as when rigor is high some willingness to sacrifice relevance is appropriate.

Worrisome Trends

The last 50 years have seen an enormous change in the kind and amount of organizational research that is done. It has become a big business outside of universities and a major activity at leading business schools. There is no question that the field has progressed and that a great deal has been learned about organizations and people at work. But there are worrisome trends today that promise to take the field further away from research that informs *both* theory and practice.

Rigor over Relevance

Many of today's organizational researchers in business schools have been trained, groomed, and rewarded for doing carefully controlled, theoretically driven research studies. New PhDs are expected to have made professional presentations and have one or more *A*-journal publications under review. These expectations put students' emphases during graduate school on lab studies, secondary data analyses, and literature reviews. Field studies and action-research are simply too time consuming and practice driven to fit the resume-building stratagems of most graduate students. The same is true for junior faculty members in business schools who are expected to have five or more *A*-journal publications in order to get tenure.

Nowhere is this traditional approach more evident than in organizational behavior where today's young scholars concentrate on laboratory research and simulations. Often they are trained in experimental social psychology (absent its historical connections to Lewinian action research). They are interested in studying social interaction, conflict resolution, and antisocial behavior such as lying and prejudice. These topics are surely relevant to how people are and should be managed. But the contrived situations that they put people in for very short periods of time—often involving deception and doing trivial tasks—have little resemblance to the reality of an organizational setting. In some cases, the research does not even involve human beings; instead, computer simulations are developed to measure the effects of things such as lying or negotiation strategies. The end result is that this type of research scores high on internal but low on external validity.

Are the findings from most of the research that is done today in business schools something that can guide practice? We do not think they can or should. It is simply too big a leap from the laboratory and computer to the situations that actually exist in organizations. Many of the scholars state that they intend eventually to validate their ideas in field settings, but we don't see it happening: The academic environment simply doesn't support it. Missing is the open dialogue about the merits of different methodologies that we found in our years at Yale and Michigan. What is also often missing in business schools is the preference for subject matter and methodological diversity in faculty staffing and promotion. Indeed, because of the way business schools operate today, there is little support and encouragement for younger faculty members to make the transition to fieldwork and applicable research; and it is not clear that it fits their skills or personalities.

Relevance over Rigor

Until recently knowledge production about organization behavior was primarily the province of the universities. Today, by contrast, think tanks and training companies (such as the Hudson Institute and the Center for Creative Leadership), consulting firms, and professional associations (such as the Society for Human Resource Management and American Society for Training and Development) are actively in the research game.

They churn out technical reports, conduct internet-based surveys, and offer insights about almost everything we in academia study. They are quicker to market and do not hesitate to say how the results should drive management practice. Often the details concerning sample construction, measurement properties, and the evidence behind insights are tucked into the back of their reports, if present at all. In many instances, the research doesn't stand up to critical research design scrutiny, but that doesn't seem to matter to practitioners, who often are not aware of the problems.

At one time companies, including AT&T, GE, and IBM, had internal research shops that worked on human resource management and organizational effectiveness. Professionals in these companies would periodically sponsor university studies or partner with university-based researchers. Most of these in-house research programs are gone. So, in many instances, is the idea that a business should support research to advance developments in theory and practice for the benefit of the "field." Linkages between practitioners and universities still exist at a few places, such as CEO, that feature peer learning and knowledge exchange, but even there, support for original research seems to be waning.

What Do Organizations Want?

When buying research in the marketplace, firms have a choice: partner with a scholar to get a study done or with a consulting firm that will do a diagnostic study, recommend interventions, and implement them with a large complement of trained staff to support the change. Most firms opt for consulting firms and one-stop shopping. (Of course, there is always the suspicion that consultants find what they are looking for when doing research—problems that fit their areas of specialization. But at least they have the expertise to take action.) This trend toward "packaged" research-and-intervention is particularly pronounced in HR, where there seems to be little willingness to launch exploratory research or to study "untested" interventions and little interest in evaluating the effectiveness of interventions. In response, academics are urging practitioners to adopt "evidence-based" management; but is there any evidence that we scholars can turn out evidence that is timely and compelling?

There was a time when operating managers read research-based books, such as McGregor's *The Human Side of Enterprise* (1960) or Likert's *New Patterns of Management* (1961), where scholarship was their key selling point. Today most managers and MBA students are clueless about theory, the nuances of research design and significance levels. With short attention spans and in need of a quick fix, they turn to e-clipping and digest services that offer *USA Today*–style summaries of research findings most germane to management, no matter their source or scientific status. The *Harvard Business Review*, once academics' prime outlet for scholarly work aimed at practice, is today uncluttered with data and research results and seemingly unconcerned with the evidence base of what it presents. Needless to say, all of this works against academics who strive to balance relevance with rigor in their studies. Still, there are potential ways forward.

Future Directions

Following the principle "if you can't beat them, join them," one option is to develop more university-based research programs specifically aimed at practice. Research centers such as CEO include traditional and applied researchers as well as scholarly practitioners. University research shops that offer "theory-to-practice" services, including intervention, are especially appealing to companies that want a comprehensive "package."

Another stratagem is for researchers to partner with consulting firms that value research and thought leadership. Mirvis, for instance, has partnered with McKinsey and the Reputation Institute on global studies. CEO has partnered with Booz and Company, Mercer, Towers Watson, Heidrick and Struggles, and Korn/Ferry. With their global reach, skilled staff, and practical smarts, these consulting firms bring more than their (fair) share to the partnership.

Applied researchers in universities can also "productize" some of their tools and frameworks. This approach can open doors to new research ventures and, as cash cows, can help fund more exploratory research. Our point is that researchers who want to do useful research need to be more managerially and commercially minded or at least hire someone to better manage their research practices.

Competitive practices can also be used. Efforts can be made, via blogs and popular books, to educate managers on the value of rigorous research and the importance of evidence-based management. Fuller exposition of counterintuitive theories and research findings can pique interests. Stronger debasement of pseudoscientific work may also help. Unfortunately, the odds are not high on this front: Twenty-five years ago journalists pointed out that many of the "excellent" companies cited by Tom Peters and Bob Waterman (*In Search of Excellence*, 1982) had become unprofitable. Recently Peters confessed that he hadn't collected systematic data to support his choice of excellent companies. *Good-to-Great* firms cited by Jim Collins (2001), such as Circuit City and Fannie Mae, don't look so great in hindsight either. Despite this, their work remains very respected by practitioners.

A final option, and the one we favor, is for academics to look ahead to the "new, new" things and do useful research in areas of high impact. Prahalad's work (2004) on the "base of the pyramid" and the work of many of the other contributors to this book exemplify what can be done at the leading edge of theory and practice. This is the kind of scholarship that keeps us looking ahead, offers personal satisfaction, and is of interest to forward-looking companies that want to venture into new territory with a research partner.

REFERENCES

Argyris, C., Putnam, R., & Smith, D. (1985). *Action science.* San Francisco: Jossey-Bass.

Bowers, D. (1976). *Systems of organization: Management of the human resource.* Ann Arbor: Institute for Social Research.

Campbell, J. P., Dunnette, M. D., Lawler, E. E., & Weick, K. E. (1970). *Managerial behavior, performance, and effectiveness.* New York: McGraw-Hill.

Collins, J. (2001). *Good to great: Why some companies make the leap—and others don't.* New York: HarperBusiness.

Gouldner, A. W. (1962). Anti-minotaur: The myth of a valuefree sociology. *Social Problems, 9,* 199–213.

Guskin, A. E., & Chesler, M. A. (1973). Partisan diagnosis of social problems. In G. Zaltman (Ed.), *Processes and phenomena of social change.* New York: Oxford University Press.

Hackman, J. R., & Lawler, E. E. (1971). Employee reaction to job characteristics. *Journal of Applied Psychology, 55,* 259–286.

Lawler, E. E., & Mirvis, P. H. (1981). Measuring the quality of work life: How Graphic Controls assesses the human side of the corporation. *Management Review, 70*(10), 54–63.

Lawler, E., Nadler, D., & Cammann, C. (Eds.). (1980). *Organizational assessment.* New York: Wiley.

Likert, R. (1961). *New patterns of management.* New York: McGraw-Hill.

Likert, R. (1967). *The human organization: Its management and value.* New York: McGraw-Hill.

Macy, B. A., & P. H. Mirvis. (1976). A methodology for assessment of quality of work and organizational effectiveness in behavioral-economic terms. *Administrative Science Quarterly, 21,* 212–226.

McGregor, D. (1960). *The human side of enterprise.* New York: McGraw-Hill.

Mirvis, P. H. (1980). The art of assessing the quality of work life. In E. Lawler, D. Nadler, & C. Cammann (Eds.), *Organizational assessment* (pp. 471–489). New York: Wiley.

Mirvis, P. H., Ayas, K., & Roth, G. (2003). *To the desert and back: The story of one of the most dramatic business transformations on record.* San Francisco: Jossey-Bass.

Mirvis, P. H., & Lawler, E. E., (1977). Measuring the financial impact of employee attitudes. *Journal of Applied Psychology, 62,* 1–8.

Mirvis, P. H., & Louis, M. R. (1985). Self-full research: Working through the self as instrument in organizational research. In D. N. Berg & K. K. Smith (Eds.), *Exploring clinical methods for social research.* Beverly Hills, CA: Sage.

Mirvis, P. H., & Marks, M. A. (1991). *Managing the merger.* Englewood Cliffs, NJ: Prentice Hall. (Republished in 2003 by Beard Books, Frederick, MD).

Mirvis, P. H., & Seashore, S. E. (1979). Being ethical in organizational research. *American Psychologist, 34,* 766–780.

O'Toole, J. (1971). *Work in America: Report of a special task force to the U.S. Department of Health, Education, and Welfare.* Cambridge, MA: The MIT Press.

Peters, T. J., & Waterman, R. H., Jr. (1982). *In search of excellence.* New York: HarperCollins.

Porter, L. W., & Lawler, E. E. (1968). *Managerial attitudes and performance.* Homewood, IL: Irwin.

Prahalad, C. K. (2004). *The fortune at the bottom of the pyramid.* Upper Saddle River, NJ: Pearson Education.

Seashore, S. L., Lawler, E. E., Mirvis, P. H., & Cammann, C. (Eds.). (1983). *Assessing organizational change: A guide to methods, measures, and practices.* New York: Wiley Interscience.

Sheppard, H., & Herrick, N. (1972). W*here have all the robots gone?* New York: Free Press.

Walton, R. E. (1972). How to counter alienation in the plant. *Harvard Business Review, 50*(6), 70–81.

ABOUT THE AUTHORS

Philip Mirvis is an organizational psychologist and senior research fellow at the Center for Corporate Citizenship. His studies and private practice concerns large-scale organizational change, the character of the workforce and workplace, and business leadership in society. He has authored ten books on his studies including *The Cynical Americans* (social trends), *Building the Competitive Workforce* (human capital), *Joining Forces,* second edition (the human dynamics of mergers), and *To the Desert and Back* (a business transformation case). His most recent is *Beyond Good Company: Next Generation Corporate Citizenship.*

Edward E. Lawler III is Distinguished Professor of Business and Director of the Center for Effective Organizations in the Marshall School of Business at the University of Southern California. He has been honored as a top contributor to the fields of organizational development, human resources management, organizational behavior, and compensation. He is the author of over 350 articles and 43 books. His most recent books include *Achieving Strategic Excellence: An Assessment of Human Resource Organizations* (2006), *Built to Change* (2006), *The New American Workplace* (2006), *America at Work* (2006), *Talent: Making People Your Competitive Advantage* (2008), and *Achieving Excellence in Human Resource Management* (2009). For more information, visit http://www.edwardlawler.com and http://ceo.usc.edu.

SEVEN

Can Relevance and Rigor Coexist?

C. K. PRAHALAD*

THE DEBATE ABOUT RELEVANCE and rigor in research is a favorite topic for academics. For as long as I can remember, this debate has been vigorous but inconclusive. This discussion is not limited to the focus of academic research and methodological preferences but also about the way the results of our research are communicated. Many practitioners find the language of academic journals overly (and often unnecessarily) complicated. Further, there is seldom an action bias in academic research. The next steps, for example, What can a manager do with these conclusions? How can she operationalize the results of academic research? have often remained unanswered. I have, over the past 25 years, avoided this debate about rigor and relevance. Early in my research career I made a clear choice: My primary audience was practitioners. My research, as a result, was focused on what I felt was relevant to managers and I chose outlets for my work that were practitioner oriented. Viewed from this perspective, I have been an academic "outlier." I believe that was probably the reason that the organizers of this workshop invited me to write a chapter in this book. They asked me to reflect on my personal journey as a researcher.

The Research Focus

My research focus has evolved over time. Shown in Figure 7.1 are the major punctuations in my overall research journey starting with *The Multinational Mission* (1987) to *The New Age of Innovation* (2008). I call them punctuations as each of these books represents a milestone in my journey. Each book was preceded by a series of articles, mostly in managerially oriented publications.

---

* Because of his untimely death, C. K. Prahalad did not have the opportunity to edit his chapter after the workshop in which it was discussed. It was edited by the author-editors and the publisher.

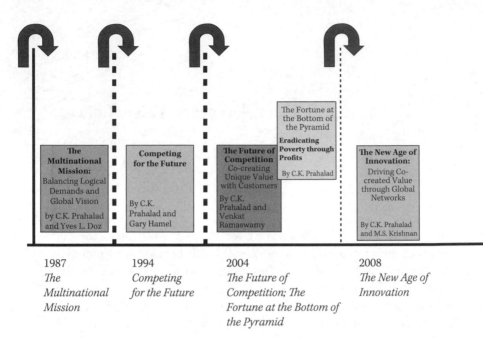

1987	1994	2004	2008
The	Competing	The Future of	The New Age of
Multinational	for the Future	Competition; The	Innovation
Mission		Fortune at the Bottom of	
		the Pyramid	

FIGURE 7.1 Evolution of My Work

Most often, we also made a large number of presentations to managers in order to test and refine these concepts. These were intended to test the validity of the concepts with managers. This process represented a method for "review" of the usefulness of the research on a massive scale. Each book represented the culmination of a program of research as well as a vehicle for presenting both the findings and a distinct point of view.

For example, in *Multinational Mission*, we argued that the *tension between the need for global integration (GI) and local responsiveness (LR)* is inherent in the nature of a global corporation. This framework has stood the test of time. Whether it is called "glocal," or some other term, this tension is debated even today. Similarly, *Competing for the Future* developed a perspective on strategy as a process for resource accumulation and leverage, not just resource allocation. The concepts of strategic intent, core competence, core products and platforms, and strategic architecture are now part of the business vocabulary. But both these books were pre-Internet. So I embarked on the implications of the rapid spread of the Internet, which resulted in both *The Future of Competition* and *The New Age of Innovation*. As a result of these studies, we developed the concepts of personalized co-creation of value, the nodal firm, and innovation as being focused on one consumer experience at a time ($N = 1$), and resources for this effort to be marshaled from a large number of institutions—an innovation ecosystem ($R = G$). The book *Fortune at the Bot-*

tom of the Pyramid was focused on building a framework to include 4 billion poor as micro consumers and producers in global commerce. This framework builds on the work on globalization, shaping markets of tomorrow, as well as co-creation and the use of technology solutions to serve the poor. The rapid commercial spread of cell phones around the world and the speed of diffusion of a modern technology among the bottom of the pyramid (BOP) markets has surprised even the optimists.

In this research effort, spread over 30 years, I have been singularly lucky with my research partners—Professors Yves Doz, Gary Hamel, Venkat Ramaswamy, and M. S. Krishnan. They added significantly to my understanding of the issues. We pushed ourselves very hard before we decided that it was time to write a book-length manuscript. This collaboration was a critical ingredient in building new concepts.

An Approach to Research

My approach to research always starts with the preoccupation of managers. Either they are catching up with their more successful competitors ("best practices") or focusing on getting an edge over established competitors ("next practices"). I recognize that most of the managerial preoccupation is with benchmarking best practices. However, it does not take much effort to come to the conclusion that if firms only benchmarked each other, they would all look, think, and act alike. There can be no enduring competitive differentiation. At best, competitive advantage can only accrue from superior execution. So from the very beginning of my research career, I focused on next practices.[1] Next practices allow managers to focus on gaining competitive advantage by being different. This distinction is critical. Managers seeking competitive advantage should focus not on being just "more efficient" (best practices) but on being "different" (next practices). A focus on next practices does not mean that efficiency and superior execution is to be ignored or undervalued. It just says that being different is a more defensible source of competitive advantage.

Research on next practices must start with what I call "weak signals." Weak signals are about what is outside the normal industry practice. It is, for example, asking in 2000, the implications of Napster to the music industry. Napster showed that 14- to 16-year-olds loved the music but wanted to co-create their own albums. This was not an isolated phenomenon. More than 30 million were downloading music. They wanted to download one song at a

---

1. I did not in the 1980s call my work "next practices." I coined the term and started using it only after the mid-1990s.

time. They wanted music to be delivered and priced differently. It was a challenge to the traditional music industry. The questions to be asked were the following: What if we had amplified these signals? Could managers in the music industry have anticipated this shift? Why did Sony forgo the opportunity to do an "iPod?"

Research methods dictated by a focus on next practices and amplification of weak signals are very different from traditional research approaches. For example, a research bias toward next practices precludes the researcher from large-scale, longitudinal databases. By definition, next practice is not about the past; it is about the future and the likely discontinuities. Understanding weak signals is about looking for "outliers" who seem to defy current wisdom—Canon in imaging in the 1990s or Google in advertising in 2000.

Picking outliers does introduce sampling bias. It is based on the judgment of the researcher. I suggest that this bias may be less harmful than it appears at first sight as the "data itself" is often of less value than it appears. It is the extraction of the core principles that must stand the test, independent of the data from which they were derived. The goal is understanding the emerging "logic" of the industry and new business models. Therefore, the approach is to develop detailed understanding of the few outliers through case studies that extract the logical structure behind the new. The cases studies serve a single purpose—providing the raw material for extracting the logical structure. The data from the case are not about validating a hypothesis; it is about illustrating the concepts. The logical structure must have the explanatory power beyond the data that were used to extract it. The real test is in the following question: Does the theory stand on its own without the data set from which it was derived?

Let me illustrate what I mean by building a logical structure and using data as illustrations (see Fig. 7.2.). Let us use *Competing for the Future* as an example. We have to start with a single and intuitive premise:

Aspirations > Resources

This is the essence of entrepreneurship. No entrepreneur—Bill Gates (Microsoft), Sam Walton (Wal-Mart), or Murthy (Infosys)—starts with resources. They start with aspirations. This premise is self-evident. We called it "strategic intent" or "strategy as stretch." This premise goes to the heart of the assumption in the strategy literature at that time, where the dominant thesis was "fit" (fit between goals and company resources). We argued for a *misfit by design*. If we want the organization to behave in an entrepreneurial way, we had to create these goals that exceeded available resources. In a start-up, this is easy. But in an established firm, we have to build a process for creating a shared aspiration. If you grant that self-evident premise, then the rest of the book flows logically.

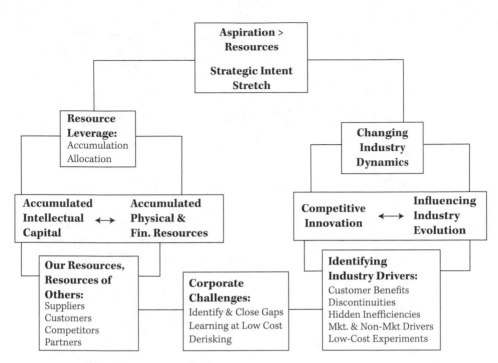

FIGURE 7.2 Structure: Competing for the Future

There are only two broad approaches to managing the misfit between aspiration and resources: (1) Accumulate and leverage resources rapidly, and (2) change industry rules such that you can have an advantage over incumbents. On the first point, we came to the conclusion that the accumulated intellectual capital (core competence) in a firm is as much a resource as its financial resources. Competence can be accumulated and leveraged. Once we recognized this, the evidence was and still is overwhelming.

On the second point, we came to a similar conclusion: that firms could change the rules of engagement. We call them new business models these days. Previously, we called them competitive innovations. We also identified that the ability to create and shape your own future (through a strategic architecture) was of great importance in changing the rules of the game. These two processes effectively reduce the risk and investment. Re-using core competencies and core products (an embodiment of core competencies) reduces both risk and investment needs. It reduces the time for new product introductions or new business creation.

Similarly, changing the industry rules allows you to reduce competitive intensity and reaction from the incumbents who are defending their established positions. It also reduces risk, investment, and time. So "derisking big opportunities" was a key theme. All the examples were illustrations of these

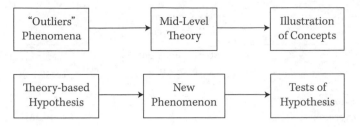

FIGURE 7.3 Research Approaches

core ideas. The validity rests on the logical structure that was extracted from field research.

The critical element of the research approach is that the *process starts with the phenomena.* It is the understanding of the outliers that allows us to construct a "mid-level theory," a map that allows managers to understand the emerging competitive landscape and navigate it. We go back to the phenomenon to illustrate the concepts. This process is very different from starting with a theory and looking at the phenomenon, as shown in Figure 7.3.

I believe it biases research when we try to fit an existing theory to a new phenomenon, which may or may not be well explained by current theory. For example, there was a deeply held belief that relative market share is a source of competitive advantage during the 1980s and 1990s. If we started with this perspective, then we would have dismissed Canon, Toyota, Honda, CNN, Microsoft, and Dell as irrelevant to Xerox, GM, NBC, and IBM. They were too small and different. We need to ask ourselves whether starting with a "theory-based hypothesis" is appropriate if our goal is to understand "next practices." The traditional approach can help us understand best practices well. But by definition, it is hard to generate a large data set when one is examining "weak signals."

Identifying Big Issues

I recognize that some may be skeptical about finding big issues that warrant a multiyear research program. I am not, as we have plenty of new problems to wrestle with. I find using the following criteria useful in unearthing big issues. The questions that follow are fairly straightforward:

How Do We Pick a Next Practice Issue?

1. Is it a big, widely recognized problem?

2. Will it affect a wide range of businesses?

3. Is there opportunity to leap frog?

4. Are there established leaders? If not, can this provide a new source of advantage?
5. Will it change the economics of the industry?
6. Is there scope for radical innovations?
7. Can this be a big opportunity for innovators?

For example, these questions reveal that emerging areas such as "sustainability" will be an integral part of the way we run businesses. Should managers look at sustainability as a regulation and a compliance issue? Is sustainability about additional costs? Can sustainability become a source of breakthrough innovations? The issue of sustainability becomes more interesting (and urgent) when you combine the need for inclusive development—adding an additional 4 billion micro consumers and micro producers—to the global economy (BOP). What additional pressures should we expect to put on the sustainability equation? Seen this way, the debate about sustainability is intimately intertwined with poverty and poverty alleviation.

This problem presents a new challenge that will not go away. No business can ignore this pressure. Without adequate water resources (both quality and quantity), many businesses will find it hard to sustain themselves; be it beverages, food, or detergents. The foregoing examination of "sustainability" is just one example of how we can identify problems that will be around for quite a long time and on which very little systematic research is done from a managerial perspective. There is voluminous research in these areas centered around public policy issues but not enough to illustrate the criticality of these issues to managers. Further, these are not seen as opportunities for breakthrough innovations.

What Kind of Impact?

It is but natural to ask what kind of impact this approach is likely to have. The managerial impact is not difficult to discern. I believe that the research stream that I have been involved in has had its share of impact on managerial practice. The question is: Can it influence academic research or is it condemned to stay outside the academic orbit? One of my colleagues and chair of the strategy group at my school did a social science citation index (SSCI) analysis of my work for the period 1995 to 2009, a period of 15 years. He found that the overall citations were around 4,684 (about 300+/year). He also identified more than 10 papers and books that each had more than 100 citations. Finally, the citations came not just from management and business articles but also from as distinctly different fields as information technology, computer science, and forestry. He thinks that this combination—sheer volume of citations, the period over which they have been referred to, the number of papers and books that exceed 100 citations each, and the range of disciplines in which the work has had some impact—is unusual. I will let the readers be the judge.

A Word of Caution

A word of caution is in order. This approach to research is not for everyone. It is risky. Given the current academic environment that primarily values traditional, empirical work and publications in specified academic journals (*A* journals), this approach can be seen as "less sophisticated" and not meeting the standards of scholarship. It was less of a problem 25 years ago. The convergence of research methods to a dominant preference was just starting to take shape then. Now it is well crystallized, not only in the academic culture in the United States but increasingly in the European academic culture as well. There is, however, room for "outliers." The fact that there is a dominant research approach and at the same time dissatisfaction with the outcomes of that approach, especially its impact on managerial practice, gives one hope.

On a personal note, I have had a lot of fun. My research has informed my teaching. It has resulted in many consulting arrangements with the chief executive officers (CEOs) of the world's largest firms. Most important, it has helped me work with some of the best minds in the business—my coauthors. I could not have imagined or asked for a more fun-filled and productive career.

REFERENCES

Hamel, G., & Prahalad, C.K. (1994). *Competing for the Future*. Boston, MA: Harvard Business School Press.

Prahalad, C. K. (2004). *The Fortune at the Bottom of the Pyramid: Eradicating Poverty through Profits*. Upper Saddle River, NJ: Wharton School of Publishing.

Prahalad, C. K., & Doz, Y. L. (1987). *The Multinational Mission: Balancing Local Demands and Global Vision*. New York: Simon & Schuster.

Prahalad, C. K., & Krishnan, M. S. (2008). *The New Age of Innovation: Driving Co-created Value through Global Networks*. New York: McGraw-Hill.

Prahalad, C. K., & Ramaswamy, V. (2004). *The Future of Competition: Co-creating Unique Value with Customers*. Boston, MA: Harvard Business School Press.

ABOUT THE AUTHOR

C. K. Prahalad was Distinguished Professor, Ross School of Business, University of Michigan. A renowned management thought leader, Dr. Prahalad contributed to the development of fundamental business concepts including strategic intent, dominant logic, core competence, and co-creation. He will always be remembered for leading thinking with respect to bottom of the pyramid markets. He is the co-author of multiple best-selling business books including *The Multinational Mission* (with Yves Doz), *Competing for the Future* (with Gary Hamel), *The Future of Competition* (with Venkat Ramaswamy), and *The New Age of Innovation* (with M. S. Krishnan). His groundbreaking paper, *The Core Competence of the Corporation* (with Gary Hamel), remains the most reprinted article in the history of the *Harvard Business Review*. His articles in the *Harvard Business Review* have won a total of four McKinsey prizes.

EIGHT

Making a Difference *and* Contributing Useful Knowledge

*Principles Derived from Life As a Scholar-Practitioner**

MICHAEL BEER

MY LIFELONG WORK as a scholar-practitioner has made a difference in the life of organizations and individuals; in a few cases, it has had a dramatic impact. Organizations and managers developed and became more effective, and the quality of work life improved. At the same time, I think I can claim that my work has had an impact on knowledge useful for theory and practice.

In this chapter, I articulate principles for developing knowledge that is relevant or actionable or both. I glean these from an examination of more than 40 years of work as a researcher and consultant, often occupying both roles at the same time. These roles have been symbiotic and have led to a broad set of activities ranging from academic research across several content domains; the development of interventions based on knowledge in the field of behavioral science; testing of these interventions through action research; and the formalization of knowledge gained through articles, books, and consulting tools. By repeating this process through many consulting projects in multiple organizational settings over a long time, I have been able to develop systemic practical theories. For example, research on large-scale corporate transformations published in *The Critical Path to Corporate Renewal* articulates a theory of organizational transformation (Beer, Eisenstat, & Spector, 1990a). My recent book *High Commitment, High Performance* provides an operating theory of high-commitment, high-performance (HCHP) organizations and how to develop them (Beer, 2009). Most academics and consultants do not engage in such a broad range of activities, and as a consequence, both

---

* Susan Mohrman read the first draft and made many helpful suggestions that found their way into this chapter. Jim Detert's comments on a later version of this chapter were very helpful as well.

147

groups struggle to develop rigorous knowledge that contributes to practice and theory.

Because the term "useful" could have different meanings to each reader, I make a distinction between two forms of useful knowledge. In this chapter, I will discuss lessons for developing both, but I will emphasize the second— actionable knowledge.

1. *Relevant* knowledge provides managers with general insights about *what* they should know, do, and be to solve practical problems in a way that achieves specified outcomes. To be useful to managers, findings from relevant research must be written in an accessible manner, but the capacity of managers to implement such research will vary widely depending on their values, skills, and context. Relevant knowledge is often a product of descriptive cross-sectional research studies. It provides academics with knowledge about *regularities* in the relationship between variables of interest. To be useful for theory, insights from this research must be placed into the context of existing literature and theory. To produce relevant knowledge, the research must focus on a managerial problem. It cannot be primarily designed to test an existing theory or validate previously identified regularities in relationships between variables.

   Knowing about relationships between managerially relevant variables does not, however, ensure effective action nor does it allow us as academics to predict with certainty the outcomes of managers trying to employ the knowledge. In short, conclusions from descriptive cross-sectional research never account for all the variance (indeed, statistically significant findings often account for relatively little variance). To be actionable, managers must contextualize relevant knowledge, something they may not be able to do, thus limiting the applicability of the knowledge. Hence the next category becomes critical.

2. *Actionable* knowledge provides guidance for *how* managers should go about solving organizational effectiveness, commitment, and performance problems. By definition, this knowledge is relevant. It is typically developed in the context of a specific organization through scholar-practitioners working collaboratively with managers to solve a problem. It provides details about the intervention that managers are advised to enact to achieve specified results—the sequence of steps they are advised to follow and the conditions that must be in place to ensure success. To be theoretically meaningful, scholars must show that the same intervention, under the same conditions, achieves the same results across multiple applications or cases. Actionable knowledge can only be obtained from action research. In my own work, our development of the Strategic Fitness Process (SFP)—an intervention that enables managers to

realign their organizations with strategy with commitment—is an example I discuss later.

In short, relevant knowledge is not necessarily actionable, but actionable knowledge is always relevant.

My Development As a Scholar-Practitioner

After receiving my doctorate in industrial and organizational psychology from Ohio State—schooled in the latest research and statistical methods—I made an unconventional career choice. I took a job at Corning Glass Works (now Corning Inc.) as a researcher in the company's corporate human resource function. Later I founded and grew the company's Organizational Research and Development Department. I regard this choice and my experience at Corning as seminal. It shaped my identity as a professional and taught me how to use consulting engagements to develop relevant and actionable knowledge.

Though initially hired to do applied personnel research, to produce relevant knowledge for human resource professionals—in effect, to be staff to staff—a number of requests by line managers for hands-on assistance in solving organizational challenges they were facing reoriented me to work as a scholar-consultant. This began a multiple-year journey that changed my identity and practice. By working with general managers, I became more concerned with general management problems—performance, strategy implementation, organization design, senior team effectiveness, and strategic management—domains that for the most part my PhD education did not deal with. Projects with which I became involved were no longer driven by my scholarly interests or existing theories but by urgent problems managers had to solve. I learned how to use grounded consulting experiences and data collection about these problems to develop both relevant and actionable knowledge—knowledge that has been useful for practice and theory.

After 11 years at Corning, I took a faculty position at the Harvard Business School (HBS) where I spent 32 years engaged in teaching, clinical field research, and action research stimulated by consulting engagements. During these years, I also learned to use less traditional research vehicles: case writing (at HBS, cases about management problems are the primary teaching and research vehicles), interaction with executives in executive development programs (particularly an executive program I developed that brought teams of managers with predefined problems to Harvard), and data gathering from participants in executive programs about problems that class discussions brought to the fore. It is the accumulation of knowledge from these different sources over 40 years that enabled me to deepen my insights about organizations and organization development first developed as a scholar-practitioner at Corning. The integration of this knowledge enabled me to develop a relevant and actionable operating theory of high-commitment, high-performance organizations and the path to developing and sustaining them over time, which was recently published as a book (Beer, 2009).

Since becoming an emeritus professor, I have been working as chairman of TruePoint Partners, a research-based management consultancy I co-founded. The firm's consulting practice, though constantly evolving, is founded on knowledge developed by me and my collaborators over the last 40 years.

Principles for Developing Knowledge for Practice and Theory

It is my professional journey that informs the principles for developing useful knowledge for practice and theory discussed in the following sections. I employ the sequence "practice and theory," to underscore that useful knowledge for practice and theory must begin with a practical problem defined by managers, not by academics. This point of departure is particularly important if the objective is actionable knowledge rather than only relevant knowledge.

Choose the "Right" Professional Context

My choice of industrial and organizational psychology as my field of study played a role in my professional journey. The field's scientist-practitioner model made it possible for me to contemplate a job in industry without violating my newly adopted professional identity, something impossible for young scholars obtaining their doctorate degrees in business schools today.

Starting my career as a practitioner played a central role in focusing my professional endeavors on problems. I could not imagine that happening had I chosen academia for my first job. Consider how difficult the norms of the academy and the promotions process make it for young scholars to choose problem-based clinical field research or action research as their primary means of inquiry. And consider how the requirement to publish in normal science scholarly journals predisposes young scholars to do research firmly placed within a theoretical framework and tradition. Such research, by definition, leads to narrowly focused theory testing rather than the development of grounded theory. Once socialized as a normal science researcher, it becomes difficult for most academics to break into other modes of inquiry even after tenure is earned.

My choice of a nontenured position at the Harvard Business School over a tenured appointment at Michigan State, when I left Corning, proved to be critical to my development as a scholar interested in managerial problems. The school's historic focus on problems in its teaching (case method) and field research encouraged my commitment to solving management problems and deepened my understanding of general management. Because case writing and course development are valued activities at HBS, I was able to use this form of research to develop practical knowledge in the fields of human resources as well as organization effectiveness and change, the focus of two different courses I developed and led (Beer et al., 1985). I might add that HBS policy at the time did not privilege publications in academic journals over publication in journals and books that speak to managers, though this may, unfortunately, be changing.

I do not argue that becoming a full-time practitioner is the only way to form the attitudes and skills needed to develop relevant and actionable knowledge. My colleague Richard Walton, whose whole career was spent in academia (Purdue and HBS), made many important contributions to practice while also contributing to the theory of high-commitment organizations. He did this by helping managers develop high-commitment organizations and through action research documenting successes and failures. Analysis of multiple cases of success and failure enabled distillation of essential design features, change processes required for success, and corporate context needed for success. His predisposition to make a difference undoubtedly was a factor in his choice to develop useful knowledge, but the environment of the Harvard Business School surely supported it. Chris Argyris, Ed Schein, Ed Lawler, Susan Albers Mohrman, Paul Lawrence, Jay Lorsch, and Richard Hackman, among others, are other stellar examples of academics that have made major contributions to practice from an academic base.

Young scholars may ask how they are to get access to organizational settings so they can develop capabilities as scholar-consultants. One way is to participate in executive development programs for senior teams who come prepared with a problem they need to solve. I developed such a program at HBS and ran it for almost two decades. It served to develop consulting skills in several faculty who participated. Because the program was designed with a follow-up session nine months later, it offered multiple case writing and research opportunities. In Chapter 9, On Knowing and Doing, Michael L. Tushman discusses a successor to this program and research that demonstrates the impact of such programs on practice. A second way for young scholars to develop their practitioner skills is to apprentice with independent consultants, small consulting firms, or applied research institutes such as the Center for Effective Organizations (CEO) or the TruePoint Center for High Commitment and Performance I recently co-founded. If business schools are to increase the production of useful knowledge, their norms will have to change to include and legitimize the types of developmental experiences outlined in the preceding paragraphs and the action research that it will produce.

Unfortunately, this legitimization is not happening, so consulting firms and not-for-profit institutes like the CEO remain the primary providers of useful knowledge.

Find a Practical Problem Which You Do Not Know How to Solve

It is not only important that the pursuit of useful information be motivated by real problems but that it be motivated by problems to which the scholar-consultant does not have an answer. I have been fortunate in my career to have had not one, but several, such opportunities. Some of them are described briefly in the following sections to give the reader a "feel" for the type of work that leads to knowledge useful for practice and theory. I employ these examples later to illustrate the principles I will discuss.

The Medfield project. Shortly after arriving at Corning, I received a call from a small manufacturing plant in Medfield, Massachusetts. It was manufacturing medical instruments, a new business for Corning. The plant was the only non-union factory in the company, and its managers wanted to ensure it stayed that way. All had worked in Corning's unionized plants and worried that unionization would lead to work practices they abhorred and that would undermine the manufacture of high-reliability instruments. The plant's leaders had read Douglas McGregor's *Human Side of Enterprise* (McGregor, 1960) and wanted to become a "Theory Y" plant. Could I help? I said yes. My PhD dissertation was an empirical study aimed at testing the relationship between Theory Y leadership behavior and various human outcomes, so I was thoroughly familiar with Douglas McGregor's theory. But as soon as I hung up the phone, I realized that I knew nothing about *what* the practice of Theory Y management looked like or *how* to help the plant's leaders transform the organization. Knowing the theory at the level of abstraction specified in McGregor's book did not provide actionable knowledge.

The resource I had was the literature—Fred Herzberg's ideas about the importance of challenging work and the then-emerging practice of job enrichment (Hertzberg et al., 1959) as well as the participative management literature. Such top-down theories must, of course, be contextualized when developing interventions for a particular organization, but my familiarity with the academic literature played an important role in this and other action research projects throughout my career. Additionally, I found useful information about practices at Non-Linear Systems, a small manufacturing company in California founded as a high-commitment system.

My lack of knowledge about how to help the Medfield plant change the way it organized and managed work and people released a lot of productive energy in devising interventions. In this and other action learning projects, practical problems I did not know how to solve took me out of my comfort zone and sent me in search of multiple sources of knowledge, a path that made me and my work more relevant. My experience suggests that the search for theories and practices when confronted with practical problems is an important development experience. Professional schools who want to develop scholars capable of developing useful knowledge will have to provide such experiences. Unfortunately, that is not happening in most professional schools, and therefore, such knowledge is not being developed.

Numerous interventions were made: workshops for managers, removal of an assembly line and the creation of whole jobs, quality control delegated to operators, coaching for first line supervisors, the posting of profit and loss as well as other performance measures on the bulletin board, information sessions with doctors who explained to employees how the instrument was used with patients, and visits by employees of one another's departments that unexpectedly led to identification of manufacturing process problems and their improvement. At the end of three years, the operating and cultural environment had changed dramatically as measured by multiple methods: participant observation, interviews and surveys conducted by a colleague in my department acting as an independent researcher, and the views of higher-level managers.

What useful knowledge did this project develop, and how did it find its way into practice? The Medfield model helped introduce high-commitment management practices to Corning's other plants. Two decades later, long after I left Corning, its new director of quality said that they were rediscovering that what was learned at Medfield was crucial to Corning's corporate quality initiative. Useful knowledge gained at Medfield informed the development of General Foods' high-commitment Topeka dog food plant when I was asked to come and share our experience. Two articles were written: one in an academic journal (Beer & Huse, 1972), and one in a managerial journal (Huse & Beer, 1971). Insights from this project also informed later work and writing.

The EPD project. Because of the credibility I developed with the Medfield project, a new general manager of Corning's Electronic Products Division (EPD) approached me for help. In our first meeting, he framed his problem as follows:

We have had some difficult times in my division over the past two years. Sales have been down due to the general economy and the effects on the electronics industry. But our problems are greater than that. Our business is becoming fiercely competitive. To deal with the downturn in business we have had to reduce the number of people and expenses sharply. This has been painful, but I think these actions have stemmed the tide. We are in control again. But the business continues to be very competitive, morale is low, there is a lot of conflict between groups that we can't seem to resolve. There is a lack of mutual confidence and trust. The organization is just not pulling together and the lack of coordination is affecting our ability to develop new products. Most of my people believe that we are having conflicts because business is bad. They say that if business would only get better we will stop crabbing at each other. Frankly, I am not so sure if they are right. The conflicts might be due to pressures we are under but more likely they indicate a more fundamental problem. Can you and your group help determine if the conflict between groups is serious and what might be done about it? (Beer, 1976)

I said I would help without knowledge about the potential causes of intergroup problems or approaches to solving them. My staff and I employed interviews and a questionnaire to collect data. Based on these data, a set of recommendations to management was made and largely accepted. These asked the senior team to meet to clarify strategy, adopt a strategic management process (at the time I did not know that was the term for what we were proposing) for prioritizing new product development initiatives, redesign the organization as a project team/matrix, and undergo team development to improve their efficacy as a team. At the end of three years EPD had transformed itself, its rate and speed of new product development increased materially, its revenues and profits increased, its culture changed, and its general manager had been promoted to a bigger job on the strength of changes in organization and performance he had achieved.

The EPD project produced many grounded insights about the systemic nature of organizations as well as about key barriers to strategic alignment and the interventions needed to overcome them. My ability to make inferences and develop insights from a combination of observations and more formal data collection grew over the years. It is a skill that, in my view, professionals who seek to develop useful knowledge must find a way to develop, but one that most business schools do not teach or encourage.

Insights gained from the EPD project informed both academics and managers via a symposium at a professional meeting, the development of a best-selling Harvard case (Beer, 1976), and the development of two executive programs about organizational effectiveness and strategic change. And the EPD project contributed significantly to the later development of the Strategic Fitness Process discussed in a following section of this chapter.

Corporate renewal project. Failed efforts at Corning to translate success-ful change projects in several organizational subunits into a corporate trans-formation led me to undertake a field study of corporate transformation after I had moved to Harvard. The efforts of corporations to transform in re-sponse to Japanese competition offered the opportunity. We identified six large corporations reported by the media to be undergoing a corporate trans-formation. We gained access and began to collect data: interviews, archival data, and questionnaires. On the basis of these data, we were able to rank order the companies in terms of their relative progress in the transformation and to identify the ingredients for a successful transformation. For the pro-fessional interested in developing useful knowledge for practice and theory, methodological flexibility is essential. In this case, a cross-sectional study was the only way to test ideas that I developed at Corning.

We learned that top-down programs were a false start that delayed prog-ress in five of the companies and that a strategy of unit-by-unit change or-chestrated by senior management was the key to success in the leading company. By comparing subunits undergoing change across all the compa-nies, we were also able to identify the process of leadership and change that worked at the subunit level. Findings resulted in the book *The Critical Path to Corporate Renewal* (Beer, Eisenstat, & Spector, 1990a), a finalist for the Acad-emy of Management's 1991 Terry Book Award and the winner of an award for best book on executive leadership. What I learned at Corning helped me and my co-authors identify patterns in these companies. In addition to the book, an *HBR* article that was accessible to managers was written (Beer, Eisenstat, & Spector, 1990b). In this instance, relevant knowledge written accessibly led to dramatic changes in at least one corporation. The chief executive officer (CEO) of ASDA (a U.K. grocery chain), who successfully transformed that company and its 200 stores, read the book and employed the unit-by-unit change strategy outlined in it. The *HBR* article has also found its way into many texts on change and has helped my colleagues at TruePoint and me inform clients about how to lead corporate transformations. And the devel-opment of cases about ASDA (Beer & Weber, 1997) led to further insights about corporate transformations and, in turn, led to the development of a theory of change (Beer & Nohria, 2000).

Interestingly, though *The Critical Path to Corporate Renewal* presents a comprehensive theory of corporate change, my impression is that it has had far more influence in the world of practice than in academia, illustrating the divide between the two worlds.

The BD project. Would I help Becton Dickinson (BD), a global medical tech-nology company, "become a company capable of strategy implementation"? That was the question I was presented with by the company's CEO and VP of

Strategy and Human Resources. BD was having problems implementing its global and business unit strategies. Using my insights about strategic alignment gained in the EPD project and insights from our study of corporate renewal, Russ Eisenstat and I developed what we have since called the Strategic Fitness Process. The process, ultimately implemented by BD in some 35 organizational units—the corporate organization as well as business and operating units—enables senior teams and consultants to collaborate in a co-investigation of the organization's effectiveness and plan change. SFP guides senior teams through a series of steps that includes (1) development of a two- to three-page statement of strategic direction; (2) commissioning a task force of eight high-performance and high-potential people to interview 100 key people across all parts of the organization as well as customers and other stakeholders; (3) hearing the truth about barriers to strategic alignment (a structure and process are specified to ensure the truth gets on the table safely); (4) a three-day meeting that enables the senior team to diagnose, redesign, and change the organization; (5) critique of the senior team's plan for change by the task force; (7) mobilization of the organization through engagement and communication; (8) recycling the process to assess progress. Using insights gained in multiple applications of the process, we developed a manual describing these steps in detail to provide actionable knowledge to practitioners (Eisenstat & Beer, 1998).

Through the development of cases about many organizations that employed SFP, we have been able to identify common "silent" barriers to effective strategy implementation and to identify conditions for successful implementation of the process. The formal research involved two research designs. In the first, we conducted a content analysis of what task forces in a dozen organizations reported to leadership teams. These findings are the basis for an emergent theory of organizational effectiveness. In the second, independent researchers were engaged to write cases on a dozen organizations who had implemented SFP. An analysis of these cases by a team of the consultants involved and the independent researchers provided an evaluation of SFP and identification of the conditions for its success. This research has been published in the *Sloan Management Review* and *Harvard Business Review* (Beer & Eisenstat, 2000; Beer & Eisenstat, 2004). Three successive CEOs at Becton Dickinson employed SFP soon after they took charge to develop their strategic change agenda. The process is still employed in the company, and top management is employing it again to identify barriers to growth and innovation. Moreover, SFP has become part of TruePoint's practice and has been employed in well over 200 organizations in some 50 corporations around the world.

Have a Bias for Action Research

For the following reasons, I argue that action research is the best way to develop actionable knowledge.

- The process of collaborative problem formulation, diagnosis, and action between managers and scholar-consultants enables the development of systemic grounded theory about causes of problems and means for change that cannot be accomplished through distanced, more narrowly focused, but more precise positivistic methods. On the other hand, normal science is best at validating these theories.

- Interventions, including the initial entry into the organization and conversations with management about their problems, allow the action researcher to observe the response (acceptance or resistance) of individuals, groups, and the organizations to the intervention, revealing truths not observable in normal science. That is because normal social science methods rely on what managers say to researchers—their espoused theory—which is almost always different from how they actually behave—their theory in action.

- A bias for action leads to the development of social technologies such as SFP. These technologies provide managers with what Fritz Rothlisberger called "walking sticks" (Rothlisberger, 1977). They make knowledge useful to practitioners who may not otherwise have the insights or skills to lead change. For example, SFP has helped managers who saw the need to change but did not know how to engage the total system in such a learning process, an essential leadership capability. Moreover, because social technologies provide detailed guidance for managers and consultants, knowledge is made accessible. For example, SFP has been applied in different industries in several parts of the world by managers who may not naturally have been inclined to do so and in the process have developed new attitudes and capabilities.

- Social technologies enable the development of predictive theories. Because they specify outcomes and guide managerial behavior to achieve these outcomes, deviations by managers are measurable. This enables revaluation of the social technology and leads to insights about context, values, and skills required to achieve specified outcomes. Multiple applications of a social technology such as SFP have led to a predictive theory of change, one that specifies behavior and context required for achieving specified outcomes.

- Action research enables innovations in organizing, managing, and leading. Managers do this, of course, when they create new managerial practices.

However, by collaborating with managers in this process, the researchers can add value. They bring to the conversation extant knowledge from the field of management and arguably improve the new practice. The Medfield and EPD project at Corning reframed for senior executives what was possible in managing people and aligning the organization with strategy. So did a union-management intervention at Corning not described in this chapter. Similarly, the development of SFP at Becton Dickinson reframed for its senior executives how to think about strategy execution and gave them a systemic organizational learning practice they might not have developed on their own. More important, through its use over the years, values and culture have changed.

Maintain an Open Aperture in the Inquiry

The development of useful and usable knowledge requires researchers to have a systemic perspective best achieved by focusing the inquiry on gaps in organizational outcomes—performance, behavior, or both—and to be open to multiple causes. The inquiry cannot be restricted to a small a priori set of content domains, theories, or measurement tools that are of interest to the researcher. To invoke an age-old story, the applied researcher cannot be the drunk looking under the street light for his key because that is where the light is. The inquiry has to consider multiple levels of analysis: individual, interpersonal, group, intergroup, the organizational context, and the context in which the organization is operating. Though clearly all of us have favorite theories that influence where we look, the researcher must guard against that predisposition, one that is deeply baked into our development as academics.

My experience with Corning's EPD again illustrates this point. The presenting symptom (quoted earlier in this chapter) was interfunctional conflict. It would have been easy to define EPD's problems that way and suggest well-known and popular intergroup interventions of that time (Blake & Mouton, 1965). By focusing on gaps in performance—the inability of the division to develop new products quickly and effectively—and searching for multiple causes, the diagnosis ultimately also included organizational design (a functional organization that did not enable coordination), senior team efficacy, the top leader himself, and the strategic management process for reviewing new product development initiatives.

Inquiries must, of course, be informed by knowledge from academic research and theories (Bartuneck & Schein, 2010). Scholar-practitioners bring some of this knowledge with them but a search of the literature is also called for. In my experience, however, it is best for the literature search to *follow* an initial foray of data gathering and analysis of the situation by the scholar-consultant to avoid narrowing the aperture. This principle is again illustrated by the EPD project at Corning. After an initial data gathering and discussions with my team about root causes and potential interventions, I located an article in *Administrative Science Quarterly* (*ASQ*) by Paul Lawrence and Jay Lorsch in which they first reported their research on differentiation and integration (*D* and *I*), ultimately published as *Organization and Environment* (Lawrence & Lorsch, 1967). Their conceptualization of *D* and *I* in the context of market uncertainty helped explain why EPD, operating in a much more uncertain environment than other Corning businesses, was experiencing unusually severe intergroup conflict. It also offered important findings about the role of "integrators" in cross-functional teams we had been contemplating. It reinforced our conclusion that organization design and role changes were needed. Beginning with this frame, however, would have focused the intervention on organization design and missed essential top team issues and the importance of the change process itself (Schein, 1969). I cannot overemphasize, however, how comforting it was to understand the problems of EPD in the larger context of the Lawrence and Lorsch theory.

Make the Inquiry Collaborative

That collaboration is essential to the development of relevant and actionable knowledge is widely accepted and understood (Shani et al., 2008). In my experience that collaboration will not develop unless the inquiry is focused on an issue central to the general manager's agenda. That means that discussions have to start with performance gaps and the manager's hypothesis about cause.

The Medfield project focused on management's concern with building a culture that they felt they needed to succeed in the labor-intensive, high-quality medical instrument business. The EPD project focused on a more immediate performance problem: speed of product development and collaboration needed to increase the rate of new product development. The Becton Dickinson project focused on the inability of the company to implement its strategy. In the following list, I discuss four desired outcomes collaboration enables and illustrate how collaboration in these projects affected the development of useful knowledge.

1. *Develops commitment to inquiry and action.* Start by helping managers clarify the gap between current and desired performance and behavior and focus inquiry on diagnosis of why the gap exists. The success of the Medfield, EPD, and BD projects can be attributed to their focus on goals developed with management. All three projects spanned several years

and its managers continued to employ the perspective and methods that they had helped to develop.

Can relevant knowledge made accessible to managers create commitment to action? Despite the awards *The Critical Path to Corporate Renewal* received, the relevant knowledge it imparted was, to my knowledge, employed by only one company, ASDA, the U.K. grocery chain where case research helped us extend our theory of change (see Corporate Renewal Project earlier in this chapter). An extraordinary intellectually inclined leader is the reason. Unfortunately, such leaders are not the norm.

2. *Enables researcher to learn from management.* My collaborators and I learned a great deal from managers in the action research projects described in this chapter. For example, the Strategic Fitness Process developed at Becton Dickinson was inspired by a process approach to strategy development that the company had institutionalized. SFP was designed to complement that process.

The design of SFP is a product of collaboration, in this case a constructive debate between the CEO and me, the scholar-consultant. Until challenged by the CEO in a high-profile meeting, the strategic alignment process did not start with strategy. It was an inquiry into barriers to effectiveness. That conversation led us to begin the Strategic Fitness Process with the senior team defining a statement of strategic direction. This statement legitimized SFP and increased commitment to it, despite the company's conflict-adverse culture at the time. As one senior executive said, "strategy is important to us, therefore learning about barriers to execution is important." And SFP changed over time as we learned with managers about situational contingencies. For example, when a task force objected vehemently to an action plan produced by its senior team, we learned from the general manager's response to resolve differences by breaking the senior team and task force members into mixed groups to develop alternatives. It is now part of the SFP toolkit.

3. *Enables management to learn from researchers.* In all three action research projects described earlier, management learned from us as scholar-consultants. In the Medfield project, we brought in knowledge about practices such as job enrichment and participative management. In the EPD project, we brought in knowledge about organization design and intergroup interventions. Perhaps most important in all three action research projects, we brought in values that became embedded in these organizations through the implementation of new practices. Nowhere was that more clear than at Becton Dickinson where almost all of the senior managers were strategy consultants who did not appreciate the

importance of engaging their people to learn about effectiveness problems blocking strategy implementation.

4. *Enables longitudinal research.* As William James said many years ago, truth emerges over time. It is a function of unfolding events that reveal new facets of the situation. Action research allowed us to be deeply immersed in the organizations over an extended period of time. That allowed me to learn things about the organization and its leaders I did not know at the start of projects. It also allowed evaluation of interventions over time. Our mental models of problems and interventions applied became richer and more comprehensive. Consider how repeated applications of the Strategic Fitness Process at Becton Dickinson allowed us to change the process (see earlier discussion). Over time our understanding of why the process works—its active ingredients—has changed significantly. The rational mental map of alignment we started with has been enriched by other frames: leader legitimacy, emotional engagement, meaning, and leadership development.

Create Structure and Processes for Collaboration

Collaboration over a sustained period of time requires a structure and process by which clients and scholar-consultants co-investigate the client system. It is a way to have periodic conversations about the problem to be solved, the inquiry method, findings and action to be taken. Such a collaborative structure serves as a container for what may become difficult conversations from which both the client and consultant can learn. Without such a container, clients may avoid such conversations, ignore data, or deny them if they are threatening, as such data almost always are in inquiries that ultimately make a difference. And the same container enables scholar-practitioners to learn about the client system. Without such a structure and process for collaboration, the client will not be committed to action and researchers can become distanced from the ever-changing concerns of leaders and the very phenomena they want to understand and study. When scholar-practitioners become distanced, they can easily drift into framing the research in academically interesting but practically unsatisfying ways (Beer, 1982).

There are an endless number of arrangements for collaborations that have and can be developed. In this chapter, I discuss briefly how the Strategic Fitness Process described earlier enables client commitment to change and research. We developed the process to avoid some well-documented pitfalls to client ownership of change: denial and dependence on consultants (Schein, 1969; Argyris, 1970).

By asking top teams to craft a short statement of strategic direction, we ensure that the inquiry has a relevant and useful focus. We have learned that when clients appoint a task force composed of their best people to conduct interviews (with approximately 100 people across the system), it is more difficult for senior teams to deny or ignore the data. In a "fishbowl" structure, task force members discuss findings as a group while senior management sits in an outer U and listens. In this structure, task force members feel safe to speak truth to power. Because top teams, not consultants, conduct the diagnosis in collaboration with consultants and develop action plans then subjected to critique by task force members, SFP increases the quality of the action plan and commitment to it.

Organizational learning processes such as SFP are an aid in collecting data. The quality of the data obtained by task forces, with relatively little training, is as good as that obtained by field researchers, in my experience. With guidance of scholar-consultants and a specified method, themes are developed by a rigorous analysis of interview data collected by the task force. Interviews can be subject to more comprehensive and rigorous analysis by researchers after the fact. I have used task force reports to write rich cases about organizations before, during, and after the intervention (usually over a period of several years), making comparative analysis possible. Employing the same method in multiple organizations has enabled us to generalize findings.

The promise of methods such as SFP that involve clients in data collection is that they enable the development of knowledge clients can use immediately while providing scholar-practitioners with a data set for theory development. If the consultant is not inclined to do the hands-on research, independent researchers can be invited to participate and observe the phenomena.

Use Multiple Methods to Triangulate on the Truth

Multiple methods are essential when developing knowledge useful for theory and practice. Interviews or participant observations or both are the primary methods in problem-centered field or action research. In all four of the projects, these methods led to a grounded map of the territory—a rich theory of the case. In three of the projects, I employed survey data and operating and financial data as well as formal content analysis to hone the emerging theory.

In the EPD project, employee survey data measuring the quality of the collaboration and coordination between each of pair of functions enabled us not only to confirm interview data, but important, to identify where the interfunctional tensions were greatest and, based on this information, to target the parties for an intergroup intervention. These data also enabled more formal evaluation of the change effort and analysis later reported in an academic symposium (Beer et al., 1971).

In the BD project, where SFP was employed, a content analysis of task force findings in 12 organizational units yielded six "silent" barriers to effectiveness. By doing the same analysis for 12 additional task forces in other companies we were able to say with some certainty that these are generic barriers to effectiveness. It was our deep and long-term relationship with each of these organizations, however, that enabled us to understand how these barriers work together to undermine strategy implementation. What has emerged is a theory of organizational effectiveness.

In the corporate renewal field study we triangulated on the truth by employing interviews, survey, and archival data in six companies. Moreover, our data collection included many interviews deep in the organization—in some companies, over 100. And employees were surveyed at multiple levels of the organization.

Cases are an important research tool that served me well. I used many of my own cases together with cases written by others to develop the operating theory of high-commitment, high-performance organizations outlined in my recent book (Beer, 2009).

In field and action research the researcher is one of the instruments by which data are gleaned, processed, and interpreted. For this reason the researcher has a responsibility to question interpretations and conclusions continuously. Partnering with an independent researcher who is not involved as a consultant and whose primary role is data analysis is one way. Presenting findings and conclusions to others and asking them to critique one's work is another. Allowing time to elapse detaches one and enables one to reformulate interpretations and conclusions. By returning to old cases and research findings, I have been able to draw deeper and in some cases different conclusions.

Be a Groundhog

Scholar-practitioners have to be focused on one or two domains of practice. That is because they have to develop distinctive capabilities—deep knowledge, often tacit knowledge, and skill—in order to be able to deliver value to clients. And scholar-consultants, by definition, become deeply knowledgeable about and skilled in organizational change; that capacity enables them to learn, better than others, about connections between their area of practice and other domains, thus leading to an ever-richer grounded and systemic theory about the phenomena on which their practice is focused.

It is this accumulation of knowledge over time that has enabled me to paint an ever-richer picture of what it takes to develop a high-commitment, high-performance organization. The Medfield project taught me about the sources of low commitment and what it takes to embed high-commitment practices in an organization. The EPD project broadened my horizon to include strategy and began my journey of inquiry into facets of the organization critical for strategy implementation: the senior team, organization design, inadequate strategic performance management, and the role of human capabilities. As I and my team began to focus on changing Corning as a corporation, I began to appreciate the problem of corporate transformation, in particular the problem of spreading change from unit to unit. That led to the corporate renewal research.

When Becton Dickinson's senior management presented me with their challenge—to help it become a company capable of strategy implementation—I was able to employ all of my experiences and insights to formulate the problem systemically and develop SFP as an intervention.

Be a Boundary Spanner

For knowledge to be useful for practice and theory, it is important for the professional to develop multiple identities and be comfortable operating in and speaking to multiple audiences: managers, internal and external professionals such as organization development (OD) and strategic management practitioners who advise managers, educators who teach aspiring practitioners, and academics. I have always been driven by my desire to be relevant to all these communities, and this motivation has helped me produce knowledge useful to each.

I write for practitioner journals and produce cases and articles that I and others use to teach MBAs and executives. I also speak to managers as well as internal and external consultants. At the same time, I have written for referred journals aimed at academics interested in applied problems and have been active in professional associations such as the Academy of Management and the Society of Industrial and Organizational Psychology, delivering papers and organizing and/or participating in symposia. I also consistently serve on the editorial board of one or more journals. My purpose is to stay in touch with the academic literature and to encourage editorial policies friendly to research useful for practice and theory.

Being a boundary spanner has been a challenge. While practitioners welcome practical knowledge, I have found that academics are much less welcoming. The dominant normal science paradigm makes it hard to publish my findings and ideas in the most prestigious academic journals—the so-called *A* journals. Instead, I present my findings and ideas in books. They are much better vehicles for the rich narrative needed to present relevant and actionable knowledge that emerges from field and action research. The fact that I get almost no requests to speak about my work in academic settings, other than conferences on change, reflects how big the divide is between normal science academics and those interested in producing relevant and actionable knowledge.

To thrive in two worlds requires a strong sense of purpose and identity, something that I have had to develop over the years. It requires a passion for solving real world problems and at the same time for contributing to theory. I have been helped in this by developing a network of like-minded scholar-practitioners who are rigorous thinkers and practically minded, although their number has declined since the 1960s and 1970s. My home at the Harvard Business School has also been an important source of support and inspiration.

Conclusion

I have used my lifelong experience as a scholar-consultant and field researcher to develop principles for those who wish to develop knowledge useful for theory and practice. I hope this narrative will be helpful to those aspiring to fashion such a professional identification. The work of developing useful knowledge is challenging. As I have tried to show, it requires passion for both making a difference *and* developing theory. It requires readiness to be drawn into ill-defined practical problems that one does not fully know how to approach or solve, to be comfortable with or foolish enough to live with uncertainty. And one has to be able to live in two worlds with different norms and rules for knowing.

It is not clear to me that all individuals are cut out for such a career. As I have tried to show, my career was shaped by my early choice of a professional context, work inside a corporation as a researcher and consultant though I do not argue that choosing to work inside an organization is the only path, nor that such a path is as open today as it was in the 1960s and 1970s. Academics seeking an identity as scholar-practitioners do, however, have to find ways to embed themselves in real world situations where they collaborate in solving managerial problems. As mentioned earlier, collaborating with research-oriented consulting firms and not-for-profit research centers is one way. Developing relationships with corporate human resources (HR) professionals or line executives attending university executive development programs or developing executive programs with a component of action learning is another. The choices I made were undoubtedly influenced by who I am as a person, by my preference for learning inductively, and by my passion to make a difference in the worlds of ideas and management practice.

As I have tried to show, the dominant academic paradigm and the career system that supports it do not make it easy to develop as a scholar-practitioner, though the creation of the Scholar-Practitioner Award of the Academy of Management and appeals by several academy presidents have helped. For years I have thought that the marketplace for ideas will cause academia to change. The opposite has happened. Business schools have become less relevant and generally eschew the development of actionable knowledge, in sharp contrast, I might add, to the values of medical schools. The task of developing relevant and actionable knowledge has increasingly fallen to other institutions—consulting firms and not-for-profit organizations such as the Center for Effective Organizations.

A career focused on developing knowledge useful for theory and practice will require courage to be different and creativity in shaping such a career. Aspiring scholar-practitioners must avoid blindly following the path to promotion required by the academy. They must make a *conscious choice* about competencies they want to develop and the place where these can be developed. Most important, they must decide that making a difference matters and find ways to integrate that purpose with their interest in academic research and theory.

REFERENCES

Argyris, C. (1970). *Intervention theory and method.* Boston: Addison-Wesley.

Bartunek, J. M., and Schein, E. H. (2010). "Organization development scholar-practitioners: Between scholarship and practice." In E. E. Lawler and Mohrman, S. A. *Useful knowledge* San Francisco: Berrett-Koehler

Beer, M. (1976). Corning Glass Works: The electronic products division (A), Case: Harvard Business School Press.

Beer, M. (1982). Computer vision. In M. L. Hakel, M. Sorcher, M. Beer, & J. L. Moses (Eds.), *Making it happen: Designing research with implementation in mind.* Beverly Hills, CA: Sage.

Beer, M. (2009). *High commitment, high performance: How to build a resilient organization for sustained advantage.* San Francisco: Jossey-Bass.

Beer, M., & Eisenstat, R. (2000). The silent killers of strategy implementation and learning. *Sloan Management Review.*

Beer, M., & Eisenstat, R. (2004, December). How to have an honest conversation about your strategy. *Harvard Business Review.*

Beer, M., Eisenstat, R., & Spector, B. (1990a). *The critical path to corporate renewal.* Boston: Harvard Business School Press.

Beer, M., Eisenstat, R., & Spector, B. (1990b, November–December). Why change programs don't produce change. *Harvard Business Review.*

Beer, M., & Huse, E. (1971, September–October). Eclectic approach to organization development. *Harvard Business Review.*

Beer, M., & Huse, E. (1972). A systems approach to organization development. *Journal of Applied Behavioral Science, 8*(1), 79–101.

Beer, M., & Nohria, N. (2000). *Breaking the code of change.* Boston: Harvard Business School Press.

Beer, M., Marcus, S. & Pieters, G. (1971). Improving integration between functional groups: A case in organizational change and implications for theory and practice. Symposium, Division of Industrial and Organizational Psychology, American Psychological Association, Washington, DC.

Beer, M., Spector, B., Lawrence, P. R., Mills, D. Q., & Walton, R. E. (1985). *Managing human assets.* New York: Free Press.

Beer, M., & Weber, J. (1997). "ASDA" (A) (A1) (B) (C): *Case Discussions.* Boston: Harvard Business School Press.

Blake, R. R., & Mouton, J. S. (1965). The union management intergroup laboratory: Strategy for resolving intergroup conflict. *Journal of Applied Behavioral Science, 1*(1), 25–57.

Eisenstat, R. & Beer, M. (1998). *Strategic fitness process handbook.* Burlington, MA: TruePoint.

Hertzberg, F., Mausner, B. & Snyderman, B. (1959). *The motivation to work,* (2nd ed.) New York: Wiley.

Lawrence, P. R., & Lorsch, J. W. (1967). *Organization and environment: Managing differentiation and integration.* Cambridge, MA: Graduate School of Business Administration, Harvard University.

McGregor, D. (1960). *The human side of enterprise.* New York: McGraw-Hill.

Rothlisberger, F. J. (1977). *The elusive phenomena,* Cambridge: Graduate School of Business Administration, Harvard University.

Schein, E. H. (1969). *Process consultation: Its role in organization development.* Boston: Addison-Wesley.

Shani, A. B., Mohrman, S. A., Pasmore, W. A., Stymne, B., & Adler, N. (2008). *Handbook of collaborative management research.* Los Angeles: Sage.

ABOUT THE AUTHOR

Mike Beer is founder and chairman of TruePoint, a research-based management consultancy firm, and Cahners-Rabb Professor of Business Administration, Emeritus, at the Harvard Business School. Mike's research and practice are in the fields of organization effectiveness, organization change, and human resource management. He has authored or co-authored many articles and ten books. His most recent, published in 2009, is *High Commitment,*

High Performance, which has received several awards from professional associations. Mike has been a consultant to senior management in numerous companies and teaches and speaks in a variety of forums. He began his career at Corning Inc., where he founded and led its Organization Research and Development Department.

NINE

On Knowing and Doing

A Perspective on the Synergies between Research and Practice*

MICHAEL L. TUSHMAN

The Challenge of Knowing and Doing: A Personal Context

My career has been one of deliberately linking research (knowing) and practice (doing). As an undergraduate student at Northeastern University, I worked for five years as a co-op student at General Radio. This distinguished electronics firm was one of the first of its kind and was, at the time, the leading test equipment firm in the industry. However, during this period, the company began to fail in the face of technological change and the entrance of new competition (HP, among others). My carpool friends were about to be laid off. They faced the trauma associated with a historically dominant firm floundering in the face of a rapidly shifting competitive arena. As it turned out, making the same products better simply drove the firm more quickly out of business. I observed General Radio's inertial responses to these competitive shifts and the disastrous consequences for its employees and stakeholders.

These experiences at General Radio led me to leave an electrical engineering career and move to graduate school to try to understand just what happened. For 30 years now, I have been working to answer the questions my carpool colleagues asked so many years ago. Just why do successful firms often fail at technological transitions? Why were seasoned executives rendered so incompetent at this particular transition? While my specific research questions have evolved over time, the central theme of my research has been rooted in this General Radio experience; that is, on trying to better

---

* This chapter builds on Tushman et al. (2007) and on Walsh et al. (2007).

understand how and why firms fail to adapt in the context of technological transitions.

After Northeastern, I went to graduate school at Cornell University. At the School of Industrial and Labor Relations, I worked with a heterogeneous faculty committee (William F. Whyte, Leo Gruenfeld, and Mike Beer). While these colleagues could not have been more different as scholars, they were each interested in research shaping the real world. My master's thesis on leadership and change in a Corning manufacturing plant built on the extant literature on change. But it was also substantially informed by emergent political and cultural issues I observed in the field (Tushman, 1978). This experience illustrated the benefits of a close relationship between the world of research and the world of practice. The phenomena taught me to look in places and at questions that were not central to the field at the time. I also experienced issues and tensions that occur at this boundary between knowing and doing. For example, early in my fieldwork, I was pressed by the plant general manager to shape my research to his needs and to provide him with inside information gained from my interviews. My committee helped me sort through these boundary issues associated with the locus of data and research question ownership.

Because of my interest in technology, innovation, and organizations, I left Cornell and enrolled in a PhD program at MIT. Working with another heterogeneous faculty committee (Tom Allen, Paul Lawrence, Ed Schein, and Ralph Katz), I replicated this work at the interface between the phenomena and research.[1] My dissertation explored the relations between informal communication networks and performance in research and development (R&D) settings. I gathered network data from Owens Corning and was able to show that differential performance in R&D teams was associated with communication networks that were contingent on task characteristics (e.g., Katz & Tushman, 1979; Tushman, 1977). While the research was well received academically, I was challenged by several R&D managers to translate my research in a way that might be useful to them. I was further challenged by these managers to broaden my work from simply studying R&D settings. These managers observed that if I was really interested in understanding innovation, understanding R&D settings was insufficient. They pushed me to move from the R&D laboratory to the organization as the unit of analysis.

These early experiences made clear the benefits (as well as challenges) of having the phenomena shape the questions I asked and the data I gathered. Over the past 30 years I have, with colleagues and doctoral students, worked

---

1. Indeed, MIT is rooted in its history of respect for research affecting practice. MIT's motto is "mens and manus."

at the interface between research and practice; more specifically, between building our field's stock of knowledge of innovation and organizational change, and accentuating our field's impact on practice. I have been working out my own research-based responses to my carpool friends and to those R&D managers who challenged me to link our field's research to their real world innovation issues.

In distinct contrast to this active linking between research (knowing) and practice (doing), our field has been drifting toward a greater bifurcation. Knowing has increasingly been uncoupled from doing. This increasing gap is problematic. It has the potential to push our research to greater internal validity at the cost of stunting external validity. Our field runs the risk of having great answers to less and less interesting problems. As our field retreats from managerial relevance, other disciplines and professions move into that vacuum (Bazerman, 2005; Bennis & O'Toole, 2005; Pfeffer & Fong, 2002). This lack of coupling between our research and our ability to speak to practice affects our legitimacy with students and our external constituencies (see also Khurana, Nohria, & Prenrice, 2005; Rynes, Bartunek, & Daft, 2001). Further, this bifurcation affects both what and how we train doctoral students (e.g., Polzer et al., 2009; Tushman & O'Reilly, 2007).

Business Schools: Toward Knowing and Doing

To fairly evaluate the relative importance of business schools' research and impact on practice, we must first be clear about the role of professional schools in general and business schools in particular. What, if anything, differentiates a business school (or school of medicine or law) from conventional academic departments? To understand these differences, we draw on insights from the history of science where there has long been a tension between "basic" and "applied" research (Stokes, 1997).

In his book *Pasteur's Quadrant* (1997), Donald Stokes draws on the history of science in general and Louis Pasteur's contribution in particular to develop a taxonomy of types of research (see Fig. 9.1). In this framework, research is categorized in three ways: (1) as a quest for fundamental understanding (basic research), (2) as development of knowledge motivated by considerations of use (applied research), or (3) both. Stokes shows how some research is simply driven by a quest for understanding with no thought of specific use (e.g., Niels Bohr and the discovery of the structure of the atom). Other research can be undertaken simply to develop applied uses (e.g., Thomas Edison and the invention of the phonograph). Yet other research, which Stokes favors, proceeds with both a quest for fundamental understanding and a desire to apply the findings (e.g., Pasteur and the development of microbiology).

Considerations of Use?

		No	Yes
Quest for Fundamental Understanding?	Yes	Pure Basic Research (e.g., Bohr)	Use-inspired Basic Research (e.g., Pasteur)
	No		Pure Applied Research (e.g., Edison)

FIGURE 9.1 Stokes's Quadrant Model of Scientific Research

Stokes's (1997) classification scheme can be used to inform the debate on the aspirations of business school research (see Fig. 9.2). Whereas conventional academic disciplines are typically about a quest for understanding (rigor) with little thought of use (relevance), business schools and professional schools, more generally, are about both; that is, about operating in Pasteur's Quadrant. Consulting firms, unlike business schools, are about meeting clients' needs (relevance) but have little concern with carefully controlled research (rigor). The implication of this taxonomy for business schools is straightforward. In business schools, research should be judged both by its quality—how rigorously it is designed and conducted—as well as the degree to which it provides understanding of the phenomena being studied. Stokes refers to this as "purposive basic research" (1997, p. 60) and observes that this research can be highly fundamental in character when it has an important impact on the structure or outlook of a field (e.g., Porter's work on competitive strategy, Bazerman's work on decision making and systematic deviations from rationality, or Kaplan's work on activity-based accounting). Basic research and applied research are not mutually exclusive undertakings.

Consistent with Mintzberg's (2004) and Bennis and O'Toole's (2005) call for relevance and rigor, and Ghoshal's (2005) plea for faculty research that respects discovery-driven research as well as integrative- and application-oriented research, Stokes's framework imposes high standards on faculty in professional schools. Whereas the evaluation of rigor is straightforward in traditional academic domains (Does the research meet the standards of peer review?), the evaluation of professional school research is more complex in that this assessment must attend to both academic rigor as well as manage-

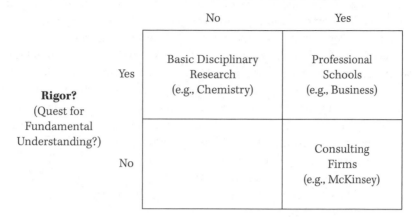

Relevance?

(Considerations of Use?)

		No	Yes
Rigor? (Quest for Fundamental Understanding?)	Yes	Basic Disciplinary Research (e.g., Chemistry)	Professional Schools (e.g., Business)
	No		Consulting Firms (e.g., McKinsey)

FIGURE 9.2 Business School Research

rial relevance. In the business school context, this implies that our research must meet the joint criteria of internal as well as external validity. Further, Stokes's insights have implications for doctoral training. Doctoral students need to have their research questions anchored on the phenomena even as they explore questions through systematic multidisciplinary training (e.g., Polzer et al., 2009).

A Point of View on Knowing and Doing

My early research experiences at Corning and Owens Corning illustrated the benefits and challenges associated with research informed by conversations with the phenomena. Encouraged by my faculty advisors to work at this boundary, I have evolved an implicit model on the co-evolution of knowing and doing. These knowing-doing relationships have had an important effect on my research as well as my MBA, executive, and doctoral teaching (see also Adler et al., 2009; Tushman et al., 2007). Although these experiences are idiosyncratic to me, my students, and my colleagues, they may have broader implications.

Over the past 30 years, I have experimented with several executive education program designs with colleagues at Columbia, INSEAD, Stanford, and Harvard (most intensively with Jeff Pfeffer and Charles O'Reilly). These alternative designs have had important impacts on our research streams as well as on our ability to affect practice. Our early, more traditional, executive education designs were loaded with content; faculty delivered their material over a five-day program. We quickly received feedback that while the content was of interest, participants wanted to link our field's researched-based knowledge to their own unique innovation, leadership, and change issues. In response to this request, we built in more application work and began to encourage intact teams to come to campus to work their issues throughout the program. We encouraged both intra as well as inter team sharing and collaboration. These active linkings between knowing and doing were highly valued by participants even as we learned more about the relevance of our research. Further, these more engaged relationships brought us closer to those leadership, innovation, and change issues where our field's research had little to say. For example, my research on the consequences of total quality management (TQM) on innovation outcomes (e.g., Benner & Tushman, 2002, 2003) was directly rooted in contentious conversations with executive education participants from Alcoa.

More recently, O'Reilly and I have developed both custom and open executive programs for senior teams. Senior teams come to campus for three or more days to work their specific innovation and change issues. Faculty content is tailored to a particular firm and its particular issues. Roughly half the time is spent in content sessions; the other half is spent in facilitated teams linking faculty content to their specific issues. These action-oriented, senior team executive programs provided a context where we were able to sharpen and extend our research questions, improve our access to the field, and directly link research to practice.

The most extensive and sophisticated action-learning version of our executive education work has been with IBM. Under the sponsorship of Bruce Harreld, IBM's senior vice president of strategy, we have collaborated over a five-year period on strategic leadership forums (SLFs). Although we learned how to construct these workshops over time, the fundamental design of intact senior teams sponsored by a corporate executive was set. The senior sponsor commissioned the scope of the work, chose the teams, and agreed to sponsor the outcomes associated with the workshop. The SLFs often had a corporate or line-of-business issue as a theme (e.g., cross line of business innovation or developing emerging business opportunities).

For these IBM SLFs, senior teams came to campus for three days armed with prework and a preliminary performance or opportunity gap articulated by the senior sponsor and general manager. During an SLF, faculty present and link content to cases for roughly half the SLF. The rest of the time is in facilitated workshops where intact teams directly link classroom material to their specific managerial challenge. Teams present their diagnostic work and their implementation plans to each other. There is much learning in the feedback sessions in which each team gets feedback from the other teams on the depth and quality of their diagnostic and change work. Over this three-day workshop, teams and their leaders gained substantial consensus on root causes, action plans, and next steps. Not only do the feedback sessions help individual teams with their strategic issues, but listening to multiple teams helped senior executives induce IBM-wide issues relating to innovation and change. Senior IBM executives initiated each workshop, participated for the three days, and were, in turn, actively involved in following up on work initiated at these workshops.

In return for this long-term faculty involvement, IBM's senior leadership provided support and access for faculty and PhD student research projects. For example, dissertation research by Benner, Smith, and Kleinbaum all had their roots in these collaborative executive education relationships (e.g., Benner & Tushman, 2003; Kleinbaum & Tushman, 2007; Smith & Tushman, 2005). Similarly, my work with O'Reilly has been shaped by these relationships (e.g., Harreld, O'Reilly, & Tushman, 2007; O'Reilly, Harreld, & Tushman, 2009; Tushman et al., 2007). Although these research projects were distinct from our executive education work, the results of the research were reported in subsequent SLFs. We have replicated these senior team–action learning relationships with a range of firms including BOC, the United States Postal Service, Siebel Systems, Irving Oil, and Agilent Technologies.

For example, during this custom program relationship with Harvard Business School (HBS), IBM had initiated a corporate strategy of simultaneously competing in multiple time horizons. As we worked in our custom programs sessions, it quickly became clear that these executives were searching for organization architectures that could exploit and explore both within business units and across the corporation. They were also grappling with the characteristics of those senior teams that could handle the contradictions associated with competing in different time frames. These observations and resulting conversations led directly to data collection on organization design choices and innovation (e.g., O'Reilly, Harreld, & Tushman, 2009; Tushman, Smith, Wood, Westerman, & O'Reilly, 2011), on interdependent innovation (Kleinbaum and Tushman, 2007), and on senior teams and contradiction (e.g., Smith & Tushman, 2005). With each of these phenomena-informed challenges, senior managers, doctoral students, and faculty developed research designs and data requirements that students were able to independently execute.

These senior team, action learning executive education designs facilitate a virtuous cycle between faculty and doctoral students collaborating with managers in research, and managers collaborating with faculty in shaping practice. The type of executive education design has had an important impact on our ability to shape practice and on the participants' ability to inform as well as host our research. The more action oriented the program,

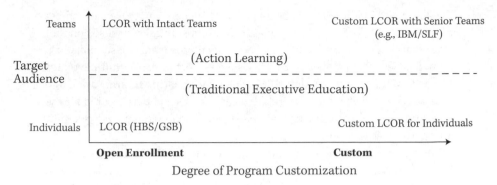

FIGURE 9.3 Experimenting in Executive Education Designs

the greater the quality of our relationship with these firms. In turn, the more senior teams trusted us, the more they understood our research agenda, the greater our ability to impact practice, and the greater their ability to connect with and help support our research and our students' dissertations (see Fig. 9.3).

Some Observations

1. Through executive education programs, I have been able to leverage our field's research to influence practice. My most productive relations with executives are all rooted in using our field's frameworks and literature to help solve real managerial issues.[2] Because our field's work adds substantial value to managers, relationships in executive education contexts open up the opportunity for faculty to learn what is managerially important but where our literature is silent. This ability to be taught what phenomena are important and then use these relationships to explore these phenomena is one of the great benefits of engaged scholarship (e.g., Van de Ven, 2007). Those most-productive knowing-doing relationships start with our adding value through researched-based insight (doing) and then moving to our research (knowing).

2. The more PhD students are involved in these executive education workshops, the more they interact with managers who are grappling with the phenomena, the more they understand the reality of innovation, leader-

---

2. Because the congruence model (see Nadler & Tushman, 1998; Tushman & O'Reilly, 1997) is able to integrate so much of our field's research, managers have found this model especially helpful in solving their challenges.

ship, and change.[3] This deeper understanding leads, in turn, to well-anchored and insightful research questions (Lawrence, 1992). Although it is clearly not necessary to be in the field to induce important research questions, those doctoral students who know both the literature and the phenomena may be better equipped to ask relatively more provocative research questions. Finally, direct access to managers facilitates our students' access to high-quality data (see also Tushman et al., 2007).

3. The longer relationship, the greater the trust and respect between managers and the researchers. The more faculty understand and respect the practitioners' need for performance and the more practitioners understand and respect the faculty's need to ask important research questions and gather reliable data, the more these relationships provide a setting for the co-production of knowledge and organizational impact.

4. These knowing-doing relationships affect our MBA, executive education, and PhD teaching. As executive education–research relations mature, we have been able to write cases, create leadership videos, and bring executives to class, as well as have executives host student field projects. Further, to the extent that our work with firms shapes those firms, we are more deeply informed on the phenomena we teach. These rich examples infuse and enliven our abilities as teachers.

5. The greater the action orientation of executive education programs, the greater the potential to develop relations such that our research and impact on practice are both enhanced. Executive education programs differ by degree of customization and the level of participant. The most action-oriented form of executive program we have employed is custom programs oriented to senior teams (see our discussion of the IBM custom program earlier in this chapter). These programs have been associated with the greatest impact on practice and with the greatest involvement of senior executives in our research questions, our data, and the interpretation of those data. It is in these action learning settings that we have co-produced action in these firms as well as co-produced innovative research (see Tushman et al., 2007).

Yet Some Concerns

With all the benefits of active collaboration between faculty and practitioners, there are also important boundary issues and areas of concern associ-

---

3. Doctoral students are involved in all LCOR programs as workshop facilitators. I introduce the students' research interests early in the program so participants get the importance of research to our community. Students are free then to approach participants about their research.

ated with these collaborations. These issues are rooted in the blurring of boundaries between the university's independent pursuit of research and the firm's local pursuit of practice: the possible distorting effects of faculty incentives in executive education programs, asymmetries in required skills and the associated need for faculty development and mentoring, and executive education administration in action-oriented executive programs.

1. Who owns the research question, who owns the data, who has access to the data, and who controls the interpretation, writing, and publication of the papers associated with these faculty-firm collaborations? Is it possible to test research questions in settings where the firm is buying executive education? These are all fundamentally important questions that get at roles and boundaries between universities and external organizations (e.g., Bok, 2003; Brief, 2000; Walsh et al., 2007).

   In order for these engaged scholarship relationships to flourish, they must be rooted in the firm's respect for independent faculty research. Independent research requires that faculty own the research question, the data associated with addressing the research question, as well as the decision where to publish the research (while protecting the firm's confidentiality). Custom clients must understand that an important piece of the relationship with the business school is to support and encourage faculty research.

   It is vital to have PhD students well integrated into these relationships between business schools and executive education clients. PhD students need to have access to custom program work on campus. These boundaries were tested several times. For example, a custom client balked when we asked that a PhD student sit in on our content sessions. We reiterated the importance of our research to the custom program client and our doctoral student's centrality to this research. We observed that if the student could not sit in on the meeting, neither could the faculty. These misunderstandings were resolved in a fashion that clarified the synergistic relations between the firm's need for confidentiality and impact and the faculty's research requirements.

2. Another major boundary issue is the question of consulting on campus. To what extent is action learning the same as faculty consulting? Does action research on campus inappropriately use the university to host faculty consulting projects? While custom programs do have an action component, they are not consulting projects. Work on campus may be facilitated, but it is limited to the work on campus. Where faculty control the content in traditional executive education programs, they share control with custom clients in action-learning programs. Indeed one of the

reasons that firms would use these modes of executive education is to get access to faculty research and the independence of faculty who have no vested interests as consultants. While relations on campus may well lead to subsequent consulting relationships (where the client has control of the questions and the pace of the relationship), these subsequent relationships are distinct from the faculty, PhD student, and executive education participant roles in on-campus programs.

3. For action-learning relationships to flourish, faculty must be willing to co-create these executive programs with the client firm. Custom programs inherently give more power to the client firm in both content delivered and program design. Further, faculty must be willing to teach for practice as they actively facilitate the linking of the program's content to the participants' specific needs. Further, faculty must be willing to teach not only their material but be prepared to make linkages across faculty content domains. This mode of teaching as well as program administration is more difficult than traditional executive education programs. The role of faculty director and program administration are much more client focused in these action-oriented custom programs. Faculty compensation models must be adjusted to account for the extra time involved in the teaching, facilitation, and design involved in action-learning programs.

4. Finally, faculty interest and skills in these active collaborations are not equally distributed. If these action-oriented executive education programs are to flourish, all faculty must be given the opportunity to work at the knowing-doing boundary. Issues of inequity of opportunity will dampen these boundary spanning experiments. As some senior faculty will be differentially capable of working these interfaces, they must take a proactive role in helping their senior and junior colleagues develop their integrative skills, their skills in translating research in ways that managers can understand, and their skills in actually helping managers solve real problems informed with our field's research.

Executive Education as a Lever in Shaping Practice and Research

Given the reciprocal relations between knowing and doing as well as doing and knowing, executive education is of particular relevance to business schools and their faculty. Executive education is a setting where practitioners come to campus to make a connection between faculty research and their own managerial challenges. In these settings, there is an enhanced opportunity to forge long-term collaborative research-practice relations.

Because these relationships develop on campus, they can be rooted both in research as well as in managerially anchored issues. Executive education settings are then a potentially important venue for developing engaged scholarship (Van de Ven, 2007; Van de Ven & Johnson, 2004).

Rigor and relevance, then, need not be separate but, rather, can be seen as interdependent activities in service of powerful theory and informed action (Huff, 2000; Weick, 2004). Action learning executive education workshops are one concrete way to embody this co-production of knowledge and practice. These enhanced individual learning and organizational outcomes are built on active collaboration between faculty and firms in program design as well as in linking program content to organizational outcomes. Through action learning workshops, we have been able to develop relations with a set of firms such that our field's research has had a real impact on practice. Equally important, this interaction with practice has had a substantial impact on my research and that of my students, and has increased the quality of my teaching.

These relations between business schools and thoughtful firms have the potential to create virtuous cycles of knowing and doing (see Fig. 9.4). A meta research question anchored these cycles for me (e.g., What are relations between technical change and organizational evolution?) and hosted a range of more concrete research questions (e.g., What are the relations between competence-destroying change and executive team succession?). Our field knows much in these broad domains (Tushman, 2004). Executive education

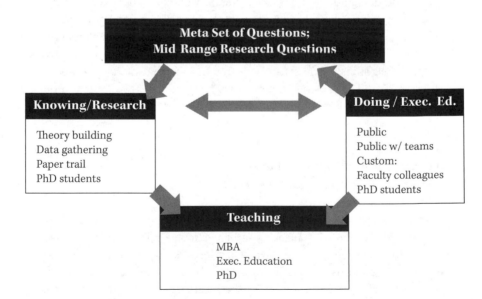

FIGURE 9.4 Knowing / Doing Cycles Affect Research, Practice, and Teaching

provides the setting where we can share this research with practitioners. In these educational settings we can make the knowing-doing link.

Relationships formed in action-learning settings, in turn, have shaped my research questions even as they have affected how I understand innovation and organizations. Doing has directly affected my knowing. Finally, both my action-learning work and my research directly affect the quality of my MBA, PhD, and traditional executive education work. As these business school–firm relations matured, the linkage between my research and practice become tighter and the co-production of research became more effective. Executive education workshops are contexts that help forge research-practice partnerships that permit these virtuous cycles to flourish (see also Kaplan, 1998, for a discussion of this virtuous cycle in the accounting and control area).

Yet business schools systematically underleverage executive education. At a time when firms are calling for more relevance and more customization, business schools remain in the modular, lecture-discussion format. While this traditional approach often is associated with participant satisfaction, the impact of these traditional executive programs on practice is equivocal (Anderson, 2003; Conger & Xin, 2000; Pfeffer & Fong, 2002). Further, since traditional executive programs do not encourage the development of relations between faculty and participants, the link to faculty research is stunted.

The concept of action-learning workshops, of active collaborations between business schools and firms, is generalizable. This action-learning approach requires clear and well-defined relationships and expectations. Faculty must take practice seriously and firms must take seriously supporting faculty research. This action-learning model is not new. It is similar to action-learning approaches hosted within firms (e.g., GE's workout and IBM's ACT; see Kuhn & Marsick, 2005; Tichy & Sherman, 1993; Ulrich, Kerr, & Asheknas, 2002). Other business schools are also leveraging executive education contexts for faculty research (e.g., MIT, Duke, LBS, INSEAD, IMD, among others). It is also similar to the consulting and executive education practices of a range of consulting firms (e.g., Argyris & Schon, 1996; Beer, 2001). What is different about action-learning workshops hosted within business schools is its emphasis generating powerful ideas and subjecting these ideas to rigorous inquiry. While consulting firms do generate powerful ideas, they are less equipped or motivated to subject these ideas to rigorous testing. Action-learning workshops position business schools to operate in Pasteur's Quadrant; to be able to excel in both research-based insight as well as practical impact.

While action-learning workshops may be an underleveraged opportunity for business schools, there are important issues that these executive education designs raise. Action-learning designs raise issues on the appropriate boundary of business schools (Kaplan, 1998; Walsh et al., 2007). For research to flourish in action-learning relationships, faculty must own the research questions as well as the data gathered in service of these research questions. Bartunek (2002) observes that faculty must be in the firms, not of the firms. The extent to which faculty get co-opted by the sponsoring firm, the quality of the research will suffer (e.g., Bok, 2003; Brief, 2000; Hinings & Greenwood, 2002). Further, these action-learning workshops can not be confused with faculty consulting. Rather, action-learning workshops are co-created workshops, conducted on campus and managed by executive education staff. Faculty present content tailored to the client's issues, teach to practice, and actively facilitate the linking of content to practice. Finally, these boundary spanning opportunities must be made available to all faculty who are interested in developing their skills to work at these interfaces. Issues of faculty inequity will assure that these experiments will fail.

While action-learning workshops are associated with a set of issues and concerns, they are a vehicle that has the promise to bridge the divide between our research and the world of practice, or between rigor and relevance. This form of executive education complements traditional executive education formats. Action learning is a highly generalizable activity for business schools and for business school faculty. Firms want more customization, and our field has generated enormous knowledge that deserves the opportunity to shape practice. Action learning promises high leverage for both faculty and firms. With this leverage also comes the opportunity for increased faculty insight and provocative research. Although there are real boundary issues to be resolved, my experience suggests that executive education in general and action-learning workshops in particular have the potential to move business schools more firmly into Pasteur's Quadrant of knowing and doing; toward building powerful theories and fundamental ideas that impact practice.

REFERENCES

Adler, P., Benner, M., Brunner, D., MacDuffie, J., Staats, B., Takeuchi, H., Tushman, M., & Winter, S. (2009). Perspectives on the productivity dilemma. *Journal of Operations Management, 27*, 99–113.

Anderson, L. (2003, September 8). Companies still value training: Development: Survey shows that investing in executives has a big future. *Financial Times*, p. 5.

Argyris, C., & Schon, D. A. (1996). *Organizational learning II: Theory, method and practice*. Reading, MA: Addison-Wesley.

Bartunek, J. (2002). Corporate scandals: How should the Academy of Management members respond? *Academy of Management Executive, 16,* 138.

Bazerman, M. (2005). Conducting influential research: The need for prescriptive implications. *Academy of Management Review, 30,* 25–31.

Beer, M. (2001). Why management research findings are unimplementable: An action science perspective. *Reflections, 2,* 58–65.

Benner, M. J., & Tushman, M. (2002). Process management and technological innovation: A longitudinal study of the photography and paint industries. *Administrative Science Quarterly, 47*(4), 676–706.

Benner, M. J., & Tushman, M. (2003). Exploitation, exploration, and process management: The productivity dilemma revisited. *Academy of Management Review, 28*(2), 238–256.

Bennis, W., & O'Toole, J. (2005, May). How business schools lost their way. *Harvard Business Review,* 96–104.

Bok, D. (2003). *Universities in the marketplace: The commercialization of higher education.* Princeton, NJ: Princeton University Press.

Brief, A. (2000). Still servants of power. *Journal of Management Inquiry, 9*(4), 342–351.

Conger, J., & Xin, K. (2000). Executive education in the 21st century. *Journal of Management Education, 24*(1), 73–101.

Ghoshal, S. (2005). Bad management theories are destroying good management practices. *Academy of Management Learning & Education, 4,* 75–91.

Harreld, B., O'Reilly, C., & Tushman, M. (2007). Dynamic capabilities at IBM: Driving strategy into action. *California Management Review, 49*(4), 1–22.

Hinings, C. R., & Greenwood, R. (2002). Disconnects and consequences in organization theory. *Administrative Science Quarterly, 47,* 411–421.

Huff, A. (2000). Citigroup's John Reed and Stanford's Jim March on management research and practice. *Academy of Management Review, 14,* 52–64.

Kaplan, R. (1998). Innovation action research: Creating new management theory and practice. *Journal of Management Accounting Research, 10,* 89–118.

Katz, R., & Tushman, M. (1979). Communication patterns, project performance, and task characteristics: An empirical evaluation and integration in an R&D setting. *Organizational Behavior and Human Performance, 23,* 139–162.

Khurana, R., Nohria, N., & Prenrice, D. (2005). Management as a profession. In J. Lorsch, A. Zelleke, & L. Berlowitz (Eds.), *Restoring trust in American business.* Cambridge, MA: American Academy of Arts and Sciences.

Kleinbaum, A., & Tushman, M. (2007). Building bridges: The social structure of interdependent innovation. *Strategic Entrepreneurship Journal, 1*(1), 103–122.

Kuhn, J., & Marsick, V. (2005). Action learning for strategic innovation in mature organizations. *Action Learning: Research and Practice, 2*(1), 29–50.

Lawrence, P. R. (1992). The challenge of problem-oriented research. *Journal of Management Inquiry, 1,* 139–142.

Mintzberg, H. (2004). *Managers not MBAs: A hard look at the soft practice of managing and management development.* San Francisco: Berrett-Koehler.

Nadler, D., & Tushman, M. (1998). *Competing by design: The power of organizational architectures.* New York: Oxford University Press.

O'Reilly, C., Harreld, B., & Tushman, M. (2009). Organizational ambidexterity: IBM and emerging business opportunities. *California Management Review, 51*(4), 75–99.

Pfeffer, J., & Fong, C. (2002). The end of business schools? Less success than meets the eye. *Academy of Management Learning and Education, 1*, 78–95.

Polzer, J., Gulati, R., Khurana, R., & Tushman, M. (2009). Crossing boundaries to increase relevance in organizational research. *Journal of Management Inquiry, 18*(4), 280–286.

Rynes, S. L., Bartunek, J. M., & Daft, R. L. (2001). Across the great divide: Knowledge creation and transfer between practitioners and academics. *Academy of Management Journal, 44*, 340–355.

Smith, W. K., & Tushman, M. L. (2005). Managing strategic contradictions: A top management model for managing innovation streams. *Organization Science, 16*(5), 522–536.

Stokes, D. E. (1997). *Pasteur's Quadrant: Basic science and technological innovation.* Washington, DC: Brookings Institution Press.

Tichy, N., & Sherman, S. (1993). *Control your destiny or someone else will.* New York: Currency Doubleday.

Tushman, M. (1977). Special boundary roles in the innovation process. *Administrative Science Quarterly, 22*, 587–605.

Tushman, M. (1978). Task characteristics and technical communication in R&D. *Academy of Management Journal, 21*, 624–645.

Tushman, M. (2004). From engineering management/R&D management to the management of innovation, to exploiting and exploring over value nets: 50 years of research initiated by IEEE-TEM. *IEEE Transactions on Engineering Management, 51*(4), 409–411.

Tushman, M., & O'Reilly, C. (1997). *Winning through innovation: A practical guide to leading organizational change and renewal.* Boston: Harvard Business School Press.

Tushman, M., & O'Reilly, C. (2007). Research and relevance: Implications of Pasteur's Quadrant for doctoral programs and faculty development. *Academy of Management Journal, 50*(4), 769–774.

Tushman, M., O'Reilly, C., Fenollosa, A., & Kleinbaum, A. (2007). Towards rigor and relevance: Executive education as a lever for enhancing academic relevance. *Academy of Management Learning and Education, 6*(3), 345–362.

Tushman, M. L., Smith, W., Wood, R., Westerman, G., & O'Reilly, C. (2010). Organizational designs and innovation streams. *Industrial and Corporate Change. 19*(5), 1331–1366.

Ulrich, D., Kerr, S., & Asheknas, R. (2002). *The GE work-out: How to implement GE's revolutionary method for busting bureaucracy and attacking organizational problems—fast.* New York: McGraw-Hill.

Van de Ven, A. (2007). *Engaged scholarship: Creating knowledge for science and practice.* New York: Oxford University Press.

Van de Ven, A., & Johnson, P. (2004). *Knowledge for science and practice.* Minneapolis: Carlson School of Management, University of Minnesota.

Walsh, J., Tushman, M., Kimberly, J., Starbuck, W., & Ashford, S. (2007). On the relationship between research and practice: Debate and reflections. *Journal of Management Inquiry, 16*(2), 128–154.

Weick, K. (2004, August). *On rigor and relevance of OMT.* Paper presented at the Academy of Management Symposium, San Francisco.

ABOUT THE AUTHOR

Michael L. Tushman is the Paul R. Lawrence, Class of 1942 Professor at the Harvard Business School. At HBS, Tushman is the co-chair of the DBA program in management and is the faculty chair of the Advanced Management Program. Tushman also co-chairs the Leading Change and Organizational Renewal executive eduction program. His research focuses on the impact of technological change on organizational evolution, innovation streams and ambidextrous designs, and the characteristics of senior teams that can deal with paradoxical strategic requirements.

PART III

Pathways: Research to Practice

TEN

Academic-Consultant Collaboration

Doing Research across the Divide

RUTH WAGEMAN*

SOME TEN YEARS AGO, an unusual research collaboration began. A trio of senior consultants, deeply experienced in working with chief executives, reflected on countless observations of wheel-spinning, conflict-ridden leadership teams and wondered whether it really had to be that way. The popular press writings on top teams provided help . . . of a sort. These works described similar patterns: conflicts among members never surfaced effectively, chief executives driving an agenda with no signs of team ownership of the strategy, repeated returns to the same sticky issues. But the underlying message in these works was less helpful: That's just how it *is* with teams of top leaders (e.g., Katzenbach, 1997a, 1997b).

So far, the story is not unusual: Observant practitioners noted a pattern of dysfunction and an opportunity to provide help to clients. They began exploring a significant opportunity to build a new practice for their firm.

Then the story becomes unusual. These senior consultants turned to an academic colleague to find out whether scholarly research on top teams might guide interventions to improve their functioning. With a literature review of upper-echelons research (Hambrick, 2000; Hambrick & D'Aveni, 1996; Hambrick & Mason, 1984) and another academic colleague drawn into the mix, this group collectively reached a conclusion: Existing research is informative about leadership team dysfunctions, but the field is wide open for some inventive new understandings of how to help such teams become more effective.

What motivated the consultants (Debra A. Nunes, Mary Fontaine, and James A. Burruss of Hay Group) was a growing frustration that chief execu-

* I would like to thank Richard Hackman and Jim Burruss for their help with a version of these ideas presented at the annual meeting of the American Psychological Association held in Boston in 2008; and Mary Fontaine and Deb Nunes for their contributions to our analysis of the enablers and obstacles to consultant-academic collaboration.

tive officers (CEOs) were taking popular writings as license to live with dysfunction in their leadership teams. What drove the academics (Richard Hackman at Harvard and me, then at Dartmouth) was a conviction that what is seen as "normal life" in upper echelons—zero task interdependence, competition for a coveted top job, no clear team purposes—are circumstances under which *no* other team would be expected to function effectively. Moreover, these conditions, we suspected, were eminently malleable. Our shared conviction became the following: It doesn't have to be that way. Would we be interested in undertaking some field research together, with the aim of developing a diagnostic model for leadership teams that would inform a top teams consulting practice? We would.

We undertook a study of what became a sample of 120 leadership teams of organizations around the world, which headed whole businesses or major business units (Wageman et al., 2008a). Teams were in the sample for a variety of reasons: Some were led by CEOs who sought help with ineffective leadership teams; others had undertaken strategic and structural changes to their organizations and wanted advice about the implications for how their leadership teams operated. Some were poor performers, whereas others were fundamentally sound.

We assessed their effectiveness in providing quality leadership to the enterprise. Sixteen expert observers, all consultants working with leadership teams, drew upon an array of archival, survey, and observational data to rate each team on Hackman's (2002) three criteria of effectiveness: (1) how well the team served its main constituencies, (2) the degree to which the team showed signs of becoming more capable over time, and (3) the degree to which the net impact of the team was more positive than negative on the well-being and development of the individual leaders who made up the team.

We also assessed the design and leadership of each team to identify those features that most powerfully differentiated superb from struggling leadership teams. Members of all teams completed the Team Diagnostic Survey (TDS) (Wageman, Hackman, & Lehman, 2005), which captures a team's main design features, the quality of its work processes, the behavior of the leader, and the quality of members' relationships. Finally, for many of the leaders in the sample, we also had social motive profiles (McClelland, 1985) and competency assessments (Spencer & Spencer, 1993).

The collaboration began in 1999. Around 2003, our intention to write a book for senior leaders began to crystallize, and our writing efforts began in 2005. The book *Senior Leadership Teams: What It Takes to Make Them Great* was released in early 2008. All told, this collaboration was nine years in the making. What I aim to do in this chapter is use the lessons of our experiences—both positive and negative—to generate some hypotheses about the *condi-*

tions under which academic-consultant collaboration will produce rigorous research that informs high-quality interventions in social systems.

Players

To draw general lessons from this particular academic-consultant collaboration, it helps to know who the players were. Mary Fontaine heads the Leadership practice of Hay Group and is one of the founding members of Hay Group's McClelland Center for Research and Innovation. Mary has her PhD in business administration from the University of North Carolina at Chapel Hill and spent some time as a professor at Duke University. She has spent more than 20 years consulting in the field of leadership and organizational effectiveness.

Jim Burruss is also one of the founding members of the McClelland Center. He earned his PhD in clinical psychology at Harvard University, studying and working with David McClelland. He has for 30 and more years applied his understanding of human motivation to helping organizations in both the private and public sectors around the world.

Deb Nunes is vice president at the McClelland Center. She has a master's degree in counseling and personnel psychology from Western Michigan University and an MBA from Boston University. Deb's clients are primarily large global companies, and she has spent more than 20 years helping CEOs and the heads of major business units implement their strategies.

Each of these consultants has a long history of using rigorous research directly in his or her practice. Each is deeply invested in the continuing improvement of his or her own practice, and all three regularly draw upon basic research—such as work on the physiological bases of social motives inspired by McClelland's research (e.g., Schultheiss, Campbell, & McClelland, 1999)—when speaking with clients about their leadership challenges.

Richard Hackman and I were both full-time academics when this collaboration began. Richard is a professor of social and organizational psychology at Harvard. He has conducted research on team dynamics and performance, leadership effectiveness, and the design of self-managing teams and organizations, among many topics. His book on leading teams (Hackman, 2002) was the starting place for our model of leadership team effectiveness. At the time our collaboration began, I was a member of the faculty of the Tuck School of Business at Dartmouth College. I remain an academic scholar in part of my professional life as visiting faculty at Harvard in the Psychology Department. I also have worked for the last several years as the director of research for Hay Group, continuing to work with Deb, Jim, and Mary.

We five were, as a group, a leadership team of sorts—one that shared responsibility for creating, launching, and implementing a research project intended to produce findings that guide effective action. Like all leadership team members, we also had our own individual responsibilities—to write and publish the work, for example, or to build a new top teams practice. So it seems appropriate to use our own research-derived model of leadership team effectiveness to analyze our collaboration.

Product

How did our own collaboration stand on the three criteria of team effectiveness? For Criterion 1, the key question for our collaboration is the following: Was the work useful both for advancing theoretical knowledge about senior leadership teams and for informing practice aimed at improving the effectiveness of such teams? We produced a book written for senior leaders about how to create effective leadership teams (Wageman et al., 2008a) that draws upon our research findings and our collective observations of the challenges of leading teams of leaders. Our aspiration was to draw upon the rich observational wisdom of the consultants and the conceptual models of the academics to provide a useable framework for leaders about how to improve the effectiveness of their leadership teams. The book offers working leaders myriad examples of CEOs struggling with the challenges of leading leadership teams as well as vivid descriptions of how they overcame them, organized around our key research findings.

If one takes online and in-person reviews seriously, the book has been well received among practitioners. As we have not created a journal article for a peer-reviewed outlet, the evidence is not clear that the research achieves the standards of academic rigor and influence on theory that are among the main aspirations of scholarly research. A research article about the difficulties of leading teams of leaders is published in a volume on leadership (Wageman & Hackman, 2010). Several popular-press articles for executives have been published from the work as well (Bolster & Wageman, 2009; Nunes & Wageman, 2007; Wageman et al., 2008b; Wageman, Wilcox, & Gurin, 2008). But the principle evidence of the *usefulness* in consulting of our collaborative research is this: A significant top teams practice within Hay Group has grown around the work, and the interventions used within that practice are built explicitly on the implementation model that came out of our collaboration. Overall, I'd suggest this collaboration scores pretty well on Criterion 1, always allowing that the longitudinal evidence (Does the consulting practice actually improve the functioning of top teams?) is largely anecdotal.

For Criterion 2, our question is the following: Did the team operate in ways that at a minimum avoided significant downward spirals over time, and—better still—showed signs of developing increasing capability? This criterion requires a little expansion, because it forms the frame for my analysis of the contributors to and detractors from scholar-consultant collaboration more generally.

I draw on the model of team performance proposed by Hackman and Morris (1975; see also Hackman & Wageman, 2005). The model posits that team effectiveness is a joint function of three performance processes: (a) the level of *effort* group members collectively expend carrying out task work, (b) the appropriateness of the *performance strategies* the group uses, and (c) the amount of *knowledge and skill* members bring to bear. Associated with each of the three performance processes is both a characteristic "process loss" (Steiner, 1972) and an opportunity for positive synergy, or a "process gain." That is, members may interact in ways that depress the team's effort, the appropriateness of its strategy, and the utilization of member talent; alternatively, their interaction may enhance collective effort, generate uniquely appropriate strategies, and actively develop members' knowledge and skills.

To assess our standing on Criterion 3, I interviewed the core members of our collaboration, so that I could legitimately speak on behalf of the team. Was the net impact of the collaboration, on balance, a positive contribution to our well-being and learning? The answer was an unequivocal "yes." It may be a significant lesson for scholar-consultant partnerships more generally that each member of the team expressed (a) significant and cherished learning from the experience, and (b) a general feeling that they miss the team and wish there were more such intensive learning experiences in their lives.

Process: Enablers and Obstacles in Consultant-Academic Collaborations

Our collaboration had both strengths and weaknesses on the three processes. Based on our experience, I offer some practical lessons about what helped us and what got in the way, and pose some practical principles for creating conditions for effective collaboration between academic scholars and consultant practitioners.

Lessons from Effort Levels in Our Collaboration

Two key effort-related patterns characterized our work. First, whenever we had our periodic team meetings, we typically spent a whole day together, examining quantitative findings from analysis of the TDS data (primarily the responsibility of the academics) and exploring those patterns based on direct observations from working with those teams (primarily the work of the consultants). Almost without exception, the engagement of members at these meetings was very high. We worked hard at developing our insights without glossing over real differences in our perspectives. The behavioral signs of deep commitment to the project within the meetings were very strong.

However, we also showed some significant process losses around effort. Often each of us committed to some analysis or pre-reading in preparation for the next meeting. When we convened, we invariably found that several or all of us had failed to do our "homework." For example, the quantitative analyses were prepared in advance and circulated to the team, but members had not actually read or thought about the material in advance, and we wasted considerable time at each meeting reading materials in silence as we sat around a conference table. Levels of pre-work even declined over time, as the team members who typically did come prepared early on learned that others might not, and thus a downward spiral began. Moreover, these meetings were well spaced out in time (once every two months or so). To underscore the significance of this process loss: It took us nine years from the beginning of the project before we wrote a complete draft of the book.

This pattern of timing is not unique to this collaboration. In my now considerable experience conducting research with consultants, the rhythm frequently evolves this way: short, intensive bursts of focus by the team between long periods of little or no progress and poor preparation in advance of the collaborative work. Even my own dedicated team of researcher-consultants at Hay Group fell into this pattern. Our collaborative project with Tim Hall and other colleagues at Boston University (BU) studying the impact of career complexity on leadership development (Wolff et al., 2008) also unfolded this way, though it had periods of real acceleration late in the game. Our wholly internal projects comparing the challenges faced by chief executives in India, China, and the West (North America and Western Europe) (Gutierrez, Spencer, & Zhu, 2009) and our research on the coming leadership drought (Wolff, Fontaine, & Wageman, 2009; Wolff, Callahan, & Spencer, 2009) showed similar stop-start patterns. What contributed to these effort patterns—both the positive energy at meetings and the long lulls in concentrated effort?

Enabler: Convene for a purpose that is highly consequential for both consultants and scholars. We labored hard on this project across a span of years because we all deeply wanted to solve the problem of how to enhance the effectiveness of leadership teams. I believe it is significant that the phenomenon and the research question came *first* from the consultants, and after an exploration of the research literature, then became an intriguing puzzle for the academics. I don't mean to assert that the order of events has to happen that way. But that sequence meant that the subject of the research was without question one of some urgency and importance to astute practitioners. They *needed* to understand why CEOs had such ineffective teams. The leaders they worked with were feeling the pain, and the consultants' deeply held professional values drove them to want answers. The scholars in the group *needed* to find out if their own understandings of teams in organizations could provide some leverage on leadership teams given the very real differences from other teams we understood well. As a consequence, there was a superb fit of people's values with the collaborative purpose and a powerful drive to work toward answers.

In my observation, few academic-consultant collaborations begin this way. More typically, the research question comes from the academics, shaped by the scholar's own interests rather than a pressing practical problem for consultants and their clients. Because Hay Group owns extensive databases (millions of assessments of working leaders around the world), I am often the recipient of requests for data from doctoral students and faculty. The next study of emotional intelligence across industry sectors, or Leader Member Exchange-based theory about leadership styles, or a further refinement of learning styles in groups is unlikely to gain much traction among consultants, when the underlying problem addressed is so obscure or small. Although providing access to data is certainly a great way for consulting firms like Hay Group to contribute to the development of new knowledge about organizations, these requests are not, in my view, ideal opportunities for true collaboration between consultants and academics.

But just as often, a "pressing problem" identified by consultants is something already pretty well explored in the research literature, and thus is of little interest to a scholar seeking a great topic—though it can be of great interest to consultants who want some new and marketable intellectual property to sell. As research director, I also am the recipient of many requests from colleagues about "what we should study": cross-cultural collaboration, matrix organizations, virtual teams, globalization, or family-owned businesses. These ideas about what would make for useful research are born from the expressed frustrations and challenges of working leaders. But they represent already well-trodden research ground. Consultants cannot know that because the problems are articulated in lay language or business jargon unrelated to academic search terms one would use to find relevant research (for example, at Google Scholar). And that is not what a typical consultant would do, in any case. I hope my consultant colleagues will forgive the generalization, but reaching out to academics or seeking scholarly knowledge about a client problem is not typical behavior among consultants. One of my chief complaints over the last several years of working closely with management consultants is that they do not read much. Typically, the first reaction when they face a novel problem in practice is to ask other practitioners if they have faced that problem and already have a methodology for tackling it. Their second instinct is to invent something based on their own ideas and experience. Asking these questions—Has anyone ever studied this problem systematically? What does research have to say about it?—is far down the list.

When consultants do look to the scholarly literature for insight, they often are disappointed and frustrated. Organizational scholars may study real problems, but those problems are framed using language that practitioners will not recognize. With a foot in both camps, one useful role I have found myself playing is finding and summarizing the scholarly research relevant to a problem facing clients. For example, I might be asked: Has anyone done a study of what it takes to transition between a line leadership role and a matrix role? No. But they *have* studied why organizations design matrix structures, and the challenges they create. They also have studied informal influence processes and peer-to-peer collaboration across functions, behaviors associated with effectiveness in a matrix leadership role. Taken together, different streams of research in distinct literatures can create a sturdy platform for a knowledgeable approach with clients. But the skill required to find these studies and synthesize them is an academic one. It is a critical path to making research useful, and one that scholarly writers could undertake more often.

The danger of these intergroup differences is that consultants and academics fall into stereotyping each other. The academics, fruitlessly seeking opportunities to pursue their research projects, receive a lukewarm response and come to view consultants as anti-intellectual or uninterested in evidence. Consultants, seeking readily applicable frameworks that speak directly to a client's problems, view researchers as clueless about reality or interested in novelty at the expense of utility. And both groups miss opportunities to find the *shared consequential purposes* that underlie each of their concerns.

A key resource that consultants can bring to a research collaboration is knowledge of what their clients' struggles are—that is, what would be *useful*—as well as the language clients use to describe those struggles, which ultimately will be needed to express findings in usable terms. A key resource that researchers bring is the skill of developing problems into researchable questions—and knowledge of what already has been learned by others (see Table 10.1 for a summary of the benefits and risks of academic-consultant collaboration). Bringing those two resources together requires a deep conversation about purposes—a collaborative definition of a project that both surfaces and satisfies the main needs of both sides of the collaboration.

TABLE 10.1 Benefits and Risks of Academic-Consultant Research Collaborations

Benefits	Risks
Access across many organizations, many different manifestations of a phenomenon, enhanced generalizability	Language differences and potential fault lines in the team
Combination of problems working leaders encounter *and* skill in posing researchable questions	Conflicting rhythms of the work of consultants and researchers, leading to inappropriately disaggregating tasks
Direct path into practice	Mishandling the learning-production balance
Intrinsic motivation: fun and personal learning	Conflicts over intellectual property rights

Obstacle: The rhythms of research work and consulting work are conflicting . . . as are the incentives. For all our drive to get answers to a pressing problem, we lost a lot of momentum as we worked together. The clues to why we suffered effort-related process losses lie, I think, where such effort problems usually do: the features of the work and the features of the incentives in our organizations.

The consultants were deeply experienced individuals who had profound insight into leadership and group dynamics. Those characteristics made them ideal partners in research that reached into new theoretical territory. It also made them very expensive and rarely available. It is highly costly for a consulting firm to invest senior consultants' time in research-based development of a new methodology. Only when the potential market is large, and the method is a substantial new approach applicable to many clients—not a refinement of existing practice—is the investment of time and money worth it to a consulting firm. Time spent on research is time not billing.

That fact, in my view, is why most consulting firm "research" consists largely of analysts surveying leaders and other practitioners about "best practices," rather than engaging in predictive research about influences on individual, group, and organizational effectiveness. It simply is not viewed as cost effective to develop that kind of rigorous basis for client work. Many decision makers in organizations will buy consulting practices that have no research basis, so why spend that kind of money on it? That certainly was not the stance of Mary, Deb, and Jim—but more junior consultants with less political capital could not have made the choice to spend their time on a long-term research collaboration. That choice is far more easily made by the academics in the group, who are expected to concentrate their time on groundbreaking projects.

Moreover, the natural rhythm of research work is completely different from the rhythms of consulting. Consulting work is done largely on the time schedule of the client, requiring unexpected travel, rapid preparation and engagement, and moving on to another client. Research work, by contrast, is much more amenable to planning and also requires dedicated and uninterrupted days to stay with a conceptual problem or a series of analyses, to work through interpretation, and above all to capture in writing what is being learned. Watching consultants try to fit these activities in between client engagements, I've come to be very skeptical about the idea of consultants doing research part-time as a second requirement of their jobs. The result is either that no substantive research ever gets done, or as in our own collaboration, the uninterrupted days are so rarely possible that it takes years and years to get the work completed.

Where I *have* seen success in moving a collaboration at a good pace is in instances where the academics in the collaboration take the main responsibility for analysis, interpretation, and writing—the key pieces of the work that require uninterrupted attention. For example, research team members at Hay Group, including Steve Wolff, Guorong Zhu, and Betzaluz Gutierrez, worked with Tim Hall and Kathy Kram at BU using a unique longitudinal database of complete career information on 57 senior leaders, conducting a series of studies about how career complexity influences leadership development. Those data hung around in a half-coded state for years while the consultant-researchers were obligated to respond to shorter-term demands and were able to turn their attention to the data only in brief spurts of activity. It was when the academic collaborators could take on much of the burden of coding and crafting a paper that the work came to fruition (Wolff et al., 2008), with the consultant-researchers providing their contributions where and when they could.

An alternative job design would be to release consultants for an extended period from any responsibility to clients so they can focus on research. The virtues of that strategy are in the many opportunities to bring their rich field knowledge into the research throughout the process. But I have never yet seen a deliberate attempt to design a researcher-consultant job that allows the individual some months of research time in between periods concentrated on consulting work. The usual expectation is that one will do both, every week or even every day. And under those conditions, only the consulting gets done.

Lessons from Our Performance Strategies

We found that senior leadership teams often fall into mindless habitual routines in how they work together, such as marching at speed through a largely tactical agenda, or conducting their meetings by having each individual give a presentation about what is going on in his or her part of the organization. Frustrated CEOs cite slippage in coordination and an inability to execute agreed-upon plans as the most common process loss. Rarely do such teams ask these questions: What does this have to do with our strategic agenda? Are there better ways we could use this time together? We, too, lapsed into some ineffective routines and fell prey to an inability to carry out our plans.

For example, the core members of the team began to meet regularly, at one- or two-month intervals, for a half or full day starting around 2002. At each meeting, we discussed the observations of the consultants from the teams they had worked with most recently; and we explored patterns in the latest set of analyses from the growing top teams database. Five years in, it became increasingly obvious that, while we were deepening our personal understanding of leadership teams with each encounter, we had not yet put one single word on paper.

Writing a book together was at the center of our aspirations, precisely because we believed that a book stood the best chance of making our research usable to working leaders around the world. We hoped to bring together in the book the systematic conceptual understanding of leadership teams from our scholarly approach with the rich observations and myriad examples of real working leaders, to provide a set of road maps for leaders to design and lead their leadership teams well. Yet for all the energy we had for the subject and for all the richness of learning, in five years we had not written one word. I believe there are some lessons in these process losses—and how we ultimately changed them—for scholar-consultant collaborations more generally.

Enabler: Provide protected time and space for research. The long and intensive meetings this diverse group had and the habitual work we did together—not disaggregated—were a critical positive contribution to making the research usable. The consultants in the team acquired a precious and rare resource in their busy work lives: time to reflect, compare notes with each other, and explore alternative understandings of leadership teams. They could apply the emerging lessons about leadership teams immediately in their own work. Rather than waiting for the book to be written—all the lessons wrapped up and synthesized—they could alter their practice and incorporate new insights in real time. In that sense, the development part of our R&D undertaking—building a top teams practice—was happening simultaneous with, rather than only after, the research.

The strategy we developed—working with quantitative findings as the basis for a rich discussion of direct observations—allowed the consultants to reality test the patterns in the data for what it might mean in practice. At the same time, it inspired those of us responsible for the quantitative analysis to undertake new explorations of the data based on insights from ongoing practice. It was in dialogue, *not* sequential or disaggregated action, that we achieved both conceptual depth and practical relevance.

Enabler: Collect data as a core part of the consulting process. While consultants have superb access to organizations, they often face the same obstacles as academic researchers in gathering data: Completing questionnaires, participating in interviews, and permitting observation of meetings are all well down the priority list of people at work. However, when data collection is a part of the diagnostic process, data accumulate as a direct function of the organization's own priorities: their desire for consulting help.

In our research, every team the consultants worked with completed the TDS, and many of the leaders in those teams also were assessed as individuals. As a consequence, no special effort was needed to get the systematic data to generate quantitative findings. At the same time, the rich qualitative observation that made sense of those patterns was also in hand, through direct work of the consultants with the teams. We could then seek systematic evidence of patterns we hypothesized from consultant observations by analyzing the accumulating data from new teams added to the database, all as the consulting work unfolded.

Many management consulting firms operate in this fashion: collecting systematic data, perhaps conducting structured interviews with senior leaders, or distributing unit-level questionnaire assessments. The accumulated data offer wonderful opportunities for useful research. However, when researchers seek access to databases—as opposed to working in dialogue with consultants to define and tackle problems of shared interest—the work usually results in findings of interest only to scholars.

Obstacle: Emergent norms mishandled the learning-production balance. Our collaboration, like any scholar-consultant collaboration, posed a major dilemma that our team took a long time to address: (1) No one individual in the group had the knowledge and skill to capture the combination of conceptual and observational richness that our team brought together in its discussions. (2) But writing is not a group task. Who was going to draft an account of our team's collective understanding, and how?

For years, our team had emergent norms that favored learning and did not hold us to account about producing anything. I do not mean to suggest that learning is a relatively trivial goal for such collaborations. Rather, production and learning have to be managed as a balancing act. The learning was deeply motivating, but we were not capturing the learning to make it available to others.

In early 2005, or what turned out ultimately to be the calendar midpoint of our nine-year collaboration (Gersick, 1988), we finally addressed the unspoken problem of how to prepare a manuscript about what we had learned as a team. To put it excessively kindly, I introduced a team coaching intervention (Hackman & Wageman, 2005). I wrote a letter to the team describing my observations of what we were and were not doing well, pointed out that we had written nothing, and asked if we should abandon the idea of a book given that none of us felt competent to write it. To the eternal credit of my colleagues, what resulted was a mature, competent, creative, and focused discussion of whether we wanted to write a book, whether we really could, and if so, how.

Two creative breakthroughs came out of that conversation. First, we invented a uniquely suited approach to writing the book. One chapter at a time, we held a day-long meeting, all tape recorded, to address a structured set of questions: (1) What are the key quantitative findings? (2) Based on direct observation, what do we see as the main challenges facing CEOs in getting a needed design condition in place for their teams, and what vivid examples do we have to illustrate these challenges? (3) What are some key actions that help a CEO get that condition in place for his or her team, and what vivid examples do we have of CEOs doing so in distinctly different ways?

The recordings of these discussions became the basis for me to write an extended chapter outline, which the group then discussed, refined, and expanded in the first part of its next meeting. Then we tackled a new chapter. We asked a professional writer, Scott Spreier, a journalist and senior consultant who participated in our meetings, to interview the appropriate consultants to flesh out the stories and expand the chapter outlines. All of us had a hand in commenting on the drafts, and Deb and I took the lead in revising the main chapters into final drafts for submission to the publisher. In this way, we managed to avoid group writing on the one hand, and we avoided disaggregating responsibilities for each chapter or parts of the work on the other. At the same time, we created repeated opportunities to combine the conceptual and observational richness our team had as a whole in creating each chapter.

The second creative breakthrough came as we crafted the structure of our book. We realized that the causal model that underpinned our analysis (see Fig. 10.1) might not be the ideal way to talk to leaders about how to *create* conditions for a great leadership team. Rather, we saw that there were natural interdependencies among conceptually distinct factors in team design that needed to be addressed together in implementation. For example, while clear team purposes are conceptually distinct from having a team that is a bounded and stable entity, in reality a CEO tackling one issue (What is this

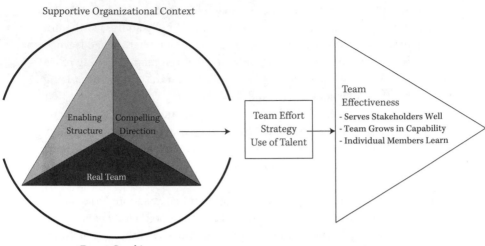

FIGURE 10.1 Conceptual Model of Influences on the Effectiveness of Leadership Teams

team for?) must simultaneously consider changing the team boundaries (Who *is* my leadership team? Do I have more than one?). As a consequence of our midpoint crisis, we developed a wholly new implementation model for leaders (see Fig. 10.2) that became the shape of the book—and the core of Hay Group's leadership teams practice.

The lesson from our midpoint crisis is straightforward but crucial: Choose a natural breakpoint in the work, and ask members of the collaboration to look explicitly at their task performance strategies and what is and is not working (Hackman & Wageman, 2005). A well-conducted review of the collaborative process sets the stage for creative breakthrough and for using well precisely those unique capabilities that brought the group together in the first place.

Lessons from the Use of Talent in Our Collaboration

Use of diverse abilities is the main aspiration of most consultant-scholar collaborations: to combine the distinctive capabilities and resources of both groups to produce knowledge that is both rigorous and usable. It was also the aspect of our process that was, I believe, our chief strength. What conditions contributed to our ability to use our respective talents well?

Enabler: Compose the collaboration for the optimum mix of members. To have an effective collaboration of any kind, the team has to be composed well

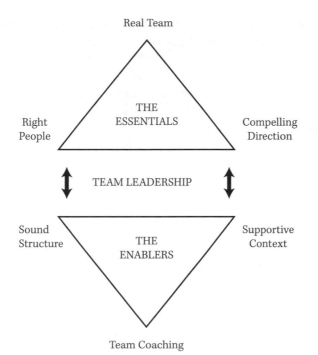

Real Team

THE
ESSENTIALS

Right
People

Compelling
Direction

TEAM LEADERSHIP

Sound
Structure

THE
ENABLERS

Supportive
Context

Team Coaching

FIGURE 10.2 Implementation Model for Creating Effective Leadership Teams

in the first place (Gruenfeld, 1998). When I teach about optimum levels of diversity, I typically borrow Richard's heuristic of "neither so alike that all are peas from the same pod," nor "so different that they cannot speak the same language" (Bowers, Pharmer, & Salas, 2000). For scholar-consultant collaboration, the larger risk is that the team will err on the side of too *heterogeneous*, with obvious fracture lines between the two groups (Chatman & Flynn, 2001; Lau & Murnighan, 2005).

Our team composition helped us to avoid the fracture line problem of diversity. We had a mix of clinical wisdom and conceptual skills on *both* sides—resulting in an overlap in capabilities between the two groups, even while we each also had some specialized abilities. That is, we had two scholars with some consultant-like characteristics and three consultants with researcher-like characteristics. Richard and I both have done our research primarily in the field, habitually studying research questions with obvious practical implications and using direct observation as a key part of our typical methodology (and sometimes a fair bit of intervention as well). At the same time, the consultants in the team all either had conducted research themselves or had a long history of using rigorous research directly in their practice.

As a consequence, this collaboration started with a high platform for recognizing and valuing the special expertise members could bring to bear on the work. When we convened again long after the book was written, it was easy for each of us to identify surprises or major changes in our thinking that occurred as a consequence of working across academic-consultant lines. For example, Jim underscored how his practice had changed from intervening directly in conflicts in leadership teams to addressing first the inevitable lack of clarity in the purposes of such teams—an important conceptual breakthrough for him. I learned to interpret and understand the problems that chief executives articulate from working with Deb and her vivid examples throughout our collaboration.

I do not believe that this enabler is unrealistic. I have reflected on the better and worse experiences I have had over the years in conducting field research. In all the most positive experiences, I had found (mostly unintentionally) a collaborator inside the organization who had a PhD in organizational behavior or a related field and who had sustained an interest in research. Indeed, many consulting firms have internal research groups that can support the building of relationships between the firm and academic collaborators. Such people are not, I find, all that rare. I hope what they find in me is a scholar who has a genuine interest in understanding how people experience the phenomena I study and who is open to co-defining the research questions we study together.

Purposes

My analysis has been about consultant-academic collaborations with which I am personally familiar, for the sake of having the observational data that would allow me to harvest lessons from experience. Let me close with some observations about a more general question from others I have observed at a greater distance. Are there particular purposes and methods for which academic-consultant collaborations are especially well suited and—just as important—*not* well suited?

Danger Zones

Some collaborative purposes can inadvertently create conflicts and tensions in the relationship between academics and consultants. I will not assert that these conflicts are insurmountable, but given the natural difficulties of such collaborations for even well-crafted purposes, I would at least urge caution in undertaking them. The two main categories of purposes that strike me as fraught with problems are (1) developing a new instrument (such as measure of individual, group, or organizational phenomena), and (2) assessing the effectiveness of consulting practice.

Developing an instrument. Intellectual property issues in this kind of collaboration will likely become divisive, unless the academics in the collaboration are willing to participate in the development of an instrument that will then become unavailable for their own use. Typically, the aims of academics include the publication of the psychometric properties of the instrument in peer-reviewed journals and the promotion of its use in research. And researchers want to be free to use our own methods and ideas without constraint.

Consulting firms, by contrast, seek a sustainable competitive advantage from protected intellectual property. If a diagnostic instrument can be readily imitated and sold by others, it is not a sustainable advantage (Reed & Defillippi, 1990). Any instrument that is published in an academic journal, with information about how to use it, will be adopted and sold by other consultants, so long as it taps something marketable to clients. It is in the best interests of a consulting firm to keep an instrument from being published and to hold the copyright so that it can be sold exclusively by its makers.

The concerns of both parties are very real. Small and independent consultants who have no R&D function, in particular, are hungry for new things to sell and will adopt anything in the public domain if it looks useful. Academic scholars have lost the legal right to use their own methodologies when they were copyrighted and sold by consultants.

In our own collaboration, we did refine and test the final version of the Team Diagnostic Survey, and it is published in a peer-reviewed journal—but its use in the practice is not a main source of competitive advantage for Hay Group, about which I will say more in a following section.

Assessment of effectiveness of existing practice. I hear frequent requests from consultants and clients for more evaluation of the impact of consulting practices. Usually, that takes a form such as: We need to prove that our consulting work improves firm profitability; can you academics help? Leaving aside the whole array of methodological and conceptual reasons why that kind of research is largely impossible, I want to underscore the inherent conflict between academics and consultants about what would be interesting findings from an evaluation study. For an academic, finding that a popular intervention or consulting approach does *not* produce any significant change in effectiveness is potential fodder for an interesting paper and an opportunity to explode some myths. For the consultant, such an outcome risks the destruction of precious intangible assets, such as reputation with clients, as well as of a tangible asset, a core consulting methodology. Positive evidence is a problem for neither, but it may not make for a particularly compelling research article unless the underlying *theory* of the practice is genuinely novel.

I do not mean to imply that consulting interventions should be excused from rigorous assessment. But practice evaluation is not a good basis for academic-consultant collaboration, except, perhaps, where consultants themselves, seeking rigorous assessment designs, turn to academics for advice about their own attempts to test and refine their intervention practices.

Sweet Spots

There are two lessons I have gained from my observations about purposes for which academic-consultant collaboration may be especially fruitful.

Developing a research instrument that supports the practice—and produces a growing database for future research. Joint development of measurement methodologies can be a source of ongoing collaboration between academics and consultants, when the continuing use of the instrument is *not* a main source of income for consultants. In the course of our research, for example, Richard and I refined and finished the published version of the TDS, but we continue to hold the copyright as we want it available to researchers and educators.

This arrangement was possible because the principle source of sustainable competitive advantage for the consultants is the intervention *practices* built around the research findings, and not the diagnostic instrument itself. Those practices are not readily imitable by novices but are highly dependent on rich experience and high-level capability.

Our consultant colleagues continue to use the TDS with top teams as a diagnostic instrument for assessing the design and leadership of such teams. As a consequence of this arrangement, there are two continuously growing databases—one of top teams held by Hay Group and one of a broad array of different types of teams held by the academics—that can provide the basis for future research collaborations.

Exploring an important problem that takes one into new theoretical and practice territory. Richard Walton articulated this idea 25 years ago when he called for identifying questions with "dual relevance" (Walton, 1985). An appropriate research question for consultant-academic collaborations is one that addresses both a *gap in theory* and an *undeveloped area of practice*. These kinds of questions can find a welcoming scholarly audience, thereby meeting the external requirements for the academics in the collaboration, and can also find a grateful client population, satisfying the consultants' constituencies.

Just as important is that those kinds of problems create the curiosity, puzzlement, frustration, passion, annoyance, and determination that keep both consultants and academics invested in making the project work. When the consultants are personally bothered by a dysfunction they observe and are looking for insight about how they can help, *and* when the academics are puzzled by an inexplicable pattern and are looking for insight about how to understand it, they will exercise the influence it takes to get the resources and the protected space needed for the collaboration. They will invest in improving their own team as a performing unit and manage the conflicts in work rhythms and incentives that might otherwise get in the way of successfully working across the consultant-academic divide.

REFERENCES

Bolster, C. J., & Wageman, R. (2009, February). Compensation committees and senior leadership teams. *Trustee*.

Bowers, C. A., Pharmer, J. A., & Salas, E. (2000). When member homogeneity is needed in work teams: A meta-analysis. *Small Group Research, 31,* 305–327.

Chatman, J. A., & Flynn, F. J. (2001). The influence of demographic heterogeneity on the emergence and consequences of cooperative norms in work teams. *Academy of Management Journal, 44,* 956–974.

Gersick, C. J. G. (1988). Time and transition in work teams: Toward a new model of group development. *Academy of Management Journal, 31,* 9–41.

Gruenfeld, D. H. (Ed.). (1998). *Research on managing groups and teams: Composition.* Stamford, CT: JAI Press.

Gutierrez, B., Spencer, S. M., & Zhu, G. (2009). Thinking globally, leading locally: Chinese, Indian, and Western leadership. Manuscript submitted for publication.

Hackman, J. R. (2002). *Leading teams: Setting the stage for great performances.* Boston: Harvard Business School Press.

Hackman, J. R., & Morris, C. G. (1975). Group tasks, group interaction process, and group performance effectiveness: A review and proposed integration. In L. Berkowitz (Ed.), *Advances in experimental social psychology* (vol. 8, pp. 45–99). New York: Academic Press.

Hackman, J. R., & Wageman, R. (2005). A theory of team coaching. *Academy of Management Review, 30,* 269–287.

Hackman, J. R., & Wageman, R. (2008). Working at the intersection: Insights from an academic-consultant collaboration about senior leadership teams. Workshop presented at the annual meeting of the American Psychological Association, Boston.

Hambrick, D. C. (2000). Fragmentation and other problems CEOs have with their top management teams. *California Management Review, 37,* 110–131.

Hambrick, D. C., & D'Aveni, R. A. (1996). Top team deterioration as part of the downward spiral of large corporate bankruptcies. *Management Science, 38,* 1445–1466.

Hambrick, D. C., & Mason, P. A. (1984). Upper echelons: The organization as a reflection of its top managers. *Academy of Management Review, 9,* 193–206.

Katzenbach. J. R. (1997a, November–December). The myth of the top management team. *Harvard Business Review,* 82–91.

Katzenbach, J. R. (1997b). *Teams at the top: Unleashing the potential of both teams and individual leaders.* Boston: Harvard Business School Press.

Lau, D. C., & Murnighan, D. K. (2005). Interactions within groups and subgroups: The effects of demographic faultlines. *Academy of Management Journal, 48,* 648–659.

McClelland, D. (1985). How motives, skills, and values determine what people do. *American Psychologist, 40,* 812–825.

Nunes, D. A., & Wageman, R. (2007, December). *What every CEO wants to know: Six conditions to create an effective top team.* White Paper Series. Washington, DC: Human Capital Institute.

Reed, R., & Defillippi, R. J. (1990). Causal ambiguity, barriers to imitation, and sustainable competitive advantage. *Academy of Management Review, 15,* 88–102.

Schultheiss, O. C., Campbell, K. L., & McClelland, D. C. (1999). Implicit power motivation moderates men's testosterone responses to imagined and real dominance success hormones and behavior. *Hormones and Behavior, 36,* 234–241.

Spencer, L. M., & Spencer, S. M. (1993). *Competence at work: Models for superior performance.* New York: Wiley.

Steiner, I. D. (1972). *Group process and productivity.* New York: Academic Press.

Wageman, R., & Hackman, J. R. (2010). What makes teams of leaders leadable? In N. Nohria & R. Khurana (Eds.), *Advancing leadership.* Boston: Harvard Business School Press.

Wageman, R., Hackman, J. R., & Lehman, E. V. (2005). The Team Diagnostic Survey: Development of an instrument. *Journal of Applied Behavioral Science, 41,* 373–398.

Wageman, R., Nunes, D. A., Burruss, J. A., & Hackman, J. R. (2008a). *Senior leadership teams: What it takes to make them great.* Boston: Harvard Business School Press.

Wageman, R., Nunes, D. A. , Burruss, J. A., & Hackman, J. R. (2008b, January). Behind the seniors: How you can help a CEO get the top team on a path to excellence. *People Management,* 38–40.

Wageman, R., Wilcox, I., & Gurin, M. (2008, October). The demise of the heroic CEO and the rise of senior leadership teams. *Pharmaceutical Commerce.*

Walton, R. E. (1985). Strategies with dual relevance. In E. E. Lawler III, A. M. Mohrman, S. A. Mohrman, G. E. Ledford, & T. G. Cummings (Eds.), *Doing research that is useful for theory and practice* (pp. 176–203). San Francisco: Jossey-Bass.

Wolff, S. B., Callahan, A., & Spencer, S. M. (2009). The coming leadership gap: Leadership challenges affected by the predicted competency shortage. Paper presented at the annual meeting of the Academy of Management, Chicago.

Wolff, S. B., Fontaine, M., & Wageman, R. (2009). The coming leadership gap: An exploration of competencies that will be in short supply. *International Journal of Human Resources Management, 9,* 250–274.

Wolff, S. B., Zhu, G., Hall, D. T., & Meras, M. (2008). Impact of career complexity on adaptability: A longitudinal study of senior executives. Paper presented at the annual meeting of the Academy of Management, Anaheim. Manuscript submitted for publication.

ABOUT THE AUTHOR

Ruth Wageman is Director of Research for Hay Group and Visiting Scholar in the Department of Psychology at Harvard University. Professor Wageman received her PhD from Harvard in 1993; she received her bachelor's degree in Psychology from Columbia University in 1987, and returned there to join the faculty of the Graduate School of Business, making her the first female alum of Columbia College to join Columbia's faculty. She also has been a member of the faculty of the Tuck School of Business at Dartmouth. Her research, teaching, and consulting interests include the design of effective leadership teams, the theory and practice of leadership development, and the effectiveness of self-organizing teams with civic and political purposes.

ELEVEN

Integrating Theory to Inform Practice

Insights from the Practitioner-Scholar *

RAMKRISHNAN (RAM) V. TENKASI

TRADITIONALLY, THE CHALLENGE of connecting academic theory and research to practice was seen as the exclusive responsibility of the research-scholar. Academics were asked to devise clever ways to make such bridging possible through the contextualization of their research results so that it has enhanced meaning for practitioners (Tenkasi, Mohrman, & Mohrman, 2007); to write in a compelling and interesting style that captures the minds, hearts, and consciences of practitioners (Bartunek, Rynes, & Ireland, 2006; Green, 2004; Van De Ven & Schomaker, 2002); and to contribute to an evidence-based management infrastructure that builds evidence-based practice capabilities among managers (Rousseau, 2006).

Recent decades have seen several intermediates emerge between the world of research knowledge and its application. These intermediates have changed society's perception of the research-scholar, who has gone from the primary or sole agent responsible for translating and applying scholarly knowledge to one of several agents involved in the process. Several intermediate bundlers and co-producers of knowledge, including practitioner-scholars, consulting firms, and professional groups, now serve as alternative pathways for translating and integrating scholarly knowledge to practice (see Chapter 1, Research for Theory and Practice). The focus of this chapter is one such intermediate agent—the practitioner-scholar—and how he or she applies theory and research knowledge to practice in order to produce outcomes for an organization and, in this process, at times advances scientific knowledge.

The PhD program in organization development and change at Benedictine University is one of several executive doctoral programs (alongside programs

---

* This chapter builds on earlier work by Tenkasi and Hay (2004, 2008) and Hay, Woodman, and Tenkasi (2008).

at Case Western Reserve, Pepperdine, and George Washington universities) that teaches working professionals how to be practitioner-scholars. As a core faculty member with Benedictine's PhD program over the past ten years, I have been able to observe and follow select graduates as they resume their work as full-time employees. I have seen how they use their theoretical and research knowledge to address issues of organizational change and resolve other business problems.

Drawing on these observations, this chapter focuses on five questions concerning practitioner-scholars as intermediate agents and alternative pathways in the research-to-practice translation value chain (Chapter 12, Organization Development Scholar-Practitioners). The questions are: (1) Who are practitioner-scholars? (2) How do practitioner-scholars translate and apply theoretical and research knowledge to resolve organizational problems? (3) How effective is the practitioner-scholar as an intermediate agent in translating and applying such knowledge? (4) How viable are practitioner-scholars in partnering with academics to conduct research that can reinform theory? and (5) What insights can traditional academics who want to shape organizational practice gain from practitioner-scholars as alternative pathways in the translation value chain?

Who Are Practitioner-Scholars?

Practitioner-scholars are actors who have received traditional academic training and who apply their knowledge of theory and research to an organization's particular challenges to resolve business problems. Unlike traditional academics, practitioner-scholars are full-time organizational employees and thus are primarily committed to practical concerns and advancing organizational causes. Only as a secondary consequence do they feel responsible for advancing a theoretical and empirical understanding of the phenomenon of concern (Tenkasi & Hay, 2004, 2008). Astley and Zammuto (1993) label practitioner-scholars as an intermediate cadre of professionals who, by virtue of belonging to both the practice and academic communities, can effectively bridge the incommensurate worlds of scholars and practitioners. Huff and Huff (2001) label practitioner-scholars intermediate boundary spanners who have one foot in the world of practice and the other in the world of theory and research.

The Mode 2 knowledge producer, as described by Gibbons and Nowotny (Gibbons et al., 1994; Nowotny, Scott, & Gibbons, 2001, 2005), is a prototype of the practitioner-scholar who combines theoretical knowledge with applied practice knowledge to solve particular organizational problems. As opposed to Mode 1 knowledge producers who seek to find generalizable laws across contexts in a nonengaged, basic scholarship way (Gibbons et al., 1994; Van De Ven, 2007; Van De Ven & Johnson, 2006), Mode 2 knowledge producers are closely tied to applied contexts. They are charged with achieving concrete results by creating actionable knowledge that can advance organizational causes. Their point of contact is closer to practice and involves investigating problems of high interest and practical import that sometimes cut across disciplines (Van De Ven, 2007; see also Chapter 1, Research for Theory and Practice, this book).

In Mode 2 knowledge environments, theoretical knowledge is tested not in the abstract but rather under concrete, local circumstances. This approach is to ensure that the theoretical knowledge is socially robust and produces consequential outcomes. The Mode 2 knowledge producer's primary concern is solving problems, as that is what their organizations reward them for (Tinnish & O'Neal, 2010; Wasserman & Kram, 2009). They produce generalizable knowledge only as a by-product. Examples of Mode 2 knowledge producers are traditionally trained PhDs in the life sciences who work for pharmaceutical firms to develop drugs. Their main interest is producing effective drugs to combat the disease area they work in; their secondary interest is contributing to the body of literature on scientific theories on their particular concerns. In the context of organizational sciences, graduates of executive doctoral programs who continue working in organizations post-education are an example of these intermediate cadre of "boundary spanners" who can close the "relevance gap from both ends of business and science" (Huff & Huff, 2001, p. 50). Practitioner-scholars can also be classified as a subtype of the "engaged scholar," as defined by Professor Van De Ven (Van De Ven, 2007; Van De Ven & Johnson, 2006). They can simultaneously play the role of the detached outsider and the attached insider (Evered & Louis, 1981; Mahoney & McGahan, 2007). Knowing outside research can provide evidence of the persuasiveness and boundary conditions of the problem, whereas knowing the inside situation and its contingencies can concretely ground the research in a particular situation (Mahoney & Sanchez, 2004).

The idea of the practitioner-scholar as an important intermediate agent between the scholar and practitioner—one with both outside and inside knowledge—goes back to Aristotle. The second century (BC) Greek philosopher initially taught the need to separate theory and practice and treated the spheres of scientific knowledge and those of experience and craft as separate, distinct domains (Aristotle, 1962). This divide became the primary assumption underlying Western scientific thought (Chalmers, 1999; Parry, 2003). But in later writings, Aristotle suggested that only by combining theory and practice can people solve consequential problems of science and society (Aristotle, 1961; Tenkasi & Hay, 2008). He labeled the combined knowledge of theory and practice *phronesis*, or practical wisdom (Dunne, 1993; Peters,

1967, p. 157). The person who is able to combine and apply such knowledge is the *technites*, or master craftsperson.

The scholar *(lógios)* appeals to scientific knowledge. Her strength is finding generalizable principles and explanatory reasons underlying a situation by invoking the larger scientific discourse of cause and effect *(episteme theoretike)* drawn from multiple contexts. However, the *lógios* lacks specific knowledge about and experience in particular contexts. In contrast, the practitioner *(cheirotechne)* derives her knowledge from experience *(empeiria)* with the specifics of a situation. She has the craft *(techne)* of getting things done in her context. But she does not know the general principles of cause and effect that underlie the situation, and engages in local activities as mostly unreflective, habitual forms of practice (Bourdieu; 1977; Bunge, 2004; Schon, 1995).

To truly change situations, such as helping a patient afflicted with disease, one needs both kinds of knowledge, concluded Aristotle—such as a physician who understands both the general principles of medicine and also the particulars of the patient's situation. This combined knowledge, or *phronesis*, mirrors the integrated knowledge and pluralism suggested by contemporary scholars (Pettigrew, 2001; Van De Ven, 2007; Van De Ven & Johnson, 2006). This integration is required to yield the kind of actionable knowledge that can address complex and wicked problems.

Applying Theoretical and Research Knowledge to Resolve Organizational Problems?

We see that the practitioner-scholar's intermediate role has both historical and contemporary precedent in Aristotle's concept of *phronesis* (1961) and Van De Ven's (2007) notion of engaged scholarship. But less is known about the specific ways in which the Mode 2 knowledge producer *(technites)* successfully integrates knowledge of the general with the particulars of an organizational context in order to inform practice. To understand this integration, we turn to an inductive qualitative study reported in detail in earlier publications (Hay, Woodman, & Tenkasi, 2008; Tenkasi & Hay, 2004, 2008). The study sought to understand not only the theory and practice the practitioner-scholar brings to the table, but also how he or she goes about linking theory to practice in organizational projects.

The 11 practitioner-scholars surveyed were graduates of Benedictine University's executive PhD program in organization development and change, the program I have worked with as a core faculty member since 1998. Typical Benedictine students are in senior-level positions as skilled practitioners who want to bring meaningful change to their organizations. They come from diverse industries and positions: presidents and chief officers of large and small firms in technology, finance, nonprofits, and so on; vice presidents who manage human resources and organizational effectiveness; doctors who lead medical departments and hospital systems; and consultants with major and minor consulting firms. Their common interest (beyond the status and career advancement that a PhD brings) is, in most cases, to gain theoretical and research knowledge in order to improve their organizations or client systems.

Interviews were completed with 11 practitioner-scholars, whom I knew well as the chair or active member of their respective dissertation committees. I had continual contact with them as they pursued additional projects related to their dissertations or postdoctoral projects unrelated to their dissertations. The practitioner-scholars represented a purposive sample and were asked to recount organizational projects in which they had applied their theory and research knowledge to achieve business outcomes. Typical outcomes were customized business models and new techniques or processes that were implemented as a result of the project. Theoretical outcomes were mostly academic presentations, conference proceedings, and in a few cases, journal publications and books written independently by the practitioner-scholar or co-authored with a PhD program faculty member.

The 11 cases were analyzed using an iterative approach of going back and forth between the data and the emerging theory to develop a model (Eisenhardt, 1989; Elsbach & Sutton, 1992; Silverman, 2001; Yin, 1994). Six contrast interviews completed as part of an earlier project were also enfolded in the systematic case analysis (Tenkasi & Hay, 2004). Four of the interviewees were business researchers with no scholarly affiliation, and two were academics who had little experience in organizations but who had engaged in organization-based projects. The analysis broadly revealed that practitioner-scholars use both their theory and research knowledge and their familiarity with local cultural conventions to approach organizational projects. They combined their formal knowledge of theory and research principles from articles, books, and expert opinion with local knowledge of the organization's power relationships and cultural norms to manage and move projects forward (Tenkasi & Hay, 2004).

Of more pertinence to this chapter, however, were the subjects' strategies for integrating theory and research knowledge to produce outcomes while achieving academic results. To illustrate these dynamics, I will rely on two of the 11 cases that best illustrate the dynamics of theory-to-practice integration. The first case involves creating self-managing teams at a cable production firm to achieve manufacturing excellence. The second case involves improving the effectiveness of the research and development function at a high-tech firm. Practitioner-scholars tended to use theory and research to inform practice in four key ways. Their chosen way depended on whether their respective projects were in the definition and planning stage, the implementation stage, or the realization/closure stage of the project life cycle (Pinto & Prescott, 1988).

Three key and interdependent dynamics compose the project definition and planning stage: framing the problem, conjecturing an appropriate pathway to resolve the problem, and influencing and legitimizing the pathway as the right course of action. Two key dynamics compose the implementation stage: activating the conjectured pathway and making sense of the pathway. Demonstrating the impact of the conjectured pathway was most commonly associated with the project realization/completion stage. The practitioner-scholars also used two metastrategies—turns and scaffolding— to inconspicuously embed theory and research into the background of the organizational projects across all stages.

Project Definition and Planning Stage

Framing the problem. The practitioner-scholars frequently used theory and research findings to frame and give direction to a broadly expressed change mandate from the organization's leadership looking for the resolution to a perceived organizational crisis or the realization of a desired future state. They typically used framing to structure an otherwise equivocal phenomenon in more concrete, precise terms (Weick, 1979). In interviews with the practitioner-scholars, it was clear that CEOs and other top-management members expressed the desire for a future state and sometimes mandated a resolution to an organizational crisis, but not with clear specifics. It is frequently at this point when the practitioner-scholar steps in, using her theory and research knowledge to analyze the situation and frame and define the problem in more precise terms (Van De Ven, 2007).

One practitioner-scholar took the CEO's vision to make his manufacturing plant a center of excellence by defining the program as one of bolstering the aging workforce's effectiveness and productivity through principles of motivation and employee involvement (Lawler, 1986). In a second case, the practitioner-scholar framed the CEO's mandate to make the research and development organization more effective as better systems and processes for knowledge management.

Conjecturing the appropriate pathway to resolve the problem. After top management accepted the practitioner-scholars' framing as an appropriate problem definition (Van De Ven, 2007), the practitioner-scholars used their theory and research findings to conjecture a pathway (Bunge, 2004) most suitable for resolving the problem in light of the local contingencies. In the first case of the CEO's mandate for the manufacturing plant to become a center of excellence, the practitioner-scholar could have addressed the issue using various mechanisms, including better manufacturing processes or materials management, both scientifically validated pathways to achieve manufacturing excellence (*Best manufacturing practices report*, 1998). But the practitioner-scholar saw that the real issue was motivating an aging workforce and enhancing their effectiveness through principles of employee involvement. She thus chose self-managing teams as the best mechanism to involve employees and increase their productivity.

She made this choice based on several local considerations. First, the older workforce had high levels of camaraderie and a collective identity as a group distinct from their supervisors. The practitioner-scholar saw that the best way to heighten awareness of quality, cost, and schedule was to let the employees take ownership of these issues through self-governing teams instead of relying on supervisory mandates, which had been ineffective in the past. Second, the practitioner-scholar chose the team-based design to allow for multiskilling and job rotation, which would give team members variety and challenge in an otherwise routine environment. Pathways such as technological enhancements to the old assembly-line format or better material management techniques would not have alleviated employee boredom or solved quality problems because these pathways didn't take into account the company's specific social dynamics.

This dynamic was also evident in the case of the second practitioner-scholar, who framed the problem of enhancing R&D effectiveness as one of better systems and processes for knowledge management. After reviewing several models for knowledge management, she found that the sociotechnical systems (STS) approach was most suitable. STS addressed the interface of knowledge elements pertaining to the social, technical, and environmental systems, and also engaged the workforce in designing such a system—a wise strategy given the CEO's desire to involve a large swath of the R&D function in the change. The practitioner-scholar skillfully matched the CEO's practical requirement of broad employee engagement with a theoretical model that allowed for the same. Asking managers from several R&D functions to join the central design team was attributed to the CEO's mandate, although it was also clearly required by the STS approach.

Influencing and legitimizing the chosen pathway. Conjecturing the pathway and considering why one mechanism works better than others also helps to legitimize the pathway because it is based on both theoretical and practical considerations. Influencing and legitimizing frequently involved distributing articles and books from practitioner sources that carry legitimacy in the business world, such as the *Harvard Business Review* or *Sloan*

Management Review, and readable article summaries from academic sources such as the *Academy of Management Journal* and *Organization Science*, condensed by the practitioner-scholar. Occasionally, the practitioner-scholar also brought in experts, including practitioners with hands-on experience in implementing the conjectured pathway in similar environments and scholars who had written practical books or articles on the topic. Sometimes the experts were hired as consultants to guide the project, but in most cases we observed, they came in as additional sources to influence and legitimize the chosen pathway and acceptance of it among concerned stakeholders.

Project Implementation Stage

Activating the conjectured pathway. Once the causal pathway or preferred strategy for change was established and accepted by relevant stakeholders, the fourth function of theory and research in informing practice was in activating the conjectured pathway. To activate the project, the practitioner-scholar often used the theoretical, research, and practice literature, including expert opinion on the chosen platform (whether self-managing teams or nonroutine STS), as guiding frameworks. This approach frequently meant creating training programs for the community to enact the details of the chosen pathway for change that preceded implementing the intervention. Often practitioner-scholars also used training programs as preassessment forums, using survey instrumentation, qualitative interviews, or in several cases, both, to create baseline information before enacting the change.

Making sense of the activated pathway. Practitioner-scholars used surveys, interviews, systematic observations, and in one case, personal diary recordings to monitor and assess the pathway's ongoing progress. Sometimes the practitioner-scholars used the same instruments as during the preintervention stage. In other cases, they created new surveys and interview questions based on the ongoing assessment of the activated pathway's implementation. For example, the self-managing team project used a constant comparison qualitative design. The practitioner-scholar compared the evolution of six self-managing work groups as they transitioned into effective self-managing teams at different speeds over a six-month period. Her use of triangulated methods (Jick, 1979) over six time periods included surveys, interviews, and analyzing the team members' diary entries. These methods helped her develop new insights and create questions that aided her in the ongoing assessment process. They also enabled her to design appropriate interventions for the lagging teams to catch up.

Likewise, for the STS knowledge management project, the practitioner-scholar used systematic research methods such as surveys and interviews to assess whether the quality of internal deliberations—an intervention created within the teams—helped them meet monthly goals in cost, quality, and schedule over one year. In this case, she used the systematic research methods to test a hypothesis instead of finding evolutionary insights, as with the self-managing teams. Whether hypothesis-driven or based on evolutionary insights, the practitioner-scholars' hallmark was using systematic research methods to gauge the efficacy of the conjectured pathway. Practitioner-scholars on the whole engaged in fact-based decision making (Pfeffer & Sutton, 2006), paying attention to the data rather than getting trapped by ideologies, beliefs, or conventional wisdom.

Project Realization/Closure Stage

Demonstrating impact of the chosen pathway in achieving the change. Finally, the practitioner-scholars applied research knowledge to demonstrate impact. Applying systematic research methods to activate and make ongoing sense of the conjectured pathway also helped demonstrate that the organizational project successfully achieved practical results, whether that meant changing mindsets, behavior, or other hard metrics. A selection bias is clearly at work in the successful projects we chose to study. Nonetheless, for these projects, demonstrating business impact required collecting and analyzing data using systematic research designs in the project execution phase. Practitioner-scholars frequently used quantitative evidence to indicate behavior and attitude change before and after the implementation of the program. They also used quantitative evidence to show shifts in hard performance measures before and after change. Likewise, the practitioner-scholars used qualitative data, particularly context-sensitive quotes or verbatim comments, to show changes in perspective or behavior. For example, the practitioner-scholar who set up self-managing teams used many quotes from team members to demonstrate that they were engaged in the kinds of behaviors involved in team self-management.

Turns: A Meta-Strategy for Relating Theory to Practice

In most cases, what was most salient and needed attention in the minds of management was the business problem. Our interviews with practitioner-scholars suggest that consulting is seen as adding value to the organization's business problem, whereas research is seen as an abstract act that is not practically relevant. For many practitioner-scholars, *research* was a term they preferred not to use but rather to integrate into the process. As one aptly summarized,

My CEO wants us to become a center of manufacturing excellence.... I have convinced him that the best way to achieve it is to create self-managing teams. He wants them to happen, and if I tell him I want to conduct a research project on testing a theory of self-managing team effectiveness, I will probably be out of the door tomorrow. We don't have the luxury of presenting a research proposal but have to build research principles into the way we consult. But if I do write a few articles from this project, he is okay with it as long as I show practical results. That is what is most important to him. If I gain research knowledge that is fine, as long as it does not come in the way of organizational needs.

Turns are reframing moves and tools that help make an element more familiar, legitimate, and palatable to the concerned audience. To do so, turns locate the element in a community's "systems of meaning" (Fleck, 1979). In our observation, successful practitioner-scholars used theory-to-practice turns to make the unfamiliar familiar to the practitioner community during all stages of the project. We found several instances of theory- and research-to-practice turns that helped a community accept theoretically informed and research-based activities. Self-evident examples of theory-to-practice turns include (1) turning knowledge of current literature into information from best practices in the industry and other organizations; (2) turning representative sampling across level, function, and gender into a strategy for broader employee involvement; (3) turning action-research processes of implementation into learning from experience; and (4) turning principles of valid and reliable research (systematic data collection, comparative research designs, and rigorous analytical strategy) into foolproof strategies to assess bottom-line impact.

Practitioner-scholars used these turns to influence a business, not an academic, audience. Reframing for a business audience carries a more pragmatic goal: to present the academic import of the theoretical action in a way that is intelligible to the business audience, who will be motivated to construe and continue with the research for being practically relevant. Framing research activities in terms similar to familiar corporate activities exemplifies the underlying logic of practitioner-scholars who use turns to legitimate activities informed by theory and research principles. Translating in this way helps the organizational community to accept theory- and research-driven activities.

Scaffolding: A Meta-Strategy to Achieve Theoretical and Research Outcomes

In a few cases, practitioner-scholars used another, less common meta-strategy known as *scaffolding* across a project's life cycle. Commonly associated with construction, the word *scaffolding* typically means a "platform made for workers to stand on when they want to reach higher parts of a building to add on to or modify the structure of the building" (*Cambridge Dictionary*, 2003). For practitioner-scholars, scaffolding means carefully selecting a theory-based platform that helps frame the problem at hand, guides practice, and has the potential to realize subsequent theoretical and empirical outcomes by seeking to answer new research questions. For example, the practitioner-scholar who framed the CEO's vision to make the manufacturing plant a center of excellence used scaffolding in reorganizing the workforce into self-managing teams. She used the theory-based platform of self-managing teams to direct action and conduct systematic research on the gap she identified in the teams' research literature; that is, What is the evolutionary pathway in becoming a self-managing team? Why can some teams but not others successfully transition into self-management? Why are some faster at it?

The practitioner-scholar who applied principles of STS theory to knowledge work in the R&D organization also used scaffolding. Her platform held practical ramifications to guide the process and also theoretical ramifications potentially to chart new territory for sociotechnical theory. It assessed how an R&D project team's deliberations affect the team's success as well as knowledge transfer and assimilation processes in and between multidisciplinary teams. In doing so, she was able to extend STS's application from routine to nonroutine work.

One of the practitioner-scholars' defining qualities was reflecting on appropriate causal mechanisms in ways that accounted for both the general and the local. This ability enabled them to produce outcomes for the organization and to add to the larger body of knowledge. Considering both the general and the local distinguished practitioner-scholars from practitioners, who often mimic the latest technique or fad and apply it indiscriminately to their local environment without fully grasping the underlying theory or conducting research to direct their efforts. The practitioner-scholar's approach also differed from the scholar's approach. The scholar applies her theoretical understanding of organizations and conducts research on an abstract problem without fully considering local dynamics or how useful the findings may be for improving the organization's causes (Tenkasi & Hay, 2004, 2008).

Effectiveness of the Practitioner-Scholar As an Alternative Pathway in the Research-to-Practice Translation Value Chain?

Practitioner-scholars, post-PhD, clearly appreciate using scholarship and the principles of systematic research design for approaching organizational problems. Frequently they use academic research to frame problems and to conjecture appropriate pathways to resolve them. The practitioner-scholar applies both theoretical and research knowledge to activate the pathway and to make sense of its progress, as well as to demonstrate the conjectured pathway's impact. In this sense, the practitioner-scholar is a sound theory and research-to-practice translator, and an effective intermediate agent. Their research- and theory-driven practical projects sometimes lead to policy and practical changes in their concerned organizations.

But by using Van De Ven's (2007) different levels of engaged research—namely, informed basic research, collaborative basic research, design and evaluation research, and action/intervention research—my sense is that most practitioner-scholar organizational projects lean toward the latter half of the continuum: design and evaluation research, and action/intervention research. In Thomas Kuhn's (1970) terms, most practitioner-scholars' organizational projects fit the description of incremental research set within established paradigms, which furthers the paradigm one step at a time. In other words, most of these projects apply recognized bodies of thought to solve the problem at hand. That is, the extant literature and research instruments could be applied to self-managing teams, nonroutine STS, transformational leadership, mergers and acquisitions, or joint ventures and alliances.

This approach is important in the research-to-practice value chain and an appropriate step for the practitioner-scholar. However, organizations have often been sources of paradigm-breaking administrative innovations that reconfigure practice and become the focus of much academic research. The research community then strives to find and formulate theory for innovations such as matrix structures, strategic business units, cross-functional teams, total quality management, six sigma, communities of practice, and other organizational innovations. It is hoped that the practitioner-scholar can also help create and document such paradigm-breaking innovations, bringing back to the academic domain her insights on new organizational arrangements. This sharing of new knowledge with the academic community, I believe, can be the practitioner-scholar's next evolutionary step. Currently, however, most practitioner-scholars serve more to apply theoretical and research knowledge to their problem. This creates mid-range theories for their own use within their organizational contexts. Fewer practitioner-scholars are creating original knowledge and approaches that can inform the broader research and practice communities.

Creating theories about phenomena takes time and experience. Most practitioner-scholars are practical individuals with practical projects to complete. Benedictine's PhD program does offer an introductory philosophy of science course that offers a big-picture view of how research and knowledge production activities change over time, thus changing concepts and methods.

But I don't believe this is sufficient for helping practitioner-scholars consider the ontological and epistemological issues underlying knowledge-production activities. In a related vein, if the hallmark of a successful boundary spanner is his ability to disseminate lessons from theoretically informed practical organizational projects to reinform theory, then after graduating, most practitioner-scholars are less successful.

A recent survey by Benedictine doctoral students Tinnish and O'Neal (2010) examined the publishing activity of 110 practitioner-scholars from four executive doctoral programs in the United States. The results suggest that only about 30 percent had published since completing the doctoral program. A majority of the publications were conference papers and nonacademic publications. Among respondents, practitioner-scholars on academic career paths published more than practitioner-scholars who worked in organizations. The sample included 24 practitioner-scholars in academic positions and 86 practitioner-scholars working with organizations. The key barriers to publishing among those working with firms were little incentive from their current organization to publish, not enough time, unable to identify the right forums to publish in, and lacking confidence that their submissions would be accepted for publication after putting in the required time and energy.

The practitioner-scholar's primary role as a consumer and applier of extant theoretical and research knowledge touches on an important question impacting all the organizational sciences, particularly regarding its education and training objectives. Two questions of concern, as skillfully raised by O'Toole in Chapter 20, On the Verge of Extinction, are Should the field enrich itself by including the education of practitioner-scholars and that of basic research scholars? And should this be done in one program and institution or in different institutions and programs?

My belief is that the organizational sciences would benefit from training a cadre of practitioner-scholars alongside research scholars because both groups represent mutual synergies. Practitioner-scholars faithfully apply theoretical and research knowledge to solve organizational problems, whereas research scholars play the upstream role of producing the theoretical and research knowledge that gets applied.

Institutions such as Case Western Reserve University offer both traditional and executive PhD programs as parallel tracks. In the public health field, Johns Hopkins University pioneered the Doctor of Public Health (DrPH) degree for public-health practitioners several years ago alongside its traditional PhD in public health. Further, joint projects and common mentors foster interaction between research scholars and practitioner-scholars, serving as mutual learning forums for the two student groups. These examples demonstrate the viability of hosting two parallel streams in the same institution.

How Viable Are Practitioner-Scholars As Partners to Academics in Conducting Relevant Research?

When operating independently, practitioner-scholars are mainly appliers of extant theoretical and research knowledge. But when they partner with academics, they may be convinced to try out new concepts and approaches. Academic/practitioner-scholar partnerships can reinform theory, particularly if the new approaches make intuitive and practical sense for organizational projects.

In a change project that involved setting up enterprise resource planning (ERP) systems in a major engineering firm's global facilities, I convinced a practitioner-scholar, a key member of the design team, to analyze social networks to assess the strength of network ties among and between units in two facilities. We were testing the hypothesis that facilities with strong network ties between and within units will more readily accept and use a newly launched ERP system. At least in the available literature, no one had assessed internal social networks and the strength of internal network ties within and between change recipients to predict the success of a change. Our test on a pilot basis confirmed our hypothesis, and the results of our study were published in an academic journal (Tenkasi & Chesmore, 2003). The other facilities in the global organization that wished to implement the ERP system drew on our study to change their social networks.

Practitioner-scholars are comfortable with publishing their project work as long as they receive appropriate and insightful guidance from academic partners. In fact, in Tinnish and O'Neal's (2010) survey of practitioner-scholars, 78 percent of respondents expressed interest in publishing in the future from their current organizational research projects and 46 percent were actively trying to publish.

Working with practitioner-scholars, particularly those in line and senior executive positions, brings the benefit of gaining access to carefully collected internal firm data that are not readily available to outsiders. One practitioner-scholar, a senior director of technology strategy at a Fortune 500 high-tech firm, accessed internal firm records on 780 interorganizational relationships (joint ventures, partnerships, and alliances) over a ten-year period. He accessed information on whether the interorganizational relationship (IOR) was successful based on several organizational metrics (achieving internal and external expectations from the IOR in terms of financial measurements, length of time the relationship lasted, and stock price impact). He also tested the association of both partner characteristics (profile of the IOR partner–firm age maturity, firm financials, and so on) and the partnerships' dynamics (relationship secrecy, relationship formality, time to build the relationship,

relationship type, relationship strategic value, and so on) as independent variables garnered from the internal database. By systematically analyzing the firm's history, he found several key insights that led to major changes in the firm's IOR strategy, particularly regarding asymmetrical IORs and how to successfully work with smaller firm partners for interorganizational relationships. This practitioner-scholar is currently working on joint publications that provide a theory of strategic technology partnerships.

Another practitioner-scholar, the head of the Gastroenterology Department at a major medical hospital and university research center, offered to create an experiment for the hospital's CEO, who worried about the effectiveness of a new clinic that integrated traditional and alternative medicine. Patients at the integrative medicine clinic reported overall satisfaction with the physicians and therapeutic interventions, but their overall cure rate had not improved compared with patients at the traditional medicine clinic. The practitioner-scholar, a strong proponent of the knowledge-based theory of the firm (Grant, 1996; Nonaka, 1994), firmly believed in the efficacy of integrated knowledge over specialized disciplinary knowledge for solving medical problems. He was puzzled as to why the cure rates were much lower in the integrative clinic compared to the traditional clinic. With his investigative spirit and my suggestions as his mentor, he chose to focus on patients with one type of disease, those with a particular musculoskeletal disorder. This disorder was the most common condition among those who attended the integrative clinic. It also had several comparison cases in patients who went only to the traditional clinic.

The practitioner-scholar accessed the hospital's existing records on comorbid conditions of 600 patients—300 of whom attended the integrative medicine clinic, the other 300 of whom attended the traditional clinic. By accessing this data and conducting systematic quantitative and qualitative investigations, he proved that patients at the alternative clinic were much sicker when beginning treatment than the patients at the traditional clinic, which explained why those at the alternative clinic did not have higher cure rates. Based on his important analysis, the hospital decided to continue operating the integrative medicine clinic.

Overall, practitioner-scholars who hold line positions are better positioned to change things within the organization, much more so than industrial and organizational psychologists in staff positions. Although these staff members fill a useful consultative role, they do not have as much power or authority to move things within the organization as do executive PhD scholars, particularly those who occupy line roles and continue to do so after completing the program.

Insights for Academics Who Want to Influence Organizational Practice

Our experiences with practitioner-scholars suggest that they use theory and research knowledge to inform practice and produce outcomes of dual relevance. However, we also see that theory and research knowledge, a critical component and one of the scholar's strengths, is just one of a set of "know that" (knowing about something) and "know how" (knowing how to do something) (Ryle, 1949) in successfully impacting organizational practice. In connecting with organizations, the scholar brings certain kinds of "know that" (current literature, social science theory, principles of research design) and certain kinds of "know how" (designing research and data analysis). But he or she must understand the importance of merging this knowledge with the "know that" (contextual conventions, norms, rules, power relationships, routines, and established procedures) and "know how" (influencing, legitimizing, project management) specific to the organization.

Further, like the practitioner-scholar, the traditional academic must reframe her research ideas and methods in terms palatable to a practitioner audience. In particular, using devices like turns and scaffolding to translate academic and research elements for the practitioner audience is useful for this purpose. Likewise, when a scholar presents a research proposal on academic problems that he or she wants to investigate in a practical setting, the scholar must present the research question in a way that appropriately frames and defines the problem at hand and also shows how the investigative or intervention process is the suitable pathway for resolving the problem. Academics must also be able to demonstrate impact on intended outcomes. Firms are most interested in reaching practical outcomes; keeping this in mind would well serve the scholar who wants to impact organizations.

However, we believe that the best way for traditional scholars to impact organizations is to create a collaborative management research structure between the theoretically well-versed scholar and the theoretically aware, but also organizationally well-informed practitioner-scholar. The collaborative structure between scholar and practitioner-scholar is needed because applying theory and research knowledge to address organizational problems inevitably occurs in local practice contexts.

Further, it is crucial that collaborative research structures account for different sets of "know how" and "know that." We see at least four roles in collaborative research communities that invoke different sets of "know how" and "know that." First, we need a set of actors familiar with the *universals* (the larger scientific discourse pertaining to theory and research) who can articulate what is known and what needs to be known to advance knowledge from a theory and research vantage. The scholar can fill this role.

Second, actors are needed who are familiar with the *particulars* of the organization—local theories of action, organizational history, social dynamics, norms, and power relationships—that the practitioner-scholar is adept at. When these two sets of actors unite, collaborative research communities can find appropriate causal mechanisms that can move the system to its desired state, achieving practical outcomes while enhancing scientific theory.

Third, to put causal pathways into motion, we need actors with credibility, legitimacy, and influence in the organizational system, particularly among top management and other stakeholders. These actors have deep practical knowledge of how to move projects in the organization. The practitioner-scholar might be able to fill this role, depending on his or her place in the organization. Finally, we need actors who can adeptly translate theory regarding its practice implications and can frame practice contingencies in terms of their theoretical potentials that require both the scholar and practitioner-scholar.

Interrelating theory and research to practice can helpfully lead to mutual sense making. Practitioner-scholars frequently use theory to activate and make sense of practice. And when executing practical organizational projects, practitioner-scholars' evolving practice insights reenable them to make sense of the theory at hand. This important reciprocal dynamic leads to relevant outcomes for practice and theory.

To me the critical contribution of collaborative research systems is facilitating these dynamics. Further, I believe collaborative research communities should deliberately create sense-making forums to optimally assess and understand the interplay of theory and practice in projects to lead to dual outcomes. An example of one such structure comes from Mohrman, Gibson, and Mohrman (2001), who describe interpretive forums that bring together scholars and practitioners to mutually pursue useful research and practical outcomes. Set up as forums to aid mutual perspective taking (Boland & Tenkasi, 1995), they are meant to join members of the research and practice worlds to reflect and interpret information.

By letting varied interpretations and objectives surface, these forums allow their members to reflect on their and others' views of a situation, collectively reexamine, and come away with better interpretations that take into account each other's viewpoints. Such forums may include sessions to craft the research effort to ensure that an organization's practical concerns and academic research concerns are taken into account, sessions to jointly examine and interpret data patterns, and sessions in which members draw and discuss possible action implications of the research findings.

Depending on an organization's openness to research, such collaborative research communities can propose an overt negotiation process between scholars and practitioner-scholars. The negotiation process would aim to develop a shared agenda for investigating organizationally hot theoretical and practical issues (Adler & Shani, 2001). Some contexts may require the practitioner-scholar to educate key managers beforehand on systematic research's benefits in creating organizational outcomes (while advancing scientific outcomes) and on a collaborative structure's unique strengths in enabling these outcomes. In organizations not as receptive to research, practitioner-scholars might frame the collaborative enterprise mainly as a consulting project. After this, they can incorporate theory and research elements into the background in a way that complements the organization's practical needs (Werr & Greiner, 2008). One caveat: The organization should see the research by-products as legitimate, and the collaborative team should get appropriate permissions for publications from the data.

Conclusion

The growing number of executive PhD programs in the United States and worldwide, as well as the number of working professionals from diverse positions who are enrolling in these programs, show that practitioner-scholars play a key role in organizations today (Tinnish & O'Neal, 2010; Wasserman & Kram, 2009). At least some practitioner-scholars can play the role of the *technites*, carefully blending the traditions of theory and practice to address problems of scientific and social concern (Tenkasi & Hay, 2008). Their work can then be built upon in academic/practitioner-scholar collaboration. For at least the past 300 years, traditional science has carried on Aristotle's legacy of separating theory from experience and knowledge from action (Chalmers, 1999; Parry, 2003). But today's practitioner-scholars can live out Aristotle's second, lesser-known legacy, heralding a new era of integrating theory and practice.

REFERENCES

Adler, N., & Shani, R. (2001). In search of an alternative framework for the creation of actionable knowledge: Table-tennis research at Ericsson. In R. Woodman, W. Pasmore, and A. B. Shani (Eds.), *Research in organizational change & development* (vol. 13, pp. 43–79). Greenwich, CT: JAI Press.

Aristotle. (1961). *Metaphysics* (Vol. 1, Bks. 1–9; Vol. 2, Bks. 10–14). (H. Tredennick, Trans.). Loeb Classical Library. Cambridge, MA: Harvard University Press.

Aristotle. (1962). *Nicomachean Ethics* (M. Ostwald, Trans.). Englewood Cliffs, NJ: Prentice Hall.

Astley, W., & Zammuto, R. (1993). Organization science, managers, and language games. *Organization Science, 3*, 443–460.

Bartunek, J. M., Rynes, S., & Ireland, R. D. (2006). What makes management research interesting, and why does it matter? *Academy of Management Journal, 49*, 9–15.

Best manufacturing practices report. (1998). Retrieved October 1, 2006, from http://www.bmpcoe.org.

Boland, R. J., & Tenkasi, R. V. (1995). Perspective making and perspective taking in communities of knowing. *Organization Science, 6*(4), 350–372.

Bourdieu, P. (1977). *Outline of a theory of practice.* Cambridge: Cambridge University Press.

Bunge, M. (2004). How does it work? The search for explanatory mechanisms. *Philosophy of Social Sciences, 34*(2), 182–210.

Cambridge dictionary of American English. (2003). Cambridge: Cambridge University Press.

Chalmers, A. F. (1999). *What is this thing called science?* Indianapolis, IN: Hackett.

Dunne, J. (1993). *Back to the rough ground: 'Phronesis' and 'Techne' in modern philosophy and in Aristotle.* Notre Dame, IN: University of Notre Dame Press.

Eisenhardt, K. (1989). Building theories from case study research. *Academy of Management Review, 14*(4), 532–550.

Eslbach, K., & Sutton, R. (1992). Acquiring organizational legitimacy through illegitimate actions: A marriage of institutional and impression management theories. *Academy of Management Journal, 35*(4), 699–738.

Evered, R., & Louis, M. R. (1981). Alternative perspectives in the organizational sciences: "Inquiry from the inside" and "Inquiry from the outside." *Academy of Management Review, 6*, 385–395.

Fleck, L. (1979). *Genesis and development of a scientific fact.* Chicago: University of Chicago Press. (Original work published in German in 1935)

Gibbons, M., Limoges, C., Nowotny, H., Schwartzman, S., Scott, P., & Trow, M. (1994). *The new production of knowledge.* London: Sage.

Grant, R. M. (1996). Toward a knowledge based theory of the firm. *Strategic Management Journal, 17*, 109–122.

Green, S. E. (2004). A rhetorical theory of diffusion. *Academy of Management Review, 29*, 653–669.

Hay, G. W., Woodman, R. W., & Tenkasi, R. V. (2008). Closing the ODC application gap by bringing ODC knowledge closer to ODC practice. *OD Practitioner, 40*(2), 55–60.

Huff, A., & Huff, J. (2001). Refocusing the business school agenda. *British Journal of Management, 12*, S49–S54.

Jick, T. M. (1979). Mixing qualitative and quantitative methods: Triangulation in action. *Administrative Science Quarterly, 24*, 602–611.

Kuhn, T. S. (1970). *The structure of scientific revolutions* (2nd ed.). Chicago: University of Chicago Press.

Lawler, E. E. (1986). *High-involvement management: Participative strategies for improving organizational performance.* San Francisco: Jossey-Bass.

Mahoney, J. T., & McGahan, A. M. (2007). The field of strategic management within the evolving field of strategic organization. *Strategic Organization, 5*, 79–99.

Mahoney, J. T., & Sanchez, R. (2004). Building management theory by integrating products and processes of thought. *Journal of Management Inquiry, 13*, 34–47.

Mohrman, S. A., Gibson, C. B., & Mohrman, A. M. (2001). Doing research that is useful to practice: A model and empirical exploration. *Academy of Management Journal, 44*(2), 357–375.

Nonaka, I. (1994). A dynamic theory of organizational knowledge creation. *Organization Science, 5*, 14–37.

Nowotny, H., Scott, P., & Gibbons, M. (2001). *Re-thinking science: Knowledge and the public in an age of uncertainty.* London: Polity Press.

Nowotny, H., Scott, P., & Gibbons, M. (2005). Re-thinking science: Mode 2 in societal context. In E. Carayannis & D. Campbell (Eds.), *Knowledge creation, diffusion, and use in innovation networks and knowledge clusters: A comparative systems approach across the United States, Europe, and Asia* (pp. 39–51). Westport, CT: Praeger.

Parry, R. (2003). *Episteme* and *Techne.* In E. N. Zalta (Ed.), *The Stanford encyclopedia of philosophy.* Retrieved from http://plato.stanford.edu/archives/sum2003/entries/episteme-techne.

Peters, F. E. (1967). *Greek philosophical terms: A historical lexicon.* New York: New York University Press.

Pettigrew, A. (2001). Management research after modernism. *British Journal of Management, 12* (Special Issue), S61–S70.

Pfeffer, J., & Sutton, R. I. (2006). *Hard facts, dangerous half-truths, and total nonsense.* Boston: Harvard Business School Press.

Pinto, J., & Prescott, J. (1988). Variations in critical success factors over the stages in the project life cycle. *Journal of Management, 14*(1), 5–18.

Rousseau, D. M. (2006). Is there such a thing as "evidence based management"? *Academy of Management Review, 31*, 256–269.

Ryle, G. (1949). *The concept of mind.* London: Hutchinson.

Schon, D. A. (1995). Causality and causal inference in the study of organizations. In R. F. Goodman & W. R. Fisher (Eds.), *Rethinking knowledge: Reflections across the disciplines.* Albany, NY: State University of New York Press.

Silverman, D. (2001). *Interpreting qualitative research* (2nd ed.). Thousand Oaks, CA: Sage.

Tenkasi, R. V., & Chesmore, M. C. (2003). Social networks and planned organizational change: The impact of strong network ties on effective change implementation and use. *Journal of Applied Behavioral Science, 39*(3), 281–300.

Tenkasi, R. V., & Hay, G. W. (2004). Actionable knowledge and scholar-practitioners: A process model of theory-practice linkages. *Systemic Practice & Action Research, 17*(3), 177–206.

Tenkasi, R. V., & Hay, G. W. (2008). Following the second legacy of Aristotle: The scholar-practitioner as an epistemic-technician. In A. B. Shani, N. Adler, S. A. Mohrman, W. A. Pasmore, & B. Stymne (Eds.), *Handbook of collaborative management research.* Thousand Oaks, CA: Sage.

Tenkasi, R. V., Mohrman, S. A., & Mohrman, A. M. (2007). *Making knowledge contextually relevant: The challenge of connecting academic research with practice.* Paper presented at the Third Organization Studies Summer Workshop on Organization Studies as Applied Science: The Generation and Use of Academic Knowledge about Organizations, Crete, Greece.

Tinnish, S., & O'Neal, R. (2010). *Building on the scholar-practitioner legacy: An investigation into the publishing rates, enablers and obstacles to publishing in the OD field.* Lisle, IL: PhD program in Organization Development, Benedictine University.

Van De Ven, A. H. (2007). *Engaged scholarship: A guide for organizational and social research.* Oxford: Oxford University Press.

Van De Ven, A. H., & Johnson, P. E. (2006). Knowledge for theory and practice. *Academy of Management Review, 31,* 902–921.

Van De Ven, A. H., & Schomaker, M. S. (2002). The rhetoric of evidence-based medicine. *Health Care Management Review, 27*(3), 88–90.

Wasserman, I., & Kram, K. (2009). Enacting the scholar practitioner: An exploration of narratives. *Journal of Applied Behavioral Science, 45*(5), 12–38.

Weick, K. (1979). *The social psychology of organizing.* New York: McGraw-Hill.

Werr, A., & Greiner, L. (2008). Collaboration and the production of management knowledge in research, consulting and management practice. In A. B. Shani, N. Adler, S. A. Mohrman, W. A. Pasmore, & B. Stymne (Eds.), *Handbook of collaborative management research.* Thousand Oaks, CA: Sage.

Yin, R. (1994). *Case study research: Design and methods.* Thousand Oaks, CA: Sage.

ABOUT THE AUTHOR

Ramkrishnan (Ram) V. Tenkasi is Professor of Organization Change at Benedictine University in Chicago. His research and practice interests on large-scale organizational change, knowledge, and, information technology have been funded by agencies such as the National Science Foundation and Department of Defense. A recent research project supported by the National Science Foundation and the Fulbright Program elevates his analysis of large-scale change to understand the interplay of planned institutional interventions and emergent entrepreneurial dynamics in explaining the formation and rapid evolution of the Indian software industry. He is past Chair of the Organization Development and Change Division of the Academy of Management and was awarded the Fulbright Senior Research Scholar, one of 150 research awards annually granted by the U.S. government across 42 disciplines.

TWELVE

Organization Development Scholar-Practitioners

Between Scholarship and Practice

JEAN M. BARTUNEK
AND EDGAR H. SCHEIN*

WE BEGIN THIS CHAPTER by stipulating that academic-practitioner relationships and the ability of academics to communicate with practitioners
matter deeply. We and many others hope very much that academics' research findings can help to facilitate more effective management practice
(e.g., Bartunek, 2003, 2007; Hambrick, 1994; Huff, 2000; McGregor, 1960;
Rousseau, 2006; Rynes, Bartunek, & Daft, 2001; Schein, 1965, 2009a, 2009b;
Van de Ven, 2002, 2007; Van de Ven & Johnson, 2006). We also hope that academics can learn from practitioners (Bartunek, 2007; Schein, 2009a, 2009b;
Van de Ven, 2007).

Nevertheless, we realize that accomplishing such improved communication is not easy. As Pettigrew (2001, S61) stated, "If the duty of the intellectual
in society is to make a difference, the management research community has
a long way to go to realize its potential." Regardless of its difficulty, attempt-
ing to have scholarly findings facilitate practice and practice facilitate scholarly learning is important. Bad management is tangibly damaging (Adler &
Jermier, 2005; Ghoshal, 2005; Rousseau, 2006), and if academics do not speak,
less rigorously developed—but much more effectively marketed—knowledge
(cf. Ernst & Kieser, 2002) is going to be virtually the only source of management knowledge for practitioners.

There are multiple problems in linking academic management theory
with practice, and it will suffice to name just a few. Many academics do not
know how to write for practitioners (cf. Bartunek & Rynes, 2010). Practitioners do not regularly read academic journals (Rynes, Colbert, & Brown,
2002). New organization development (OD) practitioners are typically less

* We are grateful to Barbara Bunker, Susan Albers Mohrman, and Ilene Wasserman for
helpful comments and suggestions.

versed in academic knowledge than those who joined the field in the 1970s or earlier (Bunker, 2010).

How to Respond?

Abstract analyses of problems associated with academic-practitioner knowledge transfer and earnest exhortations to do better have not generally succeeded in changing the tenor of the conversation in ways that feel satisfactory. In this chapter, rather than focus on exhortations or sweeping theoretical pronouncements, we are going to focus on discrete small wins (Weick, 1984) associated with those who define themselves as scholar-practitioners. By scholar-practitioners we include scholars dedicated to developing new knowledge useful to practitioners (Wasserman & Kram, 2009), or more broadly, to "actors who have one foot each in the worlds of academia and practice and are pointedly interested in advancing the causes of both theory and practice" (Tenkasi & Hay, 2008, p. 49).

We want in this chapter to practice what we preach, to be accessible to both practitioners and academics. Thus, we have organized much of our presentation around narratives, which have become increasingly recognized as an important way of communicating information successfully to both groups (e.g., Carson, 2009; Gergen, 1994; Gergen & Gergen, 1993; Ibarra & Barbulescu, 2010; Wasserman & Kram, 2009).

We will illustrate the points we make with narratives from one or both of our own experiences as occasional organization development practitioners. These narratives have arisen in large part from lengthy conversations the two of us have had in which we have reflected on our own OD experiences over many years and explored issues that are particularly important to us with regard to academic-practitioner links.

Definitional and Conceptual Roots of OD

Our Working Definition of OD

There has been a range of definitions of OD over the years. For simplicity's sake, we will define it in this chapter as a form of helping organizations achieve greater effectiveness through various forms of "process consultation" (Schein, 1969, 1999a, 2009a). As scholar-practitioners, OD consultants do not tell an organization what to do where its human systems are involved. Rather, based on their scholarly knowledge, consultants engage members of the organization in a joint effort to help them address their concerns.

According to this definition, crucial characteristics of OD are client and consultant learning, attention to processes by which learning happens, and joint efforts to resolve issues of concern. Consultants are expected to bring process expertise. Further, they should be sufficiently knowledgeable about academic literature in the relevant social sciences to be able to work with clients on the various human and systemic problems that clients face.

Conceptual Roots of OD

OD's roots are in action research, where it is expected that research will inform practice and practice will inform scholarly knowledge (e.g., Lewin, 1951; Pasmore & Friedlander, 1982). Many interventions by OD practitioners have direct roots in academic theorizing. As just a few examples, Bunker and Alban (1997, 2006) show that currently popular large-group interventions have roots in the work of Kurt Lewin, Wilfrid Bion, Fred Emery, Eric Trist, Richard Beckhard, Daniel Katz, Robert Kahn, and others. Beer (1980) and Lippitt (1982) described ways in which systems theory, contingency theory, group development and job design models, and a host of other theoretical developments could be used to guide OD interventions. Margulies and Raia (1978) added ways in which Gestalt theory and sociotechnical systems approaches could be used in OD practice. Argyris and Schön's (1978) work on organizational learning has inspired the development of learning organizations. Schein's (2009a) recent analysis of the helping relationship draws heavily on Erving Goffman's (1959, 1963, 1967) sociological model of human interaction and the sociology of symbolic interactionism (Cooley, 1902/1922; Van Maanen, 1979).

Further, the scholarly bases for OD interventions continue to evolve. For example, Marshak and Grant (2008) and Bushe and Marshak (2009) recently showed how much current OD is based more on a dialogic approach than the diagnostic approach that characterized early OD interventions. The dialogic approach is based on Gergen's (1978) and others' critiques of positivism and emphasis on the importance of social constructivism.

Thus, the questions we ask in the following section take the scholarly roots of OD for granted. Without it, the "scholar" dimension of the scholar-practitioner role does not have meaning.

Questions for Academic-Practitioner Relationships

The following five questions address several "small" (Weick, 1984), or at least circumscribed, issues. In them, we use the terms "consultant" and "scholar-practitioner" interchangeably.

Questions and Answers

1. How extensive and deep is the consultant's academic knowledge?

For OD scholar-practitioners to be able to help facilitate practitioner knowledge and better practice, they first need to be familiar with the appropriate academic knowledge. This claim may not seem startling, given what we have said about conceptual roots of OD. However, as we noted previously and as others have commented (e.g., Bunker, 2010), newer practitioners are moving away from, rather than toward, academic knowledge.

JEAN "Several years ago I participated in a conference that primarily included practitioners. At the beginning, the organizers had us divide into groups based on the decade in which we had started becoming involved in OD and to discuss what had nurtured our involvement. All of us in the 1970s group talked about links between academia and practice. Those in the 1980s and 1990s groups included fewer links with academic roots. Most of those in the 2000s group had become involved for reasons that were personally important, but that had nothing to do with academia; sometimes they almost saw their work as anti-academic."

While lack of a link between academic theorizing and OD practice is fine in some ways, it obviously limits the possibilities of academic knowledge informing the practice of OD or of practice learnings leading back to and informing academic knowledge. Ghoshal (2005) noted that blindly following academic literature sometimes leads to bad managerial practice. Thus, we are not claiming that all academic knowledge is equally good for practice. However, some of it—as illustrated by Bunker and Alban (1997)—clearly has been crucial for the development of new practice. Consultants must therefore be able to determine what academic knowledge can be truly helpful to particular practice based on their academic education and ongoing academic participation.

We believe that if OD consultants are ignorant of relevant academic knowledge, their OD work will be less likely to accomplish good practice over the long run. (This claim, of course, can be tested empirically.) But if consultants are reasonably in touch with what academics are producing in the more formal scholarly environment and can calibrate its applicability and convert it, their knowledge—when applied in action—is likely to lead to more effective practice. Becoming aware of the applicability of academic knowledge does not mean only superficial awareness of some findings. It implies an active understanding of how one's own daily activities are informed by what researchers have found and the ability to imagine how these might be used in consulting.

ED "The other day I had an experience that reminded me of some early research. I was crossing the street, jaywalking, and thought I was safe, but there was a truck coming and it was coming pretty fast. Instead of going back I continued to cross the street. And I asked myself after I crossed the street, why had I done this? What was the deep reason psychologically why I chose to jaywalk and continue to jaywalk when I saw the truck, instead of backing up? I remembered Kurt Lewin's students' experiments that were called the Zeigarnik (1967) effect, a very clear set of studies that showed that if you give someone a task and don't let them complete it, they remember it better than tasks that were completed. We have a need to finish what we started. And that's what was happening to me in the middle of the street. I was halfway across the street and I was willing to take a chance to go the rest of the way. To back up and go back to the sidewalk felt psychologically all wrong.

"I immediately linked that to my experience consulting with the Alpha Power Company analyzing accidents with splicers and other electrical workers. I can imagine that once a splicer starts on a job, he or she wants to finish the job. And so when something comes up that suggests that maybe the job should be stopped because something unsafe has been encountered, a lot of accidents happen; as the Zeigarnik effect suggests, splicers (and the rest of us) fail to pay attention to the weak danger signals.

"I haven't seen the human need to finish what we have started written up as an important issue in safety analysis. It's often analyzed as macho-ism, loss of focus, mindlessness, productivity pressure, or cognitive rigidity but this simple Lewinian finding by Zeigarnik (1967) is, I think, underused.

"Another example from Alpha Power is a slight variation on this theme. A team was putting new utility poles in, and that meant they needed to cut the old poles and pull out the stumps. They have a particular truck that has real lifting capacity for pulling stumps. One day, a work crew building a road was coming through and they asked the supervisor whether she could get a particular stump out quickly because it prevented them from doing their job and they were in a hurry.

"Ordering the correct truck for stump pulling would take some time. The supervisor got hooked on helping them so she inquired of her crew whether the lifting device on their bucket trucks could be used. She knew that these bucket trucks could possibly lift this stump, but because she was new, she asked the other workers: 'Should we use our own truck to try to lift the stump?' And they said, 'Well, we're not supposed to, but we do it from time to time.' Her intentionality to help was now biasing her judgment as to whether she should use the local truck or not. So she decided to try it. She got into the bucket herself, attached all the things to the stump, and started pulling. The braces broke and she got thrown and seriously injured. If she had not committed herself to the helping task, she would have taken the time to get the right truck."

What does such scholarly awareness enable in practice? It enables a consultant to "see" something different beneath the surface of a set of events and to intervene based on this awareness. It makes evident that such seeing will take place much more easily if the consultant is paying attention to normal, everyday practice and being curious about it in academic terms. This type of awareness can foster academic knowledge as well. As Ed's example suggests, it can contribute to new lines of inquiry, such as in safety analyses enhancing Weick's (1990) and Langer's (1989) analyses of how mindlessness contributes to accidents.

JEAN "I have also used academic theorizing in my consulting. For example, I was once beginning some consulting with top leaders of an organization I had not worked with previously. I was familiar with Joanne Martin and her colleagues' work (Martin et al., 1983) on stories as indicators of organizational culture. In order to get to know better the top leaders of the organization and the organization itself, I suggested that the leaders start by telling stories about their organization and interpret the meanings of the stories for me. This process ended up being not only very engaging for them but also an effective way to understand some of what the organization leaders saw as their culture. For example, many of their stories were about disputes between lower-ranking organization members and higher-level managers, and the stories were told without a lot of affect. This combination led me to hypothesize that the organization was somewhat used to, and not very threatened by, conflict, and based on this conjecture, I wasn't particularly concerned with conflicts that arose during my work with the organization."

These examples raise issues about what it means to translate academic research for practice. Application doesn't come in the form of handing people research results or citations to original research and saying, "See what you can do with these," but paying attention to academic literature and actually using our knowledge of what researchers have found in an interactive way. If we know the work well enough that we recognize its manifestations when an incident occurs, then we can apply our knowledge in the immediate interaction. It is our experience that when we use concepts and theory in such a fashion, they can be particularly important in helping practitioners to frame their experiences and to provide new behavioral models as well.

Which academic disciplines should OD scholar-practitioners be familiar with now? Aspects of organizational behavior, strategy, political science, economics, social psychology, sociology, anthropology, and cognitive (and neuro-) psychology could all be helpful. Complete organizational consultants really should be very, very broad thinkers if we're really going to help practitioners, because we don't always quite know in advance where the relevant knowledge might lie.

2. As one aspect of such knowledge applied to practice, does the consultant appreciate systems dynamics adequately to intervene appropriately?

Systems thinking in one guise or another has been a central component of OD since its beginnings as an effort to work with "the whole system" (French & Bell, 1998). As Bunker (2010) has outlined, early OD work related to systems included models of open systems taken from the work of von Bertalanffy (1968) and adapted by Katz and Kahn (1966), sociotechnical systems design (Emery & Trist, 1965), and Likert's (1967) System 4 among others. Other approaches to organizational systems through the years have included Gestalt theory applied to OD (Margulies & Raia, 1978), open systems planning (Beckhard, 1969), process redesign (Hammer & Champy, 1993), systems thinking as one dimension of the learning organization (Senge, 1990), large-group interventions (Bunker & Alban, 1997, 2006; Holman, Devane, & Cady, 2007) and social network analysis (Borgatti & Foster, 2003), process management (Deming,1986; Juran, 1989), and attempts to make use of scholarly work regarding complex adaptive systems (e.g., Olson & Eoyang, 2001).

The use of systems approaches continues to evolve; large-group interventions are the first set of interventions explicitly designed to address whole systems (Bunker, 2010). Consultants must be able to anticipate the impact of their interventions not only on an immediate client but on the human systems around that client. A great deal of damage can be done by practitioners who are ignorant of the accumulated academic knowledge about how human systems work and how this knowledge might be applied.

ED "I am often asked in connection with doing a culture assessment to come visit an organization to explore the issues and decide how to proceed. I almost never agree to such a visit unless I have talked to the primary contact clients somewhere away from their organization to examine the potential impact of a consultant showing up at the organization. I want the contact client to understand that such a visit would arouse questions and possibly anxieties unless the contact client made it clear why I was showing up and owned the process by which I would be introduced into the organization. My goal in those early conversations would be to make the client very aware of the systemic consequences of different kinds of next steps such as interviews or surveys."

One of the worst examples of ignoring systemic dynamics is the consultant conducting initial interviews ostensibly to formulate a diagnosis or as the basis of a survey in order to find out how people feel. In both cases, expectations and anxieties are aroused that if not dealt with by the client will worsen the situation. The responsible scholar-practitioner would not go ahead with interviews or surveys without a thorough exploration of the possible systemic consequences. The most important of those consequences is the expectation that once employees have stated their feelings and issues, they expect management to do something about it. If managers are not prepared to deal with what they learn, morale and management credibility will decline.

> **ED** "One of the most important things I do in early consultation conversations is to tell the client what the consequences might be of intervening in his or her organization. What the client usually does not recognize is the likelihood that he or she will be viewed as part of the problem to be solved. Is he or she ready to make personal changes in his or her own behavior?"

3. How can academic knowledge be communicated in writing for use in practice?

The material in the previous sections addresses some ways that academic knowledge may be used within the context of consultation. The third question refers, primarily, to how to communicate academic knowledge to practitioners outside of a formal consulting engagement and primarily through writing.

There is some literature on this topic. For example, Bartunek and Rynes (2010) have explored how implications for practice have been written in academic journals and how they might be written in a much more effective way. Leung and Bartunek (in press) discuss ways that academic evidence may be communicated by means other than writing (e.g., through informal venues or teaching cases). But how should scholar-practitioners write if they want to be understood by both academics and practitioners?

> **ED** "There is a great difference in how I wrote about organizational culture for academics and managers in my books *Organizational Culture and Leadership* (4th edition, 2010) and *The Corporate Culture Survival Guide* (1999b, 2009c). The first edition of *Organizational Culture and Leadership* was written with fellow academics in mind. My intent was to

make it as bell clear as I could, using all my knowledge, and write it in a formal fashion. That involved putting down everything I considered relevant to the understanding of how culture and leadership are intertwined. So it's a big book, it's an academic book, and it gets used that way.

"Somewhere in the nineties I realized that, in my practice, when I got around to talking about culture, the people I was working with were misusing the term. Everyone wanted to change their culture and clearly did not understand that this was not possible in the simplistic way that people used the culture concept. So I wrote the second book called *The Corporate Culture Survival Guide* (1999b), with totally different intentions. I was now going to write to managers and use more direct language: If you want to change your culture, here's what you have to do. You first have to figure out what problem you are trying to solve and then translate the potential solution into behavioral terms. If you change the behavior and it works over a period of time, you will be gradually changing the culture. So I took some of the relevant content from the first book and rewrote it with managers in mind. In advocating this approach I was allying myself with the research findings of Leon Festinger (1957), who had convinced me that it is easier to change behavior first than to change values first.

"The two books are written differently in that the original book has to stand the test of an academic audience. If graduate students are reading the *Organizational Culture and Leadership* book, it has to be expressed clearly, accurately, and with proper referencing. There's going to be an instructor's guide. With the other book, I was really saying, 'Look, if you're going to fool around with this culture stuff, here are the ABCs.' There are fewer references, and I put more emphasis on certain things. What in the big culture book might have been a chapter toward the end that emphasizes how you produce change becomes the main focus of the *Corporate Culture Survival Guide* book.

"Almost all my contacts come from somebody who has read something I've written. People read and learn from what they read if it is clear enough. From both books, the huge lesson I have learned about how you get to be a consultant is that writing is important. It is the writing that attracts the practitioner audience, which would suggest that academics should think about writing more than one version of what they feel they know from their research.

"Writing for practitioners involves a different framework and style of communication but still necessitates building on sound academic knowledge. An example of misleading practitioners because of drawing on incorrect knowledge is contained in the OD consulting books that advocate 'stages of data gathering and diagnosis' prior to recommending an 'intervention.' While discrete 'interventions' may indeed follow data gathering, Chris Argyris (1970) made evident 40 years ago that the intervening process starts with initial entry into a system. Bob Marshak and David Grant (2008) are emphasizing something similar, the importance of conversation, dialog, and engagement as central from the beginning of OD processes.

"In other words, the initial interaction between a consultant and a client is already an intervention. If academic consultants believe that they are 'just gathering data,' they are ignoring not only the Heisenberg principle that measurement itself has an impact on a system but the whole scientific basis for double-blind research studies. I make this a central issue in my books on process consultation (1969, 1999a), so that readers are forewarned not to be seduced by the claims that long and expensive periods of diagnosis and data gathering are necessary prior to intervention. You've intervened when you first picked up the phone or showed up at the client's site."

Writing clearly is very important. Virtually all of Ed's consulting contacts have come from what people have read. Jean's practitioner contacts have also come in large part from her writing. In other words, writing is a form of intervention as well.

4. How willing is the scholar-practitioner to learn from practice?

For OD scholars and consultants to be able to speak to practice, they also need to be able to learn from practice. Knowledge that is useful for both theory and practice is not a one-way street from theory to practice. In fact, some of the most important things learned are often from practice itself. Jean had an important learning about this that she published in the Academy of Management Journal *(Bartunek, 2007, p. 1323).*

JEAN "In March 2007, I had an instructive, if sobering, experience. I was participating in a conference, Nexus for Change (nexusforchange.org), the bulk of whose attendees were designers and facilitators of "large group" or "whole systems" planned change interventions....

"At the conference, I gave a talk to a few of the participants about how external researchers and designers/facilitators of such interventions can collaborate to study the effectiveness of the interventions using a joint insider/outsider research approach.... One of the people who attended that talk was a woman who has designed a successful large group intervention and who took several important leadership roles in conjunction with the conference. I was very impressed with her initiative, creativity, and considerable competence. She came to my talk because recent changes in funding requirements required her to demonstrate successful outcomes of her intervention. Thus, she was interested in learning something about research that could help her explore outcomes.

"But while she was at my talk, she acted differently and less confidently than she had otherwise at the conference. She mentioned that she had taken a research methods class once and had barely passed it. Terms like 'research question' did not have intuitive meaning for her, but instead evoked anxiety. Certainly, the language of independent, dependent, and mediating and moderating variables was foreign to how she designed or facilitated her large group intervention; she thought much more holistically. I drew a causal model, complete with boxes and arrows, regarding a possible study of the effectiveness of her intervention. But this was not, for her and for several other attendees at the talk, a familiar or helpful way of thinking."

This experience was central to the essay and led Jean to focus on the importance of relationships between academics and practitioners that extend beyond research involvement in which the researcher is primary or consulting engagements in which the practitioner is primary. It is important to develop means for both parties to be able to interact on somewhat equal terms. Ed has also learned valuable lessons from practice that have affected both his theorizing and his research.

ED "Much of the knowledge I gained about how culture works in organizations was obtained from hours of attendance at meetings in Digital Equipment Corporation and attending annual top executive meetings in Ciba-Geigy. The evolution of the 'clinical approach' to learning about organizations arose from the frequent experience that what was observed was often unrelated to the formal reason for being there or was an unanticipated consequence of interventions (Schein, 1987, 2008). Lewin's dictum that you don't understand an organization until you try to change it was a profound insight.

"For example, I got to be a process consultant in working with Digital on their group process to help their top management team be more effective. I knew from my many National Training Laboratories (NTL) T-group experiences what a good group should be. People should listen, be respectful, not interrupt each other. In Digital I encountered emotional and interpersonal chaos and worked hard to point out the dysfunctionality of how the group worked and always was politely thanked for my punitive interventions, but nothing changed. Eventually I 'gave up' and started to pay attention to what was going on and asked myself the question: 'Why are these intelligent and nice people continuing to fight with each other and not do what I'm recommending to them?'

"And that led to the insight that they are doing something that they need to do, namely, figure out which ideas are good enough to implement. They had learned as academics and practicing engineers that the way you do that is to argue with each other and see which idea survives. And if you're also passionate, that means you're going to interrupt each other. If you accept that as their process with the goal of finding the best idea, then helping them to keep track of ideas becomes the new goal. So one day I went to the flip chart and started to write ideas down and if someone got interrupted I could say to the original speaker, 'I didn't get all of that.' I now focused on the idea instead of punishing the interrupter for interrupting. Seeing their ideas on the flip chart helped them to track things, and they found that really helpful. We all learned how important it was to use a new process (someone recording ideas on the flip chart and monitoring the idea production process) that is congruent with the goal (to process and evaluate different ideas).

"What did I learn from that? I realized that they had a culture, that this culture could be described, and that what I knew from anthropology, particularly the Kluckhohn and Strodtbeck (1961) research on how different cultures can have dramatically different value sets, illuminated for me how different subcultures worked. That insight led later to the important discovery that all organizations have three generic subcultures—an executive subculture that is all about money, an operator subculture that is all about the daily work of the organization, and an engineering subculture that is about innovation and design of the work (Schein, 1996)."

As these examples indicate, it is valuable for scholar-practitioners not to approach a client system with the assumption that existing theory is sacrosanct. Rather, working with an organization is a wonderful way to test already established academic theory and to develop new ways of thinking based on learnings from the setting. This is one valuable way of establishing two-way pathways between theory and practice.

5. How important are bridging institutions in which academics and practitioners get to know each other?

Bridging institutions are organizations in which scholars and practitioners interact in a learning context that provides academic knowledge to practitioners and experience in how to be helpful to scholars. Executive education programs both inside and outside business schools provide some bridging opportunities, but it is organizations like the National Training Laboratories and the Society for Organizational Learning (SoL) that provide the best opportunities for such mutual learning.

Both Ed and Jean have been associated with NTL and SoL. Ed conducted training for NTL for many years and Jean was, while she was in her doctoral program, a participant in NTL's Graduate Student Professional Development Program. She is currently an associate editor of the Journal of Applied Behavioral Science (JABS), *a journal published by NTL. Jean and Ed were both founding members of SoL. Jean co-authored a paper with SoL leaders about changes in their core competencies course (Bartunek et al., 2007). Ed was the founding editor of* Reflections, *the SoL journal, which is "focused on the leading edge of organizational learning in practice" and attempted in every issue to carry articles and comments from researchers, consultants, and practitioners in order to build bridges across these three communities (http://www.solonline.org/reflections/aboutreflections).*

Research centers such as the Center for Creative Leadership in Greensboro, NC, and the Center for Effective Organizations at USC can also serve this bridging function if they create opportunities for practitioners and academics to interact around real organizational problems to be solved. To be helpful to practitioners, the first step for academics is to get to know some of them and to discover not only what they do or do not know but what issues they are trying to address. Similarly, practitioners need the opportunity to get inside the heads of researchers to begin to understand how academic knowledge is generated. Sometimes these attempts illustrate the challenges associated with sharing academic-practitioner knowledge.

JEAN "In March, 2010 I participated in an NTL conference focused on developing the 'New OD.' A few people who identify themselves more with academic scholarship than practice were there, along with several people who identified themselves as scholar-practitioners and many who identified themselves primarily as practitioners. It was evident in group discussions that many of the participating practitioners are very bright and intellectually curious.

"In one group I was in, for example, several people expressed creative ideas about possible roles of design in new ways of practicing OD. However, when I mentioned that in 2007 *JABS* had published a special issue on design as applied to OD, most were not aware of it and one commented that some of the articles in it were 'tough to read.'

"I have also found that it is challenging for academic researchers to get fully integrated into SoL. Applied researchers fit in much better, in part because academic time frames are so much slower than most practitioner time frames. For example, SoL sometimes issues calls for research proposals. However, organizations in which the research would be done need for work to be done soon, rather than, say, after lengthy proposal writing and institutional review board approval processes.

"My experience is that while building links within these venues is sometimes difficult, it is extremely valuable. It is a chance for academics and practitioners both to get to know each other as people, to develop the possibility of more lasting connections, and come to know more concretely the kinds of challenges involved in linking the types of communication that may help meet the challenges."

New types of such bridging institutions are arising out of new social media. We have been involved in distance teaching, podcasts, and other forms of interaction where we met practitioners at a distance and where they could discuss with us questions about the application of knowledge. These offer the potential for less formal interaction across boundaries that at one time would be been unbridgeable. These also offer the potential for people who define themselves as scholars more than scholar-practitioners to develop some experience linking with practitioners in informal ways.

Some Closing Reflections

By means of illustrative narratives, we have answered the questions we posed in the following ways. First, if scholar practitioners are to bridge gaps between scholarship and practice, they need to know scholarship; they have to have academic knowledge to convey. This doesn't mean just citation-deep knowledge; it needs to be part of their practice. Second, especially given the initial scholarly emphases associated with OD, scholar-practitioners need to be attentive to systemic implications of any consulting work that is undertaken. Without systems awareness, work might be done that not only can sabotage an overall consulting effort but can also harm the organization. Third, we have suggested differences in ways of writing for academic and practitioner audiences. Skilled scholar-practitioners can do both types of writing. Fourth, OD scholar-practitioners need to be able to learn from practice and contribute their learnings to academic writing. Fifth, there are some formal bridging institutions between academia and practice. These are valuable, even as they reflect the difficulties involved in bridging scholarship and practice. It is worthwhile for consultants to be involved in such institutions in order to come to understand issues related to academic and practitioner approaches more fully.

We hope we have demonstrated that academia and practice have something to contribute to each other and that, though it is often difficult to accomplish, facilitating such joint contributions is important for improving both practice and the validity of our academic models of how human systems work.

REFERENCES

Adler, P., & Jermier, J. (2005). Developing a field with more soul: Standpoint theory and public policy research for management scholars. *Academy of Management Journal, 48*, 941–944.

Argyris, C. (1970). *Intervention theory and method.* Reading, MA: Addison-Wesley.

Argyris, C., & Schön, D. (1978). *Organizational learning: A theory of action perspective.* Reading, MA: Addison-Wesley.

Bartunek, J. M. (2003). A dream for the Academy. *Academy of Management Review, 28*, 198–203.

Bartunek, J. M. (2007). Academic-practitioner collaboration need not require joint or relevant research: Towards a relational scholarship of integration. *Academy of Management Journal, 50*, 1323–1333.

Bartunek, J. M., & Rynes, S. L. (2010). The construction and contributions of "implications for practice": What's in them and what might they offer? *Academy of Management Learning and Education, 9* (1), 100–117.

Bartunek, J. M., Trullen, J., Immediato, S., & Schneider, F. (2007). Front and back stages of the diminished routinization of innovations: What innovation research makes public and organizational research finds behind the scenes. *Strategic Entrepreneurship Journal, 1*, 295–314.

Beckhard, R. (1969). *Organization development: Strategies and models.* Reading, MA: Addison-Wesley.

Beer, M. (1980). *Organization change and development: A systems view.* Santa Monica, CA: Goodyear.

Borgatti, S. P., & Foster, P. (2003). The network paradigm in organizational research: A review and typology. *Journal of Management, 29*, 991–1013.

Bunker, B. B. (2010). *History of organization development and the environment.* Conference on the New OD. Silver Spring, MD: National Training Laboratories.

Bunker, B. B., & Alban, B. (1997). *Large group interventions: Engaging the whole system for rapid change.* San Francisco: Jossey-Bass.

Bunker, B. B., & Alban, B. A. (2006). *The handbook of large group methods: Creating systemic change in organizations and communities.* San Francisco: Jossey-Bass.

Bushe, G. R., & Marshak, R. J. (2009). Revisioning organization development: Diagnostic and dialogic premises and patterns of practice. *Journal of Applied Behavioral Science, 45*, 348–368.

Carson, M. (2009). The narrative practitioner: Theory and practice. *International Journal of Narrative Practice, 1*, 5–8.

Cooley, C. H. (1902/1922). *Human nature and social order.* Chicago: Free Press.

Deming, E. W. (1986). *Out of crisis.* Cambridge, MA: The MIT Press.

Emery, F. E., & Trist, E. C. (1965). The causal texture of organizational environments. *Human Relations, 18*, 21–32.

Ernst, B., & Kieser, A. (2002). In search of explanations for the consulting explosion. In K. Sahlin-Andersson & L. Engwall (Eds.), *The expansion of management knowledge: Carriers, flows and sources* (pp. 47–73). Stanford, CA: Stanford University Press.

Festinger, L. (1957). *A theory of cognitive dissonance.* Stanford, CA: Stanford University Press.

French, W. L., & Bell, C. H., Jr. (1998). *Organization development: Behavioral science interventions for organizational improvement* (6th ed.). Englewood Cliffs, NJ: Prentice Hall.

Gergen, K. (1978). Toward generative theory. *Journal of Personality and Social Psychology, 36*, 1344–1360.

Gergen, K. (1994). *Reality and relationships: Soundings in social construction.* Cambridge, MA: Harvard University Press.

Gergen, M. M., & Gergen, K. J. (1993). Narratives of the gendered body in popular autobiography. In R. Josselson & A. Lieblich (Eds.), *The narrative study of lives* (pp. 191–218). Newbury Park, CA: Sage.

Ghoshal, S. (2005). Bad management theories are destroying good management practices. *Academy of Management Learning and Education, 4*, 75–91.

Goffman, E. (1959). *The presentation of self in everyday life.* New York: Doubleday.

Goffman, E. (1963). *Stigma: Notes on the management of spoiled identity.* Englewood Cliffs, NJ: Prentice Hall.

Goffman, E. (1967). *Interaction ritual.* New York: Anchor Books.

Hambrick, D. C. (1994). What if the Academy actually mattered? *Academy of Management Review, 19*, 11–16.

Hammer, M., & Champy, J. A. (1993). *Reengineering the corporation: A manifesto for business revolution.* New York: Harper Business.

Holman, P., Devane, T., & Cady, S. (2007). *The change handbook: The definitive resource on today's best methods for engaging whole systems.* San Francisco: Berrett-Kohler.

Huff, A. (2000). 1999 Presidential Address: Changes in organizational knowledge production. *Academy of Management Review, 25*, 288–293.

Ibarra, H., & Barbulescu, R. (2010). Identity as narrative: Prevalence, effectiveness, and consequences of narrative identity work in macro work role transitions. *Academy of Management Journal, 35*, 135–154.

Juran, J. (1989). *Juran on leadership for quality.* New York: Free Press.

Katz, D., & Kahn, R. L. (1966). *The social psychology of organizations.* New York: Wiley.

Kluckhohn, F. R., & Strodtbeck, F. L. (1961). *Variations in value orientations.* Evanston, IL: Row, Peterson.

Langer, E. J. (1989). *Mindfulness.* Reading, MA: Addison-Wesley.

Leung, O., & Bartunek, J. M. (in press). Enabling evidence-based management: What can researchers do to help practitioners help their organizations? In D. Rousseau (Ed.), *Handbook of evidence-based management: Companies, classrooms, and research.* New York: Oxford.

Lewin, K. (1951). *Field theory in social science.* New York: Harper & Row.

Likert, R. (1967). *The human organization: Its management and value.* New York: McGraw-Hill.

Lippitt, G. (1982). *Organizational renewal.* Englewood Cliffs, NJ: Prentice Hall.

Margulies, N., & Raia, A. (1978). *Conceptual foundations of organizational development*. New York: McGraw-Hill.

Marshak, R. J., & Grant, D. (2008). Organizational discourse and new organization development practices. *British Journal of Management, 19*, S7–S19.

Martin, J., Feldman, M. S., Hatch, M. J., & Sitkin, S. (1983). The uniqueness paradox in organizational stories. *Administrative Science Quarterly, 28*, 438–453.

McGregor, D. (1960). *The human side of enterprise*. New York: McGraw-Hill.

Olson, E. E., & Eoyang, G. H. (2001). *Facilitating Organization Change*. San Francisco: Jossey-Bass.

Pasmore, W., & Friedlander, F. (1982). An action-research program for increasing employee involvement in problem solving. *Administrative Science Quarterly, 27*, 343–362.

Pettigrew, A. M. (2001). Management research after modernism. *British Journal of Management, 12*, S61–S70.

Rousseau, D. M. (2006). Is there such a thing as "evidence-based management"? *Academy of Management Review, 31*, 256–269.

Rynes, S., Bartunek, J., & Daft, R. (2001). Across the great divide: Knowledge creation and transfer between practitioners and academics. *Academy of Management Journal, 44*, 340–356.

Rynes, S. L., Colbert, A. E., & Brown, K. G. (2002). HR professionals' beliefs about effective human resource practices: Correspondence between research and practice. *Human Resource Management Journal, 41*, 149–174.

Schein, E. H. (1965). *Organizational Psychology*. Englewood Cliffs, NJ: Prentice-Hall.

Schein, E. H. (1969). *Process consultation*. Reading, MA: Addison-Wesley.

Schein, E. H. (1987). *The clinical perspective in fieldwork*. Newbury Park, CA: Sage.

Schein, E. H. (1996). Culture: The missing concept in organization studies. *Administrative Science Quarterly, 41*, 229–241.

Schein, E. H. (1999a). *Process consultation revisited: Building the helping relationship*. Reading, MA: Addison-Wesley-Longman.

Schein, E. H. (1999b). *The corporate culture survival guide*. San Francisco: Jossey-Bass.

Schein, E. H. (2008). Clinical inquiry/research. In P. Reason & H. Bradbury (Eds.), *Handbook of action research* (2d ed., pp. 266–279). London: Sage.

Schein, E. H. (2009a). *Helping*. San Francisco: Berrett-Kohler.

Schein, E. H. (2009b). Reactions, reflections, rejoinders, and a challenge. *Journal of Applied Behavioral Science, 45*, 141–158.

Schein, E. H. (2009c). *The corporate culture survival guide* (2d ed.). San Francisco: Jossey-Bass.

Schein, E. H. (2010). *Organizational culture and leadership* (4th ed.). San Francisco: Jossey-Bass.

Senge, P. (1990). *The fifth discipline: The art and science of the learning organization*. New York: Doubleday.

Tenkasi, R. V., & Hay, G. W. (2008). Following the second legacy of Aristotle: The scholar–practitioner as an epistemic technician. In A. B. Shani, S. A. Mohrman, W. A. Pasmore, B. N. Stymne, & N. Adler (Eds.), *Handbook of collaborative management research* (pp. 49–72). Thousand Oaks, CA: Sage.

Van de Ven, A. H. (2002). Strategic directions for the Academy of Management: This academy is for you! *Academy of Management Review, 27*, 171–184.

Van de Ven, A. H. (2007). *Engaged scholarship: A guide for organizational and research knowledge.* New York: Oxford University Press.

Van de Ven, A. H., & Johnson, P. E. (2006). Knowledge for theory and practice. *Academy of Management Review, 31*, 802–821.

Van Maanen, J. (1979). The self, the situation, and the rules of interpersonal relations. In W. Bennis, J. Van Maanen, E. H. Schein, & F. I. Steele (Eds.), *Essays in interpersonal dynamics* (pp. 43–101). Homewood, IL: Dorsey Press.

von Bertalanffy, L. (1968). *General systems theory: Foundations, development, applications.* New York: George Braziller.

Wasserman, I. C., & Kram, K. E. (2009). Enacting the scholar-practitioner role: An exploration of narratives. *Journal of Applied Behavioral Science, 45*, 12–38.

Weick, K. E. (1984). Small wins: Redefining the scale of social problems. *American Psychologist, 39*, 40–49.

Weick, K. E. (1990). The vulnerable system: An analysis of the Tenerife air disaster. *Journal of Management, 16*, 571–593.

Zeigarnik, B. (1967). On finished and unfinished tasks. In W. D. Ellis (Ed.), *A sourcebook of Gestalt psychology.* New York: Humanities Press.

ABOUT THE AUTHORS

Jean M. Bartunek is the Robert A. and Evelyn J. Ferris Chair and Professor of Organization Studies at Boston College. She is a fellow and past president of the Academy of Management, and an associate editor of the *Journal of Applied Behavioral Science*, as well as a member of the editorial boards of several other journals. Her research interests focus around organizational change and academic-practitioner relationships. She is the 2009 recipient of the Distinguished Service Award from the Academy of Management.

Ed Schein is the Sloan Fellows Professor of Management Emeritus at the MIT Sloan School of Management. He has published extensively—*Organizational Psychology* (3d ed., 1980), *Process Consultation Revisited* (1999), *Career Anchors* (3d ed., 2006), *Organizational Culture and Leadership* (4th ed., 2010), and *The Corporate Culture Survival Guide* (2d ed., 2009). He also wrote about Singapore's economic miracle (*Strategic Pragmatism,* 1996) and Digital Equipment Corp.'s rise and fall (*DEC Is Dead; Long Live DEC,* 2003), and most recently he has published a book on the general theory and practice of giving and receiving help (*Helping,* 2009). He is the 2009 recipient of the Distinguished Scholar-Practitioner Award of the Academy of Management.

THIRTEEN

Professional Associations

Supporting Useful Research

WAYNE F. CASCIO

PROFESSIONAL ASSOCIATIONS HAVE a visible, leading role to play in supporting and assimilating management-related research that has a useful impact on practice. Over the years, many reasons have been suggested for the great chasm that seems to exist between academic research and the practice of management. For purposes of this article, I adopt Gelade's (2006) definition of practitioners, namely, those who make recommendations about the management or development of people in organizational settings or advise those who do. Research is relevant to the extent that it generates insights that practitioners find useful for understanding their own organizations and situations better than before (Vermeulen, 2007).

In Chapter 1, Research for Theory and Practice, Mohrman and Lawler describe three broad perspectives on the science-practice gap:

1. From an academia-centric perspective, the gap is the result of a knowledge-transfer problem. It assumes that knowledge emanates primarily from academia and focuses on ways to make practitioners knowledgeable about the "facts" that are discovered through academic research.

2. A second perspective argues that knowledge of theory and knowledge of practice are distinct—substantively, ontologically, and epistemologically. The challenge, then, is to explore and benefit from the complementary features of these distinct forms of knowledge.

3. The third perspective views the source of the academic-practice gap as a knowledge-production problem. To bridge the gap, it argues for research approaches that engage both academics and practitioners in a collaborative-learning community. To do that, it is necessary to combine the knowledge of practitioners and the knowledge of academics from different disciplines through all stages of the research process.

Despite calls by researchers for more enlightened thinking and strategies to bridge the gap (Bartunek, 2007; Cascio, 2007, 2008; Cascio & Aguinis, 2008a; Latham, 2009; Rynes, 2007; Rynes, Bartunek, & Daft, 2001; Rynes, Colbert, & Brown, 2002; Rynes, Giluk, & Brown, 2007; Saari, 2007; Starbuck (in Barnett, 2007), it remains stubbornly resistant.

To date, professional associations have actively supported management-related research that has a useful impact on practice, albeit in different ways and with differing degrees of success. This chapter will examine what five different professional associations have done and are doing to bridge the gap. Those associations are the Society for Industrial and Organizational Psychology (SIOP); the Society for Human Resource Management (SHRM) Foundation, the Human Resource Planning Society (HRPS); the Academy of Management (AOM); and the Labor and Employment Relations Association (LERA), formerly the Industrial Relations Research Association.

Society for Industrial and Organizational Psychology

According to its website, the SIOP's mission is to enhance human well-being and performance in organizational and work settings by promoting the science, practice, and teaching of industrial-organizational (I/O) psychology. Among other activities, SIOP engages in the following:

- Supports SIOP members in their efforts to study, apply, and teach the principles, findings, and methods of industrial-organizational psychology

- Provides forums for industrial-organizational psychologists to exchange research, insights, and information related to the science, practice, and teaching of industrial-organizational psychology

For decades, SIOP has actively endorsed the scientist-practitioner model (Bass, 1974; Dunnette, 1990; Murphy & Saal, 1990; Rupp & Beal, 2007). That model discourages both practice that has no scientific basis and research that has no clear implications for practice (Murphy & Saal, 1990). Toward that end, SIOP offers preconference workshops in which academics and practitioners can work together on important problems. Sessions at the annual conference provide forums for the exchange of information related to science and practice, but SIOP has moved well beyond the conference itself to promote collaboration and a deeper understanding of issues that are important to scientists and to practitioners. It also offers a blog, the *SIOP Exchange*.

The *Exchange* makes use of an interactive blog format in which professionals in the academic and applied domains submit posts that detail the latest happenings on popular topics that generate conversation, such as hot-topic issues, findings not yet published, and applications of I/O psychology that are new and innovative. Professionals from across the world can then ask questions, provide comments, and respond to other comments in reaction to these posts. New material is posted regularly, and every post is tagged with keywords so that topics of interest are easy to find.

Beginning in 2005, SIOP began an annual two-day event known as the Leading-Edge Consortium in an effort to integrate the science and the application of I/O psychology to important organizational issues. Each consortium addresses an important issue that is relevant to science and to practice. I/O psychologists working in organizations both large and small, together with leading academics, listen to presentations, interact in small-group sessions, and have extensive opportunities to network over the two days. For example, the key themes from 2005 to 2009 were the following:

- 2005 – Leadership at the Top: The Selection of Executive Talent
- 2006 – Talent Attraction and Development
- 2007 – Enabling Innovation in Organizations
- 2008 – Executive Coaching for Effective Performance
- 2009 – Selection and Assessment in a Global Setting

In summary, SIOP has extended a welcoming hand to practitioners, and they have responded by actively participating in preconference workshops, in annual conference presentations, in the *SIOP Exchange* blog, and in Leading-Edge consortia. This active involvement of scientists and practitioners has deepened the understanding that each has of the other's "thought world" (perspectives 2 and 3 identified by Mohrman and Lawler in Chapter 1, Research for Theory and Practice), and I believe that it has enriched both science and practice.

Society for Human Resource Management Foundation

The Society for Human Resource Management is the world's largest association devoted to human resource management. Representing more than 250,000 members in 140 countries, SHRM has more than 575 affiliated chapters within the United States and subsidiary offices in China and India.

The SHRM Foundation is the 501(c)(3) nonprofit affiliate of SHRM. Steered by a 14-member board of directors composed of equal numbers of academics and practitioners, the foundation is a leading funder of human resources (HR) research grants up to $200,000 each. There is no requirement that researchers be U.S. based, and in recent years, the funding rate has been similar for researchers both inside and outside the United States. Proposals are reviewed three times each year, and whether funded or not, submitters receive detailed, constructive feedback about their proposals.

In the past 12 years, the foundation has funded more than $2.3 million in research grants for 107 research projects. Fully 88 percent of completed projects have had significant impact, including articles published in academic journals and presentations at national conferences. The journals publishing the most foundation research are *Human Resource Management*, the *Journal of Applied Psychology,* and *Personnel Psychology.*

The foundation funds original, empirical academic research that advances the HR profession. The research is targeted at an academic audience, while also having direct, actionable implications for HR practice, whether the focus is on addressing current challenges or on understanding emerging trends. The foundation will consider any topic and any methodology as long as the proposed methodology is sound and appropriate for the proposed research question(s). Those research questions typically (but not solely) take the form of theoretically derived hypotheses.

In addition, the research must have clear applicability for HR practice and help contribute to evidence-based HR. At least one academic and one practitioner review each proposal. Projects that ultimately are funded share two common characteristics: (1) they are suitable for leading academic journals; and (2) they are likely to yield practical implications for HR managers (i.e., applied outlets should be interested in the research results). The emphasis clearly is on fostering applied research with practical implications for management practice.

In considering each proposal, the committee uses the following eight criteria:

1. Overall strengths of the proposal
2. Overall weaknesses of the proposal
3. The quality of the conceptual framework
4. The quality of the methodology
5. The likelihood of the study being published in a top-tier academic HR journal
6. The likelihood of the study yielding relevant, actionable insights for practitioners
7. The likelihood of the study being completed as outlined (and within two years)
8. The appropriateness of the requested budget

In addition to funding research, the foundation also hosts academic-practitioner forums through its annual Thought Leaders Retreat, and it produces publications and educational resources to advance the HR profession. It also awards $100,000 in student scholarships each year, and makes four $5,000 dissertation awards through the HR Division of the Academy of Management.

Thought Leaders Retreat

Created by the SHRM foundation in 1999, the annual Thought Leaders Retreat brings together a select group of approximately 120 leading-edge thinkers and executives in the broad field of HR. Over one-and-a-half days, participants explore issues shaping the future of the profession and their implications for research and practice. Themes from the past six retreats were the following:

- 2009 – Positioning Your Organization for Recovery
- 2008 – Workforce 2012: Attracting and Retaining Top Talent
- 2007 – Leadership Succession in a Changing World
- 2006 – Employee Engagement: Lessons and Questions
- 2005 – HR Leadership for the Next Decade
- 2004 – HR Leadership at the Board Level

Effective Practice Guidelines

This series of monographs presents important research findings in a condensed, easy-to-use format for busy HR professionals. The overall objective is to answer two questions: (1) What do we know? and (2) What are the implications for practice? This series addresses perspective number 1 of the scientist-practitioner gap noted at the beginning of the chapter. That is, it focuses on ways to make practitioners knowledgeable about the "facts" that are discovered through academic research.

An expert who is thoroughly knowledgeable about the relevant research writes each report. Prior to publication, a committee of academics and practitioners reviews the report, usually providing multiple rounds of review and feedback. Then the report is professionally edited and laid out for easy reading. The following are the reports produced to date:

- *Employment Downsizing and Its Alternatives*
- *Learning System Design*
- *Human Resource Strategy*

- *Retaining Talent*
- *Developing Leadership Talent*
- *Implementing Total Rewards Strategies*
- *Employee Engagement and Commitment*
- *Selection Assessment Methods*
- *Performance Management*

DVD Series

Based on interviews with top executives at leading companies, these educational digital video discs (DVDs), each approximately 20 minutes in length, present case studies of strategic human resources management (HRM) in actual organizations. They also include research-based lessons for practice that other organizations can use. Each comes with a detailed discussion guide and a PowerPoint* presentation to create high-impact presentations for professional development or classroom use. The SHRM Foundation's DVDs are used in more than 400 universities in 43 countries. The following titles are available:

- *Once the Deal Is Done: Making Mergers Work (Featuring* Bupa Australia*)*
- *World Economic Forum: Creating Global Leaders*
- *Seeing Forward: Succession Planning at 3M*
- *Trust Travels: The Starbucks Story*
- *Ethics: The Fabric of Business (Lockheed Martin)*
- *Fueling the Talent Engine: Finding and Keeping High Performers (Yahoo!)*
- *HR in Alignment: The Link to Business Results (SYSCO)*
- *HR Role Models (Cisco, Blue Cross, Qualcomm)*

Finally, the foundation has sponsored two books (*Evaluating Human Resources Programs: A 6-Phase Approach for Optimizing Performance* and *Making Mergers Work*) and three short reports (*Use and Management of Downsizing as a Corporate Strategy; Strategic Research: Human Capital Challenges;* and *Connecting Research to HR Practice).*

In summary, by funding grants and providing scholarships to worthy proposals that have direct implications for management practice, the SHRM Foundation is working to close the science-practice gap. Its Thought Leaders Retreat, Effective Practice Guidelines, DVD series, reports, and books contribute further to this objective. Through multiple channels, the foundation is addressing all three of the perspectives on the science-practice gap noted at the beginning of the chapter.

Human Resource Planning Society

HRPS focuses on one broad area: strategic human resource management. On its website, HRPS describes itself as "The global association of senior HR professionals in the world's leading organizations." Its mission, vision, and strategy are similarly clear. Its mission is "to help organizations enhance their performance through the strategic management of human resources." Its vision is "to be the preferred provider of leading-edge HR knowledge in key strategic areas." Finally, its strategy is "to bring together a diverse group of thought leaders and practitioners in order to align resources to extend knowledge in selected areas."

There are many knowledge areas for which HR professionals are held accountable, but HRPS addresses what it feels are the most critical and strategic ones. Through its research, HRPS has identified five key knowledge areas that are the focus of the HRPS strategy implementation. The five areas are: HR strategy and planning, leadership development, talent management, organizational effectiveness, and building a strategic HR function.

These five areas drive the content and outcomes of all HRPS activities, from workshops and teleconferences to articles in the society's journal, *People & Strategy*, publications, and research. *People & Strategy* is a quarterly journal that contains current theory, research, and practice in strategic human resource management. It focuses on human resource practices that contribute to the achievement of organizational effectiveness. *People & Strategy* includes original articles as well as sections on current practices, research, and book reviews.

A 20-person board of directors, consisting of 18 senior HR executives and independent consultants and two academics, governs HRPS. Its purpose is to oversee the alignment of HRPS activities with the stated vision, mission, and strategy. The executive committee of the board—composed of HRPS officers, board members, and the president and CEO—is responsible for providing and guiding the strategic direction of the society.

HRPS provides a variety of educational forums and activities for its members. It hosts an annual global conference as well as a fall executive forum, attended by global chief human resource officers, vice-presidents, and directors, HR thought leaders, faculty, consultants, and senior line managers. It also provides regular webcasts. The webcasts cover HR hot topics, best practices, and analysis presented live by eminent HR thought leaders. Each is moderated to allow for a question-and-answer period.

With respect to market segmentation of the professional associations discussed thus far, SIOP tends to focus on PhD-level members, academics as well as practitioners; SHRM primarily attracts mid-level HR professionals and some senior-level HR officers; and HRPS is targeted squarely on senior-level HR officers and managers. All three provide rich opportunities for academics to interact with practitioners, and all three clearly support useful, relevant research. They provide opportunities to learn and observe firsthand the "mental models" that practitioners tend to rely on and also the theoretical frameworks that guide academic research. The operative word in the foregoing sentence is "opportunities." Systematic research that demonstrates the actual outcomes of those opportunities is sorely lacking, although anecdotal evidence suggests that there is some degree of cross-pollination.

Academy of Management

According to its website, the Academy of Management is a leading professional association for scholars dedicated to creating and disseminating knowledge about management and organizations. Founded in 1936, the AOM is the oldest and largest scholarly management association in the world. Today, the academy is the professional home of 18,889 members from 108 nations. It comprises 23 divisions and one interest group. Academy members are scholars at colleges, universities, and research institutions, as well as practitioners with scholarly interests from business, government, and not-for-profit organizations. Although most of its members are academics, as a professional association, the AOM seeks and encourages members from all walks of life who are interested in advancing the scholarship of management knowledge.

The academy's central mission is to enhance the profession of management by advancing the scholarship of management and enriching the professional development of its members. The academy is committed to shaping the future of management research and education. According to its *Statement of Strategic Direction*, adopted by the board of governors in April 2001, the mission and objectives of the AOM suggest several important activities, one of which is a major annual conference that consists of a variety of important activities, ranging from workshops to paper presentations and job-placement interviews. In 2009, more than 10,000 people attended the AOM annual conference. It provides an opportunity for members from around the world to come together to build and renew professional and social relationships.

The AOM continually seeks innovative ways to make its annual meeting a better venue for sharing and learning, for example:

- *From high-quality research.* For example, by circulating papers on the Web beforehand, creating more symposia, providing more opportunities for debate of both theoretical and applied issues, and holding theme meetings across divisions.

- *By making the annual meeting more engaging.* For example, by designing a conference within a conference, providing more virtual spaces for members to interact, arranging special sessions for doctoral students to share papers, holding orientation and "get-acquainted" meetings for new members and attendees from around the world, providing additional incentives to divisions and interest groups for innovation, and by sharing best practices across divisions.

- *By making the annual meeting more developmental for members.* For example, by holding professional-development workshop (PDW) sessions for mid-career professionals on updating methodologies and finding new research interests, by organizing more symposia and paper sessions on teaching and practice, and by creating forums for "work in progress."

- *By enabling research presented at the annual meeting to make a greater impact on organizations and the larger society.* For example, by seeking feedback from practitioners about issues in need of research, including more practitioners in division programs, and providing summaries of practice implications from journals on the AOM website.

The AOM is committed to advancing theory, research, education, and practice in the field of management. It publishes four journals, each of which broadly contributes to this objective while emphasizing a particular scholarly aspect of it. The *Academy of Management Review (AMR)* provides a forum to explicate theoretical insights and developments. Articles published in the *Academy of Management Journal (AMJ)* empirically examine theory-based knowledge. The *Academy of Management Learning and Education (AMLE)* provides a forum to examine learning processes and management education. Articles published in the *Academy of Management Perspectives (AMP)*— formerly the *Academy of Management Executive (AME)*— use research-based knowledge to inform and improve management practice. In addition, a quarterly newsletter contains news, events, and activities of the academy. Divisions and interest groups also produce newsletters.

The Academy of Management's newest publication is an annual series, the Academy of Management Annals, written to provide up-to-date, comprehensive examinations of the latest advances in various management fields. Each volume features critical research reviews written by leading management scholars. These reviews explore a wide variety of research topics per volume, summarize established assumptions and concepts, identify problems and factual errors, and illuminate possible avenues for further study. The Annals are geared toward academic scholars in management and professionals in allied fields, such as sociology of organizations and organizational psychology.

A final initiative is AOM Online. It includes current information about the academy's activities, helpful links, resources for professional development, and online discussion groups. Its goal is to be an electronic information su-persource, offering management scholars a gateway to resources they can use to create, disseminate, and apply knowledge about management and or-ganizations. Making effective use of the Web, the AOM hosts 50 electronic mailing lists, connecting nearly 10,000 people. Members host these lists at their institutions, thereby linking thousands more. At a broader level, AOM Online fulfills the following six functions. It is

- an interactive *knowledge repository* for research, teaching, practice, and professional activities
- a *learning portal* with examples, tools, discussions, and electronic com-munities to ignite ideas and foster experimentation
- a *distribution channel,* broadcasting, abstracting, and generating new information
- a *community builder,* linking members to each other and to management scholars and professionals around the world
- a *practice and policy resource,* drawing academia, educational agencies, and the private sector more closely together
- a *Web-development model* with distributed responsibility for content de-velopment by committees, divisions, and volunteers

Labor and Employment Relations Association

LERA, founded in 1947 as the Industrial Relations Research Association (IRRA), is an organization for professionals in industrial relations and human resources. The national organization has more than 3,000 members and includes more than 50 local chapters where members meet colleagues in the private, public, and federal sectors, as well as faculty from local universities and third-party neutrals. It provides opportunities for professionals interested in all aspects of labor and employment relations to network, to share ideas, and to learn about new developments, issues, and practices in the field. LERA provides a unique forum where the views of representatives of labor, management, gov-ernment, and academics, as well as advocates and neutrals, are welcome. LERA also sponsors interest sections in collective bargaining; dispute resolution; international and comparative employment relations; labor and employment law; labor markets and economics; labor studies and union research; and globalization, investment, and trade.

LERA holds an annual membership and professional-development meet-ing, as well as a national policy forum. It also grants two John T. Dunlop Scholar Awards each year. One goes to an academic who makes the best contribution to international or comparative labor and employment research. A second recognizes an academic for research that addresses an industrial relations or employment problem of national significance in the United States.

The association also publishes a number of research reports and books, as well as an annual compendium of research, annual proceedings, and a newsletter. Its biannual journal, *Perspectives on Work*, covers a variety of labor-relations topics, including law, workplace culture, labor history, the effect of economic dislocation and change on employer-employee relations, corporate governance, workplace sociology and leadership, and other issues. Expert workers, students, labor leaders, human resources managers, arbitrators, mediators, government officials, and academics write articles. The target audience consists of academics and practitioners in labor and employment relations, from both a managerial and a worker perspective.

Because the competitive and employment dynamics of different industries warrant industry-specific analysis and action, LERA established a network of tripartite (management, labor, and government) industry councils. Councils are currently organizing in aerospace, airline, automotive, construction, health care, higher education, public sector, materials, utilities, and other industries. Enabled with a major grant from the Alfred P. Sloan Foundation, this initiative represents a key structural addition to the association.

Perhaps because of the highly applied nature of the problems studied, LERA, more than any other association we have examined, affords opportunities for academics and practitioners to collaborate in a manner that enriches and deepens understanding of each other's perspectives. Both groups can contribute reciprocally to progress in addressing the kinds of problems that each faces. This problem-focused research is the sort that Mohrman and Lawler (Chapter 1, Research for Theory and Practice) referred to as "no longer defined through the narrow boundaries of disciplines and professions." Why don't more academics and practitioners engage in problem-focused research? What are the obstacles, and how can they be overcome?

Creating a Future of Relevant, Useful Research

In the conclusion to their chapter, Mohrman and Lawler (Chapter 1, Research for Theory and Practice) posed two fundamental questions: "How do researchers who have been trained by faculty who are unconcerned with bridging the gap and who are in institutions that do not reward or value it, learn to carry out more connected research? How will they come to feel that this is a legitimate route to take?" In fact, many academics place little value on doing relevant research. Palmer (2006) argued that a silent majority of them advocate disinterest in practice in order to achieve scientific objectivity.

Doing so ensures that their interests and values will not be subverted to those of management and that they will not become mere servants of those in positions of power (Baritz, 1960). To the extent that this is true, however, then one can argue, as do Tushman and O'Reilly (2007), that this self-imposed distance from practical concerns reduces the quality of our field's research, undermines the external validity of our theories, and reduces the overall relevance of the data used to test ideas.

Beyond that, many academics do not need to do relevant research, because they are not rewarded for doing it. Thus an online survey of members of the Academy of Management (Shapiro, Kirkman, & Courtney, 2007) concluded that universities' promotion and tenure systems provide disincentives for conducting and publishing practitioner-oriented research. Although professional associations may do an excellent job of providing forums that bring academics and practitioners together, and in fact they do, unless academics place a strong value on doing relevant, useful research, they will not avail themselves of the opportunities to connect with practitioners. Ultimately, therefore, it's a question of values. Commenting on the current state of management research, Starbuck (in Barnett, 2007) noted:

> People should do management research because they want to contribute to human welfare. Those who are professors of management are people of superior abilities and they should use these abilities for purposes greater than themselves . . . I also observe that many doctoral students and junior faculty are focusing on achieving social status and job security and are viewing research methods as tools to construct career success. Few of them seem apt to initiate or even to participate in significant reorientations. (Barnett, 2007, pp. 126–127)

Academics and practitioners live in different "thought worlds," distinct knowledge and practice communities. Academics typically strive to develop and refine theoretically framed, generalizable knowledge (often devoid of context). Practitioners develop and refine knowledge that enables them to solve operational problems that are immersed in context. Both parties have to work hard to appreciate the "mental models" that their counterparts live by, and some just do not want to do so.

With respect to one subset of academics, Johns (2006) noted: "Some quantitative researchers seem almost desperate to ensure that reviewers and readers see their results as generalizable. To facilitate this, they describe research sites as blandly as possible—dislocated from time, place, and space—and omit details of how access was negotiated" (p. 404). In contrast, Cascio and Aguinis (2008b) argued that, at least in the context of forecasting job performance, genuine progress is more likely if researchers focus on in situ performance, that is, specification of the broad range of effects—situational, contextual, strategic, and environmental—that may affect individual, team, or organizational performance. To be able to do that, academics must connect with practitioners and get into organizations in order to understand deeply the many variables that affect performance. Academics must see that as part of their role; they have to *want* to do it. Given the stated missions and activities of the professional associations that we have examined, it is clear that those associations want to provide visibility and recognition to relevant, useful research and to those who conduct it.

Practitioners want actionable knowledge. One of the reasons they find techniques such as the situational interview (Latham et al., 1980) and goal setting (Latham & Saari, 1982) to be actionable is precisely because they were developed and shown to work in real organizational contexts with real people. Professional associations such as SIOP, the SHRM Foundation, HRPS, AOM, and LERA are actively trying to promote actionable knowledge and to create practice-accessible knowledge through the dissemination of research reports (in understandable language and with appropriate qualifiers), together with tools and solutions, such as science-practice networking websites. Yet they can do more.

They can offer interactive sessions in which academics and practitioners can work together on important problems (Cascio & Aguinis, 2008a; Bartunek, 2007). SIOP's pre-conference workshops partially address this issue, but professional associations can and should offer more focused sessions that are truly interactive. Rynes (2007) noted that this is probably the single most important thing that our professional associations can do to narrow the academic-practitioner gap. Ultimately, however, as Tushman (Chapter 9, On Knowing and Doing) has noted, boundaries are extremely important, because if managers, and especially management teams, trust you, you can collect data. Professional associations can bring academics and practitioners together, but there are limits to what they can do. For example, they cannot ensure mutual trust, because trust only develops over time through personal interactions. Yet, if academics and practitioners do not have the opportunity to meet and to share ideas and insights, then there is almost no opportunity for further collaboration.

As a general strategy to foster relevant, useful research, professional associations should strive to achieve three broad, interrelated objectives: promote collaborative inquiry, provide opportunities for access to data, and focus less on "best" practices than on "next" practices. With respect to access to data, for example, SIOP does not actually offer data sets to researchers, but it does bring practitioners and researchers together through its many programs, and in that sense it creates opportunities for researchers to get access

TABLE 13.1 Assessment of Five Professional Associations on Three Broad
Objectives

	SIOP	SHRM Foundation	AOM	HRPS	LERA
Access to Data	4	4	3	3	4
Collaborative Inquiry	4	3	2	1	5
Next Practices	4	4	3	2	4

Sources: I would like to acknowledge the helpful input of Tom Cummings, John Boudreau, Angelo DeNisi, Gary Latham, and Bill Schiemann with regard to the entries in this table.

Note: Cell entries are based on the following scale: 1 = Needs improvement, 3 = Acceptable, but could add more innovative activities, 5 = Progressive, leading-edge activities.

to data. Table 13.1 provides a rough "scorecard" that assesses how each of the professional associations that we have examined is doing with respect to these three objectives.

As the cell entries in Table 13.1 make clear, professional associations are striving to achieve these three objectives, but there is certainly room for improvement. Whereas the AOM is oriented primarily toward academics, SHRM is heavily oriented toward mid-level practitioners— even though the SHRM Foundation has been reaching out to academics for many years. SIOP does include practitioners but primarily serves those with advanced degrees. LERA is small and focuses on employee-relations issues, and by its very nature, it promotes collaboration between academics and practitioners in the production of relevant, useful research.

Conclusion

The focus of this chapter has been on academics and what professional associations can do to help them create actionable research. Although not treated in this chapter, the other side is no less important. Why should practitioners pay attention to research findings? To be sure, consulting firms, executive-education firms, and professional societies do research. Although it may not be the kind of rigorous, peer-reviewed research that academics publish, practitioners often regard it as useful for their purposes. Most of them are unlikely to read professional journals, and managers require no certification to practice, but at least one large group of managers, HR managers, often does seek certification. The Society for Human Resource Management could incorporate more research-based content into its certification study guides and examinations, which thousands of practitioners take every year (Cascio, 2007).

At a more general level, Ian Ziskin, former chief HR officer at Northrop Grumman, noted that theory is problem solving without a customer, while practice is problem solving without a theory (Ziskin, 2009). Organizations may not be interested in supporting research and sharing data with academic researchers, but they always have problems. If academics think of research as problem solving, and frame it that way for practitioners, they may find that practitioners are more receptive to their messages.

Indeed, from an operational perspective, practitioners need solutions to the pressing problems that they face, and they will actively seek new knowledge generated through rigorous research that will help them find those solutions. At the same time, as Ziskin (2009) noted, it is not enough to show that a problem exists; academics (and practitioners) have to create "love" for that problem within the organization. To do that, think carefully about how to frame the problem, and how to address it. Make sure you can answer some fundamental questions such as these: What is the problem? Who cares? Is there a customer for that problem? What is the attention span that people have to address it? Will anybody pay for it? When we are all done, can we brief management about what we found? Practitioners see problems in broad themes and broad patterns (e.g., talent management, retention). Many experts (and non-experts) come to organizations with proposed solutions that sound the same. Like a winning strategy, you must be able to differentiate your approach from others if you want to gain access and have the opportunity to solve the problem in question.

Professional associations are actively reaching out to practitioners to solicit their participation and ideas. Some, like the SHRM Foundation, have institutionalized practitioner input and review on research projects. Bridging the academic-practitioner divide is a journey that has no finish line, but the kinds of innovations and activities that professional associations are undertaking provide cause for optimism that genuine progress can be made.

REFERENCES

Baritz, L. (1960). *The servants of power.* Middletown, CT: Wesleyan University Press.

Barnett, M. L. (2007). (Un)learning and (mis)education through the eyes of Bill Starbuck: An interview with Pandora's playmate. *Academy of Management Learning and Education, 6,* 114–127.

Bartunek, J. (2007). Academic–practitioner collaboration need not require joint or relevant research: Toward a relational scholarship of integration. *Academy of Management Journal, 50,* 1323–1333.

Bass, B. M. (1974). The substance and the shadow. *American Psychologist, 29,* 870–886.

Cascio, W. F. (2007). Evidence-based management and the marketplace for ideas. *Academy of Management Journal, 50,* 1009–1012.

Cascio, W. F. (2008). To prosper, organizational psychology should bridge application and scholarship. *Journal of Organizational Behavior, 29,* 455–468.

Cascio, W. F., & Aguinis, H. (2008a). Research in industrial and organizational psychology from 1963 to 2007: Changes, choices, and trends. *Journal of Applied Psychology, 93,* 1062–1081.

Cascio, W. F., & Aguinis, H. (2008b). Staffing twenty-first-century organizations. *Academy of Management Annals, 2*(1), 133–165.

Dunnette, M. D. (1990). Blending the science and practice of industrial and organizational psychology: Where are we and where are we going? In M. D. Dunnette & L. M. Hough (Eds.), *Handbook of industrial and organizational psychology* (2d ed., vol. 1, pp. 1–27). Palo Alto, CA: Consulting Psychologists Press.

Gelade, G. A. (2006). But what does it mean in practice? The *Journal of Occupational and Organizational Psychology* from a practitioner perspective. *Journal of Occupational and Organizational Psychology, 79,* 153–160.

Johns, G. (2006). The essential impact of context on organizational behavior. *Academy of Management Review, 31,* 386–408.

Latham, G. P. (2009). *Becoming the evidence-based manager: Making the science of management work for you.* Boston: Davies Black.

Latham, G. P., & Saari, L. M. (1982). The importance of union acceptance for productivity improvement through goal setting. *Personnel Psychology, 35,* 781–787.

Latham, G. P., Saari, L. M., Pursell, E. D., & Campion, M. A. (1980). The situational interview. *Journal of Applied Psychology, 65,* 422–427.

Murphy, K. R., & Saal, F. E. (1990). What should we expect from scientist–practitioners? In K. R. Murphy & F. E. Saal (Eds.), *Psychology in organizations: Integrating science and practice* (pp. 49–66). Hillsdale, NJ: Erlbaum.

Palmer, D. (2006). Taking stock of the criteria we use to evaluate one another's work: ASQ fifty years out. *Administrative Science Quarterly, 51,* 535–559.

Rupp, D. E., & Beal, D. (2007). Checking in with the scientist–practitioner model: How are we doing? *Industrial–Organizational Psychologist, 45,* 35–40.

Rynes, S. L. (2007). Let's create a tipping point: What academics and practitioners can do, alone and together. *Academy of Management Journal, 50,* 1046–1054.

Rynes, S. L., Bartunek, J. M., & Daft, R. L. (2001). Across the great divide: Knowledge creation and transfer between practitioners and academics. *Academy of Management Journal, 44,* 340–355.

Rynes, S. L., Colbert, A. E., & Brown, K. G. (2002). HR professionals' beliefs about effective human resource practices: Correspondence between research and practice. *Human Resource Management, 41,* 149–174.

Rynes, S. L., Giluk, T. L., & Brown, K. G. (2007). The very separate worlds of academic and practitioner periodicals in human resource management: Implications for evidence-based management. *Academy of Management Journal, 50,* 987–1008.

Saari, L. (2007). Commentary on the very separate worlds of academic and practitioner periodicals. *Academy of Management Journal, 50,* 1043–1045.

Shapiro, D. L., Kirkman, B. L., & Courtney, H. G. (2007). Perceived causes and solutions of the translation problem in management research. *Academy of Management Journal, 50,* 249–266.

Tushman, M., & O'Reilly, C., III. (2007). Research and relevance: Implications of Pasteur's quadrant for doctoral programs and faculty development. *Academy of Management Journal, 50,* 769–774.

Vermeulen, F. (2007). "I shall not remain insignificant": Adding a second loop to matter more. *Academy of Management Journal, 50,* 754–761.

Ziskin, I. (2009, December). The role of practitioners in the creation of knowledge. Panel discussion at the workshop, Doing Research That Is Useful for Theory and Practice—25 Years Later, University of Southern California, Los Angeles.

ABOUT THE AUTHOR

Wayne F. Cascio holds the Robert H. Reynolds Chair in Global Leadership at the University of Colorado Denver. He has served as President of the Society for Industrial and Organizational Psychology (1992–1993), Chair of the SHRM Foundation (2007) and of the HR Division of the Academy of Management (1984), and as a member of the Academy of Management's Board of Governors (2003–2006). He has authored or edited 24 books on human resource management, including *Investing in People* (2nd ed., with John Boudreau, 2011), *Managing Human Resources* (8th ed., 2010), and *Applied Psychology in Human Resource Management* (7th ed., with Herman Aguinis, 2011). He received an honorary doctorate from the University of Geneva (Switzerland) in 2004, and in 2008 he was named by the *Journal of Management* as one of the most influential scholars in management in the past 25 years.

FOURTEEN

Sticky Findings

Research Evidence Practitioners Find Useful

DENISE M. ROUSSEAU

AND JOHN W. BOUDREAU

What we have here is a failure to communicate.
Cool Hand Luke

Technical skill is mastery of complexity,
while creativity is mastery of simplicity.
CHRISTOPHER ZEEMAN

The hardest problem of all: how people think.
EDWIN KREBS

STICKY FINDINGS ARE RESEARCH RESULTS that grab attention, gain credibility, and are readily shared. The merits of taking aspirin after a heart attack (Smith et al., 2001) or limiting TV watching for kids (Hancox, Milne, & Poulton, 2005) are sticky findings that many people have acted on. Still, an eminently useful evidence-based idea is no guarantee of uptake. Indeed, a destructive idea often stands a better chance of acceptance and use if it captures the attention of people whose interests it serves. Consider the overreliance on stock options in management compensation as one widely popular but bad-for-business idea (Ghoshal, 2005). What is popular is not necessarily scientifically valid and vice versa. Nonetheless, for research findings to be used they need to be sticky, or perhaps more accurately put, they need to be presented in sticky ways. Our chapter's thesis is this: We need to design our research and communications with users in ways that make our findings sticky. The users we have in mind are business professionals, organizational leaders, regulators, and the general public.

269

What Makes Findings Sticky

The notion of sticky findings owes much to the idea of stickiness in fads, fashions, and innovations as popularized by Malcolm Gladwell's (2000) book *Tipping Point*. This notion is developed further by the Heath brothers, in their book *Made to Stick* (Heath & Heath, 2008). Both books base their ideas on scientific studies, embellished with stories that give their research base "legs." Appropriately, findings with legs to travel on are what sticky findings are about.

Sticky ideas have certain traits (Gladwell, 2000; Heath & Heath, 2008). They are simple. They grab attention by being unexpected. Or they are sticky because they create an emotional reaction, ranging from fear (am I messing up my kids?) to relief (ok, I'll keep aspirin in my office). Last, sticky ideas are easily communicated. Or, if the original notion is really complicated, it has been boiled down to get the key idea across. By virtue of their simplicity, emotionality, and unexpectedness, sticky ideas make for a vivid story, a catchy saying, or sometimes an easy fix to try out and share.

For example, in our courses we have found it easy to discuss prospect theory, a judgment process in which people set a reference point in evaluating alternatives (Kahneman & Tversky, 1979). Its core idea can be captured in a sticky phrase, one that we have students repeat, "losses hurt more than gains feel good." It is the gist of prospect theory, and its easy recall allows students to recognize how it applies across diverse scenarios—from purchasing decisions to change management. We aren't talking about creating the Sticky Research Diet. But taking a page from popular self-help books, we do need to find ways that make research findings memorable, communicable, and actionable.

Why We Need Sticky Findings

All chapters in this book are motivated by concern that a long-standing objective in organizational and management research remains largely unrealized: conducting research that is both scientifically advanced and used by practitioners. The persistent research-practice gap is an over-identified problem, meaning that there are lots of reasons why practitioners do not readily apply our findings. This book suggests important causes of this problem, including that scholarly research topics may be too removed from the real problems managers and organizations face. How research is produced is a cause of the research-practice gap, because typically managers are not involved in problem formulation or in the research process (the antithesis of the "engaged scholarship" Van de Ven [2007] describes). Certainly, formulating research problems with greater fidelity to the issues faced by practitioners and involving them in the process may well enhance the usefulness and stickiness of research. Involving opinion-leading users in research, in particular, can lead to their endorsement and popularization of its findings.

In this chapter, we suggest that many, perhaps most, research findings can be made sticky, if communicated in an appropriate manner, channel, and form. In this matter, we concur with the respondents to Shapiro and colleagues' (2007) survey of the Academy of Management's academic and practitioner members. The consensus of that survey's findings is that a good deal of the practical value of research findings gets lost in translation. Taking this problem to heart, we develop the notion of sticky evidence and the features we believe can make for successful research translations (including "Implications for Practice" sections of research articles [Bazerman, 2005], as well as other communiqués targeting practitioners).

Let's talk now about the underuse of organizational and management research findings by practitioners (i.e., the research-practice gap) and then about how sticky findings can help bridge that gap. Fact: *Research evidence is seldom used as a basis for management practice.* Evidence: Professional human resources (HR) managers are unfamiliar with many basic findings in that field, and often fail to act on those findings they do know (Rynes, Brown & Colbert, 2002). The classic example of under-use of research evidence is utility analysis. Utility analysis formulas developed in industrial/organizational psychology show high payoffs from improved selection. Boudreau and Ramstad (2003) observed that these utility-analysis models are seldom used by leaders, and when their use is attempted, sometimes they impact decisions and sometimes they do not (Borman, Hanson, & Hedge, 1997; Florin-Thuma & Boudreau, 1987; Latham & Whyte, 1994; Macan & Highhouse, 1994; Roth, Segars, & Wright, 2000; Whyte & Latham, 1997).

Yet, utility-analysis results seem to be more acceptable to operating executives when they are integrated with capital-budgeting considerations (Carson, Becker, & Henderson, 1998; Cascio & Morris, 1990; Mattson, 2003). These results seem more credible to managers when presented as a special case of investment analysis, including considerations such as discounting for risk and time, after-tax returns, and the costs required to invest in improved selection. Simply put, investing in improved selection is not that dissimilar from investing in any other initiative with uncertain returns, and making that clear seems to improve the stickiness of what are otherwise seen by leaders as arcane psychological calculations.

Practicing managers have little access to research evidence outside professional schools. Evidence: Managers generally rely on their peers and opinion-based management periodicals such as *Harvard Business Review* for new ideas (Rynes et al., 2002. NB: Rynes and colleagues found that less than 1 percent of HR managers at the manager, director, or VP levels read that field's three top-tier academic journals. Most [75 percent] read none of the three.)

Practitioners often do not act on the findings they do know about, and it is not clear whether they even believe them. Evidence: The most widely documented failure of uptake involves the strong and persistent preference practitioners have for intuitive methods of selection. Practitioners continue to use unreliable and invalid, ad hoc or unstandardized employment interviews, a practice that prevails over more reliable and well-validated standardized predictors or mechanical combinations of selection techniques (Rynes, 2010). Highhouse (2008) reviewed multiple studies showing that mechanical or statistical predictions of employee behavior are superior to both intuitive methods, such as the unstructured interview, and combinations of mechanical plus intuitive methods. Nevertheless, the unstructured interview remains the most popular and widely used selection procedure and has been for over the past 100 years (Buckley, Norris, & Wiese, 2000).

Educators and the textbooks they use often do not focus on research findings, fearing that it will make courses too dry. Management educators often view research as "fun squishing." Evidence: Educators and textbook writers who make inconsistent use of research in their classes and texts indicate feeling pressed to avoid being too research-y (Rousseau, 2006). Case studies are used as a teaching method frequently without any grounding of their analysis in findings supported by management research.

Complicating things further, *firms are characterized by weak and inconsistent decision management, making it difficult to systematically act on research findings.* Evidence: Firms typically have unsystematic ways of making decisions regardless of whether the decision is novel or routine (Yates, 1990). They make limited use of protocols or decision trees for common or repeated decisions from selection to performance management, to implementing change, despite evidence of both their value and the repeatable nature of many managerial decisions (Boudreau, 2010; Drucker, 1993; Yates, 1990). Boudreau (2010) suggests that this unsystematic approach may be particularly true for decisions about human capital, compared to other resources, because managers typically have much less training and accountability for understanding human capital decision frameworks than they do for frameworks for resources such as money, customers, and technology. Indeed, Lawler and Boudreau (2009) report that both HR and non-HR leaders in large companies rate business leaders lower on the degree to which they use sound principles for decisions about human capital issues than on the degree to which they do so for more traditional disciplines such as finance.

Lest the last paragraph sound like a rant against managers, let us be clear: academics are at least half the problem. Scholars in organizational and management research are often unaware or unconcerned with how potential users think. Even academic writing intended for practice is often dominated by what a layperson regards as irrelevant backstory (the five other theories considered before the current one) or in-group ("scientific") debates (from the hierarchical structure of a construct such as intelligence, to the distinction between psychological contract and social exchange theory). Academics tend to assume that if something is a problem in scholarly research, it is also a problem in practice. A lot of academics also aren't particularly concerned with communicating research findings to practitioners. Scholarly careers are based on citation rates and recognition from other academics—not practitioners. Moreover, even full-time academics, not just clinical professors and adjuncts, are reluctant to make evidence central to their teaching. Only recently are more systematic ways of using evidence being promoted in management education (e.g., Rousseau & McCarthy, 2007).

The research-practice gap itself contributes to problems in making research sticky. Academics and practitioners tend to be mutually incompetent in relating to each other. Academics don't have a good understanding of how practitioners think nor even what they do. Practitioners, an even more heterogeneous group than academics, often lack training and knowledge regarding basic organizational phenomena and limited insight into their own decision processes. People tend to be overly optimistic when evaluating the quality of their performance on social and intellectual tasks (Ehrlinger et al., 2008). In particular, poor performers grossly overestimate their performance because their incompetence deprives them of the skills needed to recognize their deficits. Surrounded as we are by peers who make the same mistakes we do, this lack of insight into our own errors leads to overly optimistic estimates of how much academics understand about practitioners and vice versa. As a first step, academics and scholarly researchers need to gain insight into the thinking and decision styles of practitioners. How might we do that? Let's consider what we need to know to make findings sticky.

Core Features of Sticky Findings

The job of the teacher is to arrange victories for students.
—Quintilian

We propose a set of core features in communiqués with practitioners that help make evidence sticky. These features reflect research on cognition and decision making, persuasion, and diffusion of innovation (Gladwell, 2000; Goldstein, Martin, & Cialdini, 2008; Heath & Heath, 2008). In specifying these features, we assume that the target practitioner audience is largely made up of novices, not experts in management and organizational research.

1. Findings must be presented in ways that appear practice related.

All people have limited cognitive capacity to process information, particularly when that information is novel or unfamiliar (Simon, 1997). Sticky findings focus on practitioner-relevant or germane content and exclude what's irrelevant. Thinking and learning occur in working memory, which is constrained in the number of bits of data that can be processed at one time. Details of interest only to researchers are distracting and should be excluded. This unnecessary backstory can include the history of the research, its methodological intricacies, or theoretical nuance. The temptation for academic writers to include background is common and can be distracting even for academic readers. It is striking how often we review scholarly manuscripts that include long and comprehensive summaries of prior work but fail to answer this question: What anomalies in prior theoretical frameworks or empirical findings would be explained by this research? Sticky findings require not only an answer to this question but that the answer be presented in practice-related ways. Similarly, use of traditional academic citation style (like "Lennon & McCartney, 1965") distracts lay readers, who tend to wonder: What does this mean? Is it important?

Generally, experts process new information in the context of existing frameworks and mental models. Nonexperts tend to process new information experientially (Chi, Feltovich, & Glaser, 1981; Chi, Glaser, & Rees, 1982). They ask questions such as these: Does this track with my experience? What would it mean if I acted on it? The presentation should address which aspects of a novice's experience, via examples, might help them understand the finding and why the novice's experiences might be misleading. For example, policy-capturing studies suggest that what people report as important to their work choices can differ from factors driving their actual choices (Karren & Barringer, 2002). Evidence indicates that watching what people do may be more informative than asking them to tell you what they do. Practitioners and students often need to experience these types of discrepancies firsthand by actually doing policy-capturing exercises and seeing for themselves how their actual choices differ from their beliefs. In this fashion, we can convey the sticky finding that relying on what people say—instead of what we observe them do—may lead us astray.

2. Express clear core principles in plain language and familiar analogies.

To be easily grasped and recalled, findings need to be expressed succinctly as facts. The principal findings of goal setting, for example, can be expressed as a fact: Specific goals tend to lead to higher performance than do general, "do-your-best" goals (Locke & Latham, 1984). Similarly with the core principle of intergroup research: Socially distant groups tend to have negative perceptions of each other (Insko et al., 1990). Again, scholarly tradition often acts against the use of plain language. A tenet of scholarly research is conservatism. Thus, scholarly writing is appropriately careful to qualify findings with many conditions and caveats. As illustrated above, the phrases "tend to" or "often" may allow the essence of the findings to be stated in direct and plain language, even while maintaining conservatism. Editors and reviewers might be more tolerant of such plain-language statements in research abstracts and practical implication sections. Creating manuscript sections specifically for such plain-language summaries might also help nonacademic readers know where to look to find the essence of the research.

To convey abstract or complicated findings in a manner novices understand, we need to get their attention. Vividness can offset complexity by drawing greater attention to a finding. A vivid, memorable presentation involves actively framing the finding in a way that a person can easily recall and share with others. In medicine, the importance of base rates (i.e., the odds of having a particular disease or condition) in accurately diagnosing a patient's ailment is recalled with the phrase "if you hear hoof beats, think horses, not zebras."

We need to be creative in expressing research findings via memorable communiqués—or collaborate with others who can. We should also consider the best media for memorable communication. Video, social media, or in-person dialogue may be more effective or a great complement to print and text. Research journals can incorporate editorial elements that explicitly invite online discussion, blogging, and other electronic interaction. A good start is for journals to make consistent efforts to translate and communicate findings to traditional press outlets. Of course, pithy findings can be still unearthed by intrepid reporters, bloggers, and online communities. Yet editors and journals could make this easier by seeding these outlets with plain-language and vividly stated findings. In whatever form, the message needs to be in plain language, accompanied by analogies and illustrations to ease user understanding, recall, and uptake. Edwin Locke's (2009) recent book *Handbook of Principles of Organizational Behavior* (2d ed.) illustrates how robust findings in organizational behavior (OB) can be readily communicated to students and practitioners in this fashion.

3. Describe causal processes and mechanisms through which a principle works in plain language with familiar analogies.

To be persuasive, findings have to make sense. Making sense means either fitting into an existing understanding people already have or inducing them to understand and think differently about something. In particular, research indicates that research findings are persuasive when people understand how or why they work (Hornikx, 2005). Mechanisms show why the findings are to be believed and how to adapt and make use of the principle in practice. For example, evidence shows that the central mechanism underlying effective goal setting is the extent of the individual's acceptance and commitment to the goal. Understanding the need for goal commitment and acceptance allows the previously described principle about goals ("difficult and specific goals typically enhance performance more than do-your-best goals") to pass the inevitable sniff test that a novice might conduct: "We set goals around here all the time. Nothing happens. Hmm, maybe people aren't buying in. Should we take a different approach to setting goals?"

Mechanisms make it possible for people to actively process a research-based principle and be mindful of how it can be used. They can then think about how the principle connects to their own experience. A finding's relevance or practicality is less likely to be discounted when the potential user understands how and why it works.

Management educators frequently find it hard to teach certain well-established research findings (Rynes, personal communication, 2008). Tough ideas to get across include the notions that human resource management can be strategic and that leadership can be learned. Sometimes the problem lies in a finding's contradiction with preexisting beliefs or experiences ("the HR Department I work with only does administration and regulatory compliance; I've never seen a leader change"). However, before we blame preexisting beliefs as the major barrier, we must first ask if we have effectively conveyed the mechanisms underlying the finding. Novices who have experienced only administrative or compliance-based HR activities can be forgiven for not understanding the mechanisms through which HR can enhance strategic success, despite all the correlations between sophisticated HR processes and financial outcomes they might have read about. Users who understand the reasons underlying such a finding are more likely to persuade themselves that the finding makes sense and that acting on it can work.

Understanding mechanisms can also help users convince others whose support they need to take action. For this purpose, the mechanisms underlying research findings might be presented in ways that have fidelity or analogy to mechanisms users already understand. For example, Boudreau and Ramstad (2007) suggest that although leaders discount strategic decisions about human resources because "people are too unpredictable," the same leaders routinely make strategic decisions about products and marketing based on research describing the likely behavior of "unpredictable people"— product consumers. Reframing research on human resources as similar to research on consumer behavior reveals connections that make it easier to see how HR research might be used. For example, researchers can frame the question of predicting employee responses to changes in supervision, rewards, or career practices as very similar to predicting consumer reactions to changes in service or product features. It is useful to identify analogies in practice that have fidelity with the logical mechanisms that underlie the research findings (Boudreau, 2010).

4. Frame research according to the end-users' interests.

Findings stick when a practitioner comes to believe that accepting or acting on them serves their interests—while not acting on them has adverse consequences. But it is not enough to argue for the benefits of acting on a finding. We need to recognize that findings sometimes fly in the face of preferred practices. They can challenge a comfortable status quo or make a person feel threatened. Recalling the maxim "losses hurt more than gains feel good," it is important to call attention to harm or the costs of *not* acting on the evidence. Physicians evaluating medical evidence show such a pattern. When medical research indicates that a current treatment causes harm, physicians are more likely to express willingness to change their current practice than when a new practice is found to provide a benefit (Aberegg, Arkes, & Terry, 2006). The persistence of the status quo is a challenge to any presentation of evidence regarding a "better practice."

Since sticky findings are communicated in ways designed to motivate reflection, recall, and use, framing them with respect to the end-users' interests is part of stickiness. Why should a potential user consider acting in new ways or make a special effort to change how decisions are made? What is the end users' interest in the finding? What will happen if the findings are not adopted? Science is not about marketing or advocacy. Still, we need more attention to the ways practitioners might interpret research findings—and design communication strategies for more effective uptake.

For researchers, this observation connects naturally to the assessment of practical significance, as opposed to statistical significance, and the admonishments to present confidence intervals, not just point estimates (e.g., Bonett & Wright, 2007). For example, findings that have probabilities as the dependent variable can often be presented as odds-ratios. Dunford, Oler, and Boudreau (2008), for example, analyzed the impact on executive retention of stock options whose strike price is above the market value (underwater options) on executive retention. They summarized one finding as follows: "If executives' portfolios were underwater by $30 per share, moving them up by $20 per share would reduce the odds of turnover by 32%" (p. 725). Findings presented as proportions of explained variance can be expressed conditionally: "Those with intelligence scores in the top 30% tend to perform this much better, on average, than those in the bottom 30%."

As a firsthand experience, we have tried teaching an MBA class the notion that socialization and training along with other organizational practices can be "substitutes for leadership." This idea comes from Kerr and Jermier's (1978) essay describing how leaders can shape their organizations via certain routine practices. That lecture turned out to be a real dud. Following the class, student feedback essentially said, "We want to be leaders" and "don't need *substitutes.*"

It turns out that "substitutes for leadership" sounded to management students like a way to "replace us." In subsequent classes, students responded much more positively to Kerr and Jermier's idea of substitutes when framed more consistently with their vision of themselves as future leaders. This framing involved presenting those substitutes as "leader extenders" instead, as a way for leaders to leave their lasting imprint on the organization ("making your mark") and a way to influence people when they couldn't be physically present ("because you can't be everywhere at once"). The mechanisms that substitute for (or extend) leadership are, of course, the very means to realize those critical values and behaviors central to a leader's vision of an effective organization. Toward the end of our class discussion, we make the point that under conditions where an incompetent leader takes the helm, the practices that substitute for leadership can help the firm be resilient until better management comes along or the leader improves. In essence, we reframe leadership substitutes as insurance against the possibility of incompetent leadership, because the insurance analogy is quite familiar to MBAs well versed in financial risk hedging.

Quality connections, interactions, and idea sharing between academics and practitioners contribute to framing findings appropriately. So, too, does insight into the learning experience of students (cf. Pace & Mittendorf, 2004). At the same time, as in the case of substitutes for leadership, multiple renditions of the same finding may be needed depending on the audience, its knowledge, experience, and interests.

5. Embed findings within practitioner decision frameworks.

The features of accessible language to present findings and to specify the underlying mechanisms (Features 2 and 3 above) are reinforced when research findings are connected to actual decisions users already face. Sometimes pertinent decisions are obvious, as in goal-setting findings that can be applied to formal performance management, or findings regarding the greater validity of structured interviews over unstructured ones that can be acted on in screening job applicants.

Generally, findings in organizational psychology have their most obvious connections in improving HR processes. This is often quite a compelling connection if the audience is HR professionals. However, many non-HR managers have little context for understanding why improved HR processes matter. A fundamental challenge may be to help non-HR leaders see the value of the improved HR processes in the first place, in order to motivate their acceptance and willingness to act on such research. It does little good for HR leaders to understand that the higher predictability and reliability of structured interviews makes them more valuable than unstructured ones, if the hiring managers they work with do not know why improved validity matters. The translation of validity into value is often where the communication breaks down.

Another challenge to evidence use comes when the ways practitioners approach their current decisions are poorly developed. For example, non-HR managers regard decisions about human capital differently from their decisions about other resources (such as money, technology, materials, and customers) for which they have been more rigorously trained and are held accountable for using logical and evidence-based decision approaches (Boudreau, 2010; Lawler & Boudreau, 2009). Managers may be less systematic or informed in their human capital decisions because the evidence is embedded in disciplines such as psychology, sociology, and organization dynamics. Such disciplines are often less familiar to non-HR managers than areas such as economics, operations, and consumer behavior—more traditional management disciplines.

Yet, when managers do pay attention to the ways they make certain decisions, their capacity to incorporate research findings into their everyday thinking and decision making increases. Grounding human capital research findings in the frameworks practitioners already use can help them incorporate bigger chunks of knowledge.

To illustrate, Cascio and Boudreau (2010) demonstrate how evidence from research on the utility and monetary value of recruitment, selection, and retention nicely fits the metaphor (and decision framework) of a supply chain. When framed this way, it is obvious that when a leader adopts a suboptimal approach to selection, that is precisely the same as choosing to reject a validated method of quality control for raw materials or unfinished goods. Other useful analogies include how job design is similar to engineering component design, how turnover is similar to inventory optimization, and how workforce flows and career paths are similar to logistics (Boudreau, 2010). Recall our earlier example noting the similarity of policy-capturing research on applicant and employee preferences to consumer behavior research. One way to get leaders to attend to such research is to point out in research translations how the value of policy-capturing findings in the arena of human capital is comparable to what can be learned from research on consumers.

For HR managers and leaders, such frameworks, routines, and metaphors often reside in the decisions and processes they use when enacting

HR programs and strategies. For example, research on motivation in areas such as goals, equity, justice, needs, learning, and social dynamics is highly relevant to decisions about reward and pay systems. Yet, HR professionals engaged in the daily challenges of designing and implementing reward systems do not naturally encounter such research. The second author once worked with a senior compensation executive in a global consumer products organization, who was also teaching a class on compensation at a local university. That executive found he could teach students from his experience developing reward systems, but he lacked a theoretical and research grounding. The second author suggested incorporating information from Pinder's (2009) research-based textbook on work motivation and then systematically connecting the theory and underlying research findings to the elements of reward system design.

This executive was one of the top rewards practitioners in the world, educated at one of the top human resource programs, but even he had not incorporated research findings into his work or his teaching. The simple idea of tying his professional rewards framework to established research findings significantly enhanced his awareness of the useful research available. One can imagine similar connections for practitioners who design and implement learning, engagement, development, communications, and a host of other HR systems. The key is to consider their existing decision systems or routines and then create the right hooks to relevant research.

6. Explicate the conditions of use.

Research communiqués that discuss concrete issues surrounding implementation make acting on the findings seem possible and perhaps easier (Bazerman, 2005). It also provides opportunity to suggest tools (e.g., checklists) and frameworks (e.g., a decision tree) that can enable use and guide action. One of the most powerful interventions in evidence-based clinical care has been the increasingly widespread use of checklists to guide nurses and physicians in adhering to the modes of patient care that the research evidence supports (Wolff, Taylor, & McCabe, 2004).

In discussing use, it is important to keep in mind the tremendous diversity of practitioners and practice situations, as well as of practitioner knowledge and experience. Usability may be aided by laying out findings hierarchically so that users can access information at the level of generality or detail that their needs and interests warrant. For example, starting with the basic principles that summarize research findings (specific goals typically motivate higher performance than do-your-best goals), through more complete summaries of overall findings (contingencies where general goals are more effective), to procedural knowledge guiding use (check to ensure goals are understood and accepted; set no more than five goals). Hierarchically organized summaries let users obtain information commensurate with their levels of interest and expertise.

Again, connecting such hierarchies to analogous approaches in more accepted management areas may help. For example, inventory optimization proceeds first by using the "80-20" rule to identify which 20 percent of inventory components create 80 percent of the impact on productivity or value. It then applies deeper analysis and attention to that 20 percent. In the same way, Boudreau and Ramstad (2007) and Boudreau (2010) have suggested first identifying the "pivotal roles" where improved employee performance makes the biggest difference to organizational success and then focusing performance management improvements there.

7. Users can easily access research findings.

Ease of access to research findings is critical for their diffusion, adoption, and use. Most managerial decisions are made with the information people already have in hand (Yates, 1990). Practitioners have to be able to find the evidence both in their personal reading and other self-improving efforts. Ready access to evidence perhaps matters most. Think about a manager who undertakes an active search for relevant scientific findings when preparing to make an important decision. The busy user needs reporting formats that can be found and used with minimum effort. Putting research findings where decision makers can get at them may increasingly require using more "virtual" media such as the Internet; blogs; social media; TED.com (Technology, Entertainment, and Design); and YouTube. As we noted earlier, scholarly journals may offer an important opportunity by explicitly calling on authors to include plain-language implications and then creating standard locations for such summaries, both in print and online.

8. Include opinion leaders' testimonies.

Human learning is largely social learning, a fact true for management and organizational practitioners as it is for professionals such as physicians (Brown & Duguid, 2001). Social networks carry new information and reinforce use of existing knowledge. The stickiness of research findings is aided by the testimony of opinion leaders and their stories and examples.

The social environment where practitioners work can help or hinder their access to and ability to use research findings. Rynes and colleagues (2002) found that HR managers most commonly look to other HR practitioners for help in solving HR problems. Local opinion leaders can hinder research uptake if they are conservative about new ideas or disdainful or illiterate about science. Research-literate leaders who embrace new ideas ease the uptake for others. When opinion leaders adopt and understand research findings, valuable opportunities emerge. Including testimony from opinion leaders in research summaries can help give the findings legs, particularly if a catchy story or notion makes that testimony and idea more attractive and shareable.

Implications for Useful Research

Building Practitioner Capacity to Use Sticky Knowledge

Useful research seems to us to be that which provides insight into the frameworks and mental models practitioners already use. In the original *Doing Research That Is Useful for Theory and Practice* (Lawler et al., 1985), similar issues were raised with regard to users' mental or cognitive "maps." Argyris (1985) noted managers develop maps that structure their thinking and decision making. Such cognitive maps exist, for example, where leaders attempt to create a successful matrix structure; their maps might reflect what such structures are supposed to accomplish and the kinds of success they realize. Noting the features of such maps, Argyris describes how qualitative methods can be used to obtain them. In his response to Argyris, Driver (1985) advises managers and academics to build these maps together so that both understand their respective jargon and mental models.

Such research might entail both qualitative description (Argyris, 1985) and more positivist investigations into the models that decision makers use. Research might investigate how professional education, in management or in other fields such as engineering, shapes the models and frameworks decision makers use. It would be useful to know whether fields more closely aligned with dominant managerial models (such as finance, operations, marketing, and risk optimization) have created more readily used decision frameworks, and whether those frameworks incorporate relevant evidence more quickly or easily. We suspect that in finance and operations research, practice is more closely aligned with research through the prevalence of concepts, such as the time value of money or the spoilage rate of goods or materials, in which managers think and solve problems. Experiments need to be conducted investigating how organization and social science research might be presented in management education as frameworks guiding common human resource and organizational decisions.

Promoting Sticky Evidence in Future Research

Stickiness requires helping a user recognize how findings apply "to me." Research findings in themselves tend to be generic, applicable to a host of managerial decisions and organizational circumstances. Sticky evidence that connects with practitioners is an essential part of the solution to the research-practice gap and to making our research useful. It calls for greater attention to the design of communications between researchers and end-users (cf. Gruber, 2006). A base of knowledge for promoting sticky evidence now exists in the emerging practice domain of communication design. This new field entails the explicit and conscious effort to attract, inspire, and motivate people to respond to communiqués, with the goal of creating benefits for them, their organizations, and communities (Eppler & Mengies, 2004). Its processes involve strategic business thinking, user research, creativity, and problem solving. Tapping into this knowledge base can aid our efforts at promoting use of organizational research.

Note that sticky findings need not be sticky for all. There are practitioners who may derive little value from even the most captivating presentation of the evidence. These might include managers with limited education, those who are intuitive rather than analytic, or the inexperienced. Drucker (1993) pointed out years ago that typical managers treat repeat decisions (such as hiring, firing, and capital investment) as unique. Recognizing the commonalities among decisions requires managers to reflect on their personal practices as a manager, something that busy people may find difficult. As such, it is more pragmatic to target the likely early adopters of research evidence, that is, those self-improving practitioners and practice communities interested in learning and innovation.

There is no shortage of bottlenecks to the uptake and use of research findings, ranging from research undertaken without practice in mind to practitioners making decisions that ignore germane and robust research findings. Sticky evidence coupled with more systematic attention to practitioner decision heuristics, frameworks, and routines offers a way forward. As sticky findings become more accessible, we look forward to the expanding use of management and organizational research by practitioners. Then, indeed, we will be doing useful research.

REFERENCES

Aberegg, S. K., Arkes, H., & Terry, P. B. (2006). Failure to adopt beneficial therapies caused by bias in medical evidence evaluation. *Medical Decision Making, 26,* 575–582.

Argyris, C. (1985). Making knowledge more relevant to practice: Maps for action. In E. E. Lawler III, A. M. Mohrman, S. A. Mohrman, G. E. Ledford, Jr., & T. G. Cummings, (Eds.), *Doing research that is useful for theory and practice* (pp. 79–106). San Francisco: Jossey-Bass.

Bazerman, M. H. (2005). Conducting influential research: The need for prescriptive implications. *Academy of Management Review, 31,* 25–31.

Bonett, D. G., & Wright, T. A. (2007). Comments and recommendations regarding the hypothesis testing controversy. *Journal of Organizational Behavior, 28*(6), 647–659.

Borman, W., Hanson, M., & Hedge, J. (1997). Personnel selection. *Annual Review of Psychology, 48,* 299–337.

Boudreau, J. W. (2010). *Retooling HR.* Boston: Harvard Business Press.

Boudreau, J. W., & Ramstad, P. M. (2003). Strategic industrial and organizational psychology and the role of utility analysis models. In W. C. Borman, D. R. Ilgen, & R. J. Klimoski (Vol. Eds.), *Handbook of psychology: Vol. 12. Industrial and organizational psychology* (pp. 193–221). Hoboken, NJ: Wiley.

Boudreau, J. W., & Ramstad, P. R. (2007). *Beyond HR.* Boston: Harvard Business School Press.

Brown, J. S., & Duguid, P. (2001). Knowledge and organization: A social-practice perspective. *Organizational Science, 12,* 198–213.

Buckley, M. R., Norris, A. C., & Wiese, D. S. (2000). A brief history of the selection interview: May the next 100 years be more fruitful. *Journal of Management History, 6,* 113–126.

Carson, K. P., Becker, J. S., & Henderson, J. A. (1998). Is utility really futile? A failure to replicate and an extension. *Journal of Applied Psychology, 83,* 84–96.

Cascio, W. F., & Boudreau, J. W. (2011). Supply-chain analysis applied to staffing decisions. In S. Zedeck (Ed.), *Handbook of industrial and organizational psychology.* Washington, DC: American Psychological Association.

Cascio, W. F., & Morris, J. R. (1990). A critical re-analysis of Hunter, Schmidt, and Coggin's "Problems and pitfalls in using capital budgeting and financial accounting techniques in assessing the utility of personnel programs." *Journal of Applied Psychology, 75,* 410–417.

Chi, M.T.H., Feltovich, P. J., & Glaser, R. (1981). Categorization and representation of physics problems by experts and novices. *Cognitive Science, 5,* 121–152.

Chi, M.T.H., Glaser, R., & Rees, E. (1982). Expertise in problem solving. In R. S. Sternberg (Ed.), *Advances in the psychology of human intelligence* (vol. 1, pp. 1–75). Hillsdale, NJ: Erlbaum.

Driver, M. (1985). Response and commentary on making knowledge more relevant to practice: Maps for action. In E. E. Lawler III, A. M. Mohrman, S. A. Mohrman, G. E. Ledford Jr., & T. G. Cummings (Eds.), *Doing research that is useful for theory and practice* (pp. 107–114). San Francisco: Jossey-Bass.

Drucker, P. F. (1993). *The effective executive.* New York: HarperCollins.

Dunford, B. B., Oler, D. K., & Boudreau, J. W. (2008). Underwater stock options and voluntary executive turnover: A multidisciplinary perspective integrating behavioral and economic theories. *Personnel Psychology, 61*(4), 687–726.

Ehrlinger, J., Johnson, K., Banner, M. Dunning, D., & Kruger, J. (2008). Why the unskilled are unaware: Further explorations of (absent) self-insight among the incompetent. *Organizational Behavior and Human Decision Processes, 105,* 98–121.

Eppler, M. P., & Mengies, J. (2004). The concept of information overload: A review of literature from organization science, accounting, marketing, MIS, and related disciplines. *Information Society, 20*(5), 1–20.

Florin-Thuma, B. C., & Boudreau, J. W. (1987). Performance feedback utility in a small organization: Effects on organizational outcomes and managerial decision processes. *Personnel Psychology, 40,* 693–713.

Ghoshal, S. (2005). Bad management theories are driving out good management practices. *Academy of Management Learning & Education, 4*, 75–91.

Gladwell, M. (2000). *Tipping point: How little things can make a big difference.* New York: Little, Brown.

Goldstein, N. J., Martin, S. J., & Cialdini, R. B. (2008). *Yes! 50 scientifically proven ways to be persuasive.* New York: Free Press.

Gruber, D. A. (2006). The craft of translation: An interview with Malcolm Gladwell. *Journal of Management Inquiry, 15*, 397–403.

Hancox, R. J., Milne, B. J., & Poulton, R. (2005). Association of television viewing during childhood with poor educational achievement. *Archives of Pediatric and Adolescent Medicine, 159*, 614–618.

Heath, C., & Heath, D. (2008). *Made to stick: Why some ideas survive and others die.* New York: Random House.

Highhouse, S. A. (2008). Stubborn reliance on intuition and subjectivity in employee selection. *Industrial and Organizational Psychology: Perspectives on Science and Practice, 1*, 333–342.

Hornikx, J. (2005). A review of experimental research on the relative persuasiveness of anecdotal, statistical, causal, and expert evidence. *Studies in Communication Sciences 5*(1), 205–216.

Insko, C. A., Schopler, J., Hoyle, R. H., Dardis, G. J., & Graetz, K. A. (1990). Individual-group discontinuity as a function of fear and greed. *Journal of Personality and Social Psychology, 58*, 68–79.

Kahneman, D., & Tversky, A. (1979). Prospect theory: An analysis of decision under risk. *Econometrica, 47*, 263–291.

Karren, R. J., & Barringer, M. W. (2002). A review and analysis of the policy-capturing methodology in organizational research: Guidelines for research and practice. *Organizational Research Methods, 5*(4), 337–387.

Kerr, S., & Jermier, J. (1978). Substitutes for leadership. *Organizational Behavior and Human Performance, 22*(3), 375–403.

Latham, G. P., & Whyte, G. (1994). The futility of utility analysis. *Personnel Psychology, 47*, 31–46.

Lawler, E. E., III, & Boudreau, J. W. (2009). *Achieving strategic excellence in human resources management.* Stanford, CA: Stanford University Press.

Locke, E. A. (2009). *The Blackwell handbook of principles of organizational behavior.* Oxford: Blackwell.

Locke, E. A., & Latham, G. P. (1984). *Goal setting: A motivational technique that works.* Englewood Cliffs, NJ: Prentice Hall.

Macan, T. H., & Highhouse, S. (1994). Communicating the utility of HR activities: A survey of I/O and HR professionals. *Journal of Business and Psychology, 8*(4), 425–436.

Mattson, B. W. (2003). The effects of alternative reports of human resource development results on managerial support. *Human Resource Development Quarterly, 14*(2), 127–151.

Pace, D., & Mittendorf, J. (2004). *Decoding the disciplines: A model for helping students learn disciplinary ways of thinking.* San Francisco: Jossey-Bass.

Pinder, C. (2009). *Work motivation in organizational behavior.* Englewood Cliffs, NJ: Prentice Hall.

Roth, P., Segers, A., & Wright, P. (2000). *The acceptance of utility analysis: Designing a model.* Paper presented at the Academy of Management Annual Meeting, Toronto, Canada.

Rousseau, D. M. (2006). Is there such a thing as evidence-based management? *Academy of Management Review, 31,* 256–269.

Rousseau, D. M., & McCarthy, S. (2007). Evidence-based management: Educating managers from an evidence-based perspective. *Academy of Management Learning and Education, 6,* 94–101.

Rynes, S. (2010). The research-practice gap in I/O psychology and related fields: Challenges and potential solutions. In S. Kozlowski (Ed.), *Handbook of industrial and organizational psychology.* New York: Oxford University Press.

Rynes, S. L., Brown, K. G., & Colbert, A. E. (2002). Seven common misconceptions about human resource practices: Research findings versus practitioner beliefs. *Academy of Management Executives, 18*(3), 92–103.

Shapiro, D. L., Kirkman, B. L., & Courtney, H. G. (2007). Perceived causes and solutions of the translation gap in management. *Academy of Management Journal, 50,* 249–266.

Simon, H. A. (1997). *Administrative behavior* (4th ed.). New York: Free Press.

Smith, S. C., Blair, S. N., Bonow, R. O., & Brass, L. M. (2001). Guidelines for preventing heart attack and death in patients with atherosclerotic cardiovascular disease. *Circulation, 104,* 1577–1579.

Van de Ven, A. (2007). *Engaged scholarship: A guide to organizational and social research.* New York: Oxford University Press.

Whyte, G., & Latham, G. P. (1997). The futility of utility analysis revisited: When even an expert fails. *Personnel Psychology, 50,* 601–611.

Wolff, A. M., Taylor, S. A., & McCabe, J. F. (2004). Using checklists and reminders in clinical pathways to improve hospital inpatient care. *Medical Journal of Australia, 181,* 428–431.

Yates, J. F. (1990). *Judgment and decision making.* Englewood Cliffs, NJ: Prentice Hall.

ABOUT THE AUTHORS

Dr. Denise M. Rousseau is the H. J. Heinz II University Professor of Organizational Behavior and Public Policy at Carnegie Mellon University. Rousseau is founder of the Evidence-Based Management Collaborative, a network of scholars, consultants, and practicing managers to promote evidence-informed organizational practices and managerial decision making. She is editor of the *Handbook of Evidence-Based Management* to be published by Oxford University Press in 2011. A two-time winner of the Academy of Management's award for best management book, Rousseau won the award in 2006 for her most recent book, *I-Deals: Idiosyncratic Deals Workers Bargain for Themselves. Psychological Contracts in Organizations: Understanding Written and Unwritten Agreement* won in 1996.

John W. Boudreau, PhD, is Professor of Management and Organization and Research Director of the Center for Effective Organizations (CEO) at the Marshall School of Business, University of Southern California. A Fellow of the National Academy of Human Resources, he has published more than 50 research articles and books, translated into Chinese, Czech, and Spanish. His scholarly work has won multiple awards from the Academy of Management's Human Resources and Organizational Behavior divisions. His practitioner work has been featured in *Harvard Business Review,* the *Wall Street Journal, Fortune, Fast Company,* and *Business Week.* He advises companies including Global 100 multinationals, nongovernmental organizations, and early-stage companies. Prior to the University of Southern California, Boudreau was a Cornell University professor for over 20 years and Director of Cornell's Center for Advanced Human Resource Studies (CAHRS).

FIFTEEN

Popular and Influential Management Books

GEORGE S. BENSON*

A QUICK TRIP through any bookstore shows that the public's interest in reading business books might only be exceeded by the willingness of gurus, academics, and executives to write them. Amazon currently sells more than 250,000 books categorized as "Management and Leadership." Simply based on sales, a number of these books appear to have captured the attention of managers in the United States and around the world. There are also numerous examples of books without seven-figure sales whose ideas have helped shape business practice. This chapter investigates whether popular and influential management books are written by university-based researchers and addresses the prospect of translating organizational research to managerial practice through management books.

The degree to which popular management books are based on sound research has been hotly debated. Over the past several decades academics and other commentators have regularly criticized popular business books for presenting unsupported conclusions and poor quality research (e.g., Pierce, Newstrom, & Cummings, 2002). Despite their sales, popular business books in general have been widely panned by academic researchers as presenting simple prescriptions, promoting trademarked phrases, and repackaging common wisdom (Argyris, 2000; Rosenweig, 2009). Popular business books are often viewed as advertisements for seminars or consulting rather than as actual prescriptive ideas based on theory and research.

To better understand how university-based researchers are competing in this marketplace for managers' attention, I collected information on books listed on the *Business Week* best-seller list from 1997 to 2009 and six different "best of" or "most influential" lists published from 1997 to 2009. These data suggest that although consultants and gurus dominate the mega–best sellers and popular culture business books, management books written by academics

* Thanks go to Aaron Moses, Bushra Ali, and Hoda Vazari for their help in collecting data and to Jeff Ferguson for his thoughts on business books with impact.

are an important market segment. I found that although most best-selling books are written by consultants and gurus, 25 percent of the *Business Week* best sellers in management from 1997 to 2009 were written by university-based authors. For the 58 management books published since 1970 that are cited on "best" and "most influential" lists, nearly 75 percent were written by authors with university appointments. I also found that management books written by academics were significantly more likely to be cited in practitioner journals and human resources (HR) trade publications than those written by consultants and gurus. In the following pages, I investigate which management books are popular; which have been influential; and how often these books are cited in the popular press, practitioner-oriented journals, and trade magazines. Finally, I review some of the writing on popular and influential management books and offer some thoughts on the prospects for research-to-practice transfer through management books.

Which Books Are Popular?

Coming up with a list of the most popular management books of all time is difficult because there are no agreed-upon or centralized means to track book sales across eras. Contemporary methods of tracking book sales by register scans (e.g., Neilson BookScan) have only been around since the 1990s, and most book sales claims come from authors and book jackets. Of all the business books that are published annually, there are a relatively small number that break through into popular culture and become mega–best sellers. Books such as *The 7 Habits of Highly Effective People*, *Who Moved My Cheese?* and *What Color Is Your Parachute?* rank among the highest selling books of all time. Other self-reported best sellers include *In Search of Excellence* with 6 million sold and *Good to Great* with 4.5 million copies sold.

The 625 different books that appeared on the *Business Week* best-seller lists from 1997 to 2009 are a mixture of new releases and old favorites. In fact, consistency in the list of top sellers over the years led *Business Week* to begin a separate list for "Long-Running Best Sellers" for both paperbacks and hardcover books in the early 2000s. Relatively few of the books on the *Business Week* list, however, actually deal with management, strategy, and leadership. Books on management topics make up only 17 percent of the total and are overshadowed by a huge number of books on personal finance, investment strategies, and self-help. University-based authors were responsible for around a quarter of the best-selling management books (management, strategy, and leadership). Table 15.1 lists the management best sellers written by authors with current or past university affiliations.

TABLE 15.1 *Business Week* Best Sellers, 1997–2009, by Authors with University Affiliations

Management Books	Author	Year	Months as Best Seller
Our Iceberg Is Melting	Kotter, Rathgeber, and Mueller	2006	22
The Innovator's Dilemma	Clayton Christensen	1997	20
Primal Leadership	Goleman, Boyatzis, and McKee	2002	11
The Leadership Challenge	Kouzes and Posner	2001	6
The No Asshole Rule	Robert I. Sutton	2007	6
Confidence	Rosabeth Moss Kanter	2004	4
Management Challenges for the 21st Century	Peter Drucker	1999	3
The Dance of Change	Peter Senge	1999	3
Blue Ocean Strategy	Kim and Mauborgne	2005	3
The Heart of Change	Kotter and Cohen	2002	3
Leading Change	John P. Kotter	1996	2
The Daily Drucker	Peter Drucker	2005	2
The Innovator's Solution	Christensen and Raynor	2004	2
The Fifth Discipline	Peter Senge	1997	1
The Essential Drucker	Peter Drucker	2001	1
Emotional Intelligence	Daniel Goleman	1997	1
The Leadership Engine	Tichy and Cohen	1998	1
Business: The Ultimate Resource	Daniel Goleman et al.	2003	1
The HR Scorecard	Becker, Huselid, and Ulrich	2001	1
Working with Emotional Intelligence	Daniel Goleman	1998	1
Evolve!	Rosabeth Moss Kanter	2001	1
A Sense of Urgency	John P. Kotter	2008	1
Geeks and Geezers	Bennis and Thomas	2002	1
Organizing Genius	Bennis and Biederman	1997	1
The Mind of the C.E.O.	Jeffrey E. Garten	2001	1

Which Books Are Influential?

To gauge which books managers rate as influential, I surveyed executives and examined published lists of "best" or "most influential" business books. First I worked with the eePulse company based in Ann Arbor, Michigan, to pose the question to a large sample of executives through the *Leadership Pulse* survey. The *Leadership Pulse* is a short-format survey regularly conducted with a group of more than 10,000 self-selected executives. These executives are primarily based in the United States and represent a variety of industries and functional backgrounds. A single question was added to a regular survey conducted in January 2010 that asked, "We would like some nominations for books that have had the greatest impact on your management practice or leadership style."

Of the 470 survey respondents, 300 executives listed a total of 224 different books. As an indicator of the inherent subjectivity of what makes a "best" business book, only 44 books were cited by more than one respondent. The list of books most often cited as influential largely overlaps with the *Business Week* best sellers over the last 12 years. All 15 books listed by four or more respondents also appeared on the *Business Week* best-seller lists from 1997 to 2009. (See Table 15.2.)

TABLE 15.2 *Leadership Pulse* Survey of "Best" Books with More Than Three Mentions

Title	*Author*	*Mentions*
Good to Great	Jim Collins	53
The 7 Habits of Highly Effective People	Stephen Covey	14
Execution	Bossidy and Charan	10
QBQ! The Question Behind the Question	John Miller	7
The One Minute Manager	Ken Blanchard	7
Blink	Malcolm Gladwell	5
First, Break All the Rules	Buckingham and Coffman	5
The Five Dysfunctions of a Team	Patrick Lenconi	5
The Leadership Challenge	Kouzes and Posner	5
The Tipping Point	Malcolm Gladwell	5
In Search of Excellence	Peters and Waterman	4
Servant Leadership	Ken Blanchard	4
The Goal	Eliyahu Goldratt	4
The Servant Leader	Robert Greenleaf	4
What Got You Here Won't Get You There	Marshall Goldsmith	4

As a second measure of the influence of management books, I used existing "all time" and "most influential" lists. I compiled six "best" lists from various sources which contained a total of 166 books. Each of the lists was selected based on different criteria, but focused on some combination of the most "important," "influential," or "best" business books of all time. Of the 166 books on the influential lists, approximately half (81) could be categorized as management topics. The six "best" lists included the following:

- *The 100 Best Business Books of All Time* (2009) New York: Penguin.
- *The Best Business Books Ever* (2007) New York: Bloomsbury.
- *Business: The Ultimate Resource* (2002) Cambridge, MA: Perseus.
- "Best Business Books of the 20th Century" (2000) New York: HarperBusiness.
- "20 Most Influential Business Books from 1981–2000" (2000) New York: Forbes.
- *The Ultimate Business Library* (1997) New York: AMACOM.

Table 15.3 details the management books published after 1970 that appeared on three or more of the "best" lists (see the Appendix later in this chapter for a complete list of the "best" books). Although there was significant divergence across the lists, a small number of important books appeared on multiple lists. Two books, *In Search of Excellence* and *Reengineering the Corporation,* appeared on all six lists. *Competing for the Future* appeared on five of the lists and Demming's *Out of the Crisis* appeared on four. These influential books are twice as likely to be written by university-based authors as the *Business Week* best sellers.

Half of the 58 management books published after 1970 that appear on the influential lists were written by authors holding university positions. Although these individuals vary in the degree to which they might be called traditional academics, they all have (or have had) university affiliations.

"Most Influential" Authors with Current University Appointments

Chris Argyris	Daniel Goleman	Jeffrey Pfeffer
Joseph Badaracco	Rosabeth Moss	Michael Porter
Christopher Bartlett	Kanter	C. K. Prahalad
R. Meredith Belbin	Robert Kaplan	Barry Posner
Warren Bennis	John Kotter	Edgar Schein
Leonard Berry	James Kouzes	Donald Schon
Adam	Henry Mintzberg	Peter Senge
Brandenburger	Barry Nalebuff	Robert Sutton
Clayton Christensen	Ikujiro Nonaka	Hirotaka Takeuchi
Reg Evans	David Norton	Noel Tichy
Sumantra Ghoshal	William Ouchi	Michael Useem

TABLE 15.3 Most Commonly Listed "Best" Management Books, 1970–2009

Title	Author	Year	Number of Lists*
In Search of Excellence	Peters and Waterman	1982	6
Reengineering the Corporation	Hammer and Champy	1993	6
Competing for the Future	Hamel and Prahalad	1994	5
Out of the Crisis	W. Edwards Deming	1982	4
Built to Last	Collins and Porras	1994	3
Competitive Strategy	Michael Porter	1980	3
Corporate-Level Strategy	Goold and Campbell	1994	3
Leaders: Strategies for Taking Charge	Bennis and Nanus	1985	3
Management Teams	R. Meredith Belbin	1984	3
Managing Across Borders	Bartlett and Ghoshal	1989	3
Managing on the Edge	Richard Pascale	1990	3
Organizational Culture and Leadership	Edgar H. Schein	1997	3
Organizational Learning	Argyris and Schon	1978	3
Planning for Quality	Joseph M. Juran	1988	3
The Art of Japanese Management	Pascale and Athos	1981	3
The Change Masters	Rosabeth Moss Kanter	1983	3
The Competitive Advantage of Nations	Michael Porter	1990	3
The Fifth Discipline	Peter Senge	1997	3
The Innovator's Dilemma	Clayton Christensen	1997	3
The Mind of the Strategist	Kenichi Ohmae	1982	3
The Nature of Managerial Work	Henry Mintzberg	1973	3
The Rise and Fall of Strategic Planning	Henry Mintzberg	1994	3
Toyota Production System	Taiichi Ohno	1988	3

*Books with equal number of citations are listed alphabetically.

Another 15 books were written by former academics or individuals with previous university affiliations. Notable gurus counted among the "former" academics include Tom Peters, who spent "seven years at Stanford Business School to get my PhD in organizational behavior," as well as Gary Hamel (London Business School, Michigan, and Harvard) and Michael Hammer (Massachusetts Institute of Technology). Also included in this list is Jim Collins, who was formerly on the faculty at Stanford.

Which Books Transfer to Practice?

To better gauge the diffusion of the different books into popular culture, HR practice, and teaching through business journals, I searched for mentions of the popular and influential books in three different types of publications. Full text searches were done for the book titles and in some cases the first author's last name. Articles that mentioned the book were counted and used to compute citations per year since the books were published (or since 1984 for older books). First, newspapers and magazine articles were searched using LexisNexis to search major U.S. publications. Second, ABI/Inform was used to search *Training and Development* magazine and *HR Magazine.* Third, mentions in business journals were collected for: *Harvard Business Review, Sloan Management Review, and Organizational Dynamics.*

Data on the number of mentions in these publications suggest that these three types of publications (popular press, practitioner journals, and HR trade associations) tend to focus on different types of books and authors. General newspapers and magazines are most likely to mention books written by nonacademic consultants and gurus with 19.72 mentions per year for the average book published. However, books written by academically affiliated authors were close behind with an average of 15.46 mentions per year. Actual managers (in the form of ex-CEOs and billionaires) were the least likely to be mentioned in newspapers and magazines. These data indicate that although academic books cited as "best" or "influential" have gained some traction, the mass media still gravitate toward books written by consultants and gurus.

A different pattern emerges, however, when examining which books are mentioned in practitioner journals and HR trade magazines. Books written by authors with academic affiliations are two and a half times more likely to be mentioned in practitioner journals such as *Harvard Business Review* and more than twice as likely to be mentioned in HR trade magazines than books written by consultants and gurus. (See Table 15.4.)

Examining the ten most mentioned books in each of these three types of publications further illustrates these differences. Newspapers and magazines

TABLE 15.4 Book Mentions per Year by Author for Influential Management Books

	Number of Books	Newspapers and Magazines	Practitioner Journals	HR Trade Magazines
Consultant/Guru	26	19.72	0.95	0.25
CEO/Billionaire	4	8.61	0.48	0.06
Academic	28	15.46	2.41	0.61

were far more likely to mention books that have crossed over into popular culture such as *Freakonomics, The Tipping Point, Blink*, and *The Black Swan*. When newspapers and magazines mention management books, they are most likely to mention the most popular books written by consultants including *Who Moved My Cheese?* and *The 7 Habits of Highly Effective People.*

The books most often mentioned in practitioner journals and HR trade magazines, on the other hand, are dominated by books written by academics. Eight of the ten books most often appearing in practitioner journals were written by university-based researchers, with books by Harvard faculty appearing most frequently. Among all the popular and influential management books investigated, *The Balanced Scorecard* stands out as one of the most frequently mentioned across all three types of publications, indicating the broad impact of this book on popular culture, teaching and HR practice. (See Table 15.5.)

What Makes a Book Popular or Influential?

Given the number of business and management books that are published annually, it is difficult to say definitively what causes a business book to break through to mass popularity. The role that news media and marketing play is clear from watching the success of books such as *Freakonomics* and *Blink,* which have been featured in popular magazines and newspapers at least daily (on average) since they were released. Word of mouth and popular appeal also play a role. Peters and Waterman were apparently surprised by the mass sales of 1982's *In Search of Excellence.* The publishers were unhappy when McKinsey distributed 15,000 prepublication copies of the book, thinking that the authors had given away a significant proportion of their potential sales (Newstrom, 2002). It turns out that these prepublication copies primed interest in the book as people wanted to know what everyone was talking about. Although it is difficult to peer into the black box of popular appeal, the mass market management books appear to have some characteristics in common.

TABLE 15.5 Top 10 Citations per Year for Popular and Influential Management Books

Newspapers and Magazines	Number of Citations	Practitioner Journals	Number of Citations	HR Trade Magazines	Number of Citations
Freakonomics	415	Competitive Advantage	12.21	The Fifth Discipline	3.67
Blink	414	The Balanced Scorecard	8.77	The Balanced Scorecard	3.23
The Tipping Point	244	Competing on Analytics	6.50	Action Learning	3.12
The Black Swan	201	The Fifth Discipline	5.92	In Search of Excellence	1.96
Who Moved My Cheese?	153	The Innovator's Dilemma	5.58	The One Minute Manager	1.96
The 7 Habits of Highly Effective People	138	Competitive Strategy	4.28	Emotional Intelligence	1.75
Good to Great	127	In Search of Excellence	4.16	The Change Masters	1.32
The Balanced Scorecard	111	Blue Ocean Strategy	4.00	Good to Great	1.00
The Will to Manage	85	The Knowledge-Creating Company	3.07	Megatrends	.96
Why We Buy	82	Built to Last	3.07	Competitive Advantage	.83

Notoriety

For popular books in particular, the number one factor in book sales appears to be the author's notoriety. The influence of notoriety is clear, for example, when looking at the number of billionaires, CEOs, and other famous people who have published business best sellers over the past 12 years. Twenty-six different CEOs (and former CEOs) published *Business Week* best sellers from 1997 to 2009. The list also includes a number of coaches, politicians, and others who have translated their fame into best sellers.

The *Business Week* best-seller lists over the past 12 years also reveal multiple repeat authors. These are authors who have created their own brands and books series around certain topics. Among management consultants, serial authors include Ken Blanchard (seven books) and Steven Covey (five books). Tom Peters and Jim Collins have built audiences that vault any new release onto the best-seller lists. Among university-based authors, Michael Porter and Warren Bennis have created personal brands for all their books.

Target Audience

The most popular business books of all time and the very top sellers in the *Business Week* list are all geared toward mass audiences. Books such as *The One Minute Manager, Who Moved My Cheese?* and *Getting to Yes!* tend to straddle the line between management and self-help and are widely read by more than business people. Sales are also driven by the integration of the material into common corporate training classes. *Who Moved My Cheese?* is a parable on coping with change that is easy to ask participants to pre-read and is regularly used in both in-house training and off-the-shelf courses; it claims sales of more than 20 million copies. *The 7 Habits of Highly Effective People* has been integrated into a series of course offerings widely offered in Fortune 500 firms.

Timing

Many of the books cited as "best" or most "influential" reflect the times in which they were published. The early 1980s was a time of transformation in American manufacturing, in which a competitiveness gap was perceived and the economy was easing out of a recession and the "malaise" of the 1970s. It was a perfect time for *In Search of Excellence,* which provided some specific prescriptions and optimism that large corporations could be transformed with "a bias for action" and willingness to challenge bureaucracy. The other most influential books of the 1980s dealt with quality (*Out of the Crisis*; *Planning for Quality*) and Japanese management (*The Art of Japanese Management*; *Japan Inc.*).

Similarly, the 1990s were a time of rapid technological change, internationalization, and evolution toward a knowledge- and service-based economy. The internet revolution and tech bubble were in full swing and books such as *Complexity, The Knowledge-Creating Economy,* and *Intellectual Capital* reflected the zeitgeist. Disruptive technologies were on everyone's mind when *The Innovator's Dilemma* was released in 1997. The most influential books of the times reflect the times but also help to define certain ages in retrospect.

Style

Although the most popular and influential management books of all time are generally defined by a "breakthrough idea," many are also notable for their simplicity. Newstrom (2002) notes, "Many books that were successful in the marketplace, selling millions of copies and sustaining interest over a period of years had one distinguishing feature above all others: readers could reiterate their major conclusions or recommendations in very few words." Pagel and Westerfelhaus (2005) conducted a detailed analysis of the reading habits of managers and concluded that above all else they preferred simple "business" writing and expressed distaste for "academic" writing. The preferred writing is characterized by "(a) short length, (b) concise word usage, (c) direct presentation of main points, (d) the presence of concrete examples and/or the absence or abstract concepts, and (e) simple language" (p. 430).

Are They Based on Research?

The management, strategy, and leadership books published by university-affiliated authors and reviewed for this study cover a wide range of topics and vary significantly in the degree to which they are based on research. For example, Goleman's original *Emotional Intelligence* largely presents the work of other brain researchers as derived from peer-reviewed articles, whereas the follow-up *Working with Emotional Intelligence* presents original work. Bob Sutton's *The No Asshole Rule*, described by *Publishers Weekly* as "meticulously researched," aligns with academic research but is largely supported with nonacademic examples. Kim and Mauborgne's *Blue Ocean Strategy* uses a series of case studies to illustrate their theory developed in a series of papers published predominantly in *Harvard Business Review*. The contrast in the degree to which they are research based is particularly stark among the *Business Week* best sellers from 1997 to 2009. *The Innovator's Dilemma* presents the details of Christensen's groundbreaking research on organizational survival in the disk storage industry, whereas Kotter's *Our Iceberg Is Melting* is a parable about organizational change that details the ground breaking beneath a group of penguins.

Moving beyond the books by university-affiliated authors, any discussion of management books, research, and practice must acknowledge that the best-selling management books of all time (and many of those cited as best or most influential) are not research based. They do not present research findings and in many cases do not suggest that the books are based on anything more than personal observation. Some popular books have been criticized as not only unsupported by research but actually spreading bad advice (Argyris, 2000).

Of all the management books over the last 40 years, Peters and Waterman's *In Search of Excellence* is the leader in simultaneously capturing the attention of managers and the derision of business researchers. The publication of *In Search of Excellence* is commonly cited as a watershed for business publishing and the market for business gurus in general. The eight easy-to-understand principles with explanatory examples have generated a whole series of similar books over the last 30 years that presents a set of defining principles or characteristics of high-performing companies.

The book was also notable in presenting the eight attributes based on empirical research used to identify the companies. The book describes how the *In Search of Excellence* companies were identified by assessing objective performance measures. This same formula has since been applied in a number of other popular and influential books most notably *Built to Last* (Collins and Poras) and *Good to Great* (Collins). The research used to select the companies and the practices for *In Search of Excellence* was criticized almost immediately ("Oops! Who's Excellent Now?" *Business Week*, 1984) and has been the subject of several systematic critical analyses in the 27 years since its publication (e.g., Hitt & Ireland, 1987; Rosenzwieg, 2009).

It now appears that the methods to select the companies were less systematic than presented. In 2001, an article appeared in *Fast Company* with Peters on the byline that contained the admission that "I confess: We faked the data." Peters wrote:

> *Search* started out as a study of 62 companies. How did we come up with them? We went around to McKinsey's partners and to a bunch of other smart people who were deeply involved and seriously engaged in the world of business and asked, Who's cool? Who's doing cool work? Where is there great stuff going on? And which companies genuinely get it? That very direct approach generated a list of 62 companies, which led to interviews with people at those companies. Then, because McKinsey is McKinsey, we felt we had to come up with some quantitative measures of performance.

Peters was surprised by the negative publicity over the admission and quickly backtracked by claiming that he had been the victim of an "aggressive headline" and that the words had come from Allan Weber, *Fast Company* senior editor who had actually written the article after lengthy interviews with Peters. "Get off my case...We didn't fake the data," Peters later said (Byrne, 2001). Peters writes:

> Was our process fundamentally sound? Absolutely! If you want to go find smart people who are doing cool stuff from which you can learn the most cutting-edge principles, then do what we did with *Search*: Start by using common sense, by trusting your instincts, and by soliciting views of "strange" (that is, unconventional) people. You can always worry about proving the facts later.

The primary criticism leveled against books with high-performance principles and other books is that company examples are selected first and the measures used to identify the companies are reverse engineered. Jim Collins describes that for *Good to Great*, the 11 companies were selected in part based on superior stock returns and that the conclusions drawn come "directly from the data" (p. 10). Although making no criticism of the practices that good companies use to transform themselves into great ones, Resnick and Smunt (2008) attempted to reproduce Collins's results and concluded that the selection of the companies was most likely "data-mining."

However, the influence (and sales) of these books is undeniable and a detailed critique of their methods may be missing the point. The practicing manager values research differently than university faculty, and the success of these books has created a market and opened up the discussion as to what the "high-performance" practices should be. Julia Kirby (2005), senior editor at *Harvard Business Review*, summarized the impact of *In Search of Excellence*:

> As management consultants, Peters and Waterman sat at the intersection of scholarship and practice, and cast the gauntlet down in each direction: They challenged managers by claiming that varying managerial actions and attributes could account for the differences between winners and losers. At the same time, they challenged researchers by claiming that the problem of isolating the drivers of high performance was tractable. Did they get the answers right? Probably not... In the end the impact of *In Search of Excellence* is less that it solved the problem than that it put the problem on the table.

Prospects for Research Transfer

A great deal of frustration and pessimism has been expressed among management scholars in writing, conferences, and this book over the difficulty they have in transferring research findings into practice through traditional outlets, including management books. It is clear that more academic researchers have a difficult time competing with consultants, journalists, gurus, and former CEOs in both book sales and name recognition. However, I think many researchers both overstate the actual impact of popular business books and discount the role that rigorous research has played in the evolution of management practice in today's large organizations around the world.

Granted, there are well-documented examples of *Business Week* best sellers that have helped to spread ideas that not only lack research support but may actually be damaging in practice. Forced ranking systems, overuse of short-term incentive rewards or stock-based compensation, and a fixation on "total quality" and "reengineering" have all been popularized through business books with significant negative repercussions. However, many of the popular business books that have drawn criticism from management researchers have either limited application to practice or actually align with practices supported by rigorous research. While instructive fables (e.g., "the hedgehog") and platitudes (e.g., "think win/win") are easy to remember and appealing, they are not particularly actionable. In many cases, the criticism leveled against popular management books is not against the practices they advocate but the methodology used to derive them. Setting clear goals, using validated selection practices, and creating a culture of empowerment are all sound practices supported by research—regardless of how the authors arrived at the conclusions.

Focusing on best sellers to compare the impact of academic versus popular management books also might not be the best measure of the transfer of research to practice. First of all, many research-based books by academic authors are intended for smaller audiences of professionals in human resources, organizational development, training, and other specialized areas rather than managers in general. For example, it is clear that books such as *HR Champions*, *The HR Scorecard*, and *Beyond HR* have changed the way that HR managers think about practice even though they have sold a fraction of the biggest best sellers. The notion that academic authors cannot compete with mass market business books ignores the fact that there have been many innovations in employee selection, organizational design, team-based work, goal setting, training, job design and other practices over the past several decades with firm peer-reviewed research foundations and adopted by managers in part because of books that were not best sellers or on all-time lists. The widespread use of goal setting, team-based work, or high-involvement work practices in manufacturing has had positive impacts on organizations but represents an accumulation of research and writing in many formats rather than a single breakthrough book.

For many researchers such as Beer, Prahalad, Lawler, and Gratton represented in this book, works targeted toward practitioners serve as punctuation points or summaries of a career's worth of work that also includes academic and practitioner journal articles, teaching, cases, textbooks, consulting, speeches, and interviews. I suggest that genuine changes in management practice are more likely to emerge from this steady drumbeat of examples and findings rather than the single best-selling books. The presentation and repetition of research findings across formats allows managers of different generations, educational backgrounds, and industries to discover and apply the principles in ways that suit them best—whether that comes from a 300-page book or a short workbook and diagnostic survey.

There are many good examples of research transfer through books, but organizational researchers should note the popularity of recent books on the psychology of decision making. Half of the popular books on decision making are written by academics who effectively translate peer-reviewed research for managers. Another third of the best-selling books on decision making are by professional writers, such as Malcolm Gladwell, who read academic research and repackage it for mass consumption. Robert Cialdini is a great example of programmatic research-to-practice writing; his two books on the *Business Week* list (*Influence* and *Yes!*) on the psychology of persuasion are supported by numerous original peer-reviewed articles and a textbook.

The findings presented in this chapter should be tempered by numerous limitations of measuring and comparing the popularity and influence of business books. First, this research ignores the large market in textbooks, which are not only "best sellers," but also important formats for transferring research to practice. Second, the lists of "best" or "influential" are inherently problematic, and no doubt important books have been left off and books have been included that are idiosyncratic to particular lists. Similarly, categorizing the popular and influential books by subject was arbitrary in certain cases. I categorized academic authors by whether they had a faculty affiliation, but the distinction between academic and consultant or guru is inexact and subjective. Finally, selecting only best sellers and "best of all time" lists also focuses on single books by individuals and overlooks the changes in business practice that are based on cumulative research and writing. For example, very few of the books identified as most influential dealt with work teams, job design, and incentive rewards, whereas the arguably largest change in business practice over the last 30 years has been the adoption of "high-performance" work practices in the United States and Europe.

Given the intense competition in the marketplace for business books, are management books a viable means to transfer organizational research into practice? In 2002, Pfeffer and Fong conducted a similar analysis of popular and academic business books and concluded that, "only a small fraction of the business books that presumably influence management are actually written by academics" and that "business books are not a major source of books that directly influence management thought" (p. 87). I would suggest that although consultants and gurus dominate the mega–best sellers and popular culture business books, management books written by university-based academics are more likely to be cited by journals specifically oriented towards managers and are more likely to be cited as influential over the long term. So even though management books written by university researchers have a tough time competing for mind share among the general public and practitioners, there is reason to believe that management books are a viable and important means to transfer academic research to practice.

Appendix

Management Books Published Since 1970 on "Best" Lists

Title	Authors	Year	#	Best Ever	Business	Ultimate	100 Best	Forbes	Harpers
In Search of Excellence	Peters and Waterman	1982	6	1	1	1	1	1	1
Reengineering the Corporation	Hammer and Champy	1993	6	1	1	1	1	1	1
Competing for the Future	Hamel and Prahalad	1994	5	1	1	1	1	1	
Out of the Crisis	W. Edwards Deming	1982	4	1	1	1	1		
Built to Last	Collins and Porras	1994	3	1	1			1	
Competitive Strategy	Porter	1980	3	1	1	1			
Corporate-Level Strategy	Goold and Campbell	1994	3	1	1	1			
Leaders: Strategies for Taking Charge	Bennis and Nanus	1985	3	1	1	1			
Management Teams	Belbin	1984	3	1	1	1			
Managing Across Borders	Bartlett and Ghoshal	1989	3	1	1	1			
Managing on the Edge	Pascale	1990	3	1	1	1			
Organizational Culture and Leadership	Schein	1997	3	1	1	1			
Organizational Learning	Argyris and Schon	1978	3	1	1	1			
Planning for Quality	Juran	1988	3	1	1	1			
Riding the Waves of Culture	Trompenaars and Hampden-Turner	1997	3	1	1	1			
The Age of Unreason	Handy	1990	3	1	1	1			
The Art of Japanese Management	Pascale and Athos	1981	3	1	1	1			
The Borderless World	Ohmae	1990	3	1	1	1			
The Change Masters	Kanter	1983	3	1	1	1			

Title	Authors	Year	#	Best Ever	Business	Ultimate	100 Best	Forbes	Harpers
The Competitive Advantage of Nations	Porter	1990	3	1	1	1			
The Fifth Discipline	Senge	1990	3	1	1	1			
The Innovator's Dilemma	Christensen	1997	3	1			1	1	
The Mind of the Strategist	Ohmae	1982	3	1	1	1			
The Nature Of Managerial Work	Mintzberg	1973	3	1	1	1			
The Rise and Fall of Strategic Planning	Mintzberg	1994	3	1	1	1			
Toyota Production System	Ohno	1988	3	1	1		1		
Blur	Davis and Meyer	1998	2	1	1				
Good to Great	Collins	2001	2				1	1	
Intellectual Capital	Stewart	1997	2	1	1				
Leading Change	Kotter	1996	2	1			1		
Managing	Geneen	1985	2	1	1				
On Becoming a Leader	Bennis	1994	2	1			1		
The Will to Manage	Bower	1996	2	1	1				
Being Digital	Negroponte	1995	1	1					
Co-Opetition	Brandenburger and Nalebuff	1996	1	1					
Competitive Advantage	Porter	1985	1					1	
Complexity	Waldrop	1992	1	1					
Control Your Destiny or Someone Else Will	Tichy and Sherman	2005	1				1		
Discovering the Soul of Service	Berry	1999	1				1		
Emotional Intelligence	Goleman	1997	1	1					
Execution	Bossidy, Charan, and Buck	2002	1				1		
First, Break All The Rules	Buckingham and Coffman	1999	1				1		

(Continued)

Appendix (*Continued*)

Title	Authors	Year	#	Best Ever	Business	Ultimate	100 Best	Forbes	Harpers
Information Rules	Shapiro and Varian	1998	1	1					
Japan Inc.	Ishinomori	1988	1					1	
Leadership Is an Art	Depree	2004	1			1			
Liberation Management	Peters	1992	1		1				
Managing Transitions	Bridges	1991	1	1					
Natural Capitalism	Hawken, Lovins, and Lovins	1999	1	1					
The Art of Long View	Schwartz	1997	1	1					
The Balanced Scorecard	Kaplan and Norton	1996	1				1		
The Discipline of Market Leaders	Treacy and Wiersema	1997	1	1					
The Five Dysfunctions of a Team	Lencioni	2002	1				1		
The Great Game of Business	Stack and Burlingham	1994	1				1		
The Knowing -Doing Gap	Pfeffer and Sutton	2000	1				1		
The Knowledge-Creating Company	Nonaka and Takeuchi	1995	1	1					
The Leadership Challenge	Kouzes and Posner	2001	1				1		
The Leadership Engine	Tichy and Cohen	1998	1						1
The Machine That Changed the World	Womack, Jones, and Roos	1991	1	1					
The New Corporate Cultures	Deal and Kennedy	1999	1	1					
The Radical Leap	Farber	2004	1				1		
The Six Sigma Way	Pande, Neuman, and Cavanagh	2000	1					1	
The Wisdom of Teams	Katzenbach and Smith	1993	1						1
Theory Z	Ouchi	1981	1	1					

RESEARCH APPROACH

I examine which business books are popular based on *Business Week* best-seller lists from 1997 to 2009. The source of the *Business Week* best-seller data is proprietary and the list has changed format over the years. For each of the 625 books I investigated the degree to which they (1) dealt with management topics and (2) were written by current and former academics. Second, using frequent appearance on "best of" lists as a proxy for influence, I compiled a list of 161 books cited among the most influential of all time. I also categorized these books by subject and collected data on whether these books were written by current and former academics. Finally, I gathered citation counts on popular and influential management books in various publications to gauge the size of their impacts on business practice. I counted the number of times the books were mentioned in popular newspapers and magazines, HR trade magazines (e.g., *HR Magazine*), and academic bridge journals (e.g., *Harvard Business Review*) to better understand the pathways through which popular and influential business books written by academics and nonacademics might influence business practice.

REFERENCES

Argyris, C. (2000). *Flawed advice and the management trap.* Oxford: Oxford University Press.

Byrne, J. (2001, December 3). The real confessions of Tom Peters. *Business Week.*

Hitt, M., & Ireland, D. (1987). Peters and Waterman revisited: The unending quest for excellence. *Academy of Management Executive, 1*(2), 91–98.

Kirby, J. (2005). Toward a theory of high performance. *Harvard Business Review, 83*(7), 30–39.

Newstrom, J. (2002). In search of excellence: Its importance and effects. *Academy of Management Executive, 16*(1), 52–56.

Pagel, S., & Westerfelhaus, R. (2005). Charting managerial reading preferences in relation to popular management theory books. *Journal of Business Communication, 42*(4), 420–448.

Peters, T. (2001, November 3). The real confessions of Tom Peters. *Fast Company.*

Pfeffer, J., & Fong, C. T. (2002). The end of business schools? Less success than meets the eye. *Academy of Management Learning and Education, 1,* 78–95.

Pierce, J., Newstrom, J., & Cummings, L. L. (2002). Reflections on the best sellers: A cautionary note. In J. Pierce & J. Newstrom (Eds.), *The manager's bookshelf: A mosaic of contemporary* views (pp. 25–30). Upper Saddle River, NJ: Prentice Hall.

Resnick, B., & Smunt, T. (2008, November). From good to great to... *Academy of Management Perspectives,* 6–12.

Rosenzwieg, P. (2009). *The halo effect... and eight other business delusions that deceive managers.* New York: Free Press.

ABOUT THE AUTHOR

George S. Benson is an Associate Professor at the University of Texas at Arlington and an Affiliated Researcher with the Center for Effective Organizations. George earned his PhD from the University of Southern California in the Marshall School of Business. He also holds degrees from Washington and Lee University and Georgetown University. He previously worked as a research analyst at the American Society for Training and Development in Alexandria, Virginia.

SIXTEEN

Commentary

Observations Concerning Pathways for Doing "Useful Research"

GARY P. LATHAM

THE SPECIFIC HIGH GOALS of the workshop on which this book is based were, in my opinion, threefold: (1) Determine whether there is consensus among the presenters and discussants as to whether the interrelated academic fields of human resource management (HRM), industrial-organizational (I-O) psychology, and organizational behavior (OB) are in serious trouble from the standpoint of widening the scientist-practitioner gap. (2) Identify the causes for the gap if the gap is getting larger rather than smaller. (3) Provide prescriptive solutions on ways to at least minimize, if not eliminate, the gap between these two groups.

The Problem

The workshop participants were predominately senior scholars whose academic careers exemplify the practice of science for the purpose of improving organizational behavior. Although his name was not invoked during the workshop, all of the participants have had careers that exemplify Kurt Lewin's credo (1945) of no research without action, no action without research. "Useful research" was implicitly defined by some, and explicitly defined by others, as research that significantly influences and is influenced by practice in organizational settings. The desired reciprocal influence of these two domains has been discussed elsewhere (Latham, 2001a, 2001b), as have disagreements with this viewpoint (Hulin, 2001).

There was strong, if not unanimous, consensus among the workshop participants that the three interrelated fields—HRM, I-O, and OB—currently are in trouble. The problem is the ongoing widening rather than narrowing of the gap between science and practice. As an example, Rousseau and Boudreau

(Chapter 14, Sticky Findings) point out that behavioral scientists have known for decades (e.g., Wagner, 1949; Ulrich & Trumbo, 1965) that an unstructured interview is unreliable and hence lacks validity for hiring employees. Despite this well-known fact, unstructured interviews continue to be widely used for selection around the globe. This practice results in both Type I and Type II errors. That is, applicants who are not qualified for the job are hired while qualified applicants are rejected. Consequently, many organizations suffer needlessly low productivity and high employee turnover.

The narrowing of the scientist-practitioner gap through research that is used by the public warrants attention because we are citizens of this globe first and foremost, and secondarily scientists, practitioners, or scientist-practitioners. It is arguably unethical for behavioral scientists to restrict their findings to scholarly journals when they have answers to so many organizational ills. Imagine the outcry of the public if the medical profession remained silent regarding their knowledge of action steps for preventing cholera, measles, mumps, or polio.

As I noted in my first presidential column in *The Industrial Psychologist* (Latham, 2008), when the public perceives a problem, they are likely to turn to economists, engineers, legislators, physicians, theologians, and the like. They are even likely to turn to weather forecasters before they consider turning to behavioral scientists for answers. This is because, for the most part, we have not made ourselves known. Yet we in the behavioral sciences have accumulated a vast amount of knowledge that can be beneficial to the public. What discipline or profession knows as much as HRM, I-O, or OB about the productivity of individuals and teams, job satisfaction, leadership, motivation, quality of work life, work-life balance, performance management, reward systems, and decision making, let alone reliable and valid methods for hiring people? What right do we have, as citizens of this world, to take little or no action to promulgating this knowledge to people who are in need of it?

Causes of the Problem

The reasons for the science-practitioner gap are exposed in the chapters throughout this book. In no particular order of importance, the causes include the following:

1. Research findings are seldom shared with practitioners. They appear in, and are written in a style appropriate for, scholarly journals only. Hence, as Rousseau and Boudreau (Chapter 14, Sticky Findings) point out, the research results rarely grab the attention of or gain credibility with the public.

2. As Cummings points out (Chapter 18, How Business Schools Shape (Misshape) Management Research), the values entrenched in business schools

and departments of psychology make explicit the necessity for conducting research that is publishable in scholarly journals. In most universities, there is little, if any, appreciation by deans and department chairs for presentations to or publications for the public. The extent to which the findings of a behavioral scientist are put into practice is deemed irrelevant in most academic institutions. Consequently, most behavioral scientists are far more comfortable with description than they are prescription.

3. As Benson notes (Chapter 15, Popular and Influential Management Books), the books that do influence organizational behavior are, for the most part, written by CEOs (e.g., Jack Welch), professional consultants (e.g., McKinsey), or by professional writers who lucratively reframe research findings in ways understandable to the public (e.g., Gladwell). These books sell well despite the fact they are widely criticized by behavioral scientists for being incorrect in the prescriptions offered. For example, Dan Pink, a professional writer, has repackaged Deci's (1975) research for consumption by the public. Pink's (2009) book erroneously propagates the view that people cannot motivate others and that they can only motivate themselves. Worse, the book argues incorrectly that giving employees a monetary incentive for a job well done typically decreases rather than increases their job performance. The fault for creating the void in the marketplace that allows these people to provide misinformation to the public is largely, if not solely, our own.

4. Collaboration between researchers and practitioners can sometimes be difficult, as shown in Chapter 10, Academic-Consultant Collaboration. As noted elsewhere in an article co-authored with my spouse, a former VP of HRM for J. P. Morgan Chase, Canada (Latham & Latham, 2003), behavioral scientists and HR managers often view one another as pursuing self-serving interests. The HR, I-O, or OB researcher is often perceived by managers to be pursuing narrowly defined interests that will likely affect an easily measured dependent variable and hence lead to a journal publication. HR managers and other organizational decision makers are often perceived by behavioral scientists as wanting to pursue fuzzily defined goals that will somehow affect the "bottom line" and hence lead to a salary increase, if not a promotion. Working together could jeopardize the attainment of their respective goals—a rational reason perceived by both parties for maintaining the two solitudes.

5. Most practitioners are unaware of the benefits that can be derived from using behavioral science theories in the workforce (see Chapter 11, Integrating Theory to Inform Practice), for philosophical concerns underlying this issue). This is unfortunate because behavioral science theories provide highly useful frameworks that enable managers to predict, explain,

and influence the behavior of subordinates, peers, and supervisors. For example, few things can kill the effectiveness of a team faster than perceptions by team members of an in-group versus an out-group, and the feeling that some people on the team are getting a better deal than others. Graen's (Graen & Uhl-Bien, 1995) theory of leader-member exchange and Folger and Cropanzano's (1998) theory of organizational justice provide useful checklists for preventing the occurrence of these phenomena.

Prescriptions

If medical doctors can write prescriptions based on science for the public, so can we. Cascio (Chapter 13, Professional Associations) describes institutions that can minimize the science-practice gap in the absence of assistance from most universities. One institution that he described is the Society for Industrial-Organizational Psychology, known as SIOP by most behavioral scientists. SIOP is unique in that nearly half of its 7,000 or so members are academics from either HRM or OB departments in business schools or departments of psychology. The other half are practitioners who work full-time as external or internal consultants. McHenry, an organizational psychologist employed full-time by Microsoft served as SIOP's president from 2006 to 2007. I served as president from 2008 to 2009. To increase the probability that research findings are used by the public, SIOP is currently doing the following:

1. At SIOP's instigation, the Alliance for Organizational Psychology has been formed consisting of three societies: European Work and Organizational Psychology (EAWOP), Division 1 (Work and Organizational Psychology) of the International Association of Applied Psychology (IAAP), where I am currently president elect, and SIOP. Among the Alliance's primary goals is to conduct research useful for global organizations (e.g., the Red Cross, the United Nations, and the World Health Organization). White papers will soon be issued by the Alliance for use by policy makers on such topics as dealing with an aging workforce. Division 1 of IAAP has a representative to the UN; SIOP also has applied for nongovernmental organization (NGO) status.

2. SIOP has become the source for evidence-informed practice for the Society for Human Resource Management (SHRM). SHRM's members include over 250,000 human resource professionals in over 150 countries. SIOP will produce four articles a year that are relevant to and understandable by human resource professionals.

3. SIOP will soon be publishing an annual review of "Science You Can Use: Evidence-Based Principles and Management." This annual book series will

consist of chapters written exclusively for practitioners. It will be showcased by SHRM.

4. As a result of the workshop on which this book is based, a web link will be set up for informing practitioners of significant findings by behavioral scientists. This site will also provide easy access for sharing best practices among practitioners.

5. A menu for accessing up-to-date reviews and critiques of mainstream HR-relevant books will be available on the SIOP webpage.

6. Practitioners are SIOP's face to the public. It is they who apply research-based findings to the real world on an ongoing basis. It is they who distinguish SIOP from other scholarly societies such as the Academy of Management. Consequently, SIOP has formed an Awards Committee to develop an early career professional award to be given annually. A mentoring program for practitioners is already in place, as is an annual award for Distinguished Contributions to Psychology as a Profession. An annual award is also given for Distinguished Contributions to Psychology as a Science.

7. SIOP's annual Leading Edge Consortium targets a topic of interest to practitioners that is co-chaired by a scientist and a practitioner.

8. A wiki site has been established from which practitioners can access and download practice-based presentations, papers, and tutorials presented at the SIOP annual meeting.

I close this section by stressing what I believe are pathways leading to useful research for organizational leaders and their employees. These comments are based on recommendations I have made elsewhere (Latham, 2007a, 2007b; Latham & Latham, 2003).

1. Margaret Mead, a sociologist, was fond of saying: "Never doubt that a small group of thoughtful people can change the world. Indeed, it's the only thing that ever has." The majority of the thoughtful authors of the chapters in this book began their careers in the late 1960s and early 1970s. Our generation played a major role in the implementation of the 1964 Civil Rights Act, America's exit from Vietnam, and the decision by President Johnson not to seek reelection. In short, that generation embraced the need for change in the mores of society.

As Rousseau commented at the workshop, the impediments to useful research that confront us today are merely ones of change management. Academic deans and department chairs serve at the pleasure of the faculty. If we want them to change the values by which scientists are rewarded, we can readily do so at the time of their selection and again when their term as dean or department chair is to be renewed. The hurdles to overcome in bringing about this change in university values are relatively small in comparison to the change interventions we fought for implementation in the 1960s. The risk in doing so is especially small relative to riding on the "freedom trains" from the northern to the southern United States. This is especially true in light of the fact that there already are deans of business schools who embrace the need for disseminating research findings in useful ways to the public and rewarding their senior faculty members for doing so (e.g., Roger Martin, Rotman School of Management, University of Toronto). These deans can be helpful in getting the Association to Advance Collegiate Schools of Business (AACSB) to see the necessity for valuing and rewarding academic activity that benefits organizational behavior and human resource management.

2. Set mutually interdependent goals for scientists and practitioners by focusing on the dependent rather than the independent variable. A solution for fostering collaboration between scientists and practitioners is to focus on specifying the issue of concern to organizational decision makers, then setting interdependent goals for improving the dependent variable. For example, I have never approached a manager with a request to do research on goal setting, an independent variable. However, I have worked with lots of managers on ways to improve productivity, a dependent variable.

3. Be proactively reactive. "Are we doing this for Gary or for Weyerhaeuser?" I heard this question on numerous occasions soon after becoming Weyerhaeuser's first staff psychologist. Their suspicions were the result of me taking the initiative to attack a company issue that I believed needed to be resolved. Not until I stopped, looked, and listened before speaking was I seen as a valuable resource to a team. I learned to listen intently to concerns of organizational decision makers before I offered suggestions. This ability to listen led to an invitation to join ad hoc teams that were formed to problem solve an issue of concern to one or more members of senior management. In short, my expertise was soon seen as useful.

4. Become bilingual. Many behavioral scientists are perceived by the public as having mastered the language of obfuscation. We are often viewed as making straightforward explanations complex. Consequently, we make it easy for us to be ignored by the public. Many of us add to our lack of credibility with the public by hedging the most straightforward conclusions with contingencies followed by whining for more research.

In learning to become bilingual as a staff psychologist and later as an external consultant, I stopped doing "research" and I started doing "projects" and interventions for managers. I stopped showing the results of statistical analyses, and instead I showed documentations of the effectiveness of an intervention through the presentation of graphs. I consciously worked on ways to phrase and present material in memorable ways for clients. I chose language that I believed would capture the attention and imagination of decision makers with little concern for the precision in language required by a scholarly audience. In time, I became bilingual.

5. Educate the other solitude. I seldom if ever pass up the opportunity to teach an Executive MBA class or a module in our business school's executive education programs. I pose questions to the managers (e.g., Do you think bias can be minimized if not eliminated in a performance appraisal?), encourage strong debate, and then immediately involve them in an experiment to obtain an answer. The participants love the suspense, and I do too. The result is invariably knowledge useful to them and to fellow behavioral scientists. The result is often an invitation from one or more class participants to collaborate on a project of interest to them and to me in their respective organizations (e.g., increasing job attendance, building trust between the manager and a team, developing leaders), as well as a journal publication for behavioral scientists (e.g., Latham & Seijts, 1997).

6. We should remember that gaining entry to an organization for the purpose of doing useful research is not difficult. In fact, it is all but a fait accompli for behavioral scientists employed in an academic setting. A university is an organization like any other organization in that there are typically unions, machinists, maintenance workers, electricians, and professionals. There are usually recruitment and selection problems as well as negotiation and conflict resolution issues; there are labor-management disputes and the need for minimizing grievances. There are a multitude of training opportunities, not to mention opportunities for leadership development. There is almost always an HR department that is overworked and understaffed, a department that would welcome the assistance of experts in the behavioral sciences. The opportunities for conducting research that will be truly useful for, and hence appreciated by, clients employed at a university are virtually endless.

For example, Collette Frayne's doctoral dissertation not only won an award from SIOP and the OB Division of the Academy of Management, it was subsequently published in a top-tier journal (Frayne & Latham, 1987). Her dissertation topic was on training in self-management for unionized hourly workers for the purpose of increasing their job attendance. Her research was perceived to be highly useful by the employees, their respective bosses, and the Union Executive Committee, all of whom were employed at the University of Washington. Similarly, Nina Cole's dissertation on the application of procedural justice principles when taking disciplinary action had the support of management and labor at the University of

Toronto because it was seen as highly useful for both parties. And as was the case with Frayne's dissertation, it too was appreciated by behavioral scientists as evidenced by its publication in a top-tier journal (Cole & Latham, 1997).

Conclusion

That the public does not see the behavioral sciences as useful is no one's fault but our own. That they would value what we do if we took the time to explain the results of our research to them is readily apparent by the huge success of professional writers, such as Gladwell and Pink, who have stepped up to fill the void in information that we have created. It is more than ironic, it is sheer chutzpah for us to subsequently carp among ourselves that these professional writers, who are not behavioral scientists, misrepresent our findings in one or more ways.

To hide behind the entrenched values of misguided deans and department chairs as an excuse for not taking the action needed to disseminate findings from the behavioral sciences that are useful for the public is disingenuous for a generation of scholars who are masters of change management. This generation of scholars, who emerged in the 1960s and 1970s, was unafraid of entrenched authority figures in that era. What credibility can we now have with one another, let alone subsequent generations of scholars, in expressing our helplessness today, 40 to 50 years later, in bringing about change in academic reward systems?

Not mentioned directly at the workshop, but nevertheless hinted at by several speakers, was a perception among senior scholars that the present generation is doing research less useful than ours. If that is true, where does the fault lie? If that is true, who trained the present generation of scholars? The answer is rarely a dean or department chair. The answer in most instances is us.

The superordinate goal of this book is to serve as a beacon of light for the next generation of behavioral scientists to see ways of, and the necessity for, conducting "useful research." It is up to our generation to remove the impediments to them doing so.

REFERENCES

Cole, N., & Latham, G. P. (1997). The effects of training in procedural justice on perceptions of disciplinary fairness by unionized employees and disciplinary subject matter experts. *Journal of Applied Psychology, 82,* 699–705.

Deci, E. L. (1975). *Intrinsic motivation.* New York: Plenum.

Folger, R., & Cropanzano, R. (1998). *Organizational justice and human resource management*. Thousand Oaks, CA: Sage.

Frayne, C. A., & Latham, G. P. (1987). The application of social learning theory to employee self management of attendance. *Journal of Applied Psychology, 72,* 387–392.

Graen, G. B., & Uhl-Bien, M. (1995). Relationship based approach to leadership: Development of leader-member exchange (LMX) theory of leadership over 25 years: Applying a multi-level domain perspective. *Leadership Quarterly, 6*(2), 219–247.

Hulin, C. (2001). Applied psychology and science: Differences between research and practice. *Applied Psychology: An International Review, 50,* 225–234.

Latham, G. P. (2001a). The reciprocal effects of science on practice: Insights for the practice and science of goal setting. *Canadian Psychology, 42,* 1–11.

Latham, G. P. (2001b). The reciprocal transfer of learning from journals to practice. *Applied Psychology: An International Review, 50,* 201–211.

Latham, G. P. (2007a). *Work motivation: History theory, research and practice.* Thousand Oaks, CA: Sage.

Latham, G. P. (2007b). A speculative perspective on the transfer of behavioral science to the workplace: "The times they are a changin." *Academy of Management Journal, 50,* 1027–1032.

Latham, G. P. (2008, July). Message from your president. *The Industrial Psychologist.*

Latham, G. P., & Latham, S. D. (2003). Facilitators and inhibitors of the transfer of knowledge between scientists and practitioners in human resource management: Leveraging cultural, individual and institutional variables. *European Journal of Work and Organizational Psychology, 12,* 245–256.

Latham, G. P., & Seijts, G. H. (1997). The effect of appraisal instrument on managerial perceptions of fairness and satisfaction with appraisals from peers. *Canadian Journal of Behavioural Science, 29,* 275–282.

Lewin, K. (1945). The Research Center for Group Dynamics at the Massachusetts Institute for Technology, *Sociomety, 8,* 126–135.

Pink, D. H. (2009). Drive: The surprising truth about what motivates us. New York: Riverside.

Ulrich, L., & Trumbo, D. (1965). The selection interview since 1949. *Psychological Bulletin, 63,* 100–116.

Wagner, R. (1949). The employment interview: A critical summary. *Personnel Psychology, 2,* 17–46.

ABOUT THE AUTHOR

Gary P. Latham is the Secretary of State Professor of Organizational Effectiveness in the Rotman School of Management, University of Toronto, a Past President of the Canadian Psychological Association and the Society for Industrial-Organizational Psychology (SIOP), and the President Elect of Work and Organizational Psychology, a Division of the International Association of

Applied Psychology. In addition to being awarded the status of Fellow in each of those three scholarly societies, he is a Fellow in the Association for Psychological Science, the National Academy of Human Resources, the Royal Society of Canada, and the Deputy Dean of Fellows in the Academy of Management (AOM). He is the recipient of the Scholar-Practitioner Award from AOM, and the only person to receive both awards for Distinguished Contributions to Psychology as a Science as well as a Profession from SIOP. His 2009 book, *On Becoming the Evidence-Based Manager,* copublished by Davies Black and SHRM, received the science to practice award from the AOM.

SEVENTEEN

Practitioner Perspectives

*Comments from a Panel Discussion**

DAVID NADLER

IAN ZISKIN

EDWARD E. LAWLER III

MICHAEL BEER

SUSAN ALBERS MOHRMAN

THE FOLLOWING COMMENTS come from a discussion at the December 2009 book workshop. David Nadler and Ian Ziskin, both of whom are long-term supporters of and participants in the research of the Center for Effective Organizations, were asked to provide a practitioner's perspective.

David Nadler has been an academic, a consultant, and a senior executive. He served on the faculty at the Graduate School of Business, Columbia University. In 1980, he founded the Delta Consulting Group and was CEO of the firm for 20 years. In 2000, he managed the acquisition of Delta by Mercer, a Marsh & McLennan Company, and continued to run Mercer Delta through 2005. In 2007, he was appointed vice chairman of the Marsh and McLennan Companies, a global professional services firm.

Ian Ziskin is president of EXec EXcel Group LLC, a consulting firm he founded after a highly successful 28-year career as a business executive. He is the former corporate vice president, chief human resources and administrative officer for Northrop Grumman Corporation.

Prior to this panel discussion, both Nadler and Ziskin listened to the chapter overview presentations and participated in the discussions on the first day of the workshop. We begin with some summary comments from Nadler and Ziskin about their perspectives on relevance and the gap between academic research and practice.

---

* Video clips from this panel and other discussions at the workshop are available at: http://ceo.usc.edu/book/useful_research_advancing_theo.html.

I believe strongly that trying to understand organizations and the patterns of behavior within them requires real intimacy and engagement with the phenomena. I don't know how you study it from a distance with real understanding because it has tremendous complexity.

I also think it requires relationships over time because the phenomena play out over time. It is difficult to go into an organization and look at something for a short period of time, even a couple months, and understand what's going on. One of the great experiences I had was my relationship with the Xerox Corporation, which went on for more than 21 years. When you're in a place 21 years, you understand the context, and it gives you a perspective on what's really happening. It also leads you from problem to problem.

Most of my thinking and writing has not been because I thought "what do I want to do next," but because I was in a situation that posed new questions to me. During my consulting career I usually had at least three major clients at any one time, and each of them at some time or another posed the next big problem to me. The best cases were where we learned together. In most of these cases, I wasn't trying to prove something, but it was more that I saw things that I didn't understand and the client also didn't understand. We said, "Why don't we try to learn about this together, and we'll see what insights we produce?" These were the paths of inquiry that were the most productive. I found, both as a producer and consumer of knowledge, that model building versus prescription was more helpful. If I could understand a situation, rather than just telling the client what he or she should do, I ended up giving them tools to solve similar problems in the future. In addition, frequently the prescription didn't apply because there were so many "what if's" or "if then's." What I wanted to have, and still want to have, are conceptual tools that will be useful to me and my client.

The thing that I've been struggling with all day is the question of pathways, access, and distribution. I think there is a huge translation issue between academia and the world of leading and managing organizations. Frankly, although I subscribe to journals and I look online at the publications, occasionally just for sadistic value, I read to a business colleague the title of an article and the abstract. Usually, they just scratch their heads and tell me that they can't figure out what the author is talking about. And I can almost pick the article at random because they all have that quality to them. It is simply a different language system. That language system may be fine for academics to communicate to academics; I'm not denigrating it. But as a practitioner, that very same language system makes it very difficult to access knowledge.

Do I read? Yes, I read. But I have so many things to read as part of my business life that I frequently will just scan the table of contents of a journal online and see if there's something interesting. Usually it's not. I have information overload. So what is useful to me? I want information on demand. When I have a problem I'd like to be able to get to the useful knowledge about that problem. What I don't have today is an easy way to get to that, other than asking someone who works for me to go do a scan of the literature.

IAN ZISKIN

I've been fascinated by the discussion, which for me has largely centered on what appears to be reconciling competing priorities between these notions of theory and practice. And so as an adopted member of the club, now that I've been here for the day, I'd like to offer a theory even though I'm a practitioner. One of the things that dawned on me was that theory might be viewed as problem solving without a customer. And practice might be viewed as problem solving without a theory. And honestly, I think you need both.

As I've been listening to the debate and the discussions and the very good presentations, one thing that's come through to me is a sense of frustration on your parts, wondering whether or not the things that you're doing are relevant and useful. It's a good question to ask. It's always a great question to ask. But I would encourage you to be much more positive about your contribution, in the past as well as the present and the future. Why do I say that? In our organization, we have about 125,000 people. About 43,000 of those people are engineers and computer scientists. So it's highly intellectual work. We also have a couple of thousand PhDs in our company. And one of the things that we like to talk about is highly valuing the free electrons. These are the people who have the outside-the-box ideas that nobody at first blush might think are very practical or pragmatic. But many of the things that they talk about, the arguments that they make, and the issues that they push for end up to be game changers, either in terms of the technology, which in turn becomes product and service that we deliver, or in terms of how the organization simply runs better and more effectively.

I think many of the things that you've been talking about today, they've been game changers to a lot of industries and a lot of organizations. I would encourage you not to lose that. That's my first point.

My second point is that, like everything in life, there's a balance to be struck. And I know that as academicians, the notion of frameworks is important to you and the work that you do. I'd offer a pragmatic framework to think about that has five pieces to it. So let me just quickly run through them.

One is just making sure that you understand the question, What is the problem? You've talked a lot about that today. It's very simple, but it's probably the most important question. The second question I think is equally important, which is, Who cares? Is there a customer for the problem that you have identified? The third question is, What is the attention span that people have to address it? This question may be the hardest one, and I'll come back to it. The fourth question is, Will anybody pay for it? And the fifth question is, When we're all done, can we be brief about what we found?

Most of the frustration that I hear in the room today is not about the importance of the issues that are being researched, analyzed, and addressed. It is about the question, Does anybody have a willingness or an attention span or the resources to do something with findings once in fact they're delivered? And to me, that's really all about attention span. I've been working in companies for almost 28 years now. Certainly I've seen a pattern that many of you are experiencing as well, which is that the attention span of people has been significantly reduced due to resource constraints and time pressures. Projects and studies that might have been endorsed and invested in years ago, which would have been longitudinal in nature and taken multiple years to complete, are not being undertaken because no one has the patience to wait for those findings anymore.

Many of you are concerned about the issue of relevance. To me, relevance in some ways translates into rapid prototyping, cycle time reduction, and quick turnaround from identification of the problem to the solution. I think organizations today are actually more thirsty for great problem solving. Maybe the term "research" does not relate well to everybody, but "problem solving" certainly does. It's the speed with which those problems get addressed that I think fundamentally is the issue.

The last point I'll make is that I take note with many academicians with whom I interact. They go to great pains to think through the problem that they're going to address, as well as the research methodology that they're going to employ to address it. I would suggest to you that most practitioners tend to see problems in high-level themes and broad patterns. They don't necessarily differentiate in the same way you do at the micro level and the things that you're studying and analyzing, compared to many other people out there. So I think you need to allow for the possibility that many practitioners often see multiple research studies, multiple requests for resources to address that research, as not necessarily unique.

People are coming to us with things that sound very much the same, even though in your minds they may not be. So I would strongly encourage you to think about either how to band together with other people who have like interests (to minimize the number of external requests that are coming in for companies), or how to differentiate your concept, theory, and problem that you believe you can solve from that of others. I don't mean to be negative or condescending in any way. It's just not the way that many of the practitioners who are being approached are thinking about the problem.

ED LAWLER

David, let me follow up on one thing you mentioned; it has always seemed to me that one of the things you do exceptionally well is produce action-oriented tools, concepts, and materials. How do you think about producing not just knowledge, but knowledge that translates into or gets translated into tools and useful guides for people in the world of practice?

DAVID NADLER

My core process for creating concepts or tools is reflection. I'm doing some work and I'm involved in some phenomena, and I push myself to step back and reflect on what's happening. Often it's reflecting on what's working and what's not working and then figuring out what I can learn from that and what might be generalizable beyond the specific case situation. I'm fundamentally searching for insight. Over the years, I often sought to bring outsiders in to reflect on the same issues from a different perspective than I would have. There's value to looking at the same problem through different lenses with different perspectives. I also used my client situations to test out ideas as part of the development process. When I had insights, I first tried to teach or present to a client before I ever wrote anything. I could come in to a client and say, "I have some ideas. Can I talk to you about them? Will you tell me what do you think about them?" And so it was back and forth between a potential consumer. Similarly, I'd say to my colleagues, "Let's take this idea. Talk to your clients about it."

ED LAWLER

An article is one kind of product, but you have developed other kinds of products as well—surveys and diagnostic guides.

DAVID NADLER

I developed tools because I wanted to operationalize my insights and enable others to apply them—whether they be diagnostic or prescriptive insight. Part of my approach to working with clients was to give them things they could use to understand and solve problems, as opposed to doing it for them or doing it to them. It was a collaborative consulting model, as opposed to a "study and recommend" model where the consultant says, "We're going to come study you, and then tell you what your problem is and what you should do about it." Instead, my consulting approach from the beginning conveys the following: "We're going to help introduce you to some tools that we could use together to help you understand the problems and then help you figure out solutions because then you'll be more committed to the solution and to making it happen. You'll have deeper understanding and a greater commitment than in a traditional study and recommend model."

ED LAWLER

I always saw you as having an actionable orientation, but a codeveloped actionable orientation.

DAVID NADLER

Absolutely. That's a good description.

IAN ZISKIN

I relate very much to the model and approach that Dave was talking about. He's obviously been a well-known successful practitioner of this for a very long time. And I think one of the reasons why it has been successful is—certainly in my organization and I think in other companies as well—the notion of codevelopment and iterative process, some experimentation and testing out of certain ideas before springing it on the entire organization, so you have a chance to see if it works and improve it. And because of the iterative nature of it, I think there's this sense of progress and responsiveness in short time frames, where again those cycle times are significantly reduced. I'm sure there are many things that you're all conducting as research that require multiple years to get right. And I'm not pooh-poohing that in any way. But to the extent that you're feeling resistance from corporations and dealing with that in today's environment, I think that's in part why.

MIKE BEER

Ian, in your presentation you talked about problem solving and research. I think if the academics in the room are ever going to bridge the boundary you have been talking about all day, it is actually going to be by helping Ian Ziskin solve problems. And that to me is a world of exploiting; in terms of Jim March's ideas, that's exploiting what the field knows. And we know an awful lot. We can also actually push the boundaries, so that there are some pieces of the work we're doing that we actually feel are exploring things that will inform the field and inform our doctoral students. But one can only get there after one has a relationship. And then one can get to a place where these relationships help in exploring stuff we don't know, the boundaries of the field, both idea wise and then getting data. So this relationship is what you both have been talking about, and relationship building is really important to us in the academy.

DAVID NADLER

I think you're absolutely right. You have to build confidence in your client so that you can actually help them, that you can add some insight, that you can do it in a language system and a time frame that makes sense for them. Then that gives you permission to ask broader questions and to explore other things. I like to find the places where the client has some energy about a problem that concerns him or her that lines up with where I can help them or where I have intellectual interest.

IAN ZISKIN

If I could build on that, one of the things that I've seen among the most effective academicians who are doing work inside companies, not unlike effective consultants who are doing work inside companies, is that it's not enough to be able to articulate and point out that a problem exists. You have to be able to create a love for the problem. And it's a strange word to use when you think about the problem. But academics are great because they get a great idea and, by the time you show up at the companies that you're wanting to work with, you love the problem. That's a good start. But the people that you're selling to have a lot of problems. They may not have the same love for the one that you've identified, even though they may recognize that it, in fact, exists. If it's C on a long list, that's really the one that's the biggest itch for me that I need to have scratched. And having you be able to help us think through how to frame that problem, how to address it in a practical way but in a way that also produces some concrete research that you can use to replicate and expand that notion to others—that's the real sweet spot. But not everybody's good at that.

SUSAN ALBERS MOHRMAN

Underlying some of our discussion and some of the papers is an assumption, on the one hand, that somehow all the wonderful things we've learned in management research aren't getting to people in corporations. On the other hand, I feel that when I deal with managers, they know a heck of a lot because they're managing and they're learning a lot of stuff by experience. I would like your perspective on what is needed, if anything, to get the research that's been done to the people that work and manage your organizations or the organizations you come in contact with?

IAN ZISKIN

First of all, I don't know if management is a profession, but it's certainly practiced. And people are heavily invested, in terms of development, to be more effective managers and leaders in companies like ours and many others all over the world. So organizations like ours have a very high interest in making managers better. First and foremost, the entire workplace experience is driven by the person's relationship with their immediate boss. And if that's a mess, everything else you do in the organization that might be spectacular gets lost in the sauce.

The place where I think we may be missing the boat a little bit, in terms of your question, Susan, is that there are a lot of messages out there. I think most people who work in companies today crave simplification. And honestly, there have been a number of references made during the discussion today to some of the more popular books and popular consultant tools. And almost invariably, when people talk about those, there's this tendency to kind of wrinkle your nose up and pooh-pooh what's been done.

I honestly don't know the quality of the academic rigor and research that's behind many of these tools. But to be brutally honest with you, most people like me don't care. What they care about is solving problems in organizations. This problem happens to be how to improve the quality of your managers and your leaders. So there is nothing wrong with having great research, and you do. I think the challenge is, how do you package it, and how do you communicate it in a way that is simple sound bites that people can pay attention to, run away from it, and go do something else because they're multitasking, and come back to it? I find that much of the academic literature does not do that. It's hard to digest.

DAVID NADLER

I'm more on the optimistic side. Over the years (now decades), I've interacted with companies, and I've seen that, by and large, managers are more informed and more enlightened than they were. I remember going to the Ford Motor Company with Ed Lawler when we were doing the projects around quality of work life. And we were talking about the idea of what happens on the assembly line and how it's so boring and how workers drop bolts into the line to stop it because that adds variety, knowledge, and challenge to their otherwise unmotivating and unfulfilling jobs. And the managers looked at us and said, "We don't care." Today, if you go into those companies, at least the ones that I deal with, the thinking is very different. Many of the concepts that we have written about, spoken about, and taught to our students are now part of the accepted general wisdom. People believe that teams are a useful way of organizing work, that we do indeed want to empower our people, or that we ought to think about reward systems in terms of what behavior you want to have. A lot of progress has been made in introducing the insights of organizational behavior into companies. In part, we may be victims of our own success. The basic ideas that we advocated for decades are now accepted as common wisdom by many, so the question is, conceptually, "What have you done for me lately?"

PART IV

Barriers and Enablers

EIGHTEEN

How Business Schools Shape (Misshape) Management Research

THOMAS G. CUMMINGS

BUSINESS SCHOOLS (BSs) are the professional home of most management researchers. Consequently, they can have an enormous effect on the conduct and output of faculty research and, ultimately, on whether it is useful for theory and practice. Recently there has been considerable criticism and debate about BSs' mission, operation, and value to students, business firms, and larger society (e.g., Bennis & O'Toole, 2005; Khurana, 2007; Mintzberg, 2004; Pfeffer & Fong, 2002; Starkey & Tiratsoo, 2007). Concurrently, there have been spirited discussions about the relationship between management research and practice—whether management research should contribute to theory and practice, the extent to which it does, and how this can be accomplished (e.g., Ford et al., 2005; Hambrick, 1994; Huff, 2000; Rynes, Bartunek, & Daft, 2001; Starkey & Madan, 2001; Van de Ven & Johnson, 2006; Walsh et al., 2007).

In this chapter, we draw on these different perspectives to identify key forces affecting BSs today. We show how those forces shape important aspects of BSs, which in turn influence the kind of management research that is conducted. This provides a clearer picture of the barriers and enablers that exist in BSs to produce knowledge that is useful for theory and practice. We focus on management research, such as human resource management, organizational behavior, organization theory, and strategy. Research from other disciplines in BSs, such as accounting, finance, and marketing, tends to translate more directly into practice than management research. We also center our discussion on BSs that are located in research universities, where most management research is produced.

Based on the material in this book, we first briefly review the features of research that is useful for theory and practice. This review provides a reference point for discussing how BSs can inhibit or promote that approach to inquiry. Next, we identify forces having a significant effect on BSs' functioning and performance and show how they can create, often unintentionally, barriers to doing research for theory and practice. Finally, we identify ways that BSs can overcome these barriers and enable this form of research.

Research Useful for Theory and Practice

Evident throughout this book is the considerable attention that has been paid to understanding how management research can contribute to theory and practice (see Chapter 1, Research for Theory and Practice). Referred to as "action research" (Lewin, 1946), "engaged scholarship" (Van de Ven & Johnson, 2006), "action science" (Argyris, Putnam, & Smith, 1985), or "collaborative research" (Adler, Shani, & Styhre, 2004), among other names, this action-oriented research has features that promote joint contributions to theory and practice (see Chapter 8, Making a Difference *and* Contributing Useful Knowledge; Chapter 4, A Ten-Year Journey of Cooperation; and Chapter 2, Crossing Boundaries to Investigate Problems in the Field). This type of research is characterized by the following features:

- *Rigorous and relevant.* This research explicitly seeks to create knowledge that is both rigorous and relevant. It applies scientific methods to collect and analyze data and test theories, while striving to capture the conditions and reality that practitioners face.

- *Collaboration between researchers and practitioners.* Action-oriented research is grounded in a collaborative partnership between researchers and practitioners. Both sides are actively involved in the research to varying degrees, from defining the research problem, to choosing appropriate methods and theories, to analyzing and interpreting the results, to applying them to theory and practice development. The effectiveness of this collaborative community rests on mutual trust, openness, and respect among participants. This promotes active listening and sharing different perspectives and expertise among members; it helps them constructively address conflicts that invariably arise when views and opinions differ; it takes full advantage of this diversity to gain a more comprehensive understanding of the research problem.

- *Messy problems grounded in practice.* This research tackles complex real-world problems that are not easily understood or resolved. Such messy problems have multiple underlying causes that are interrelated in complicated ways. This complexity makes it extremely difficult to comprehend and address them applying the expertise of either researchers or practitioners acting alone. Messy problems need to be studied from multiple theoretical and practical perspectives using different methods and approaches. This interdisciplinary research permits triangulation of methods and views, which can lead to richer, more valid explanations and more effective solutions.

- *Long-term and intense.* Action-oriented research inherently takes time and energy both to create and sustain an effective partnership between researchers and practitioners and to understand and devise solutions to messy problems. Researchers and practitioners come from different professional cultures and it takes considerable time and effort to develop and maintain trust, openness, and respect between them. Moreover, this relationship is likely to be psychologically intense as participants share diverse views and confront and resolve the conflicts that invariably arise. It takes hard work to develop the strong social bonds needed for collaborative research, and the quality of the research outcomes depends heavily on the quality of the partnership. The nature of the research problem also demands long time commitments. Messy problems must be studied up close and over time to discover the causal mechanisms underlying them and to design, enact, and assess possible solutions. This requires substantial time collecting and analyzing data, testing different theories, and trying out possible solutions, particularly in the context of collaborative inquiry where participants must share, understand, and reconcile different perspectives.

Barriers to Research Useful for Theory and Practice

Given its dual focus on theory and practice, action-oriented research seems ideally suited to generating management knowledge in business schools. It provides both the rigor and relevance necessary to create scientific knowledge to inform good practice. It assures that business professionals will be guided by evidence-based knowledge that is applicable to the problems they face. Yet this form of inquiry is relatively scarce in BSs. Indeed, the kind of management research predominate today has almost the opposite characteristics. It is researcher driven and theory oriented. It applies rigorous methods to well-defined problems studied from afar over relatively short time frames. Relevance plays a secondary role as do practitioners who are treated as subjects and passive recipients of research knowledge rather than as collaborators. Typically, the research findings advance scientific knowledge while having modest to no consequences for management practice (e.g., Pfeffer & Fong, 2002; Rynes, Bartunek, & Daft, 2001; Starkey & Madan, 2001).

To explain how management researchers have come to eschew action-oriented research in favor of theory-oriented research, we examine how BSs

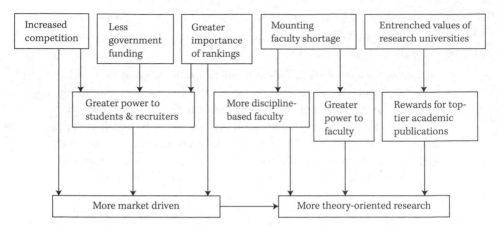

FIGURE 18.1 Forces Shaping the Kind of Research Encouraged in Business Schools

influence the kind of research that faculty do. We organize this analysis around five powerful forces affecting BSs today: (1) increased competition, (2) less government funding, (3) greater importance of media rankings, (4) mounting faculty shortage, and (5) entrenched values of research universities. As shown in Figure 18.1, these conditions have set off a chain of events in BSs that results in particular forms of research being favored over others. This analysis reveals strong barriers to the kind of management research that is likely to be useful for theory and practice.

Increased Competition

Business schools are facing increased competitive pressures as their sheer number swells throughout the world (Starkey & Tiratsoo, 2007). Originating mostly in the United States and Canada, BSs have proliferated in recent years in Asia, Australia, Europe, Latin America, and the United Kingdom. Those in the top tier compete globally and nationally for students and funds, whereas others confront stiff local or regional competition. Add to this the growing number of organizations unaffiliated with established universities that are entering the business education market. Consulting and training firms, for-profit colleges, and corporate universities are all seeking inroads into business education, often through distance learning and other forms of nontraditional instruction. Realizing that business education is big business, they are extending their reach beyond executive education to business degrees (Pfeffer & Fong, 2004).

On the demand side, student applications and enrollments have become much more erratic and difficult to predict (Starkey & Tiratsoo, 2007). This can be seen in the fluctuating popularity of different kinds of degree programs, such as the full-time, part-time, and executive MBA programs. This volatility in demand has a lot to do with the rapidly growing global market for business education, in addition to jolts in the economy and job market. Not only are BSs proliferating globally but also is the sheer number of students from different countries seeking business degrees. This means that BSs are increasingly competing with schools from different countries for students worldwide. Changes in exchange rates, visa restrictions, disease patterns, political conditions, and the like can affect student demand for business education in complex and unpredictable ways. Thus, BSs are discovering that the global marketplace is far more complex and uncertain than the more traditional domestic market.

As shown in Figure 18.1, faced with increasing competitive pressures, BSs are becoming more market driven; they are also giving greater power to students and recruiters, which in turn feeds this market focus. These two aspects of BSs affect management research in the following ways.

More market driven. Faced with increasing competitive pressures, BSs have become far more market driven, paying greater attention to things like the bottom line, market share, industry reputation, and short-term results (Khurana, 2007; Trank & Rynes, 2003). This market focus is evident in the growing application of business rhetoric to BSs, where business education is referred to as an "industry," students as "customers," other BSs as "competitors," and new programs as "revenue sources." Faced with fierce global competition and uncertain student demand, BSs are aggressively cutting costs and seeking new ways to boost income. Class sizes, faculty pay, staff support, and infrastructure expenses are being closely scrutinized to minimize costs. Efforts to enhance revenues include increases in student fees, new educational programs and services, broader student diversity, overseas expansion, identity branding, and alliances with other BSs and corporations (Starkey & Tiratsoo, 2007).

The relationship between this market focus and faculty research is closely tied to the important role that research has come to play in determining BSs' prestige. Starting with the Ford Foundation's highly influential report in the late 1950s (Gordon & Howell, 1959), which admonished BSs for being too vocational and lacking a scientific knowledge base, BSs have put enormous resources and effort into becoming legitimate research institutions (Khurana, 2007). Typically, they have encouraged research that draws on and emulates established academic disciplines—theoretically based, methodologically sophisticated, and empirically sound (Pfeffer & Fong, 2002). This kind of research, which is generally published in top-tier academic journals, has become the gold standard and a primary determinant of BSs' prestige (Armstrong, 1995; Armstong & Sperry, 1994; Becker, Lindsat, & Grizzle, 2003).

Moreover, within the university, a BSs stature rests largely on its research eminence. Given the reputational benefits of research, the more market driven BSs have become, the more they favor and support the kind of inquiry just described. Theory-oriented research confers prestige on BSs, which translates into better students and faculty, more external funding, better job placements, and more resources and autonomy within the university.

Greater power to students and recruiters. Increased competition also has enhanced the power of students and recruiters, which in turn has contributed to BSs becoming more market driven. Students' main reason to earn a business degree is the expectation of future career success, typically gauged in terms of compensation (Pfeffer & Fong, 2002). Thus, students seek to attend BSs with strong capabilities in career training and job placement. On the recruiting side, firms hire business graduates because they have been pre-screened for business achievement and acquired knowledge and skills to start a business career successfully. Therefore, recruiters want to hire graduates from BSs that excel at selecting and training students for career success.

Growing competition and more erratic enrollments have led BSs to become more and more responsive to student and recruiter needs. This responsiveness can be seen in how receptive they have been to student calls for more simplified teaching materials, less theoretical and more job-focused coursework, better job placement support, and reduced grade pressure (Rynes & Trank, 1999). BSs have been equally if not more responsive to recruiter demands for graduates with more vocational skills and technical training needed for early career success. All of this gives students and recruiters more influence over BSs' decision making, which contributes to the short-term market focus we see in many schools today.

The challenge for BSs is balancing market-driven demands for prestige bestowed by theory-oriented research with student and recruiter demands for less theory and more job-related training. One solution that seems to be emerging, at least tacitly, is a two-tier faculty system that partly reconciles these conflicting demands. The top tier includes faculty who excel at research; because they have high career mobility, they receive high salaries, reduced teaching loads, generous research support, and tenure-track status. The second tier consists of more teaching-oriented faculty including the growing cadre of clinical and adjunct instructors, many of whom teach full-time. Because their career prospects are mainly in the local market, they have relatively modest salaries, large teaching loads, reasonable teaching support, and generally are not tenure track. This two-tier system helps to jointly optimize the research demands of academe and the vocational demands of students and recruiters. It enables BSs to gain the benefits of both theory-based research and job-relevant education.

Less Government Funding

As shown in Figure 18.1, another major force affecting BSs is the steady decline of public financial support for higher education. Over the past few decades in the United States, for example, federal support for higher education has decreased in constant dollars and percentage terms while demand has grown significantly (Beauvais, 2007; Sonnenberg, 2004). This has increased financial pressures on BSs and made them more reliant on student tuition, corporate donations, and company subsidies for employee tuition.

The growing financial dependency on students and companies has enhanced their power over BSs' decision making, which in turn has added to BSs being more market driven. As discussed previously, BSs are paying closer attention to student and recruiter needs, so they can attract the best students and place them in the top companies. This market focus is particularly sensitive to BSs' prestige because it affects with which schools students and corporations choose to associate. Given theory-oriented research's contribution to schools' prestige, growing financial pressures reinforce BSs' support for this kind of research.

Greater Importance of Rankings

Probably the most visible factor affecting BSs today is the proliferation of rankings by popular magazines and newspapers. These publicly pit BSs against one another on such dimensions as student selectivity, diversity, and satisfaction; job placements, starting salaries, and recruiters' assessments; and faculty research, alumni ratings, and financial return on student educational expenses. Although there has been considerable debate about the validity of these various rankings, they are highly visible and widely read and can have significant effects on BSs (e.g., Corley & Gioia, 2000; DeAngelo, DeAngelo, & Zimmerman, 2005; Fee, Hadlock, & Pierce, 2005; Khurana, 2007; Zimmerman, 2001). Students consider the rankings when they choose a school, as do alumni when they consider gift-giving, recruiters when they make hiring decisions, and new faculty when they choose which school to join. Rankings also can affect a school's status and funding within its university. Therefore, administrators and faculty increasingly take rankings seriously and expend considerable time and effort to maintain their school's ranking, move it higher, or stem a drop by trying to turn things around.

The explosive growth of media rankings contributes directly to BSs becoming more market driven. It forces them to compete intensely with each other for reputational advantages, which can be enormous. Rankings can affect the quality of students and faculty that BSs can attract, the success of student job placements, the amount of external funding, and a school's status in the business education profession and within the university. These benefits positively feed on themselves, with high ranking promoting success and success promoting high ranking. Thus, rankings play an increasingly important role in decisions about curriculum, enrollment, and resource allocations. They also are motivating BSs to pay closer attention to their external image by investing considerable time and resources in public and corporate relations, alumni communications, career placement services, and in some cases, gaming the rankings to get a leg up on the competition.

The media rankings add indirectly to BSs' market focus by giving greater power to students and recruiters. For example, the *Business Week* rankings, which arguably are the most influential, are heavily weighted by student and recruiter assessments. Consequently, BSs increasingly pay close attention to these key stakeholders' feedback, so they can quickly counter any negative reactions that might adversely affect the rankings. It is common, for example, for schools to modify their curriculum and placement practices quickly when negative feedback is encountered. More proactively, BSs have been known to remind students that it is in their best interest to rate the school highly; they have given key recruiters preferential access to top students and special treatment during their recruiting efforts. These responses underscore the power that media rankings have given to students and recruiters; they show how market driven BSs have become in responding to their needs.

BSs' hyperattention to media rankings is strengthening their support for theory-oriented research. Indeed, some of the rankings include measures of research impact. *U.S. News and World Report's* rankings, for example, contain input from deans, which likely takes into account a school's research stature (Pfeffer & Fong, 2002). Even the venerable *Business Week* recently added a measure of research influence to its rankings. There is evidence showing that student and corporate ratings of BSs' prestige take into account schools' research reputations (Armstrong, 1995; Armstrong & Sperry, 1994), which as discussed previously, are based heavily on theory-oriented research. Research productivity can serve an important signaling function. It can provide a concrete indicator about a business school's status, especially when there is imperfect information about its overall capabilities (Besancenot, Faria, & Vranceanu, 2008).

Mounting Faculty Shortage

One of the most challenging forces affecting BSs is a severe shortage of faculty, especially those holding doctoral degrees (Association to Advance Collegiate Schools of Business [AACSB] International, 2008a). BSs are producing far fewer PhDs than they did a decade ago, and a good number of them are finding more attractive alternatives to working in a business school (AACSB

International, 2002, 2003; Zimmerman, 2001). Among the large contingent of scholars that comprised the first wave of PhDs employed in BSs during the 1960s and 1970s is a growing number of faculty who are choosing to retire or work part-time. Both of these trends are projected to accelerate in the coming years (AACSB International, 2008a). As shown in Figure 18.1, this mounting faculty shortage is resulting in BSs employing more discipline-based faculty and giving faculty greater power.

More discipline-based faculty. To address the faculty shortage, BSs are increasingly hiring from the disciplines of economics, psychology, and sociology (Pfeffer & Fong, 2002). The knowledge base and research methods of these social sciences are closely aligned to the management field. Moreover, for many of these scholars, the job prospects are far better in BSs than in disciplinary departments.

The growth of discipline-based faculty contributes to management research becoming more theory oriented. These scholars reinforce the long-held belief in BSs that this kind of research is the path to academic legitimacy. They promote research that is theory driven and methodologically sophisticated, which has become the standard for publication in top management journals (Pfeffer & Fong, 2002). This disciplinary focus is also finding its way into the training of doctoral students in BSs. Students in top programs increasingly supplement their business education with a minor or major in one of the disciplines. Faculty hiring decisions are more and more based on these PhDs having disciplinary knowledge and skills, which helps to assure that future management research will continue to be theory oriented.

Greater power to faculty. The growing faculty shortage is also giving faculty more power in BSs. This shift is especially the case for faculty publishing in top academic journals. They are the primary source of a school's research reputation. Because they are in short supply, they can command high salaries and research support as well as reduced teaching loads. These researchers' growing power is contributing in part to the two-tier faculty system described earlier. It affords them freedom to do research without being overburdened with teaching and student demands. Their enhanced power also influences key decisions about faculty hiring, promotion and tenure, and rewards, all of which favor the kind of theory-oriented research at which these scholars excel.

Entrenched Values of Research Universities

Business schools have had an uneasy relation with the research universities that house them (Starkey & Tiratsoo, 2007). Periodically, they have faced university concerns about student quality, curriculum rigor, resource allocations, financial contributions to overhead, and the like. The most persistent and possibly critical issue, however, centers on questions of academic legitimacy. From BSs' inception on university campuses, they have encountered skepticism from many disciplinary departments about the quality of their faculty and research. They have been accused of being little more than vocational schools closely aligned with the interests of big business.

Because these negative and partly erroneous perceptions can adversely affect BSs' access to resources and autonomy to make decisions, BSs have worked hard to remedy them. This can be seen in the strides BSs have taken to adhere to the values of research universities. These ideals promote scientific rigor as the path to knowledge, generally through disciplinary research that is theoretically and methodologically sound (Pfeffer & Fong, 2002; Starkey & Tiratsoo, 2007). These values are deeply embedded in university practices and behaviors. As shown in Figure 18.1, they are reflected in university reward systems, which are closely tied to top-tier academic publications, a visible measure of research rigor. BSs have followed suit linking such publications to pay increases, promotion and tenure, endowed chairs, and research support. This reward system sends a powerful message to faculty that theory-oriented research, which is the primary path to top-tier publication, is valued and rewarded.

In summary, we have analyzed five important factors affecting BSs and shown how they set off a chain of events that influence faculty research. They create conditions within BSs that heavily favor theory-oriented research. When taken together, the forces create almost a "perfect storm" to thwart the kind of action-oriented research addressed in this book.

Enablers to Research Useful for Theory and Practice

Overcoming these barriers to action-oriented research is challenging, to say the least. The forces affecting BSs and the resulting chain of events are likely to persist, if not heighten, in the coming years. To address these barriers to more action-oriented research, BSs can (1) professionalize their research focus, (2) broaden their reward and career practices, and (3) enhance their engagement with practitioners.

Professionalize Research Focus

As discussed previously, BSs have sought legitimacy and prestige by emulating the theories and methods of discipline-based departments, thus doing more and more theory-oriented research. Although to some extent this emphasis has produced the intended effect, it also has led to a growing disconnect between BSs' research and the management profession it intends to inform, as many critics have pointed out (e.g., Bennis & O'Toole, 2005; Ford et al., 2005; Pfeffer & Fong, 2002; Porter & McKibbin, 1988; Rynes, Bartunek, & Daft, 2001). One promising solution is for BSs to become more like other university-based professional schools such as medicine and law (Pfeffer & Fong, 2004; Sherman, 2009; Trank & Rynes, 2003). Research would be aimed at creating knowledge relevant to the management profession; it would provide a scientific basis for professional learning and practice (Lorsch, 2009; Pfeffer, 2009; see Chapter 9, On Knowing and Doing, this book).

This proposed shift toward "profession-oriented" research fits well with BSs' competence in creating scientific knowledge. It brings that research expertise to bear on important issues of ongoing relevance to management, thus giving BSs a competitive advantage over other providers of management education and knowledge, such as consulting firms and schools that focus on teaching. Profession-oriented research can help to differentiate science-based management education from training and storytelling (AACSB International, 2008b). Its rigorous theorizing and empirical testing stand in stark contrast to the unsubstantiated claims and hyping that are so prevalent in nonacademic sources of management knowledge. It provides the evidence-based knowledge needed to guide wise management practice (Pfeffer & Sutton, 2006, 2007; Rousseau & McCarthy, 2007; see Chapter 14, Sticky Findings, this book).

Profession-oriented research can promote greater tolerance and appreciation for diverse theoretical and methodological approaches to creating management knowledge. Because it focuses research on a common domain or subject matter, no particular discipline, theory, or method is privileged over others. What matters is the quality of the research (rigor) and its contribution to understanding the phenomenon in question (relevance) (Pettigrew, 2001). The management domain is diffuse, complex, and changing; consequently the greater the variety of research approaches, the better are the chances of comprehending it. BSs could enable this diversity by providing a broad umbrella under which different forms of inquiry prosper and productively interact (Starkey, Hatchuel, & Tempest, 2004). They could create a supportive milieu for both basic research and more applied forms of inquiry. Moreover, they could promote useful exchanges and collaboration among researchers from different perspectives, all focused on gaining a shared understanding of the management domain.

Broaden Reward and Career Practices

Rewards are powerful determinants of behavior, even in scholarly settings like BSs. As discussed earlier, BSs have tended to reward top-tier academic publishing, which reinforces theory-oriented research. Although action-oriented research can lead to high-level publication, it generally takes longer, is messier and more difficult to conduct, and has a higher level of publication uncertainty than theory-oriented research (Van de Ven & Johnson, 2006). If BSs want both types of research to inform management knowledge, which is essential in my view, they must expand their reward practices to account for these features (AACSB International, 2008b; Starkey & Madan, 2001; Tushman & O'Reilly, 2007). One reasonable solution is to design two parallel reward systems, one geared to theory-oriented research and the other to action-oriented inquiry. Each would have its own performance measures, assessment cycle, and reward pool, though some overlap between the two systems seems sensible. The theory-oriented reward system is pretty much in place at most BSs, whereas the action-oriented system would need to be designed from scratch. This system would require developing measures of research impact that go beyond simple counts of journal quality, citations, and the like; perhaps metrics tied to effects on practice (AACSB International, 2008b). The assessment-reward cycle would probably need to be extended beyond the typical calendar year to account for the longer time it takes to do this research and to assess its consequences. Clearly, there are numerous practical challenges to measuring and rewarding action-oriented research. BSs might start by borrowing from the reward practices of those academic departments where long-term field research is more the norm, such as anthropology, political science, and sociology.

Consistent with these changes in reward practices, BSs can expand how they view faculty careers to support both theory- and action-oriented researchers (Ashford in Walsh et al., 2007). Currently, the careers of tenure-track faculty are seen pretty much within a context that presumes that theory-oriented research will be the norm throughout a career. At research universities, this assumption makes sense during faculty's early career stages, when tenure and promotion are likely to depend on publishing in top-tier academic journals. It is questionable, however, during later career stages for those faculty members doing action-oriented research. They require career practices that value and support long-term engagement with practitioners around messy management issues. To support these scholars, BSs can be more flexible in how they structure and support faculty careers, perhaps creating different career tracks for theory and action researchers, like the dual reward systems suggested above. In early career stages, even though most faculty members would be on a theory-oriented career track, BSs could create small opportunities for engaging with practice for those wanting to develop in this direction. In later career stages, faculty continuing to do theory-oriented research would stay on that track much like they do today, while action researchers would move to a career track more consistent with their research. This career track would focus outward toward organizations and management rather than inward toward disciplines and other academics. It would include a combination of research, teaching, and service that emphasizes practice (see Chapter 6, Rigor and Relevance in Organizational Research). This dual career system would be flexible so faculty members could move between tracks depending on their changing interests and capabilities.

Enhance Engagement with Practitioners

To create useful knowledge, the quality of the relationship between researchers and practitioners can be as important as the content of the research itself. BSs can create mechanisms for facilitating faculty engagement with practitioners. These enable the two sides to explore opportunities for joint learning and research. They increase the chances that researchers will study important issues facing management, and that practitioners will learn the right lessons from the results and how to apply them. BSs are developing a variety of ways to relate to the practitioner community (Starkey & Madan, 2001). We describe approaches that seem particularly relevant to action-oriented research in the following sections.

Action-learning executive education workshops. These workshops evolved from traditional executive education programs (Tushman & O'Reilly, 2007; Tushman in Walsh et al., 2007; see Chapter 9, On Knowing and Doing, this book). They are a response to the common plea from participants for a closer connection between the academic content presented and the problems they face at work. To better link knowing with doing, the workshops tailor content to a specific firm, which sends teams of senior executives to campus for a few days. About half the time is spent in content sessions, and the other half in teams applying the content to company issues. Faculty design and deliver the content and facilitate the team sessions.

These action-learning workshops can help practitioners better understand and apply research to real problems. They can provide researchers with closer access to firms and better understanding of the important problems they are facing. These benefits in turn can lead to innovations in management practice and research that address key management issues and provides actionable results. To achieve these outcomes, researchers' and practitioners' roles, relationships, and expectations need to be explicit and well defined; each side must appreciate the other's views and goals (Kimberly in Walsh et al., 2007).

Joint interpretive forums. BSs can bring together researchers and practitioners to discuss and reflect on particular issues or information. Joint interpretive forums generally are organized around a particular research project, management issue, or common topic (Mohrman, Gibson, & Mohrman, 2001). They can last from a few hours to a couple of days, and can recur periodically or be one-shot events. These face-to-face forums are highly interactive and can facilitate perspective taking and collective learning among participants, which in turn can broaden researchers' and practitioners' thought-worlds and appreciation for each other's perspectives. Depending on the forum's purpose and design, participants may jointly interpret research results, explore their relevance to practice, identify emerging areas for management inquiry, and make preliminary plans for action-oriented research projects.

Research suggests that joint interpretive forums are especially effective in helping participants conceptually understand the usefulness of research findings (Ginsburg et al., 2007; Mohrman, Gibson, & Mohrman, 2001). To assure that the results are subsequently implemented, however, "perspective taking" must occur between researchers and practitioners. This means that each side must recognize and understand the other's values, meanings, and beliefs. This type of understanding enables a researcher to translate research results into a practitioner's meaning system and organizational context.

Knowledge networks. These link BSs and companies into an interactive partnership that seeks to align research with practice (see Chapter 4, A Ten-Year Journey of Cooperation; and Chapter 13, Professional Associations). The network provides a collaborative structure for researchers and practitioners to determine a research agenda that captures both of their interests, to design and fund promising research projects, and to apply the findings. One of the oldest and most successful knowledge networks is the Marketing Science Institute (MSI) currently headquartered in Cambridge, Massachusetts (Starbuck in Walsh et al., 2007). Founded in 1961 by Wharton's dean, it aims to bridge the gap between marketing research and practice. Today, MSI connects executives from around 70 global firms with researchers from over 100 BSs worldwide. MSI identifies research priorities through member polling and global discussions. It then circulates them to researchers who submit research proposals; about 35 projects are funded each year. Research results written in practical language are disseminated promptly to members. MSI has its own publication series and routinely holds and co-sponsors a variety of conferences and workshops to discuss research findings, explore how to implement them, and encourage applied research. These events are highly interactive and facilitate meaningful dialogue between researchers and practitioners. Research sponsored by MSI often appears in top academic journals and wins prominent awards.

Executive doctoral programs. These alternative doctoral programs are aimed at working professionals with extensive practical experience (Hart et al., 2004; Hay, 2004). They generally offer a blend of practice, theory, and research in a format that enables students to work full-time while pursuing their studies. Executive doctoral programs are not intended to educate academic researchers but scholar-practitioners who can serve as boundary spanners linking the worlds of academe and business (see Chapter 11, Integrating Theory to Inform Practice). Graduates typically continue to work in business or government, enter management consulting, or seek employment in BSs as clinical or adjunct faculty.

Executive doctoral programs are growing in number and size (Bisoux, 2009). Although they are relatively new in business education, they can offer new and potentially valuable ways to engage with practitioners. Graduates of these programs are likely to be strong proponents of evidence-based management, and they can extend that perspective to the organizations in which they work or consult. They can encourage leaders to ask hard questions about the efficacy of different management innovations; they can show them how to measure and assess the consequences of their decisions. Graduates can play an important role in disseminating research findings to practitioners. They can use their dual perspective to translate research results so practitioners can understand and use them, something academic researchers typically are unwilling or unable to do. Graduates of these programs can help BSs deal with the growing shortage of faculty with doctoral degrees. They can bring their academic and business expertise into the classroom to help students tie theory to practice. They can facilitate collaborative research between academics and practitioners to create useful knowledge.

Because executive doctoral programs are so new to business education, there is little information on which to judge their effectiveness in preparing students to be scholar-practitioners. Few of the programs are housed in research-based BSs, and there is likely wide variation in the quality of their students and curriculum. To their credit, a growing number of these doctoral programs are working diligently to develop and legitimize their role in management education. They encourage their students to participate regularly in professional conferences such as the Academy of Management; their administrators and faculty meet periodically with their counterparts in other programs to share problems and solutions and to develop a common set of professional practices.

Business school research centers. These provide a formal structure for connecting BSs to the practitioner community (see Chapter 1, Research for Theory and Practice). Research centers generally are organized around a domain that fits a particular constituency within industry, such as human resources, marketing, finance, and the like. Emphasizing a particular domain provides them with identifiable and potentially receptive partners for sharing knowledge, gaining access to firms, and sponsoring research and related activities. Research centers serve as a hub for academics and practitioners, periodically bringing them together to discuss research knowledge and its practical applications, to identify key emergent problems, and to facilitate networking among practitioners so they can share their experiences and learn from one another. Research centers may have their own professional staff that conducts action-oriented research and generates useful knowledge, such as the Center for Effective Organizations at the Marshall School of Business, University of Southern California; or more commonly, they may be a virtual organization that draws on the research of business school faculty and links it to the practitioner community.

Research centers are a particularly effective way for BSs to engage with practitioners. They have a distinct identity, an applied research competence, a specific practitioner base, and ongoing relationships with it. Because they have a foot in both academic and practitioner worlds, research centers know the values, beliefs, and practices of each of them and can serve as boundary spanners linking them together. They can help explicate the expectations, roles, and rules that facilitate effective research partnerships between the two sides (Hatchuel, 2001).

Research centers can have problems sustaining these efforts, however, especially if they are run with professional researchers and support staff that must be funded and managed. Centers may receive deficient funding, support, and direction from BSs; they can easily become disconnected from them and treated as stand-alone appendages that operate and survive by their own wits and funding. Research centers are prone to external jolts that adversely affect their industry partners, such as the recent global recession. The demands of academe and practice are difficult to jointly satisfy, and being seen as marginal in both worlds can be stressful. Add to this the constant pressure to generate rigorous and relevant knowledge, to publish the results in respectable academic and applied outlets, to gain funding and balance a budget, and to keep all of this organized and moving forward can be daunting even to the most skilled and ardent researchers.

BSs need to address these problems strategically as a key part of an overall plan for connecting to the external world. They need to determine the unique role that research centers will play in this strategy and how they will fit with other linking mechanisms, such as student recruiting, job placement, and fund-raising. These strategic choices are essential for addressing how research centers should be funded, organized, assessed, and rewarded. They provide a context for dealing with many of the problems that research centers face. When treated strategically and provided with sufficient funds, support, and direction, research centers can be a valuable resource for satisfying the dual demands for rigor and relevance in management knowledge; they can be a powerful bridge between the academic and business communities.

Conclusion

In writing this chapter, I gained a better appreciation for the complex challenges that BSs face today and the difficulties they pose for creating knowledge that is both rigorous and relevant, the joint demands that all professional schools must satisfy. Clearly, BSs have come down on the side of rigor for the reasons identified in this chapter, and this emphasis is being reinforced through existing norms, practices, and beliefs. The enablers I described for remedying this imbalance seem promising yet face an uphill battle to overcome these inertial forces. Changing the status quo for how knowledge is created in BSs is an extremely difficult, if not impossible, task. Yet, we must meet the challenge if we truly want to create knowledge that is useful for theory and practice.

REFERENCES

AACSB International. (2002). *Management education at risk*. Report of the Management Education Task Force to the AACSB International Board of Directors. Tampa, FL: AACSB International.

AACSB International. (2003). *Sustaining scholarship in business schools*. Report of the Doctoral Faculty Commission to the AACSB International Board of Directors. Tampa, FL: AACSB International.

AACSB International. (2008a). *Business school faculty trends 2008 report*. Tampa, FL: AACSB International.

AACSB International. (2008b). *Final report of the AACSB international impact of research task force*. Tampa, FL: AACSB International.

Adler, N., Shani, A., & Styhre, A. (Eds.) (2004). *Collaborative research in organizations*. Thousand Oaks, CA: Sage.

Argyris, C., Putnam, R., & Smith, D. (1985). *Action science: Concepts, methods and skills for research and intervention*. San Francisco: Jossey-Bass.

Armstrong, J. S. (1995). The devil's advocate responds to an MBA student's claim that research harms learning. *Journal of Marketing, 59*, 101–106.

Armstrong, J. S., & Sperry, T. (1994). The ombudsman: Business school prestige— research versus teaching. *Interfaces, 24*(2), 13–22.

Beauvais, P. (2007). The fifth freedom: Access to postsecondary education in America today. *American Academic, 3*(1), 1–7.

Becker, E., Lindsat, C., & Grizzle, G. (2003). The derived demand for faculty research. *Managerial and Decision Economics, 24*(8), 549–567.

Bennis, W., & O'Toole, J. (2005). How business schools lost their way. *Harvard Business Review, 83*, 96–104.

Besancenot, D., Faria, J., & Vranceanu, R. (2008). *Why business schools do so much research: A signaling explanation.* ESSEC École Supérieure des Sciences Économiques et Commerciales Research Centre, Cergy-Pontoise, France.

Bisoux, T. (2009, March–April). Solving the doctoral dilemma. *BizEd*, 24–31.

Corley, K., & Gioia, D. (2000). The rankings game: Managing business school reputation. *Corporate Reputation Review, 3*(4), 319–333.

DeAngelo, H., DeAngelo, L., & Zimmerman, J. (2005). *What's really wrong with U.S. business schools?* Los Angeles: Marshall School of Business, University of Southern California.

Fee, C., Hadlock, C., & Pierce, J. (2005). Business school rankings and business school deans: A study of nonprofit governance. *Financial Management, 34*(1), 143–166.

Ford, E., Duncan, W. J., Bedeian, A., Gintei, P., Rousculp, M., & Adams, A. (2005). Mitigating risks, visible hands, inevitable disasters, and soft variables: Management research that matters to managers. *Academy of Management Executive, 19*(4), 24–38.

Ginsburg, L., Lewis, S., Zackheim, L., & Casebeer, A. (2007). Revisiting interaction in knowledge translation. *Implementation Science, 2*(34), 1–11.

Gordon, R., & Howell, J. (1959). *Higher education for business.* New York: Columbia University Press.

Hambrick, D. (1994). 1993 Presidential Address: What if the Academy actually mattered? *Academy of Management Review, 19*, 11–16.

Hart, H., Kylen, S., Norrgren, F., and Stymne, B. (2004). Collaborative research through an executive Ph.D. program. In N. Adler, A. Shani, & A. Styhre (Eds.), *Collaborative research in organizations* (pp. 101–116). Thousand Oaks, CA: Sage.

Hatchuel, A. (2001). The two pillars of new management research. *British Journal of Management, 12* (Special Issue), S33–S39.

Hay, G. (2004). Executive Ph.D.s as a solution to the perceived relevance gap between theory and practice: A framework of theory-practice linkages for the study of the executive doctoral scholar-practitioner. *International Journal of Organisational Behaviour, 7*(2), 375–393.

Huff, A. (2000). 1999 Presidential Address: Changes in organizational knowledge production. *Academy of Management Review, 25*(2), 288–293.

Khurana, R. (2007). *From higher aims to hired hands.* Princeton, NJ: Princeton University Press.

Lewin, K. (1946). Action research and minority problems. *Journal of Social Issues, 2*(4), 34–46.

Lorsch, J. (2009). Regaining lost relevance. *Journal of Management Inquiry, 18*, 108–117.

Mintzberg, H. (2004). *Managers not MBAs: A hard look at the soft practice of managing and management development.* San Francisco: Berrett-Koehler.

Mohrman, S., Gibson, C., & Mohrman, A. (2001). Doing research that is useful for practice: A model and empirical exploration. *Academy of Management Journal, 44*, 357–375.

Pettigrew, A. (2001). Management research after modernism. *British Journal of Management, 12* (Special Issue), S61–S70.

Pfeffer, J. (2009). Renaissance and renewal in management studies: Relevance regained. *European Management Review, 6*(3), 141–148.

Pfeffer, J., & Fong, C. (2002). The end of business schools? Less success than meets the eye. *Academy of Management Learning and Education, 1*(1), 78–95.

Pfeffer, J., & Fong, C. (2004). The business school 'business': Some lessons from the US experience. *Journal of Management Studies, 41*(8), 1501–1520.

Pfeffer, J., & Sutton, R. (2006). Profiting from evidence-based management. *Strategy & Leadership, 34*(2), 35–42.

Pfeffer, J., & Sutton, R. (2007). Suppose we took evidence-based management seriously: Implications for reading and writing management. *Academy of Management Learning & Education, 6*(1), 153–155.

Porter, L., & McKibbin, L. (1988). *Management education and development.* New York: McGraw-Hill.

Rousseau, D., & McCarthy, S. (2007). Evidence-based management: Educating managers from an evidence-based perspective. *Academy of Management Learning and Education, 6,* 94–101.

Rynes, S., Bartunek, J., & Daft, R. (2001). Across the great divide: Knowledge creation and transfer between practitioners and academics. *Academy of Management Journal, 44*(2), 340–355.

Rynes, S., & Trank, C. (1999). Behavioral science in the business school curriculum: Teaching in a changing institutional environment. *Academy of Management Review, 24*(4), 808–824.

Sherman, H. (2009). Improving the relevance of university business schools: Refocusing on providing professional business education. *American Journal of Business, 24*(1), 3–6.

Sonnenberg, W. (2004). *Federal support for education: Fiscal years 1980–2003.* Washington, DC: U.S. Department of Education, National Center for Education Statistics. (NCES 2004-026)

Starkey, K., Hatchuel, A., & Tempest, S. (2004). Rethinking the business school. *Journal of Management Studies, 41*(8), 1521–1531.

Starkey, K., & Madan, P. (2001). Bridging the relevance gap: Aligning stakeholders in the future of management research. *British Journal of Management, 12* (Special Issue), S3–S26.

Starkey, K., & Tiratsoo, N. (2007). *The business school and the bottom line.* Cambridge: Cambridge University Press.

Trank, C., & Rynes, S. (2003). Who moved our cheese? Reclaiming professionalism in business education. *Academy of Management Learning and Education, 2*(2), 189–205.

Tushman, M., & O'Reilly, C. (2007). Research and relevance: Implications of Pasteur's quadrant for doctoral programs and faculty development. *Academy of Management Journal, 50*(4), 769–774.

Van de Ven, A., & Johnson, P. (2006). Knowledge for theory and practice. *Academy of Management Review, 31*(4), 802–821.

Walsh, J., Tushman, M., Kimberly, J., Starbuck, B., & Ashford, S. (2007). On the relationship between research and practice. *Journal of Management Inquiry, 16*(2), 128–154.

Zimmerman, J. (2001). Can American business schools survive? (Financial Research and Policy Working Paper No. FR 01-16). The Bradley Policy Research Center, University of Rochester, New York.

ABOUT THE AUTHOR

Dr. Thomas G. Cummings is a leading international scholar and consultant on strategic change and designing high-performance organizations. He is Professor and Chair of the Department of Management and Organization at the Marshall School of Business, University of Southern California. He has authored over 70 articles and 22 books. Dr. Cummings was formerly President of the Western Academy of Management, Chair of the Organization Development and Change Division of the Academy of Management, and Founding Editor of the *Journal of Management Inquiry*. He was the 61st President of the Academy of Management, the largest professional association of management scholars in the world with a total membership of over 19,000.

NINETEEN

Counterpoint

Now Is a Great Time for Conducting Relevant Research!

SARA L. RYNES*

ALTHOUGH I DO NOT WISH to minimize the challenges for researchers who wish to create research that is useful to both theory and practice (as outlined by Cummings in Chapter 18, How Business Schools Shape (Misshape) Management Research), I would like to take a slightly different tack by offering several pieces of evidence suggesting that the type of research championed in this book is not only highly valued now, but is likely to become increasingly valued in the future.

Evidence of the Scholarly Value of Rich Field Research

I first got interested in the usefulness of research for practice through my interaction with a (then) graduate student, Brian McNatt. Brian was motivated to get a PhD because after several years of working in public accounting firms, he had observed and experienced many dysfunctional management practices and thought there just had to be a "better way." He wanted to discover something about this better way through study and research, and then to disseminate what he had learned to managers and students through teaching. He was also highly motivated to examine his ideas in field settings (e.g., McNatt & Judge, 2004; McNatt, 2010) despite the challenges of doing so.

Discussions with Brian about his interest in producing useful research evolved into my first two publications pertaining to the academic-practice interface. In Rynes, McNatt, and Bretz (1999), my colleagues and I examined

* I wish to thank Jean Bartunek, Tamara Giluk, and Susan Albers Mohrman for very helpful comments on an earlier draft of this manuscript.

the origins, processes, and outcomes of 141 studies in four top-tier journals[1] that could not have been conducted without at least minimal collaboration between the authors and one or more organizations. "Collaboration" was rather broadly defined for purposes of this research, ranging from (at a minimum) organizations giving permission for researchers to use archival databases to fully collaborative ventures where researchers spent months on-site collecting data.

The most interesting findings from this study concerned differences in outcomes based on the number of hours academics spent at the organizational research site. Specifically, academics who spent more time at the research site reported greater personal learning from the experience. Moreover, spending more hours at the research site was also associated with higher subsequent citations by other researchers. These findings left a big impression on me and influenced my subsequent beliefs about what constitutes "good research"[2]— an attitude shift that I put into action when I later become a journal editor. The second study (Rynes & McNatt, 2001) also produced some reason for optimism about academic-practitioner collaboration in producing top-tier research: 24 percent of the top-tier articles included in our study had been initiated by organizations rather than academics, and another 26 percent resulted from organizations that responded favorably to cold calls from academics.

My early experiences as incoming editor of the *Academy of Management Journal* (*AMJ*) further solidified my growing enthusiasm for the types of research described by other authors in this book (e.g., Chapter 2, Crossing Boundaries to Investigate Problems in the Field; Chapter 4, A Ten-Year Journey of Cooperation; Chapter 10, Academic-Consultant Collaboration). Specifically, in preparation for the editorial role, I conducted a survey of incoming *AMJ* board members. Results revealed that the number one suggestion for improving the *Journal* was to "accept more innovative, less formulaic research" (Rynes, 2005, p. 12).[3] Similarly, a second *AMJ* survey (Bartunek, Rynes & Ireland, 2006)—in which board members were invited to nominate up to three empirical articles from any academic journal or book that they regarded as "most interesting"—revealed that approximately half the articles nominated consisted of intensive field studies of either one or a small number of

---

1. *Academy of Management Journal* (*AMJ*), *Administrative Science Quarterly* (*ASQ*), *Journal of Applied Psychology* (*JAP*), *and Personnel Psychology* (*PPsych*).

2. Based on the training I received as a doctoral student, early in my career I tended to value highly controlled research and was skeptical about the value of methodologies such as ethnographies, case studies, or action research.

3. In Rynes McNatt, & Bretz (1999), we found that *AMJ* authors, on average, spent less time at organizational research sites than authors publishing in *ASQ, JAP,* or *PPsych*; i.e., *AMJ* was more likely to publish studies using archival databases than observational, interview, or participation-based studies.

organizations (e.g., Barley, 1986; Dutton & Dukerich, 1991; Eisenhardt, 1989). This result is way out of proportion with the (small) overall percentage of case or multiple-case studies published in top-tier management journals (see, for example, Rynes, 2007b).

Moreover, there is other evidence that interest in intensive "small-n" field research is very high. For example, Eisenhardt & Graebner's (2007) essay on how to build theory from case studies has already been cited 224 times according to the Institute for Scientific Information's (ISI) Web of Science and 708 times based on Google Scholar, making it by far the most-cited *AMJ* paper for that year. In addition, attendance at Academy of Management (AOM) professional development workshops (PDWs) on topics such as conducting "rich" research (such as The Power of Rich PDW in 2006; see Rynes, 2007a) or research that is useful to practice (Antonacopoulou & Yu, 2009) often leave standing room only and participants flowing into the hallways. In a similar vein, examination of *AMJ*'s "best paper" award reveals that a high proportion of the recent winners have been either single or multiple-case field studies (e.g., Elsbach & Kramer, 2003; Ferlie et. al., 2005; Gilbert, 2005; Greenwood & Suddaby, 2006; Plowman et al., 2007).

Additionally, many "management laureates" (e.g., Bedeian, 1992, 2002) have written at considerable length about how their academic careers—both as researchers and teachers—have been enhanced by close engagement with practitioners and their real-world problems. Finally, many of the authors in this book have received awards for doing the kinds of research discussed in this book. For example, Ruth Wageman won the Paper of the Year Award from the Organization Behavior Division of AOM for her work at Xerox on interdependence and group effectiveness (Wageman, 1995), Amy Edmondson won the Early Career Achievement Award from the OB Division for her excellent programmatic work on teams (e.g., Edmondson, 1999; Edmondson, 2002; Edmondson, Bohmer, & Pisano, 2001), Andy Van de Ven's *Engaged Scholarship* (2007) won the AOM's Terry Book Award, and several of the authors in this book have won the prestigious Michael J. Losey Award for career contributions to human resource research and practice (e.g., Ed Lawler, Michael Beer, Gary Latham, and Wayne Cascio).

In short, the type of collaborative field research discussed in this book is disproportionately represented in terms of best paper awards, career achievement awards, and citations by other authors—not to mention that such research is almost certainly more likely to result in findings that are applied in real organizations (e.g., see Chapter 8, Making a Difference *and* Contributing Useful Knowledge; Chapter 4, A Ten-Year Journey of Cooperation; Chapter 17, Practitioner Perspectives; Chapter 10, Academic-Consultant Collaboration). Moreover, I believe that the value of this type of research will only increase in years to come, as discussed in the following section.

Why the Value of Useful Research Will Increase

I fully agree with Tom Cummings's point (Chapter 18, How Business Schools Shape (Misshape) Management Research) that business schools have become more market-driven, and I am on record as sharing a number of his concerns about the implications of an excessively market-driven focus (see, e.g., Rynes & Trank, 1997, and Trank & Rynes, 2003). However, with respect to the prospects for valuing high-quality research that is simultaneously useful to practice, I believe that the increasingly market-driven focus of business schools is primarily a positive development. Indeed, I believe that several features of the current research value system that some of us find troubling—for example, excessive and sometimes inappropriate emphasis on theory (Hambrick, 2007; Locke, 2007), fixation on ever-more esoteric quantitative methods that require stringent (and often unmet) assumptions about data (Starbuck, 2006), and empirical contributions of low practical importance (Oviatt & Miller, 1989)—are the result of business schools having become *too isolated* from market pressures, thus enabling them to indulge in self-serving, insular activities. Indeed, it was a public perception of business schools as *not* being responsive to markets (i.e., students, taxpayers, and employers) that led to instigation of the *Business Week* rankings in 1988 and the host of subsequent followers (e.g., *Financial Times, Forbes*).

Although it is possible that business school rankings may have increased the emphasis on producing quick top-tier "hits," there are a number of countervailing forces. First, the *main* emphasis of the rankings (particularly the highly influential *Business Week* rankings) has been to increase the voice of business recruiters and students. This is no bad thing in the present context because both groups would rather have business professors producing and disseminating (via teaching) research that is useful and important, rather than esoteric or trivial. In addition, various popular press rating schemes tend to "count" journals that focus more on *management* journals (versus the specialized disciplinary journals that Cummings is concerned about; see also Judge, 2003) and also bridge journals such as *Harvard Business Review, California Management Review,* and *Human Resource Management Journal.*

Second, over the past few years, I have detected a shift in the deliberations of promotion and tenure committees from simply "counting" the number of top-tier publications to factoring in the scope, importance, and impact (or expected future impact) of a scholar's work via citations (Judge et al., 2007; Adler & Harzing, 2009).[4] This shift has almost certainly been facilitated by

---

4. Of course, this trend may not be universal.

the emergence of databases capable of producing early estimates of impact. Moreover, in a world that values speed and globalization, assessments of academic impact are moving away from sole emphasis on the relatively narrow citation base represented by ISI's Web of Science to also include faster, more inclusive sources such as Google Scholar (GS) and the Social Science Research Network (SSRN). Comparisons of citation counts for the same individuals across ISI and GS reveal that GS generally produces much higher impact scores for academics who (1) write books (which tend to be based on longer-term efforts than journal articles); (2) write for more general audiences (since citations are not restricted only to top-tier journals), and (3) contribute to new journals (since it takes a minimum of six years before a new journal receives an impact factor calculation from ISI, and at least three years before its articles are included in the ISI database; Adler & Harzing, 2009). As members of the academy begin to use SSRN and GS more frequently for their speed, breadth, global reach, and ease of use (see Harzing, 2008; Harzing & van der Wal, 2008), the payoff to researchers for conducting more important, more generally accessible, and more interesting types of research is likely to correspondingly increase.

Finally, after nearly four decades of declining public investment in higher education, business schools have become increasingly dependent on the private sector for resources (Slaughter & Leslie, 1997).[5] This development further increases the value of faculty members whose research can be highlighted on school websites and featured in university fund-raising ventures. Even a casual glance at the webpages of major business schools reveals that the featured researchers are those who are studying topics of obvious importance to business and/or society. In short, the increased financial dependency of educational institutions on the private sector broadens the number of ways in which faculty members can—and really *must*—contribute value to business schools (and other university entities) and, in the process, lends support to the kinds of research championed by this book. (For an excellent discussion of how different types of research and faculty members can contribute to business schools, see Susan Ashford's essay in Walsh et al., 2007.)

Growing Restlessness for Change

Criticisms of business schools and the research they are producing have escalated dramatically over the past ten years, not only from those outside the academy (Crainer & Dearlove, 1999) but also among prominent academic

---

5. Indeed, some (such as Michigan, Virginia, and UCLA) have taken or are in the process of taking their business schools private.

insiders (e.g., Garten, 2006; Hambrick, 2007; Khurana, 2007; Mintzberg, 2005). Moreover, some of these critiques have received substantial attention. For example, according to citation counts on GS, Sumantra Ghoshal's (2005) "Bad Management Theories Are Destroying Good Management Practices" has been cited 865 times; Pfeffer and Fong's (2002) "The End of Business Schools? Less Success than Meets the Eye" has been cited 577 times; and Bennis and O'Toole's (2005) "How Business Schools Lost Their Way" has been cited 545 times. All three of these articles criticize the movement of business school research away from the context and concerns of ongoing organizations, the marginalization of stakeholders other than owners, and the reification of theories based on untenable assumptions that favor certain types of decisions and behaviors over others.

At the same time, the number of special forums calling for increased attention to the intersection of research and practice has increased dramatically over the past ten years (e.g., Burke, Drasgow, & Edwards, 2004; Gelade, 2006; Rynes, Bartunek, & Daft, 2001; Rynes, Giluk, & Brown, 2007; Stone, 2007). Attempts to bridge the gap have also emerged in HR Town Hall Meetings at the Academy of Management, best practice DVDs produced by Wayne Cascio and the Society of Human Resource Management (SHRM) Foundation, and a series of Practice Guides offered on the SHRM website. The Society for Industrial and Organizational Psychology (SIOP) has also responded to the gap with its *Science You Can Use* collaboration with SHRM, as well as the recent introduction of *Industrial and Organizational Psychology: Perspectives on Science and Practice,* a new journal that publishes "state of the science and/or practice" essays, followed by short commentaries by both academics and practitioners. Recognition for research that is useful to practice has also come in the form of awards, such as AOM's Distinguished Scholar-Practitioner award, SIOP's M. Scott Myers Award for Applied Research in the Workplace, and a variety of division-specific AOM awards.

Research that is useful to both science and practice is also being supported by new sources of funding that emphasize the necessity of working with and speaking to both communities. One such source is the SHRM Foundation, which funds individual studies up to $200,000 and has funded more than $2.5 million in research over the past ten years. Another generous source of applied research funding is the Management Education Research Institute (MERI), the foundation arm of the Graduate Management Admissions Council. MERI gives $50,000 fellowships and grants of up to $100,000 for individual studies designed to improve the process of getting management research into the hands of practicing managers through education. The National Science Foundation, too, emphasizes studies that are expected to yield important advances in principle-based understanding of organizations, as exemplified by their Virtual Organizations as Sociotechnical Sys-

tems (VOSS) and Science of Science and Innovation Policies (SciSIP; http://
www.nsf.gov/funding). Of course, the sums mentioned here are not as eye-
popping as the £1 million offered to individual researchers by the United
Kingdom's Advanced Institute of Management (the type of grant that jump-
started Lynda Gratton's research program, described in Chapter 4, A Ten-
Year Journey of Cooperation), but they are nevertheless effective vehicles for
encouraging research that is likely to be useful to practice.

Journals Are Changing

A variety of authors in many fields have noted the increasing importance of
citation rates to the fate, not only of individual scholars, but also of journals
(Christenson & Sigelman, 1985; Garfield, 2006; Johnson & Podsakoff, 1994;
Judge et al., 2007). Citation rates and impact factors are indeed issues of growing importance to journal editors, and I sympathize with editors of new
journals or those that presently do not have high citation rates.

At the same time, I think it is important to look at where the most-cited
articles have been coming from recently in management and the organization sciences. For example, the previously mentioned articles by Ghoshal
(2005), Pfeffer & Fong (2002), and Bennis and O'Toole (2005) were all published in bridge journals—specifically, the first two in the *Academy of Management Learning and Education* and the last in *Harvard Business Review.*
In addition, they were not empirical articles, but rather "thought pieces" by
well-known, respected academics.

Similarly, some of the most widely cited articles in *AMJ* in recent years
have come from essays published as part of editors' forums, rather than
from the peer-reviewed research found in later pages of the journal. Examples include Eisenhardt and Graebner's (2007) piece "Theory Building from
Cases," referred to earlier; Nicolaj Siggelkow's (2007) "Persuasion with Case
Studies" (91 cites according to ISI and 267 via GS); and Roy Suddaby's (2006)
piece on "What Grounded Theory is *Not*" (71 ISI citations and 228 via GS). In
other words, many of the recent articles that are getting the most "buzz"
in management journals are those that either address the state of the field
(which is frequently argued to need more of the type of contextualized
field research championed in this book) or that provide "how to" guidelines
for researchers who wish to design research with the kind of impact produced by Steve Barley, Jane Dutton, Kathleen Eisenhardt, Richard Hackman, Ed Lawler, C. K. Prahalad, Michael Tushman, Ruth Wageman, and others.
I believe these patterns suggest there is a great yearning among management
scholars to do research that "matters" (see also McGrath, 2007; Vermeulen,
2007).

In addition, there has been a broadening of the types of research considered appropriate for publication in several journals—all in ways that are favorable to the types of research discussed in this book. For example, in addition to the broadening of publication criteria by *AMJ*, the *Journal of Organizational Behavior* (*JOB*) has increasingly emphasized the importance of contextualization in management research since Denise Rousseau's editorship (e.g., Johns, 2001; Rousseau & Fried, 2001). Johns (2001) argues that greater emphasis on context contributes to storytelling, makes an article more interesting, and supports active processing by readers: "As long as (authors) have fairly described the institutional and organizational context of their research, readers are free to make their own interpretations about their impact" (p. 33)—something that both practitioners and academics do all the time (Czarniawska & Sevon, 2005; Rousseau, Manning, & Denyer, 2008).

Even the *Journal of Applied Psychology*, a top-tier psychology journal with a strong experimental foundation, has indicated its willingness to entertain "research that is based on content analyses, case studies, observations, interviews and other qualitative procedures" (Zedeck, 2003, p. 3). Another positive development is the recent special issue on qualitative research in *Organizational Research Methods* (Easterby-Smith, Golden-Biddle, & Locke, 2008), which was commissioned in part to help educate authors, reviewers, and editors about what constitutes "quality" in qualitative work and how such work is evaluated by reviewers and editors.

There is also recent research suggesting that some of these developments have made a difference in terms of researchers paying more attention to practitioners in discussions of their research findings. Specifically, Jean Bartunek and I recently conducted a study (Bartunek & Rynes, 2010) to determine whether or not discussion sections in five top-tier journals (*AMJ, JAP, JOB, OS,* and *PPsych*) have become more likely to include implications for practice (IFPs) since the early 1990s. Our rationale for comparing recent years (2002–2007) with the early 1990s was that the early nineties were a time of considerable activism in championing greater collaboration between researchers and practitioners. Examples include Dunnette's (1990) robust defense of the scientist-practitioner model; Murphy and Saal's (1990) book on integrating science and practice in psychology; the emergence of *Organization Science* as a journal founded, at least in part, to "enhance research relevance . . . encourage the joining of theory to practice, and anchor organization research in relevant problems" (Daft & Lewin, 1990, pp. 2, 9); and Hambrick's (1994) notable AOM presidential address, "What If the Academy Actually Mattered?" Our idea was that if these developments had made a difference, recent published research would pay more attention to practitioner concerns than research published prior to Hambrick's (1994) address.

Our comparison of discussion sections from the 1990s and mid-2000s revealed that in four of the five journals, the proportion of discussion sections including IFPs has notably increased. The biggest increase was in *Personnel Psychology* (from 34 percent in 1990s to 79 percent in 2000s), followed by *JAP* (30 percent to 58 percent), *AMJ* (27 percent to 55 percent), *JOB* (40 percent to 58 percent), and *OS* (46 percent to 47 percent). Although simply including implications for practice does not insure that research articles are useful to (or used by) practitioners (see, for example, Kieser & Leiner, 2009), it certainly is a step in the right direction.

In sum, at the same time that much top-tier management research has continued to get increasingly esoteric, there also are trends in the opposite direction. Nevertheless, more can be done, particularly in supporting research that addresses important and interesting questions (Bartunek, Rynes, & Ireland, 2006; McGrath, 2007) even if—or perhaps especially if—they don't fit neatly into already-existing theoretical frameworks (e.g., Hambrick, 2007; Locke, 2007). As Tsui (2007) observes, a "theoretical fixation tends to homogenize our research, burying potential gems of insight in a quest to integrate emergent or unfamiliar phenomena into the perspective generated by previous theory building" (p. 1373). Other actions might be to give relatively more weight to implications for practice (Bartunek & Rynes, 2010) or to create separate sections in top-tier journals for collaborative or action research (e.g., *PPsych* has long had a "practice" section, which more top journals might emulate).

Young Academics Want to Do Relevant Research

Another reason that I am optimistic about the future of research that is jointly relevant to academics and practitioners is that doctoral students tend to be particularly interested in creating research that "matters" to the broader society. In the six-plus years that I attended countless "editors' forums" at AOM, SIOP, and individual universities, I observed a real yearning among young scholars (such as Brian McNatt) to make a difference both inside and outside academia. The same is also true in our doctoral program at the University of Iowa; because many students now enter doctoral programs with considerable experience under their belts, they tend to be motivated by a desire to improve practice through their research and teaching as much—or perhaps more—than anything else.

Vermeulen (2007) expresses this longing well: "I remember (my doctoral student days) with fondness. I had already chosen to be an academic, while my friends went off to have well-paid jobs in banking, consulting, and industry. I was going to be a poor yet noble academic, not driven by money, job status, or security, but dedicated to a quest for knowledge and understanding that would enable me to help others understand and improve the workings of their organizations. I think many management scholars start out with this feeling ... However, over time ... we learn that the legitimate way to frame our academic identity is in terms of a theoretical tradition and a stream of research. And there is nothing wrong with that, unless these goals have completely replaced our desire and quest for true knowledge and understanding" (p. 754).

Vermeulen (2007) describes some of the ways that he has tried to remain true to his dream of being relevant to practice while conducting rigorous research. First, quoting March (2006), he says, "No academic has the experience to know the context of a managerial problem well enough to give specific advice about a specific situation. What an academic *can* do is say some things that, in combination with the manager's knowledge of the context, may lead to a better solution. It is the combination of academic and experiential knowledge, not the substitution of one for the other, that yields improvement" (p. 85). Thus, Vermeulen aims to tell practitioners about his research through teaching and consulting, and considers himself successful when "some of these people feel they have gained an insight they did not yet have ... that enables them to make better decisions regarding their own specific company situations" (2007, p. 75).

Another thing Vermeulen (2007) does is to force himself to "smell the beast": that is, to stay close to practitioners and the world of practice. He does this by consulting, interviewing practitioners, writing teaching cases, and evaluating future research possibilities by asking whether the managers of his "case companies" would be interested in the question. In other words, by beginning all his research projects with both extant research and practical problems in mind, he tries to build both rigor and relevance into his research projects.

While Vermeulen (2007) focuses on things young academics might do to produce more relevant (but rigorous) research, McGrath (2007) focuses on what senior faculty can do to pave the way and support them. She, like Tom Cummings, believes that borrowing from other disciplines (e.g., sociology, economics) comes at a cost to the emerging discipline of management, as well as to its interest in real-world managerial problems. However, unlike Tom, she believes that the current state of business schools is on the verge of deinstitutionalization—in large part because of the disproportionate value placed on top-tier academic research over everything else in academic reward systems. As such, McGrath is more optimistic than Tom that now is a very propitious time for taking the types of actions suggested in his paper and in the following section.

Making It Happen

As is apparent by now, I am optimistic that there is a bright future for research that advances both the science and the practice of management. Like McGrath (2007), I believe that conditions are aligned to give tremendous advantages to schools and researchers that blend the best of scientific thinking with examination of significant real-world problems. After all, this is currently the type of research that garners the greatest amount of respect, citations, awards, and influence, and I see no reason for this to change.

So, how can young scholars get started down the path toward having both academic and practical impact? The following are a few research-supported ideas:

- *Find a niche that suits you.* Eden (2008) advises young researchers to find their own personally meaningful niche: "an identifiable, circumscribed area of scholarly inquiry that can provide a good match with an individual's qualifications, interests, and career aspirations. Within these niches, individual scholars can thrive. There a newcomer can find colleagues with similar interests, form partnerships, exchange information, and in general, derive support for a career" (p. 733). With the emergence of the Internet, finding a niche—and a group of supportive colleagues with whom to share it—has never been easier.

- *Be optimistic, set goals, and have positive expectations.* Dozens of laboratory and field experiments have shown that people perform better when others have high expectations of them (Eden & Shani, 1982; McNatt, 2000) and they have high expectations of themselves (Eden & Kinnar, 1991). Similarly, people attain higher performance by setting difficult but attainable goals, a result discovered through "more than 1,000 studies conducted by behavioral scientists on more than 88 different tasks, involving more than 40,000 male and female participants in Asia, Australia, Europe and North America" (Latham & Locke, 2006, p. 332). Having a positive attitude is also reliably related to job performance (Kaplan et al., 2009) and, happily, positive affect can be acquired through practice (Fredrickson, 2009). So even though there is some truth to the concerns raised in Tom Cummings's chapter, young scholars will do better to focus instead on the wonderful research that others in this book have brought into being through optimism, persistence, and commitment to make a difference (see also Eden, 2008).

- *Don't go it alone.* As a general rule, I also recommend co-authoring research papers rather than going it alone. Co-authoring improves project quality through the give-and-take of ideas, permits the melding of complementary skills, speeds the process, and provides much-needed social support through the often arduous process of bringing research to publication. For some great ideas on writing for scholarly publication and working with co-authors, see Huff (1998).

- *Find supportive—and productive—mentors and co-authors.* Research on supervisory support and leader-member exchange has clearly demonstrated that people with supportive supervisors display higher job performance (Gerstner & Day, 1997; Liden, Sparrowe, & Wayne, 1997). Moreover, we know that positive emotions are contagious (Barsade, 2002), and that positivity is associated with higher energy, greater creativity, and better performance (Frederickson, 2009). Finally, research shows that productive faculty supervisors beget productive early-career scholars (Williamson & Cable, 2003). So, in choosing mentors and co-authors, think "positive, productive, and supportive."

- *Together, ask big, messy, exciting questions.* Daft, Griffin, and Yates (1987) examined characteristics of research questions that most differentiated between scholars' "most-versus-least significant" pieces of research (where significance was self-assessed, but then verified via independent ratings and citation counts). Studies that were most significant tended to be substantively rather than methodologically driven, and to be "characterized by less clarity and more uncertainty during the beginning stages than not-so-significant research . . . (and also) by high levels of excitement and commitment through the life of a project. . . . However, significant research projects tended to be *more* certain, clear, and orderly in the *final* publication stage than not-so-significant research projects" (p. 782, emphasis added). Now, doesn't this sound just like the kinds of research projects described in this book? And lest the idea of "big, messy questions" seems too daunting, remember that big, messy questions can be broken down into smaller pieces, and studied via multiple methods over many years (see, for example, Fredrickson, 2009; or Locke & Latham, 2002).

- *Pursue multiple projects simultaneously.* Soon after I took my first job at the University of Minnesota, Herb Heneman Jr. (for whom the AOM's Heneman Career Achievement Award in Human Resources is named) advised me that the secret to success in publishing was to "throw a lot of stuff at the wall, hoping some of it will stick." Although I suspect it is possible to throw too many things at the wall, Herb's folksy advice has been empirically confirmed in the management discipline (Taylor et al., 1984). Because studies that make solid contributions to both research and practice are more likely to be "big" studies that take a lot of time, it seems wise to balance them out with other, smaller (and where possible, related) studies. The nature of the academic publishing process is such that each individual study undergoes a lot of "down time" (e.g., waiting for human subjects approval, waiting for reviews), but with multiple projects, one study's downtime can become another's surge to completion.

- *Don't forget to get out of your office.* Campbell, Daft, and Hulin (1982) found that significant research projects often emerge from the chance convergence of different inputs, that is, researchers from different disciplines, people from different lines of work (e.g., management versus academics), or discrepant accounts between scientific and popular media. Both Tushman and O'Reilly (2007) and Vermeulen (2007) report that they get many of their research ideas from interactions with the people they teach, particularly those in executive education. The odds of discovering something truly new increase when beliefs based on current research findings butt up against contrary evidence, or practitioners ask a question to which there is no good research-based answer. Every researcher can increase her chances of finding important research questions by choosing to partake of these other experiences. So, socialize, consult, teach, and read something other than research journals.

Conclusion

Those of us who have chosen academic careers are truly blessed by being able to, far more than most employees, create a path of our own choosing (Frost & Taylor, 1996). Particularly after being granted tenure, we are far more able than people in most other occupations to do the kind of work that seems most important to us and that most deeply satisfies our souls. In this, I agree with Dov Eden (2008), who recently said: "Who but academicians do what they want to do, are free to determine where they spend their days and hours of the day, and get so many paid vacation days? Which other type of gainful employment grants so much freedom? . . . No one should be deterred by the stress and strain of an academic career. Compared to most careers, it's a piece of cake" (p. 739). Similarly, McGrath (2007) said: "Although academics moan about being busy, we have the luxury of being able to mull over questions for years, if we so please. Unlike our colleagues in the world of consulting, our ideas do not have to be immediately billable, and so can extend over longer time horizons. Academics can thus bring the potential for reflection and deeper 'sensemaking' to practical problems" (p. 1371). So, what are we so afraid of?

It seems to me that more than any other factor, producing important research that is useful to practice depends on the desire, will, and commitment to do so. Let's put on our Nikes and *just do it.* The time is right.

REFERENCES

Adler, N., & Harzing, A-W. (2009). When knowledge wins: Transcending the sense and nonsense of academic rankings. *Academy of Management Learning and Education, 8,* 72–95.

Antonacopoulou, E., & Yu, F. (2009, August 9). *Bringing practice back into our scholarship: Delivering the agenda for action.* Professional Development Workshop, Academy of Management Annual Meeting, Chicago, IL.

Barley, S. (1986). Technology as an occasion for structuring: Evidence from observations of CT scanners and the social order of radiology departments. *Administrative Science Quarterly, 31,* 78–108.

Barsade, S. G. (2002). The ripple effect: Emotional contagion and its influence on group behavior. *Administrative Science Quarterly, 47,* 644–675.

Bartunek, J. M., & Rynes, S. L. (2010). The construction and contributions of "implications for practice": What's in them and what might they offer? *Academy of Management Learning and Education, 9,* 100–117.

Bartunek, J. M., Rynes, S. L., & Ireland, R. D. (2006). What makes management research interesting, and why does it matter? *Academy of Management Journal, 49,* 9–15.

Bedeian, A. G. (1992). *Management laureates: A collection of autobiographical essays* (Vol. 1). Greenwich, CT: JAI Press.

Bedeian, A. G. (2002). *Management laureates: A collection of autobiographical essays* (Vol. 6). Oxford, UK: Elsevier.

Bennis, W. G., & O'Toole, J. (2005). How business schools lost their way. *Harvard Business Review, 83*(5), 96–104.

Burke, M. H., Drasgow, F., & Edwards, J. E. (2004). Closing science-practice knowledge gaps: Contributions of psychological research to human resource management. *Human Resource Management, 43,* 299–304.

Campbell, J. P., Daft, R. L., & Hulin, C. (1982). *What to study: Generating and developing research questions.* Thousand Oaks, CA: Sage.

Christenson, J. A., & Sigelman, L. (1985). Accrediting knowledge: Journal stature and citation impact in social science. *Social Science Quarterly, 66,* 964–975.

Crainer, S., & Dearlove, D. (1999). *Gravy training: Inside the business of business schools.* San Francisco: Jossey-Bass.

Czarniawska, B., & Sevon, G. (Eds.). (2005). *Global ideas: How ideas, objects, and practices travel in the global economy.* Frederiksberg, DK: Liber & Copenhagen Business School Press.

Daft, R. L., Griffin, R. W., & Yates, V. (1987). Retrospective accounts of research factors associated with significant and not-so-significant research outcomes. *Academy of Management Journal, 30,* 763–785.

Daft, R. L., & Lewin, A. S. (1990). Can organization studies begin to break out of the normal science straitjacket? An editorial. *Organization Science, 1,* 1–9.

Dunnette, M. D. (1990). Blending the science and practice of industrial and organizational psychology: Where are we and where are we going? In M. D. Dunnette & L. M. Hough (Eds.), *Handbook of industrial and organizational psychology* (Vol. 1, 2nd ed., pp. 1–27). Palo Alto, CA: Consulting Psychologists Press.

Dutton, J. E., & Dukerich, J. (1991). Keeping an eye on the mirror: Image and identity in organizational adaptation. *Academy of Management Journal, 34*, 517–554.

Easterby-Smith, M., Golden-Biddle, K., & Locke, K. (2008). Working with pluralism: Determining quality in qualitative research. *Organizational Research Methods, 11*, 419–429.

Eden, D. (2008). Thriving in a self-made niche: How to create a successful academic career in organizational behavior. *Journal of Organizational Behavior, 29*, 733–740.

Eden, D., & Kinnar, J. (1991). Modeling Galatea: Boosting self-efficacy to increase volunteering. *Journal of Applied Psychology, 76*, 770–780.

Eden, D., & Shani, A. B. (1982). Pygmalion goes to boot camp: Expectancy, leadership, and trainee performance. *Journal of Applied Psychology, 67*, 194–199.

Edmondson, A. (1999). Psychological safety and learning behavior in work teams. *Administrative Science Quarterly, 44*, 350–383.

Edmondson, A. (2002). The local and variegated nature of learning in organizations: A group-level perspective. *Organization Science, 13*, 128–146.

Edmondson, A., Bohmer, R., & Pisano, G. (2001). Speeding up team learning. *Harvard Business Review, 79*, 125–134.

Eisenhardt, K. M. (1989). Making fast strategic decisions in high-velocity environments. *Academy of Management Journal, 32*, 543–577.

Eisenhardt, K. M., & Graebner, M. E. (2007). Theory building from cases: Opportunities and challenges. *Academy of Management Journal, 50*, 25–32.

Elsbach, K. D., & Kramer, R. M. (2003). Assessing creativity in Hollywood pitch meetings: Evidence for a dual-process model of creativity judgments. *Academy of Management Journal, 46*, 283–301.

Ferlie, E., Fitzgerald, L., Wood, M., & Hawkins, C. (2005). The non-spread of innovations: The mediating role of professionals. *Academy of Management Journal, 48*, 117–134.

Fredrickson, B. L. (2009). *Positivity: Top-notch research reveals the 3-to-1 ratio that will change your life.* New York: Three Rivers Press.

Frost, P. J., & Taylor, M. S. (1996). *Rhythms of academic life: Personal accounts of careers in academia.* Thousand Oaks: Sage.

Garfield, E. (2006). The history and meaning of the journal impact factor. *Journal of the American Medical Association, 295*, 90–93.

Garten, J. E. (2006, December 9). Really old school. *New York Times,* Op-Ed.

Gelade, G. A. (2006). But what does it mean in practice? The *Journal of Occupational and Organizational Psychology* from a practitioner perspective. *Journal of Occupational and Organizational Psychology, 79*, 153–160.

Gerstner, C. R., & Day, D. V. (1997). Meta-analytic review of leader-member exchange theory: Correlates and construct issues. *Journal of Applied Psychology, 82*, 827–844.

Ghoshal, S. (2005). Bad management theories are driving out good management practices. *Academy of Management Learning and Education, 4*, 75–91.

Gilbert, C. G. (2005). Unbundling the structure of inertia: Resource versus routine rigidity. *Academy of Management Journal, 48*, 741–763.

Greenwood, R., & Suddaby, R. (2006). Institutional entrepreneurship in mature fields: The big five accounting firms. *Academy of Management Journal, 49,* 27–48.

Hambrick, D. C. (1994). What if the academy really mattered? *Academy of Management Review, 19,* 11–16.

Hambrick, D. C. (2007). The field of management's devotion to theory: Too much of a good thing? *Academy of Management Journal, 50,* 1346–1352.

Harzing, A. W. (2008). *Publish or perish,* version 2.5.3171, available at http://www.harzing.com/pop.htm.

Harzing, A. W., & van der Wal, R. (2008). Google Scholar as a new source for citation analysis. *Ethics in Science and Environmental Politics, 8*(1), 62–71.

Huff, A. S. (1998). *Writing for scholarly publication.* Thousand Oaks, CA: Sage.

Johns, G. (2001). In praise of context: Commentary. *Journal of Organizational Behavior, 22,* 31–42.

Johnson, L. J., & Podsakoff, P. M. (1994). Journal influence in the field of management: An analysis using Salancik's index in a dependency network. *Academy of Management Journal, 37,* 1392–1407.

Judge, T. A. (2003, January). Marginalizing the *Journal of Applied Psychology? The Industrial Psychologist, 40*(3). Retrieved from http://www.siop.org/tip/backissues/Jan03/JAn03TOC.aspx.

Judge, T. A., Cable, D. M., Colbert, A. E., & Rynes, S. L. (2007). What causes an article to be cited? Article, author, or journal? *Academy of Management Journal, 50,* 491–506.

Kaplan, S., Bradley, J. C., Luchman, J. N., & Haynes, D. (2009). On the role of positive and negative affectivity in job performance: A meta-analytic investigation. *Journal of Applied Psychology, 94,* 162–176.

Khurana, R. (2007). *From higher aims to hired hands: The social transformation of business schools and the unfulfilled promise of management as a profession.* Princeton, NJ: Princeton University Press.

Kieser, A., & Leiner, L. 2009. Why the rigour–relevance gap in management research is unbridgeable. *Journal of Management Studies, 46,* 516–533.

Latham, G. P., & Locke, E. A. (2006). Enhancing the benefits and overcoming the pitfalls of goal setting. *Organizational Dynamics, 35,* 332–340.

Liden, R. C., Sparrowe, R. T., & Wayne, S. J. (1997). Leader-member exchange theory: The past and potential for the future. *Research in Personnel and Human Resource Management, 15,* 47–119.

Locke, E. A. (2007). The case for inductive theory building. *Journal of Management, 33,* 867–890.

Locke, E. A., & Latham, G. P. (2002). Building a practically useful theory of goal setting and task motivation: A 35 year odyssey. *American Psychologist, 57,* 705–717.

March, J. G. (2006). Ideas as art. *Harvard Business Review, 84*(10), 82–89.

McGrath, R. G. (2007). No longer a stepchild: How the management field can come into its own. *Academy of Management Journal, 50,* 1365–1378.

McNatt, D. B. (2000). Ancient Pygmalion joins contemporary management: A meta-analysis of the result. *Journal of Applied Psychology, 85,* 314–322.

McNatt, D. B. (2010). Negative reputation and biased student evaluations of teaching: Longitudinal results from a naturally occurring experiment. *Academy of Management Learning and Education*, 9, 225–242.

McNatt, D. B., & Judge, T. A. (2004). Boundary conditions of the Galatea effect: A field experiment and constructive replication. *Academy of Management Journal, 47,* 550–565.

Mintzberg, H. (2005). *Managers not MBAs: A hard look at the soft practice of managing and management development.* San Francisco: Berrett-Koehler.

Murphy, K. R., & Saal, F. E. (1990). *Psychology in organizations: Integrating science and practice.* Hillsdale, NJ: Erlbaum.

Oviatt, B. M., & Miller, W. D. (1989). Irrelevance, intransigence, and business professors. *Academy of Management Executive, 3,* 304–312.

Pfeffer, J., & Fong, C. T. (2002). The end of business schools? Less success than meets the eye. *Academy of Management Learning and Education, 1,* 78–95.

Plowman, D. A., Lakami, T. B., Beck, T. E., Kulkarni, M., Solansky, S. T., & Travis, D. V. (2007). Radical change accidentally: The emergence and amplification of small change. *Academy of Management Journal, 50,* 515–543.

Rousseau, D. M. & Fried, Y. (2001). Location, location, location: Contextualizing organizational research. *Journal of Organizational Behavior, 22,* 1–13.

Rousseau, D. M., Manning, J., & Denyer, D. (2008). Evidence in management and organizational science: Assembling the field's full weight of scientific knowledge through syntheses. *Academy of Management Annals, 2,* 475–515.

Rynes, S. L. (2005). Taking stock and looking ahead. *Academy of Management Journal, 48,* 9–15.

Rynes, S. L. (2007a). *Academy of Management Journal* editors' forum on rich research. *Academy of Management Journal, 50,* 13.

Rynes, S. L. (2007b). Time flies when you're having fun. *Academy of Management Journal, 50,* 1273–1276.

Rynes, S. L., Bartunek, J. M., & Daft, R. L. (2001). Across the great divide: Knowledge creation and transfer between practitioners and academics. *Academy of Management Journal, 44,* 340–356.

Rynes, S. L., Giluk, T., & Brown, K. (2007). The very separate worlds of academic and practitioner periodicals in human resource management: Implications for evidence-based management. *Academy of Management Journal, 50,* 1046–1054.

Rynes, S. L. & McNatt, D. B. (2001). Bringing the organization into organizational research: An examination of academic research inside organizations. *Journal of Business and Psychology, 16,* 3–19.

Rynes, S. L., McNatt, D. B., & Bretz, R. D. (1999). Academic research inside organizations: Inputs, processes and outcomes. *Personnel Psychology, 52,* 869–898.

Rynes, S. L., & Trank, C. Q. (1997). Behavioral science in the business school curriculum: Teaching in a changing institutional environment. *Academy of Management Review, 24,* 808–824.

Siggelkow, N. (2007). Persuasion with case studies. *Academy of Management Journal, 50,* 20–24.

Slaughter, S., & Leslie, L. L. (1997). *Academic capitalism: Politics, policies, and the entrepreneurial university.* Baltimore, MD: Johns Hopkins University Press.

Starbuck, W. H. (2006). *The production of knowledge: The challenge of social science research*. Oxford University Press.

Stone, D. L. (2007). The status of theory and research in human resource management: Where have we been and where should we go from here? *Human Resource Management Review, 17,* 93–95.

Suddaby, R. (2006). What grounded theory is *not*. *Academy of Management Journal, 49,* 633–644.

Taylor, M. S., Locke, E. A., Lee, C., & Gist, M. (1984). Type A behavior and faculty research productivity: What are the mechanisms? *Organizational Behavior and Human Performance, 34,* 402–418.

Trank, C. Q., & Rynes, S. L. (2003). Who moved our cheese? Reclaiming professionalism in business education. *Academy of Management Learning and Education, 2,* 189–205.

Tsui, A. S. (2007). From homogenization to pluralism: International management research in the academy and beyond. *Academy of Management Journal, 50,* 1353–1364.

Tushman, M. L., & O'Reilly, C. A. (2007). Research and relevance: Implications of Pasteur's quadrant for doctoral programs and faculty development. *Academy of Management Journal, 50,* 769–774.

Van de Ven, A. H. (2007). *Engaged scholarship: A guide for organizational and social research*. Oxford: Oxford University Press.

Vermeulen, F. (2007). "I shall not remain insignificant": Adding a second loop to matter more. *Academy of Management Journal, 50,* 754–761.

Wageman, R. (1995). Interdependence and team effectiveness. *Administrative Science Quarterly, 40,* 145–180.

Walsh, J. P., Tushman, M. L., Kimberly, J. R., Starbuck, B., & Ashford, S. (2007). On the relationship between research and practice. *Journal of Management Inquiry, 16,* 128–154.

Williamson, I. O., & Cable, D. M. (2003). Predicting early career research productivity: The case of management faculty. *Journal of Organizational Behavior, 24,* 25–44.

Zedeck, S. (2003). Editorial. *Journal of Applied Psychology, 88,* 3–5.

ABOUT THE AUTHOR

Sara L. Rynes is the John F. Murray Professor of Management and Organizations at the University of Iowa. Her research interests are in human resource strategy, compensation, staffing, academic-practice relationships, and management education. She is a Fellow of the Academy of Management, the American Psychological Association, the Management Education Research Institute, and the Society for Industrial and Organizational Psychology. She received the Academy of Management's Herbert G. Heneman Career Achievement Award for Human Resource Management in 2006, was Editor-in-Chief of the *Academy of Management Journal* from 2005 to 2007, and was Chair of the Department of Management and Organizations at the University of Iowa from 1999 to 2004. She received her PhD from the University of Wisconsin.

TWENTY

On the Verge of Extinction

Some Final Reptilian Thoughts

JAMES O'TOOLE

Organizational behavior, organization theory, or organization studies, by whatever name you choose to identify our
field, is at a crossroads. A generation of scholars that
began their careers in the sixties is gradually leaving the
field. Most are doing so quietly. To quote General Douglas
McArthur, "Old soldiers never die, they just fade away."
Most of this generation is doing just that.... I am not,
myself, predisposed to leaving quietly.

—Jay Lorsch (2009)

MY FRIEND, the leadership expert Jay Conger, recently pointed out to me that
I am "officially a dinosaur" in the eyes of most of the academic community.
Well, what are friends for if not to warn you when you are in denial? Of course,
Jay went on to say that, actually, I am "among a set of dinosaurs" that includes
all of my closest professional colleagues, and Jay himself! Indeed, in the eyes of
the lab psychologists and *A*-journal scientists now in ascendancy in America's
leading business schools, the entire subspecies of scholars (like me) whose
writings are intended primarily for managers and leaders is headed toward
extinction. A great many younger scholars believe that our remnants are doomed
to die out because we lack the "rigor" to survive in a new age of social science
in which people (like themselves) write for an audience that is exclusively academic. Based on the general trend in business schools (b-schools) over the last
two decades, the prediction of our imminent extinction offered by the two
Jays (Conger and Lorsch) appears accurate. But just as we were preparing to
"fade away," something has started to happen recently that may indicate the
reports of our inevitable demise are premature. I start this chapter with a review of the alarming trends that portend our extinction and end with a few
thoughts about what might be done to "save the species."

Disturbing Trends

For many years now, my colleague Warren Bennis and I have been fretting over the rigor versus relevance issue in graduate business education (Bennis & O'Toole, 2005; O'Toole, 2009). Our main concern has been the potential, long-term consequences for business organizations when b-school professors' primary focus is on their own careers as scientists, and not on preparing students to lead the nation's economic institutions. Over the last decade or so, we have grown increasingly concerned by the fact that too many MBA programs—often those at prestigious research universities—are failing to (a) impart useful skills, (b) develop leaders, (c) instill high ethical norms, and (d) prepare mangers to deal with complex, cross-disciplinary, nonquantifiable issues. The intent of this chapter is to address the root causes of those failings and to suggest a course of action to correct them. But before getting to that proposal, it may be useful to briefly describe the origins of my own academic orientation. By making clear "where I am coming from," readers may be better able to judge the validity of the way forward that I offer later in this chapter.

Sources of My Biases

In the 1960s, like most undergraduate students in the social sciences at the time, I was raised on a heady diet of books by such once-luminary figures as William F. Whyte, Erving Goffman, Daniel Riesman, Nathan Glazer, Robert Nesbitt, C. Wright Mills, Daniel Bell, Daniel Patrick Moynihan, Seymour Martin Lipset, William H. White, Gunnar Myrdal, and J. Kenneth Galbraith. Later, I read books by the then-contemporary masters in the field of management and leadership studies, including pioneering works by Douglas McGregor, Abraham Maslow, Jay Lorsch, Warren Bennis, Paul Lawrence, Herbert Simon, James March, and James McGregor Burns. That is to say, I read works by *generalists*, scholars who wrote not just for academic audiences; in addition, their books and articles were meant to be accessible to all educated professionals. While my terminal degree is in social anthropology, I was greatly influenced by the work of these scholars, none of whom was an anthropologist. Hence, I never have thought of myself as either defined by, or limited to, the discipline in which I received my degree (or to any other single discipline, for that matter). In fact, I probably have been influenced more by the writings of John Stuart Mill than by those of any single social scientist. Throughout his career, Mill's intended audiences were the political, business, and legal professionals of his day, the practical people who were the leaders of society.

He was, at once and the same time, an economist, philosopher, historian, journalist, and practicing politician. In short, he might be called a "dilettante." Since I have worked, briefly, in government, journalism, and management consulting (at McKinsey and Company and, later, at Booz, Allen & Hamilton), I suppose the same epithet might be applied to me.

At any rate, it is from that perspective that I offer these sketchy thoughts about why those of us who engage in research meant to be useful to practitioners are a dying species, and how people like us might yet avoid extinction. To start, I don't think the reason usually offered for the wide dismissal of applied research such as ours—specifically, that it lacks quantitative rigor—is the actual cause. At least, it is not the complete story. I believe the issue is more complex and more attributable to the growing power of academic disciplines in business schools than to any other single factor. I illustrate what I mean by reference to the best-known exemplar of perceived relevance over rigor, the most famous management professor in the eyes of the business community, but one who, tellingly, is among the least cited scholars in academic journals: the late Peter F. Drucker.

Drucker As Exemplar

The catholicity of Drucker's interests defies the pigeonholing of his work: He wrote imaginatively and knowledgeably about a wide array of subjects including economics, technology, history, politics, demography (and Asian art). Most notably and profoundly, he wrote about all aspects of the corporation, explicating the complexly interrelated functions and roles of planning, strategy, marketing, organization structure, labor relations, performance measurement, and leadership. "My main point," Drucker (1985) wrote, "is that the organization is a human, a social, indeed, a moral phenomenon." In terms of the latter, he stressed not the *power* of executives but, instead, their *responsibilities* (significantly, the subtitle of his 1974 magnum opus, *Management,* is "Tasks, Responsibilities, Practices"). With the 1957 publication of *America's Next Twenty Years,* he arguably became the nation's first "futurist," a role he returned to time and again, notably in his 1976 *The Unseen Revolution* where he anticipated many of the problems corporations would encounter in subsequent years as the result of the way pensions were traditionally funded. His classic 1946 study of General Motors, *Concept of the Corporation,* was based on the rigorous, but nonscientific, research method known as "participant observation." Reissued in 1972, just as GM was starting to lose ground to Japanese competitors, the book presciently and cogently identified the cultural and organizational problems that eventually would lead to the humbling (and eventual nationalization) of that once great company. Prophetically

he concluded that "GM is an organization of managers and management...
not an innovative company." The end result was that GM was too impersonal,
too addicted to technique, and too concerned with scientific measurement
and controllable facts "when what is needed is not facts but the ability to see
facts as others see them."

Once, when Warren Bennis praised him publicly for such foresight, Drucker
(1985) offered this surprising response: "It was meant as a compliment, but I
winced because, bluntly, I was ten years premature with every one of my fore-
casts. And *that's* not a compliment. That is saying that one has had no impact."
Well, he certainly didn't have much impact on what is taught in business
schools.

In 1985, I asked six prominent thinkers to review Drucker's entire *oeuvres*
(some twenty books at the time), and to offer their critical evaluations for
publication in *New Management* magazine (where I was editor). I then sent
the six draft essays to Drucker who commented on them in his usual style:
promptly, coldly, analytically... and condescendingly! (He wasn't the easiest
person to deal with: On more than one occasion in the '70s and '80s, when
something I had written found its way into print, I received phone calls from
Peter who, in his patented, guttural growl, would tell me how "interesting"
my latest effort was—and then go on for a good half hour explaining in painful detail how I had gotten my analysis all wrong! He wasn't loveable, but he
was usually right.)

In the *New Management*'s "Peter Drucker Retrospective" issue published
in 1985, Tom Peters noted, to his "amazement and... dismay" that, on just
having read Drucker's 1954 *The Practice of Management* for the first time, he
discovered therein all the key points that he and Bob Waterman had thought
original when they presented them over two decades *later* in their best-
selling *In Search of Excellence*. Given that Drucker was the first to have said
almost everything there was to say about management, Peters (1985) thus
wondered why Drucker's name never once was mentioned by his professors
while he was a Stanford MBA student. Rosabeth Moss Kanter (1985) similarly expressed great admiration for Drucker's work, but she also wondered
why "there are no Druckerians... teaching in the tradition of the master?" In
fact, the writings of the man who is often called "the father of management
studies" not only have not been assigned in major American business schools
for many years now, his work almost never has been cited by scholars. Bennis
(1985) wrote that Drucker himself wondered if he really "belonged" in a university or business school, but defended Drucker by likening him to Alexis
de Tocqueville, who also was not easily pegged, and who similarly belonged
to the grand "world of ideas.... Unless that is understood, we risk placing
Drucker in too narrow an intellectual context and will fail to do full justice
to his unique contribution."

Limits to Social Science

I think Warren was on to the real reason for the academics' disdain for Drucker's work. It was not the absence of scientific, quantitative rigor in his books that led scholars to dismiss them; instead, the root cause has been the ever-increasing dominance of traditional, ever-narrower, academic disciplines in business schools. Unlike Drucker, no scholars today think of themselves as "professors of management," let alone as "professors of business." Today, b-school faculties are composed of self-fashioned "professors of organizational behavior" or "professors of finance," or, in most cases, as members of some narrow subset within such broader disciplinary rubrics. (The Academy of Management lists some two dozen such specialties. While such disciplinary specialization may be necessary to advance the state of scientific knowledge, it is far from clear that it benefits MBA students. Indeed, the professoriate's commonly held assumption that what is good for them is also good for b-schools, students, and the business community at large is a debatable notion, at best, as we see later in this chapter).

There are at least two fundamental drawbacks to the trend toward ever-narrower disciplinary specialization—at least from the perspective of educating MBAs to be effective leaders. First, the most-vexing issues and problems business executives face—the kinds of questions that business leaders found so relevant when Drucker addressed them—do not respect the boundaries of academic disciplines. Business leaders are seldom if ever faced with a "psychology problem" or "an economics problem"; instead, they must deal with such multifaceted, systemic problems as, *What is the most effective organizational design for my company? How can I create a business model and strategy that will effectively deliver on the "triple bottom line." How do I organize and motivate my associates to generate a steady and sustainable stream of innovation?* (Michael Tushman identifies a passel of such cross-disciplinary issues in Chapter 9, On Knowing and Doing).

The second, and perhaps more fundamental, drawback to a discipline-driven approach is that it assumes there is "a solution" to the problem being studied. Researchers would deny this, but in fact that assumption (most often unstated) is a by-product of thinking about business research in terms of "science." One thing all scientific research has in common is the quest for a theory. Behind all those complex models found in social science journals is the unstated assumption that there is something "out there" in the world of organizations equivalent to the law of gravity, theory of relativity, or laws of thermodynamics. Social science researchers are not at all deterred by the fact that they have failed to find the managerial equivalent of $E = mc^2$; indeed, it is not too great a stretch to say they have discovered very little about organizational behavior, or leadership, that can stand the true test of a scientific law (that is, the findings are replicable at all times and at all places). Instead, the findings offered in business-oriented scientific journals are far more circumscribed: They concern only what has been found true for a particular time and/or place. In effect, what organizational scientists have been doing is to keep reducing the dimensions of what they study until they are small enough to fit the available research methods. And, yes, they then end up with statistically valid findings, but those results are typically too narrow or specific to be generalizable. For example, it stretches the notion of science to the breaking point to extrapolate the findings of a lab experiment (in which a couple of dozen undergraduates serve as guinea pigs) to a generalization about all human behavior. Scientific researchers do not deny this; instead, they argue that "our discipline is still young and, surely, we will find the laws of organizations if we just keep looking. Clearly, any single study, by and of itself, tells us little. But one day, when all the results of all the studies are aggregated...."

Alas, as Peter Drucker understood, nothing as complex and multidimensional as human behavior lends itself to such reductionism. And that's probably why he was dismissed by academics: *He didn't even pretend to have a grand theory of management, of organizations, of leadership or, for that matter, of anything else.* His academic critics are, at least, technically correct when they say that "he was not a systematic thinker." In fact, he never propounded a single theory, or even a systematic set of beliefs (in Isaiah Berlin's famous construct, Drucker was more a "fox" with many ideas than a "hedgehog" with one big idea). But, to most academics, a person with no theory is no academic at all! Thus, from their perspective, Drucker's fatal shortcoming was the modesty and humility of his work. There is great irony in this: as implied earlier, Peter was extremely far from being a modest and humble man; but he was not delusional about the nature of the enterprise in which he was involved. His modest goal was to better understand organizational behavior through the analysis of relevant facts, the application of reason, and the willingness to challenge conventional wisdom. He was intent on teaching executives how to think about complex problems so as to increase the likelihood of their making effective decisions. But Drucker didn't fool himself into thinking that his rigorous study of management was the same thing as "science."

Now it must be understood that Peter collected data, analyzed it, and used it whenever it was available and appropriate to do so. The facts—*the numbers* when they were available and valid—were almost always his starting point. As much as any business professor, he understood that one can and should use statistics to correlate relationships between discrete variables. He drew on academic research in which statistical methods were used in controlled situations to tease out the various interactions of several variables. But Drucker understood the limits to such quantification. As Aristotle explained in his *Nicomachean Ethics* nearly 2,500 years ago:

> Our discussion will be adequate if it has as much clarity as the subject-matter permits, for precision is not to be sought for alike in all discussions.... It is the mark of an educated man to look for precision in each class of things just so far as the nature of the subject admits; hence it is evidently foolish to accept probable reasoning from a mathematician, and to demand demonstrative proofs from a rhetorician. (*Nicomachean Ethics*, 1953, p. 5)

Of course, the activities of business typically are more quantifiable than the activity of rhetoric. Yet, not everything about business is quantifiable, as much as we would like it to be. As a professor of ethics, for example, I would like to be able *to prove scientifically* that ethical leaders prosper and unethical ones do not. I also would like to be able to prove that socially responsible companies make more money than irresponsible ones. Alas, to the extent that such complex and ambiguous human and organizational issues (ones involving the interaction of such multidimensional variable as leadership, culture, and values) are amenable to scientific study, analyses of the available facts prove inconclusive (Vogel, 2005). All one has to do is read the *Wall Street Journal* to find examples of both successful and unsuccessful leaders who behaved ethically, and examples of both successful and unsuccessful ones who were unethical. Similarly, there appears to be no correlation between the level of a company's social responsibility, on the one hand, and its profitability, on the other.

This absence of certainty about the causal relationship between doing good and doing well is regrettable, at least from my point of view, because so many executives say that they would do the "right thing" if they knew "for sure" that it would pay to do so, or even if it would be effective. But realistically and regrettably, I have to accept the fact that the search for the "facts" that would give clear guidance with regard to broad leadership, ethical, and cultural issues is, and will remain, fruitless. Executives search in vain for guidance based on hard evidence because there are no scientific laws with regard to such soft and multidimensional subjects, nor can such laws ever be found. The available "facts" tell executives only that they are as likely to succeed taking the high, as opposed to the low, road. And that's why the most important and difficult questions that confront leaders require making *moral choices*, and not conforming to some set of scientifically determined rules or principles. Indeed, the very essence of leadership is the necessity to choose in the absence of certainty (the luxury of certainty is reserved for engineers, bureaucrats, and administrators). That's why Peter Drucker talked about management in terms of its *responsibilities*.

Inside B-Schools Today

But that is not how most management professors today view the study of leadership. In business schools, the subject now falls in the domain of social science, with an accent on the science. That trend has implications for the classroom. For example, a few years back, I engaged in a long debate about leadership with a group of professors from a leading America business school. When they asked what topics I covered in my leadership class, I mentioned that I stressed the effectiveness of leaders listening to the concerns and needs of their followers. The professors then proceeded to explain to me that there was nothing in the scientific literature to indicate that effective leaders listen to their followers. One of the professors said, "I would never teach my students anything that was not supported by scientific fact." Ergo, no listening in his class.

I believe this emphasis on applying scientific standards of proof to the study of leadership is misplaced. Not only does it lead to shortchanging business students, it also explains (paradoxically) the manifest absence of valid studies exploring the effects of leadership behavior. In this regard, I have done a little casual, nonscientific research. Working with the help of two graduates students, we undertook a review of two dozen well-documented cases describing successful organizational transformations in large corporations. Our intent was to identify how the top management teams (TMTs) in those companies led their transformations; in other words, *what they did* that made their change efforts successful. We sorted those actions into generic categories, for example, "listening to subordinates' ideas," "delegating authority for implementation," "keeping the organization focused on task." We then winnowed the list down to the handful of behaviors that almost all of the successful leaders seemed to engage in (the list included the three examples just cited, including listening, which was a behavior noted in all the cases).

We then went to the scientific literature and entered those behaviors as key words along with the words "leadership," "organizational change," and so forth, to see if our "casual empiricism" was supportable by scientific fact. Surely, we thought, some academic must have studied a *scientifically valid sample* of CEOs, TMTs, or even division heads, to discover what leadership actions, behaviors, and approaches to change are the most effective? Alas, in the dozen or so journals we examined, we found next to no studies referring to our key words (with the exception of a few tangentially related studies relating to the narrow—albeit important—leadership activities that build trust). Instead, we found many small-sample and single-organization studies of narrow "leadership" behaviors of middle managers (and students). But no studies of the behavior of real corporate leaders. I don't know why I had expected otherwise; in hindsight, I certainly can't fault my fellow professors for failing to produce scientifically valid research relating to leading large-scale organizational change. It simply can't be done. And, if I thought it could be done, I would try to do it myself!

The main reason why such studies do not exist is because the statistical methods typically employed by social scientists do not and cannot reveal the causal interactions of the multiplicity of variables involved in changing behavior in a large organization. How would one scientifically control the various factors involved in the leadership activity we call listening? The methodological problems are multifold because there are numerous ambiguous and dynamic aspects of human behavior involved in leadership: For example, there are the interactions of both leaders and followers, and corporate cultures are systems involving complex interrelationships between scores of such hard-to-measure variables as purpose, values, and trust, and such organizational capacities as the effectiveness of communications channels. Thus, it is difficult to imagine how one would ever measure the effectiveness of leadership listening in influencing the behavior of followers. And it is not simply the act of listening in and of itself that is relevant; more precisely it is listening in conjunction with other complementary activities, such as responding positively and following up on suggestions. How would one ever measure the effectiveness of such a set of behaviors?

Although there are excellent scientific studies of many specific aspects of leadership—for example, relating to the personalities of leaders—those are undertaken in isolation from other aspects of what are complexly interrelated human systems (for example, the culture of the firm), and that is like studying the human toe apart from the foot or separate from the body's circulatory and immune systems. The researcher can get partial truths, at best, but they do not add up to much that is useful or scientifically verifiable.

Certainly it is possible to undertake a scientific study of one aspect of a leader's behavior on a discrete part of a particular culture, but adding up all those parts in an attempt to understand the whole does not necessarily lead to valid conclusions. The methodological problem involves more than a logical error of faulty aggregation; it ignores the most salient fact of systems: All the parts are complexly interrelated and, thus, changes in one part cause changes in all other parts, and the nature or direction of those changes are not scientifically predictable. Hence, an interesting scientific study of a leader's efforts to create trust tells us little about the effects of the action on other aspects of the culture of an organization, nor does it predict the effectiveness of those efforts. And what may work to create trust in one organization may not do so in another (with different characteristics).

These caveats are far from being antiscience. They are actually *pro*science. In this age of creeping theocracy, it is more-than-ever necessary for all scholars to stand firm against those forces of ignorance and superstition who increasingly and stridently deny scientific evidence. That is why I believe scholars should be careful to reserve the hallowed name of science for that which is *real science*. Of course, most of the studies published in academic journals are not exercises in scientism (in fact, most could be more aptly described as collections of valid data about specific events, organizations, or populations that may be suggestive of broader interpretation). Some of this is extremely useful, and some even approaches the standards of true science (for example, the research findings of Joseph Blasi, Douglas Kruse, and Richard Freeman [2006], drawing on a U.S. Census scientifically valid sample of the entire U.S. workforce).

Moreover, I believe the effective study of organizations needs to be rigorous, evidence-based and, whenever possible, quantified. (Strategy consultants at McKinsey and Booz, Allen, & Hamilton often draw profitably on the rigorous, applied organizational research undertaken by Michael Beer, Richard Walton, Michael Tushman, Nitan Nohria, and Christopher Bartlett, all now, or formerly, at the Harvard Business School). Indeed there is a good amount of such rigorous, *applied* research readily available, and not only from the Harvard crowd and the authors of this book. But as the Drucker example illustrates, that does not make those studies "scientific." When dogs sniff fire plugs they are collecting and analyzing data, but they are not engaging in science.

In a recent blog, Tom Peters answered criticisms leveled against Bob Waterman, Jim Collins, and himself that attacked the scientific validity of the conclusions of their respective books. Candidly, Peters pled guilty to most of those charges. But he insisted that he and Waterman were innocent of having ever purported to provide "a complete success prescription based on a flawless accumulation of data that managers should follow like the ten commandments." On that score, he parts company with Collins (who has claimed the mantle of science for his work). As Peters blogs:

> The product of management studies should never be confused with the research-experimentation used to confirm Einstein's theory of relativity. That is not, nor will it ever be, the standard for the so-called social sciences. It is even a travesty to award a Nobel in economics—economics ain't physics either, as you'll discover when you check the status of your 401(k). Well, Mr. Collins apparently disagrees. Not only does he compare his research to physics, but he also claims to have discovered "Immutable laws of organized human performance." Dear God! Or, rather, God help us. (Tom Peters!, http://www.tompeters.com/dispatches/010980.php)

What is most unfortunate about Collins's absurd claim is not simply that he has invited academics to make mincemeat out of both his methods and the claims he makes about what his data "prove"; far worse, his claims distract from the fact that the general conclusions he draws tend to be spot on! Hence, his professorial critics have had a field day ripping Collins's numbers to pieces and discrediting his work in the eyes of many inside and outside of academe; all the while, what goes unnoticed is that none of them have gainsaid the wisdom of his observations (which is the real value of his work). Collins, like so many of us, feels the necessity of *proving* his observations scientifically, even when doing so is impossible or inappropriate to the task at hand.

Collins has tried to prove, for example, that certain forms of leadership behavior lead to certain kinds of organizational outcomes. Unfortunately, there is no way to "prove" that one or another style of leadership leads to more (or less) productivity, profitability, innovation, sustainability, or any other complex set of outcomes. Thus, Collins has inadvertently shown that, while it is manifestly possible to identify a few organizational or leadership variables and then to message and control them meaningfully, the end product will not be valid because the sum total of all the aspects of human behavior involved in organizational performance is too multifaceted, soft, and changing to be accurately modeled, let alone studied scientifically.

Let me be clear about the nature of my criticism. In a great many instances, traditional quantitative methods produce interesting and valid results. But there are other sources of valid knowledge that are not scientifically rigorous. In particular, if the findings are to be useful to practitioners, applied studies of leadership and management must be based on a concatenation of (often incommensurable) examples, data, facts, experience, logic, analysis, plus whatever suggestive data exist in the scientific literature. As good lawyers, journalists, consultants, and anthropologists know, the best way to discover the truth in an organization is to diversify the sources of one's information. Or, as Michael Beer (Chapter 8, Making a Difference *and* Contributing Useful Knowledge) aptly puts it, the method is *triangulation*. But even then, when all the data are analyzed, leaders must still *choose*; ultimately, they must make decisions about complex matters based not on scientific proof but on their personal values, desires, and levels of aversion to risk.

But that is not what is being taught in most b-schools today, and until recently, the situation seemed likely to get worse in terms of the preparation for leadership that MBA students will receive in the future. After all, how can today's narrowly focused business school professors be expected to train and nurture the next generation of scholars to become broad-gauged, discipline-spanning, pragmatic, systemic thinkers? And why should they do so when universities are perversely hell bent on rewarding the opposite behavior? (Here's the inside baseball on this: At large research institutions, university-wide personnel committees dominated by social science faculties are the ultimate authorities with respect to business school hire, tenure, and promotion decisions. Thus, representatives of the psychology and economics departments in Letters, Arts, and Sciences are empowered to set the academic standards by which b-school professors are evaluated.)

A Modest Proposal: Professionalize B-Schools

Is there any way to break out of this self-defeating, downward spiral? Warren Bennis and I have concluded that the best chance is to transform the institutions of graduate business education into true *professional schools* along the lines of those offering law and medical degrees. At medical schools, for example, an MD professor who specializes in developing new surgical methods—publishing her results in practitioner-oriented journals and devoting her time to the hands-on teaching of med students and interns—is viewed by her institution as the equal of a PhD biologist who spends all his time in the lab doing theoretical research and publishing in journals read only by other scientists (while never getting anywhere near an MD candidate, let alone a patient). This model has been widely adopted because medical schools see there is a need for them to provide *both* scientific research and professional training for docs.

The professional school model has been tested, and it works. Yet, at most of the nation's leading b-schools the trend is to hire, reward, and promote only the equivalent of the med school's "pure science" biology professor. In effect, the faculties at prestigious b-schools (and their wannabes) increasingly are composed of discipline-oriented professors and researchers who see themselves as economists or psychologists, both of whom know (or care) little about the practical world of business organizations or about teaching MBAs how to lead them. By way of illustration, the likes of Peter Drucker, Jim Collins, and Tom Peters would not be hired by any major business school today. Or, if hired, they would be labeled "guest lecturers" and thus marginalized as second-class professors.

Hence, Bennis and I have proposed that b-schools halt this trend by adopting a professional school model that embraces faculty pluralism. We conclude that like medical schools, b-schools need both rigor *and* relevance, and if those two characteristics can be found in a single professor, so much the better. But failing that—as most often is the case—both discipline-oriented and practitioner-oriented faculty need to be hired (and then rewarded equally to prevent the formation of the invidious distinctions that invariably arise in highly stratified, two-class systems).

Stop the Press

There may be some good news on the horizon for us threatened brontosauri. Around the time that Bennis and I first offered our modest proposal (see the previous section), a few enlightened administrators, faculty members, alumni, and students (for example, at Yale and at such "second-tier" institutions as Duquesne's Donahue, Denver's Daniels, and York's [Canada] Schulich b-schools) started connecting the dots among an alarming set of events and trends in the operating business environment (Bennis & O'Toole, 2005). Taking note of the Enron and WorldCom scandals, the deindustrialization of North America, and public calls for "sustainability" (and, later, the nationalization of General Motors and the Wall Street meltdown), they decided the time had come for them to address social, environmental, and ethical issues in their respective MBA curriculums. Subsequently, there has been a snowballing effect of those pioneering efforts: Last fall, representatives from several dozen b-schools around the world gathered in New York as guests of the Aspen Institute's Center for Business Education to share what they were learning from their new initiatives to address the cross-disciplinary concerns previously absent from their curriculums.

In a parallel effort, Harvard's Rakesh Khurana (2007) is leading a movement to make b-schools into professional schools, starting with the Oath Project in which MBA candidates across the country are voluntarily swearing to a professional code of conduct, à la the oaths taken by lawyers and doctors. And, within the last year, influential scholar Jay Lorsch (2009) has called for rethinking the way b-school professors are evaluated and promoted. Based on the med school model, business schools in large research universities would be given the same leeway as other professional schools to set their own standards of performance, for example, counting practical publications oriented toward managers (for example, serious books and *Harvard Business Review* articles) as heavily for promotion and tenure as purely scientific and theoretical research. Of course, the main accrediting body of business schools is still lagging years behind this nascent reform movement (ditto the discipline-based associations to which professors often show greater loyalty than to the universities that pay their salaries).

But business professors do not need to be passive victims of the bad policies wrought by university committees, discipline-based academic societies, or external accrediting bodies. In the foregoing, I noted that leaders ultimately must make choices about complex matters based on their personal values and desires. I believe the same is true for business school professors. We must, and we can, choose what we study and what we teach. The good news is that a growing number of young scholars appear to be choosing to study the real issues facing business organizations, for example, problems relating to governance, community, innovation, workplace civility, ethics, sustainability, and cross-cultural management—issues that are, by nature, multidisciplinary and concerned with the pursuit of the common good. The more professors choose to focus on such issues, the more relevant b-schools will become *without losing rigor.*

All told, there now seems to be some progress in that direction. Recently, I ran into a professor who had been one of the most vocal critics of the "controversial" article that Bennis and I wrote in 2005 in which we first offered our proposal concerning b-school professionalization and faculty pluralism. The professor, a past president of the Academy of Management, mentioned to me in passing that "I was outraged by your *HBR* piece. Then, a month or so ago, I read it. Actually, it's not all that unreasonable." Well, I guess that's what progress amounts to in academia!

Let me summarize my argument by quoting the words of business ethicists Rogene Buchholz and Sandra Rosenthal (2008):

> The problem is not that business schools have embraced scientific rigor, but that they have forsaken other forms of knowledge that are relevant to business organizations. To regain relevance, business schools must realize that business management is not a scientific discipline but a profession, and they must deal with the things a professional education requires. There must be a balance between rigor and relevance.

REFERENCES

Aristotle. (1953) *The Nicomachean Ethics.* Translated by J.A.K. Thomson. Penguin Books.

Bennis, W. (1985). A personal reflection. *New Management, 2*(3), 24–27.

Bennis, W., & O'Toole, J. (2005, May). How business schools lost their way. *Harvard Business Review,* 96–104.

Blasi, J., Kruse, D., & Freeman, R. (2006). Shared capitalism at work: Impacts and policy options. In E. E. Lawler III & J. O'Toole (Eds.), *America at work* (pp. 275–295). New York: Palgrave Macmillan.

Buchholz, R., & Rosenthal, S. (2008). The unholy alliance of business and science. *Journal of Business Ethics, 78,* 199–206.

Drucker, P. (1985). Memo. *New Management, 2*(3), 28–32.

Kanter, R. M. (1985). The unsolved puzzle. *New Management, 2*(3), 10–13.

Khurana, R. (2007). *From higher aims to hired hands: The social transformation of American business schools.* Princeton, NJ: Princeton University Press.

Lorsch, J. (2009). Regaining lost relevance. *Journal of Management Inquiry, 18,* 108–117.

O'Toole, J. (2009). The pluralistic future of management education. In S. J. Armstrong and C. V. Fulami (Eds.), *The SAGE handbook of management learning, education and development* (pp. 547–558). Thousand Oaks, CA: Sage.

Peters, T. (1985). The other half of the message. *New Management, 2*(3), 14–17.

Vogel, D. (2005). *The market for virtue.* Washington, DC: Brookings Institution Press.

ABOUT THE AUTHOR

James O'Toole is the Daniels Distinguished Professor of Business Ethics at the University of Denver's Daniels College of Business. Formerly, he was the University Associates Professor of Management at the University of Southern California and Research Professor in the Center for Effective Organizations. His doctorate is in social anthropology from Oxford University, where he was a Rhodes Scholar. He is author or editor of some seventeen books, including *The Executive's Compass, Leading Change, Creating the Good Life,* and, with Edward Lawler, *The New American Workplace.*

PART V

Putting It All Together

TWENTY-ONE

Reflections on Research for Theory and Practice

From an Engaged Scholarship Perspective

ANDREW H. VAN DE VEN

THIS BOOK FOCUSES on the relationships between theory and practice, research and action, and basic and applied knowledge. A core assumption is that research knowledge should be useful for advancing science and practice. As Mohrman and Lawler (Introduction and Overview) state, the central question in this book is how should such research be designed, carried out, and disseminated to achieve the twin goals of advancing both theory and practice?

This book addresses this question in a variety of ways. Amy C. Edmondson (Chapter 2, Crossing Boundaries to Investigate Problems in the Field), Susan Albers Mohrman and Allan Mohrman (Chapter 3, Collaborative Organization Design Research at the Center for Effective Organizations), and Lynda Gratton (Chapter 4, A Ten-Year Journey of Cooperation) provide three exemplars of practicing scholars who are carrying out research that has the dual purpose of generating academic knowledge and enabling more effective practice. They describe the choices they make and the tactics they employ. They are followed by Philip Mirvis and Edward E. Lawler (Chapter 6, Rigor and Relevance in Organizational Research), C. K. Prahalad (Chapter 7, Can Relevance and Rigor Coexist?), Michael Beer (Chapter 8, Making a Difference *and* Contributing Useful Knowledge), and Michael L. Tushman (Chapter 9, On Knowing and Doing), five scholars whose research careers have clearly influenced both theory and practice.

In addition, Ruth Wageman (Chapter 10, Academic-Consultant Collaboration), Ram V. Tenkasi (Chapter 11, Integrating Theory to Inform Practice), Jean M. Bartunek and Edgar H. Schein (Chapter 12, Organization Development Scholar-Practitioners), Wayne F. Cascio (Chapter 13, Professional Associations), Denise M. Rousseau and John W. Boudreau (Chapter 14, Sticky Findings), and George S. Benson (Chapter 15, Popular and Influential Management Books) examine various pathways through which academic knowledge reaches practice, including professional associations, evidence-based management resources, books, tools, and professions such as consultants and organizational development. A key institution that shapes the field—MBA programs—is also examined. These chapters plus section commentaries (Chapter 5, Walking on Three Legs; Chapter 16, Observations Concerning Pathways for Doing "Useful Research") contribute a gold mine of practical experience-based wisdom for doing research that is useful for theory and practice.

I was asked to reflect on these contributions from the perspective of engaged scholarship. To do this, I will summarize how our model of engaged scholarship addresses the question of how to do research that is useful to theory and practice. In doing so, I will indicate how chapter authors complement and extend our view of engaged scholarship. These contributions focus not only on research methods but also on building the capabilities of scholars and practitioners to co-produce and use research knowledge for theory and practice.

Engaged Scholarship

We (Van de Ven & Johnson, 2006; Van de Ven, 2007) proposed a method of *engaged scholarship* for studying complex social problems that often exceed our limited individual capabilities to study on our own. *Engaged Scholarship* is a participative form of research for obtaining the advice and perspectives of key stakeholders (researchers, users, clients, sponsors, and practitioners) to understand a complex problem or phenomenon. By exploiting differences in the kinds of knowledge that scholars and other stakeholders can bring forth on a problem, we argue that engaged scholarship produces knowledge that is more penetrating and insightful than when scholars or practitioners work on the problems alone.

Using a diamond model, as illustrated in Figure 21.1, I argue (in Van de Ven, 2007) that researchers can significantly increase the likelihood of producing knowledge that advances theory and practice by engaging others whose perspectives are relevant in each of four study activities:

- *Problem formulation.* Situate, ground, and diagnose the research problem by determining who, what, where, when, why, and how the problem exists up close and from afar. Answering these journalist questions requires meeting and talking with people who experience and know the problem, as well as reviewing the literature on the prevalence and boundary conditions of the problem.

- *Theory building.* Develop plausible alternative theories (or propositions) that address the problem as it exists in its particular context. Developing these alternative theories requires conversations with knowledge experts

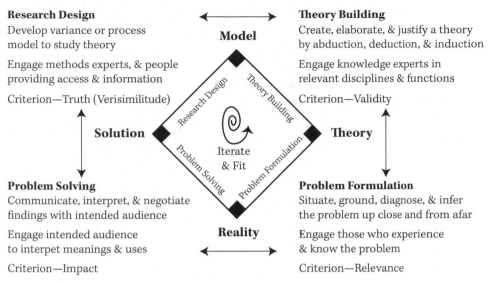

Study Context: Research problem, purpose, perspective

Research Design
Develop variance or process model to study theory

Engage methods experts, & people providing access & information

Criterion—Truth (Verisimilitude)

Model

Theory Building
Create, elaborate, & justify a theory by abduction, deduction, & induction

Engage knowledge experts in relevant disciplines & functions

Criterion—Validity

Research Design / Theory Building / Problem Solving / Problem Formulation

Iterate & Fit

Solution

Theory

Problem Solving
Communicate, interpret, & negotiate findings with intended audience

Engage intended audience to interpet meanings & uses

Criterion—Impact

Reality

Problem Formulation
Situate, ground, diagnose, & infer the problem up close and from afar

Engage those who experience & know the problem

Criterion—Relevance

FIGURE 21.1 ENGAGED SCHOLARSHIP DIAMOND MODEL

from the relevant disciplines and functions that have addressed the problem, as well as a review of relevant literature.

- *Research design.* Gather empirical evidence to compare the plausible alternative models that address the research problem. Doing this well typically requires getting advice from technical experts in research methodology, the people who can provide access to data, and of course, the respondents or informants of information.

- *Problem solving.* Communicate, interpret, and apply the empirical findings on which models better answer the research question about the problem. The greater the difference in content-specific knowledge between researchers and stakeholders, the more they need to communicate in order to understand and use the research findings. Communications might begin with written reports and presentations for knowledge transfer, then go on to conversations to interpret different meanings of the report, and then end with pragmatic and political negotiations to reconcile conflicting interests.

Engaged scholarship can be practiced in many different ways, including the four approaches outlined in Figure 21.2. These different approaches depend on (1) whether the purpose of a research study is to examine basic questions of description, explanation, and prediction or applied questions of design, evaluation, or action intervention, and (2) the degree to which a researcher

Research Question/Purpose

	To Describe/Explain	To Design/Intervene
Detached Outside	Basic Science with Stakeholder Advice 1	Policy/Design Science Evaluation Research for Professional Practice 3
Attached Inside	2 Co-Produce Knowledge with Collaborators	4 Action/Intervention Research for a Client

Research Perspective

FIGURE 21.2 Alternative Forms of Engaged Scholarship

examines the problem domain as an external observer or an internal participant.

1. *Informed basic research* is undertaken to describe, explain, or predict a social phenomenon. It resembles a traditional form of basic social science where the researcher is a detached outsider of the social system being examined, but it also solicits advice and feedback from key stakeholders and inside informants on each of the research activities (as listed in Fig. 21.1). These inside informants and stakeholders play an advisory role, and the researcher directs and controls all research activities.

2. *Collaborative basic research* entails a greater sharing of power and activities among researchers and stakeholders than informed research. Collaborative research teams are often composed of insiders and outsiders who jointly share the activities (as listed in Fig. 21.1) in order to co-produce basic knowledge about a complex problem or phenomenon. The division of labor is typically negotiated to take advantage of the complementary skills of different research team members, and the balance of power or responsibility shifts back and forth as the tasks demand. Because this collaborative form of research tends to focus on basic questions of mutual interest to the partners, it has much less of an applied orientation than the next two forms of engaged scholarship.

3. *Design and evaluation research* is undertaken to examine normative questions dealing with the design and evaluation of policies, programs, or models for solving practical problems. Variously called "design or policy science" or "evaluation research," this form of research goes beyond describing or explaining a social problem but also seeks to obtain evidence-based knowledge of the efficacy or relative success of alternative solutions

to applied problems. Evaluation researchers typically take a distanced and outside perspective of the designs or policies being evaluated. Inquiry from the outside is necessary because evidence-based evaluations require comparisons of numerous cases, and because distance from any one case is required for evaluation findings to be viewed as impartial and legitimate. But engagement of stakeholders is important so they have opportunities to influence and consent to those evaluation study decisions that may affect them. These decisions include the purposes of the evaluation study (problem formulation), the criteria and models used to evaluate the program in question (research design), and how study findings will be analyzed, interpreted, and used (problem solving).

4. *Action/intervention research* takes a clinical intervention approach to diagnose and treat a problem of a specific client. Kurt Lewin, a pioneer of action research, suggested a learning strategy of both engaging with and intervening in the client's social setting. The foundation of this learning process was client participation in problem solving using systematic methods of data collection, feedback, reflection, and action. Since Lewin's time, action research has evolved into a diverse family of clinical research strategies in many professional fields. Action research projects tend to begin by diagnosing the particular problem or needs of an individual client. To the extent possible, a researcher utilizes whatever knowledge is available from basic or design science to understand the client's problem. However, this knowledge may require substantial adaptation to fit the ill-structured or context-specific nature of the client's problem. Action research projects often consist of N-of-1 studies, where systematic comparative evidence can only be gained through trial-and-error experiments over time. In this situation, action researchers have argued that the only way to understand a social system is to change it through deliberate intervention and diagnosis of responses to the intervention. This interventionist approach typically requires intensive interaction, training, and consulting by the researcher with people in the client's setting.

Sometimes advocates of a particular research approach make disparaging remarks about other forms. This is unfortunate, because all four forms of engaged scholarship are legitimate, important, and necessary for addressing different research questions posed by science and practice (description, explanation, design, or control of a problematic situation). Which approach is most appropriate depends on the research question and the perspective taken to examine the question. Pragmatically, the effectiveness of a research approach should be judged by how well it addresses the research question for which it was intended (Dewey, 1938).

Although the four forms of engaged scholarship entail different kinds of relationships between the researcher and stakeholders in a study, engagement is the common denominator. The more ambiguous and complex the problem, the greater the need for engaging others who can provide different perspectives for revealing critical dimensions of the nature, context, and implications of the problem being studied.

Elaborating and Extending the Model

This book elaborates and extends these goals and methods of engaged scholarship in several important ways. They include insights on doing problem-driven, boundary-crossing fieldwork, spending time in field research sites to gain penetrating knowledge of a topic being investigated, appreciating the challenges and opportunities of academic-practitioner research collaborations, examining big questions that ignite academics and practitioners to pursue their alternative models on the questions, communicating and using research findings with intended audiences, becoming engaged scholars, and developing a personal identity and empathy with the stakeholders of a study. The rest of this chapter discusses each of these insights.

Problem-Driven, Boundary-Crossing Fieldwork

Edmondson's discussion of her approach in Chapter 2 (Crossing Boundaries to Investigate Problems in the Field) of starting with problems, going into the field, and reaching across boundaries is an important elaboration of engaged scholarship.

She suggests starting with problems. "Problems provide a natural connection with practice. Studying a compelling problem, researchers are motivated to care about action. Problems matter!"

She advises researchers to go into the field. "Unless you have an unusual office location, sitting at your desk is unlikely to be the most conducive situation for gaining insight into the kinds of organizational phenomena described previously. Although one can learn about an industry or company from written materials, fuller understanding and new ideas are more likely when meeting and observing people who work in that setting."

She also advises collaboration across knowledge boundaries. "In most field research sites, it takes time to understand both the organization and the industry. Collaborators who bring different perspectives and expertise can accelerate the learning needed to get up to speed and offer novel insights. For me to understand drug errors in hospitals, for example, would have been extremely difficult without working closely with the physicians and nurses in the larger research project."

Edmondson (Chapter 2, Crossing Boundaries to Investigate Problems in the Field) also makes good suggestions on using the literature for each step in the diamond model in Figure 21.1: problem formulation, theory building, research design, and problem solving.

> The literature—that is, prior research that informs and shapes the research question—plays a crucial role in helping to keep these elements working together for research purposes. The literature is an integrating force, helping to shape research to make its best contribution. Familiarity with what has come before in a given field that relates to your research question makes sure prior findings are integrated, elaborated, or refuted in the current work. More specifically, with respect to understanding a problem, finding out what others have done to understand that problem lowers the risk of reinventing the wheel.... The literature is crucial for shaping methodological and scope decisions, and hybrid approaches allow researchers to test associations between variables with quantitative data and to explain and illuminate novel constructs and relationships with qualitative data (Edmondson & McManus, 2007). When collaborating across academic disciplines, it is important to identify the literature one hopes to advance. The insights from different fields are likely to enrich one's thinking, as noted previously, but then it must be tamed and focused. The literature provides a force to focus and sharpen what one has found, before communicating it to others. This helps to avoid the trap of the overly broad or superficial observation in favor of offering precise statements on the advance that has been made.

Spending Time in Field Research Sites

Edmonson (Chapter 2, Crossing Boundaries to Investigate Problems in the Field) cautions young scholars that her approach slows you down and may even harm your career. Like Sara L. Rynes (Chapter 19, Counterpoint), I take a more optimistic view. Edmondson's approach to problem/phenomena-driven and boundary-crossing field research is well worth the time for it generates more profound and penetrating knowledge that leads to faster career advances than the status quo alternative of the researcher going it alone analyzing secondary data files in his/her office.

Time is critical for building relationships of trust, candor, and learning among researchers and practitioners. Sara L. Rynes (Chapter 19, Counterpoint) discussed the importance of spending more time on site to build direct and personal relationships with organizational participants to facilitate implementation of research findings and to increase the likelihood of making significant advances to a scholarly discipline.

One explanation for these findings is that it takes an extensive amount of direct and personal investigation to become acquainted with the dimensions and context of a phenomenon. Simon (1991), for example, argued that it takes ten years of dedicated work and attention to achieve world-class competence in a domain. While we might quibble over the amount of time it takes to achieve competence, the point is that one-time cross-sectional organizational studies only provide a single snapshot of an issue being investigated. Cross-sectional studies seldom provide researchers sufficient time and trials to become knowledgeable about their research topic.[1] Longitudinal research promotes deeper learning because it provides repeated trials for approximating and understanding a research question or topic. Becoming "world class" is a path-dependent process of pursuing a coherent theme of research questions from project to project over an extended period of time.

A basic, but often overlooked, fact of most academic research is that *researchers are exposed to only the information that people in research sites are willing to share.* Interviews in cross-sectional studies or initial interviews in longitudinal studies with research sites tend to be formal and shallow. Greater candor and penetration into the subject matter seldom occur until a sufficient number of interactions over time have occurred for participants to come to know and trust one another. Perhaps the "one-minute manager" is an unfortunate social construction of the one-minute researcher.

Candid information comes not only with familiarity and trust, but also with more knowledgeable and penetrating probes in responses to questions. Mohrman and Mohrman (Chapter 3, Collaborative Organization Design Research at the Center for Effective Organizations) state that to examine nanoscale phenomena, it takes two years or more for different disciplines to learn enough about one another's frameworks to be able to combine knowledge. Repeated interviews and meetings with practitioners in longitudinal research provide important opportunities to penetrate more deeply into the subject matter being investigated.

Of course, a series of related cross-sectional studies on the same problem or phenomenon can achieve penetrating insights as well. Mohrman and Lawler (Introduction and Overview) note that through a series of related studies, researchers can collaborate with a variety of organizations and researchers from other disciplines, apply multiple theories, and hone in on the

---

1. I also think that too many scholars dilute their competencies by conducting an eclectic and unrelated series of cross-sectional studies in their careers.

best understanding of the complex problems and phenomena in question. The QWL (quality of work life) studies in Michigan operated in this manner, drawing on the knowledge of dynamic teams of interventionists and researchers conducting related studies in multiple organizations, each of which wanted to put in place more effective work systems.

Academic-Practitioner Research Collaboration

When chapter authors described their joint academic-practitioner research projects, most seemed to reflect the second (collaborative co-producing knowledge) and fourth (action/intervention research) forms of engaged scholarship (as shown in Fig. 21.2). These two forms of engaged scholarship tend to present greater challenges than the first (basic science with stakeholder advice) and third (evaluation research). Because of this, *I tend to advise junior scholars to undertake and learn the first and third forms of engaged scholarship before launching into collaborative academic-practitioner projects. Moreover, don't launch into these studies alone; engage and rely on senior and experienced colleagues.* In addition to all the technical research skills that Edmondson (Chapter 2, Crossing Boundaries to Investigate Problems in the Field) describes, chapters by Gratton (Chapter 4, A Ten-Year Journey of Cooperation), Wageman (Chapter 10, Academic-Consultant Collaboration), and Bartunek and Schein (Chapter 12, Organization Development Scholar-Practitioners) point out that collaborative and action research projects include the challenges of finding mutual interests, boundary spanning, power sharing, and task coordination between academics and practitioners.

Gratton (Chapter 4, A Ten-Year Journey of Cooperation) discusses a number of important prerequisites for cooperation. First, however motivated individuals may be to cooperate, the actual act of cooperation is more likely to occur when they engage in a task, a big question or a vision that excites and motivates them and forms what we called the "ignition." Second, she observes that while this point of ignition can potentially pull people together, the opportunity for them to be creative also depends on the extent and breadth of boundary spanning across networks. Third, the ability to actively exchange ideas and contacts within these ignited networks depends on the habits and attitudes of individuals to cooperation, which she calls a "cooperative mindset." Finally, Gratton refers to a series of "productive practices" that enable team ideas and creativity to translate into performance and innovation. These practices require competencies in conflict resolution, commitment making, and creating opportunities for reflection.

Wageman (Chapter 10, Academic-Consultant Collaboration) provides useful advice on managing academic-practitioner research teams, which appears to apply to most boundary-crossing work teams. Based on her and Richard Hackman's academic-consultant research team experience with the Hay Group, she discusses two key process losses, "(1) failure of participants to do their 'homework' between meetings, and (2) conflicting time pressures—leading to "short, intensive bursts of focus by the team, between long periods of little or no progress, and little preparation in advance of the collaborative work" (Wageman, Chapter 10, Academic-Consultant Collaboration). Based on these experiences, she provides a number of practical suggestions for enabling collaboration and overcoming its obstacles.

The Need for Alternative Models to Examine Big Questions

Given all of the challenges and efforts discussed by chapter authors to make academic-practitioner research collaborations work, we should ask, Why do it? What kind of research problems require academic-practitioner engagement? Several contributors (Gratton, Chapter 4, A Ten-Year Journey of Cooperation; Tushman, Chapter 9, On Knowing and Doing; Edmondson, Chapter 2, Crossing Boundaries to Investigate Problems in the Field; and Beer, Chapter 8, Making a Difference *and* Contributing Useful Knowledge) argue that *the more complex the problem or the bigger the research question, the greater the need to engage researchers from different disciplines and practitioners with different functional experiences.* Engagement of others is necessary because most real-world problems are too complex to be captured by any one investigator or perspective. As Beer suggests, there are many big questions and problems that are very difficult to study in a productive way without engagement and close interaction among scholars and practitioners.

Big questions have no easy answers, and they seldom provide an immediate payoff to practitioners or academics (Pettigrew, 2001). By definition, big questions often do not have clear solutions until after the research has been conducted and policy questions have been addressed. Big questions also require a process of arbitrage in which researchers and practitioners engage each other to co-produce solutions whose demands exceed the capabilities of either researchers or practitioners. Thus, at the time of designing a research project, prospective solutions to research questions are secondary in comparison with the importance of the research question that is being addressed. As Gratton suggests, *a good indicator of a big question is its self-evident capability to ignite the attention and enthusiasm of scholars and practitioners alike* (Chapter 4, A Ten-Year Journey of Cooperation).

Study of big questions requires developing and comparing plausible alternative theories or models. Multiple models and frames of reference are needed to understand complex reality. Any given theory is an incomplete abstraction that cannot describe all aspects of a phenomenon. Theories are fallible human constructions that model a partial aspect of reality from a particular point of view with particular interests in mind. Comparing and contrasting plausible alternative models that reflect different perspectives are essential for discriminating between credible, erroneous, and noisy information. The choice of models and methods varies, of course, with the particular problem and purpose of a study. *The more complex the problem or question, the greater the need to map this complexity by employing multiple and divergent models.* Triangulation of methods and models increases reliability and validity. It also maximizes learning among members of an engaged scholarship team. Presumably different models reflect the unique hunches and interests of different participants in the research project. Sharing approaches and findings enhance learning among co-investigators. Each strategy represents a different thought trial to frame and map the subject matter. As Weick (1989) argues, undertaking multiple independent thought trials facilitates good theory building.

Communicating and Using Research Findings

Susan Albers Mohrman and Allan Mohrman (Chapter 3, Collaborative Organization Design Research at the Center for Effective Organizations) discuss Mohrman, Gibson, and Mohrman's (2001) study that provided empirical evidence of useful knowledge generated with collaborative research. Practitioners reported research as being more helpful the more they incorporated the findings into their internal sense making and organizational design processes and made changes to their organization taking the findings into account. Usefulness also related to whether the company participants experienced the researchers as having incorporated the perspective of practice into the research and whether time had been spent mutually interpreting the data patterns. Interestingly, usefulness was not related to practitioner involvement in the design and conduct of the research. This suggests that the usefulness of research knowledge depends on bridging the meaning gap between the communities of theory and practice—communities with very different contexts, beliefs, and practices. The study made clear, however, that the onus is not only on the academic researcher. Usefulness depends on practitioners and users to engage in the hard and intentional work of applying the knowledge to make changes in regards to how they function.

Rousseau and Boudreau (Chapter 14, Sticky Findings) discuss a pervasive problem of evidence-based knowledge—it is not "sticky" and hence seldom used as a basis for management practice. They discuss a number of insightful communication principles for building a practitioner's capacity to use sticky evidence-based management knowledge. They cite many studies providing evidence for these principles. If that is not convincing, Everett Rogers (2003,

p. xviii) estimates no less than 5,200 studies have examined these principles on the adoption and diffusion of innovations. He states, "No other field of behavior science research represents more effort by more scholars in more disciplines in more nations" (Rogers, 2003, p. xviii).

Given the extensive research evidence supporting the principles for communicating and implementing research findings that Rousseau and Boudreau summarize, why do so few academics and practitioners follow this evidence-based advice? I suspect that proponents of evidence-based knowledge have overlooked the role of rhetoric in communicating and implementing research findings. *Research reports are more likely to be adopted by a specific audience when they are presented in a rhetorically persuasive way.* What makes information convincing and, therefore, utilized is a rhetorical question. Rhetoric is the use of persuasion to influence the thought and conduct of one's listeners. To Aristotle, the art of persuasion comprises three elements: (1) *logos*—the message, especially its internal consistency (i.e., the clarity of the argument, the logic of its reasons, and the effectiveness of its supporting evidence), (2) *pathos*—the power to stir the emotions, beliefs, values, knowledge, and imagination of the audience to elicit not only sympathy, but empathy as well, and (3) *ethos*—the credibility, legitimacy, and authority that a speaker both brings into and develops over the course of the argument or message (Barnes, 1995). Logos, pathos, and ethos are the elements of the rhetorical triangle. Combined, they shape the persuasiveness of any communication.

Mohrman's study findings indicated that persuasiveness is in the "eyes" of the listener (not just the speaker) and requires appreciating the context and assumptions of the audience or listeners. For example, Davis (1971, 1986) argues that what influences readers to view a theory as interesting or classical is the degree to which the writer challenges the assumptions of the reader. In a nutshell, a classic work speaks to the primary concerns or assumptions of an audience, while an interesting theory speaks to the secondary concerns of an audience. Interesting theories negate an accepted assumption held by the audience and affirm an unanticipated alternative. The key rhetorical message is that knowledge transfer is not only a function of the logic and data supporting a message but also the degree to which the speaker is viewed as a credible witness and is able to stir the human emotions of listeners. Hence, from a rhetorical perspective, a researcher can increase the likelihood of influencing his or her intended audience by going beyond logos (the logical, technical research findings) to include pathos (persuasiveness and incentives) and ethos (the ethical and appropriateness) of the findings in research presentations, discussions, and reports.

Becoming an Engaged Scholar

There does not appear to be a turnkey method for learning how to do research that is useful for theory and practice. Philip Mirvis and Edward E. Lawler (Chapter 6, Rigor and Relevance in Organizational Research), C. K. Prahalad (Chapter 7, Can Relevance and Rigor Coexist?), Michael Beer (Chapter 8, Making a Difference *and* Contributing Useful Knowledge), and Michael L. Tushman (Chapter 9, On Knowing and Doing), whose work has significantly influenced theory and practice, each received their formal graduate training at schools with a fairly standard curriculum. Beyond formal training, each of their research careers and experiences followed different progressions. *This suggests that there is no one best way; instead there are many different ways to learn how to perform research that is useful for theory and practice.*

Mirvis and Lawler (in Chapter 6, Rigor and Relevance in Organizational Research) reflect on their experiences as matching the person and research (P-R fit) through socialization and career experiences over time. Lawler seems to have begun his career doing basic science (cell 1 in Fig. 21.2) and then over time expanded his repertoire by engaging in the other kinds of engaged scholarship (as shown in Fig. 21.2). Specifically, they state:

> Lawler's journey matches that of many other senior organizational behavior scholars who "end up" doing useful research. Lawler was socialized early on as a mainstream scientific researcher: exploring core psychological phenomena with traditional methods and tools. His early career experiences at Yale opened him up to other methodological perspectives and the exigencies of running a research shop at Michigan and later USC pulled him to more action-oriented scholarship and research methods.
>
> Later career writings turned from *JAP* to *HBR* and from books aimed at scholars and students to those aimed at practicing managers. As for person-environment fit, changes in his scholarly identity seemed to progress from Yale to Michigan to USC. As for his own motives for turning toward useful research, Lawler, when pressed, explained his outlook, "I get a kick out of doing work that makes people more effective and satisfied. It is rewarding to me. I'd rather do that than solve a crossword puzzle or deal with some technical issue."

Mike Beer, on the other hand, started his career as a practitioner doing a form of action research (cell 4 in Fig. 21.2), then learned basic science in his PhD program, and since has done all other forms of engaged scholarship. In Chapter 8 (Making a Difference *and* Contributing Useful Knowledge), he states:

> I have used my lifelong experience as a scholar-consultant and field researcher to develop principles for those who wish to develop knowledge

useful for theory and practice. I hope this narrative will be helpful to those aspiring to fashion such a professional identification. The work of developing useful knowledge is challenging. As I have tried to show, it requires passion for both making a difference *and* developing theory. It requires readiness to be drawn into ill-defined practical problems that one does not fully know how to approach or solve, to be comfortable with or foolish enough to live with uncertainty. And one has to be able to live in two worlds with different norms and rules for knowing.

Prahalad (Chapter 7, Can Relevance and Rigor Coexist?) and Tushman (Chapter 9, On Knowing and Doing) have also engaged in all four types of research (as shown in Fig. 21.2). However, my sense is that they have stayed closer to engaging in basic science, whereas Lawler and Beer appear to be more involved in applied research. My intentions in saying this are to show that *there are many ways and perspectives for doing research that is useful for theory and practice.* Prahalad has been an intense observer of diverse practices, which enables him to develop inventive insights on next practices. He states, "It is the understanding of the outliers that allows us to construct a 'mid-level theory,' a map that allows managers to understand the emerging competitive landscape and navigate it. We go back to the phenomena to illustrate the concepts. This process is very different from starting with a theory and then looking at the phenomenon." Prahalad's career has been one of crossing boundaries; this increases the likelihood of recognizing or creating organization and management inventions that provide a sustainable basis for contributing to and leading theory and practice.

In Chapter 9 (On Knowing and Doing), Tushman discusses how customized executive education programs are an underleveraged vehicle in reducing the rigor-relevance gap between business schools and the world of practice. His experience shows that teaching and research are inextricably linked and that executive education provides an ideal setting for engaging in use-inspired basic research (Pasteur's Quadrant in Stokes's Quadrant Model), which he argues is what business school research should emphasize. Tushman's suggestion that business school scholars focus on Pasteur's Quadrant is a nice expansion on Herbert Simon's proposal for the design of a business school (in the appendix of his 1976 version of *Administrative Behavior*). It provides a way forward to Cummings's insightful analysis of how and why business schools are in their problematic state today.

Simon (1976) proposed that a basic challenge for scholars in professional schools is to contribute to both the science and the practice of management—not either-or. He noted that the information and skills relevant to accomplishing this objective come from the social system of practitioners and the social system of scientists in the relevant disciplines. These social systems have elaborate institutions and procedures for storing, transmitting, developing, and applying knowledge. As the chapters by Cascio (Chapter 13, Professional Associations) and Benson (Chapter 15, Popular and Influential Management Books) demonstrate, academics and practitioners live in different communities, and the main way to understand each community is to participate in it.

Bartunek and Schein (Chapter 12, Organization Development Scholar-Practitioners) discuss some of the challenges of scholars becoming conversant in these different communities of science and practice. Practitioner-scholar doctoral programs have the purpose of creating such professionals who bridge management theory and practice. Tenkasi (Chapter 11, Integrating Theory to Inform Practice) discusses such a program at Benedictine University in Chicago. Such practitioner-scholar PhD programs also exist at Case Western Reserve, the University of Southern California, and the DBA program at Harvard, and it would be instructive to compare their curricula. Tenkasi uses Aristotle's "phronesis" to characterize the kind of combinatorial knowledge of theory and practice to be learned in practitioner-scholar doctoral programs. Levi-Strauss's (1966) ideas about the science of the concrete and science of the abstract could also provide challenging ways to bridge the two kinds of knowledge.

In Chapter 9 (On Knowing and Doing), Tushman, like Simon (1976), argues that significant invention in the affairs of the world calls on two kinds of knowledge: applied knowledge about practical issues or needs of a profession and scientific knowledge about new ideas and processes that are potentially possible. Invention is easy and likely to produce incremental contributions when it operates among like-minded individuals. Thus we find applied researchers who tend to immerse themselves in the problems of the end-users and then apply available knowledge and technology to provide solutions to their clients, and we find pure scientists immersed in their disciplines to discover what questions have not been answered and then apply research techniques to address these questions. In either case if researchers cannot answer their initial questions, they modify and simplify them until they can be answered. As this process repeats itself, the research questions and answers become increasingly specific contributions to narrow domains of problems and inquiry.

Research in regards to Pasteur's Quadrant requires researchers to be equally exposed to the social systems of practice and science. At this boundary, they are likely to be confronted with real-life questions that are at the forefront of the kind of knowledge and policies that—as Prahalad suggests—are used to address problems in the world. This setting increases the chance of significant innovation. As Louis Pasteur stated, "Chance favors the prepared mind." Research in this context is also more demanding because scholars do not have the option of substituting simpler questions if they cannot solve real-life problems. Engaged scholarship is difficult because it entails a host of interpersonal tensions and cognitive strains that are associated with juxtaposing investigators with different views and approaches to a single problem. But focusing on the tensions between scientists and practitioners is a mistake, for it may blind us to the very real opportunities that can be gained from exploiting their differences in the co-production of knowledge. As Tushman (Chapter 9, On Knowing and Doing), and Simon (1976) suggest, if research becomes more challenging when it is undertaken to answer questions posed from outside science, it also acquires the potential to become more significant and fruitful.

The reflective chapters of distinguished career scholars such as Lawler, Prahalad, Beer, Tushman, Schein, and Bartunek attest to this. So also do the biographical stories of 23 "Great Minds" of Management about their theory and research development journeys (Smith & Hitt, 2005). Indeed, doing engaged scholarly research that crosses the boundaries and is useful to theory and practice is a common theme in the stories of successful and highly respected scholars. The history of science and technology demonstrates that many of the extraordinary developments in pure science have often been posed by problems and questions from outside the scientific enterprise. Necessity is indeed the mother of important invention. Scholarship that engages both scientists and practitioners can provide an exceedingly productive and challenging environment; it not only fosters the creation of the kind of knowledge that solves practical problems but also makes irrelevant the argument for a gap between theory and practice in the arenas of professional and public life.

Researcher's Identity and Empathy

In conclusion, I want to emphasize that *producing research that is useful for theory and practice is not a solitary exercise; instead, it is a collective achievement.* Engagement means that scholars step outside themselves to obtain and be informed by the interpretations of others in performing each step of the research process: problem formulation, theory building, research design, and problem solving. For example, Mohrman and Lawler (Introduction and Overview) state that "combining theoretical knowledge from different disciplines with knowledge from practice . . . requires familiarity with each other's knowledge and building conceptual bridges such as prototypes or other boundary objects to link the knowledge bases" of theorists and practitioners.

For this to happen, Mirvis and Lawler (Chapter 6, Rigor and Relevance in Organizational Research) discuss a researcher's empathy for closing the theory-practice gap. "Close contact with practitioners in field studies, and their active engagement in the research process and interpretation, yields a sense of affinity and empathy across the research-practice divide. This more interactive and participatory process thrusts the scholar into the organizational system that, in traditional scientific terms, risks objectivity as the researcher 'goes native.' At the same time, it gives us a deeper and richer feel for the subject matter and people under study. In the process, the "self" becomes a research instrument that can stimulate insights into what is going on and provoke more grounded theorizing."

As Mirvis and Lawler imply, *engaged scholarship entails a fundamental shift in how researchers define their relationships with the communities in which they are located, including faculty and students from various disciplines in the university and practitioners in relevant professional domains.* Edward Zlotkowski, a leading proponent of engaged scholarship in American higher education, captures the identity and empathy of an engaged scholar.

> It's about faculty members having a profound respect for those other than themselves, whether they be practitioners or students.... There is a profound emphasis on the concept of deep respect and, I might even say, humility vis-à-vis other kinds of knowledge producers. Not because we don't have an important and distinctive role to play in knowledge production, but because we don't have the exclusive right to such production. As we begin to engage in partnerships with both our students and outside communities of practice on the basis of such deep respect, we allow ourselves to become real-world problem solvers in a way that is otherwise not possible. Indeed, I would suggest that unless we learn to develop deeper respect for our non-faculty colleagues, we run the risk of becoming "academic ventriloquists"— speaking for our students, speaking for the communities we allegedly serve—but not really listening to them or making them our peers in addressing the vital issues that concern all of us. (Edward Zlotkowski, in Kenworthy-U'ren, 2005, p. 360)

Engagement is a relationship that involves negotiation and collaboration between researchers and practitioners in a learning community; such a community jointly produces knowledge that can both advance the scientific enterprise and enlighten a community of practitioners. Instead of viewing organizations and clients as data collection sites and funding sources, an engaged scholar views them as a learning workplace (idea factory) where practitioners and scholars co-produce knowledge on important questions and issues by testing alternative ideas and different views of a common problem. "Abundant evidence shows that both the civic and academic health of any culture is vitally enriched as scholars and practitioners speak and listen carefully to each other" (Boyer, 1996, p. 15).

Conclusion

This chapter summarized our perspective on engaged scholarship and discussed how chapters in this book elaborate and extend this perspective in many important ways. The chapter also reviewed various ways to practice engaged scholarship, including basic, collaborative, evaluation, and action research as illustrated in Figure 21.2, and how to use the approach that best addresses the research question. Most doctoral students and junior faculty begin their research career addressing basic questions devoted to describing, explaining, or predicting various phenomena. I encouraged young researchers to do this basic science with stakeholder advice because such engagement produces more significant advances to knowledge than when researchers do their studies alone. Moreover, I suggested to *not* do it alone; engage and rely on senior and experienced colleagues for mentoring, networking, and accessing potential research sites and stakeholders. Engaged scholarship is a collective and developmental achievement. As researchers learn the technical and social skills of engaging stakeholders in basic science, then they can begin to address additional challenges of finding mutual interests, boundary spanning, power sharing, and task coordination between academics and practitioners in the other forms of engaged scholarship.

In the final analysis, the "proof is in the pudding." As many chapter authors have suggested, I believe that researchers who adopt the engaged scholarship model will produce research findings that make more significant advancements to theory and practice than the traditional approach of going it alone. As a result, research reports based on engaged scholarship should win out in competitive reviews for research funding, publications in journals, presentations at professional conferences, and professional training and development programs over those based on unengaged or disengaged research. The cumulative record should result in career advancements and promotions for engaged scholars at disproportionately higher rates than disengaged scholars who go it alone in conducting their research. Time will tell.

REFERENCES

Barnes, J. (Ed.). (1995). *The Cambridge companion to Aristotle.* Cambridge: Cambridge University Press.

Boyer, E. L. (1996). *Scholarship reconsidered: Priorities for the professoriate.* San Francisco: Jossey-Bass.

Davis, M. (1971). That's interesting! *Philosophy of Social Sciences, 1,* 309–344.

Davis, M. (1986). That's classic! *Philosophy of Social Sciences, 16,* 285–301.

Dewey, J. (1938). *Logic: The theory of inquiry.* New York: Holt.

Edmondson, A., & McManus, S. E. (2007). Methodological fit in management field research. *Academy of Management Review, 32*(4), 1155–1179.

Kenworthy-U'Ren, A. (2005). Towards a scholarship of engagement: A dialogue between Andy Van de Ven and Edward Zlotkowski. *Academy of Management Learning and Education, 4*(3), 355–362.

Levi-Strauss, C. (1966). The science of the concrete. In C. Levi-Strauss (Ed.), *The savage mind* (pp. 1–33). Chicago: University of Chicago Press.

Mohrman, S., Gibson, C., & Mohrman, A. (2001). Doing research that is useful to practice: A model and empirical exploration. *Academy of Management Review, 44*(2), 357–375.

Pettigrew, A. M. (2001). Management research after modernism. *British Journal of Management, 12* (Special Issue), S61–S70.

Rogers, E. M. (2003). *Diffusion of innovations* (5th ed.). New York: Free Press.

Simon, H. A. (1976). The business school: A problem in organizational design. In *Administrative Behavior* (3d ed., chap. 17). New York: Free Press.

Simon, H. A. (1991). Bounded rationality and organizational learning. *Organization Science, 2*(1), 125–135.

Smith, K. G., & Hitt, M. A. (Eds.) (2005). *Great minds in management: The process of theory development.* Oxford: Oxford University Press.

Van de Ven, A. H. (2007). *Engaged scholarship: A guide for organizational and social research.* Oxford: Oxford University Press.

Van de Ven, A. H., & Johnson, P. (2006). Knowledge for theory and practice. *Academy of Management Review, 31*(4), 802–821.

Weick, K. (1989). Theory construction as disciplined imagination. *Academy of Management Review, 14*(4), 516–531.

ABOUT THE AUTHOR

Andrew H. Van de Ven is Vernon H. Heath Professor of Organizational Innovation and Change in the Carlson School of the University of Minnesota. He received his PhD from the University of Wisconsin at Madison in 1972 and taught at the Wharton School of the University of Pennsylvania before his present appointment. Van de Ven directed the Minnesota Innovation Research Program during the 1980s and 1990s. Since 1994, he has been studying changes unfolding in health care organizations. In addition to organizational innovation and change, Van de Ven's research has dealt with the Nominal Group Technique, program planning, organization assessment, and interorganizational relationships. He is co-author of 12 books, including *The Innovation Journey* (1999, 2008), *Organization Change and Innovation Processes* (2000), *Handbook of Organizational Change and Innovation* (2004), and *Engaged Scholarship* (2007), which won the 2008 Terry Best Book Award from the Academy of Management.

TWENTY-TWO

What We Have Learned

SUSAN ALBERS MOHRMAN
AND EDWARD E. LAWLER III

IN THIS BOOK we revisit the key learnings from Lawler and others' 1985 book, *Doing Research That Is Useful to Theory and Practice*, and chronicle what has been learned since then about how to conduct research that helps organizations be more effective and advances theoretical understanding. Our intent was not to assess whether useful research has become the standard; indeed, we know that it has not. Still, during the last quarter century, many scholars have conducted research that is useful to both practice and theory, and there is growing interest and knowledge about how to do useful research. There is also a growing concern about why the usefulness of research to practice is not a more salient purpose nor an outcome that is frequently pursued in today's academic institutions. We feel this book makes an important "twenty-five years later" contribution because it establishes what is known about how to do useful research and provides an important guide to scholars who want to do it.

As was true with the 1985 book, authors brought their chapters to a workshop where we shared and discussed one another's ideas and honed the content of the book. Researchers were invited to be part of this project because their work relates to useful research. During their careers, they have conducted rigorous research that is useful to practice, and have systematically examined the gap between academic research and practice and tried to understand how it can be narrowed. In several cases, they are dedicating significant professional time to influencing the field to do more useful research. Again, as during the 1983 workshop, we were gratified by the passion that the participants hold for the topic. The thoughtful chapters they have written and their willingness to share their profound understandings of useful research is truly impressive. Most of the authors have made significant contributions to practice while holding positions in traditional academic institutions. They are proof that it can be done.

Looking back, we are struck by how key changes in the landscape of management and organizational research have made it more difficult to do work that is both rigorous, as viewed by prevailing academic standards, and relevant, as viewed by practitioners. Narrow academic specialties have proliferated, and academic career prestige and business school ratings have become tightly connected to success in theory-driven subfields that are often largely disconnected from practice. At the same time, the organizational world has been fundamentally altered by new technologies that have enabled new ways of organizing; by globalization and the emergence of strong competitors in new markets; and by the acceleration of societal, governmental, and ecological change. Organizations are continually being started, designed, and redesigned as a result of the decisions and actions of their members, who often have little knowledge of the research on organizational effectiveness. Organizational practices have largely evolved independently of academic knowledge. A disconnected academia has failed to keep up and as a consequence has had little influence on management practice.

As organizations have struggled to adapt and succeed in dynamic and challenging markets and economies, their need for useful knowledge has become stronger. Consultants, professional societies, commercial bundlers of knowledge, and many types of bridging organizations such as consortia and networks have become major providers of expertise. However, the knowledge they provide only sometimes builds on academically generated theory and research. Their typical approach to research is to survey practices and to quickly sense and provide feedback about current issues and "best practices." They create and provide "actionable" knowledge products and services that have become integral to the way many organizations seek knowledge and try to become more effective.

Despite the changing landscape, the value stream of academia has remained relatively static and simple. Researchers operate in discipline silos exploring increasingly esoteric aspects of elegant theoretical frameworks. They publish in outlets read by like-minded academics. Contact with the world of practice occurs primarily through the one-way communication that occurs in the classroom, with the assumption that teaching tomorrow's managers will eventually influence practice. Even there it is questionable whether academically produced knowledge is conveyed in a manner that impacts practice.

The chapters in this book provide a rich picture of the landscape that must be navigated by researchers if their work is to make a difference to practice. They do an excellent job of specifying the kinds of research approaches and professional activities required in order to do useful research. In Chapter 1, Research for Theory and Practice, we presented two frameworks for how academic researchers contribute to practice. The first retains the traditionally held view that knowledge flows from academic research to practice. Unlike the prevailing academic model, this model explicitly makes practice the ultimate "customer" of the knowledge that is generated and broadens the view of the value stream to include the many pathways through which academic knowledge generation can link to practice. In this framework, the task facing researchers who aspire to relevance is to determine how they will position their work in this value stream, so that the knowledge gained through their research will reach practice.

In the second framework, the value stream is reconceptualized as a complex network of actors who play different roles in advancing and applying knowledge, rather than as a linear flow from academia to practice. This network is characterized by multistakeholder and cross-boundary collaborations that enable the combination of knowledge from different actors and the co-exploration of problems and co-development of knowledge. This network model entails a complex communication system with many feedback loops and reciprocal linkages. In this framework theoretical knowledge and practice co-evolve. The challenge for academics who aspire to make a difference is determining how to engage across boundaries so that research yields knowledge that contributes to more effective organizational decisions and actions.

It is evident from the chapters in this book that researchers make many important choices about what impact they want their research to have, about how to carry out their research, and about their portfolio of professional activities. In this chapter, we briefly discuss the implications of the major themes from the chapters to help guide the choices made by scholars who want to impact practice. We have organized this discussion according to the two frameworks because we believe the key choices relate to positioning oneself in the value stream and building the network of relationships that enable the conduct of impactful research.

Connecting to the Value Stream of Organizational Knowledge

The complex organizational knowledge landscape and changing value stream that exists in organizational knowledge have emerged during the last decades as organizations have sought the knowledge they need in order to be effective. They include academic research as well as the work of other actors who generate and apply knowledge to improve organizations, and who develop intermediate products and services that make knowledge accessible to practitioners. Impacting practice is not a simple one-step influence process that consists of publishing research results that will be acted on by practitioners because they are valid. Academics must find ways for their work to move down this value stream in order for it to affect practice. The following are ways that are suggested by one or more of the chapters in the book.

Connect Directly to Practice in Doing Research

Most of the authors in this book have spent a large amount of their professional time conducting research and testing their theories in organizations. They have developed a deep understanding of the challenges that practitioners face and of the issues that are important to building effective organizations. Because they have spent time in organizations, their work has a rich sense of context. Having this sense is important because it leads to a theoretical understanding of complex issues, and it is required in order to do work that is compelling to practitioners. Sara Rynes points out that the amount of time spent in field settings is also associated with effective scholarship because it is related to greater self-reported personal learning by researchers, as well as to a greater citation rate for journal articles that result from it (Rynes, Chapter 19, Counterpoint, this book; Rynes, McNatt, & Bretz, 1999).

Utilize Nonacademic Pathways to Disseminate Research Findings to Practitioners

Many of the authors in this book regularly test the relevance of their work by writing it in a manner suitable for practitioner-oriented publications, and by presenting it to practitioner audiences in companies, professional associations and consortia, workshops, and consulting projects. In Chapter 15, Popular and Influential Management Books, George S. Benson points out that many academics who have influenced practice have used practitioner-oriented books as a way to periodically take stock of the implications of their research programs and to convey this in a practice-friendly way.

Michael Beer's career, described in Chapter 8, Making a Difference *and* Contributing Useful Knowledge, has mixed facilitating organizational development interventions that apply existing academic organizational knowledge with conducting research to discover effective intervention methodologies that improve organizational performance. His books describe change interventions and provide models of high performance systems in a manner that can be applied by practitioners. Researchers can translate the knowledge from their research into tools that can be used by practitioners. For example, in Chapter 3, Collaborative Organization Design Research at the Center for Effective Organizations, Mohrman and Mohrman recount being requested by several companies that participated in their team-based organization design research to go beyond the book that they wrote that recounted findings (Mohrman, Cohen, & Mohrman, 1995). The practitioners wanted an organizational design workbook that they could use to guide them through the process of designing and implementing a laterally focused organization (Mohrman & Mohrman, 1997).

Connect to Service Organizations That Are Situated in the Organizational Knowledge Value Stream

Many service organizations are much more closely linked to organizational practice than are most academics. For example, in Chapter 13, Professional Associations, Wayne F. Cascio discusses the opportunities for academics to be active in professional societies where they can secure funding for research on topics that practitioners view as useful and contribute to practitioner-oriented reports of research-based knowledge. Ruth Wageman (Chapter 10, Academic-Consultant Collaboration) points to the opportunities and challenges that exist when academics work in partnership with consulting firms. She points out that combining an academic's deep theoretically based knowledge with a consultant's broad experience-based knowledge of the world of organizations can result in important learning. Scholar-practitioners such as organization development consultants (Chapter 12, Organization Development Scholar-Practitioners) and executive PhDs (Chapter 11, Integrating Theory to Inform Practice) can carry knowledge from academia into organizations. Ideally, these scholar practitioners are good translators of theory into practice and practical interventions. By connecting with them, academic researchers can move their knowledge into organizations.

Develop an Ambidextrous Communication Capability

Repeatedly in this book authors point out that achieving downstream impact requires academics to break out of the internally focused communication system of academia. It requires new communication competencies, new language skills, and the establishment of deeper relationships with practitioners. While valuing research that advances theoretical understanding and provides powerful frameworks for understanding organizations, the authors in this book and the practitioners in the panel discussion agree that standard jargon-filled academic publications are aimed at other academics, are not read by practitioners, and are simply not a way to connect to practice.

To build a connection with practitioners, researchers need to communicate differently—framing knowledge using language and examples that are compelling to practitioners and that connect with their world. They need to find "sticky" concepts (Chapter 14, Sticky Findings) that are memorable and useful to practitioners. Some advocate publishing special versions of research results for practitioners, others stress the power of speeches and presentations.

Developing Relationships with Practitioners

It takes face time with practitioners to learn the language that connects with practice and the organizational logics and challenges that are embedded in practice, and to discern the key research questions that are relevant to effective practice. The relationships that are established through experiences with practitioners provide the foundation for such learning and the legitimacy to gain the access needed to explore critical issues, gather data, and garner the needed resources and attention from the organization.

The centrality of relationships to doing useful research is a theme that emerges continually. Tushman (Chapter 9, On Knowing and Doing) talks about the importance of the relationships that are developed with line managers during executive education programs that are based on action projects. These relationships lead to a two-way exchange of knowledge that allows for crafting more meaningful research questions and educational content. They also contribute to the willingness of participants to act based on academic knowledge and to support the ongoing generation of knowledge by participating in academic research.

In Chapter 12, Organization Development Scholar-Practitioners, Bartunek and Schein point out that participation in organizations and networks that bridge academia and practice is valuable. It provides an opportunity to develop relationships with practitioners and enables researchers to understand why much academic knowledge is not compelling in practice and what kind of knowledge is seen as useful.

Doctoral programs in management and organization provide little formal training in how to connect to the practice value stream. Indeed, little attention is paid to the question of whether and how researchers should relate to practice. The assumption that rigorous research must be objective and hands-off prevails.

The measures just described—particularly the development of close relationships to practice—are a departure from academic norms. Yet these measures are precisely what is mentioned when researchers describe their strategies and methodologies for doing relevant and rigorous research.

Knowledge-Combining Networks to Address Relevant Research Questions

Organizations are dynamic artifacts created by human beings to accomplish purposes. Relevance to practice is necessarily defined relative to the challenges faced by practitioners, the contexts in which they exist, the purposes they are trying to achieve, the work they must carry out and the decisions and choices they must make to accomplish their purposes. Pragmatically, this means that researchers who aspire to do relevant research must develop a deep and broad appreciation of the systems they are studying. The knowledge of a single researcher or from a single narrow discipline is unlikely to capture the complexity faced by managers (O'Toole, Chapter 20, On the Verge of Extinction). The alternative depiction in Chapter 1, Research for Theory and Practice, is of the knowledge system as a network in which many contributors to knowledge and forms of knowledge can be combined to advance organizational knowledge. Not the least of the contributors to knowledge is practice itself. This network depiction reflects the combination of knowledge from organizational practice, from intermediary knowledge providers, and from multiple theoretical and applied domains. Such a combination is necessary in order to conduct research that adequately addresses the complexity of practice and the knowledge required to advance it.

The researchers who wrote about their research programs and careers in Part I, Exemplars of Useful Research, and Part II, Bodies of Work That Have Influenced Theory and Practice, of this book without exception conducted research in a manner that takes into account the complexity of practice. They built on and combined the knowledge of multiple stakeholders. They created a network of collegial relationships that extended beyond academia and their discipline boundaries to do so. A number of themes emerge from the chapters describing their research approaches.

Conduct Problem-Focused Research

Doing research that addresses the problems that are experienced by practitioners not only leads to greater relevance, it is also likely to address important theoretical issues. This perspective is compellingly described in the engaged research framework recapped by Van de Ven (Chapter 21, Reflections on Research for Theory and Practice). It argues that problems can be identified and addressed by multiple stakeholders. New aspects of complex problems often emerge in the course of carrying out engaged research projects because close connection to the field brings to light dynamics and nuances that were not originally apparent. Edmondson describes this vividly in Chapter 2, Crossing Boundaries to Investigate Problems in the Field, where she recounts her research program investigating drug errors and other quality issues in healthcare settings. In each investigation, new aspects of the quality dynamics of teams surfaced and raised interesting theoretical and critical practical issues.

Utilize Research Methodologies That Fit the Complexity of the Systems and Issues Being Studied

This book is full of examples where multiple disciplines, multiple-level analyses, and multiple research approaches have been used to yield useful knowledge. For example, both Gratton (Chapter 4, A Ten-Year Journey of Cooperation) and Mohrman and Mohrman (Chapter 3, Collaborative Organization Design Research at the Center for Effective Organizations) found that they could not fully investigate and describe the dynamics of building effective teams without examining individual-, team-, and organization-level phenomena using both quantitative and qualitative methodologies.

The concept of adaptive research developed by Lawler for the Quality of Worklife studies anchors the high end of the continuum of complexity (Lawler, Nadler, & Cammann, 1980; Mirvis & Lawler, Chapter 6, Rigor and Relevance in Organizational Research, this book). This research program utilized many different theoretical and empirical approaches at multiple levels of analysis and from different disciplines to understand the factors that lead to high levels of performance and to satisfying and motivating work. It combined longitudinal and collaborative research methodologies linking together a complex set of stakeholders with multiple agendas to execute and evaluate interventions intended to impact system performance. It employed both quantitative and qualitative approaches from multiple-discipline perspectives to understand the dynamics in the systems and the impact of various aspects of the work systems on outcomes. Mirvis and Lawler (Chapter 6, Rigor and Relevence in Organizational Research) point out that research projects that examine complex organizational dynamics and interesting issues in the field may sacrifice some rigor, as defined from a positivistic science perspective, in the interest of relevance and the ability to shed light on complex system performance issues.

Combine Knowledge from Different Disciplines

Innovations and knowledge breakthroughs often occur at the intersection of multiple disciplines. The generation of knowledge to address complex problems often requires multiple perspectives (Van de Ven, 2007). Organizational practice is guided in large part by the experientially based knowledge and practical frameworks utilized by practitioners. It is also shaped by formal knowledge systems such as the engineering and science knowledge that guide technical organizations, and the economic knowledge and financial and accounting frameworks that underpin business decision making. To avoid being disconnected from practice, the process of generating knowledge to inform practice development requires that the frameworks of organizational practices and those of multiple academic practice be combined.

Ram Tenkasi (Chapter 11, Integrating Theory to Inform Practice) documented the strategies that are used by scholar practitioners trained in research and academic theories through executive PhD programs. They combine academic theory and research with the knowledge of practice in order to contribute to successful knowledge application to advance practice in their organizations. They find approaches to help practitioners broaden their frameworks to include academic organizational knowledge, and they find ways to frame academic knowledge to make it more context appropriate. Knowledge combination processes are foundational to useful research—both to the generation of useful knowledge and to its actionability.

Research Usefulness Is Related to the Actionability of the Knowledge That Is Created

Useful research is actionable research (Argyris, 1970). When this precept is combined with Lewin's (1948) notion that the best way to understand an organization is to try to change it, the needs of practice and scholarship become aligned. This orientation toward actionable knowledge underpins much of the research described in this book. The path from research findings to organizational action and change often entails one or more fundamental interventions into the dynamics of an organization. Interventions are not possible without internal sponsors and champions and a willingness to go through a redesign or transition process (Chapter 12, Organization Development Scholar Practitioners; Chapter 8, Making a Difference *and* Contributing Useful Knowledge).

Awareness of the frameworks that practitioners apply, the business and design challenges they face, and the dynamics of organizational change and learning is critical. It helps the researchers craft useful research and communicate research findings in a manner that connects to practitioners' frames of reference so that it can inform action and change. Many academic researchers may not have the intervention skills and knowledge to couch their knowledge within effective interventions in practice, but instead may want to team with others who do have deep knowledge of intervention and change.

Build Teams That Have the Knowledge, Capabilities, and Resources Necessary to Conduct Useful Research

Often the complexity of useful research studies requires a range of knowledge and skills that individuals do not have. Teams can be an effective way to solve this problem. The appropriate composition of a research team depends on the nature of the problem being investigated and the methodologies that are appropriate to generate the knowledge being sought. For example, the focus and methodology of the Quality of Worklife studies at the University of Michigan required that organizational development interventionists, practitioners from multiple stakeholder groups, and academics from different disciplines be on the team in order to enact the adaptive research methodology and to introduce change.

Gratton (Chapter 4, A Ten-Year Journey of Cooperation) describes the importance of having experts in visualization of research findings and models in order to investigate how organizations can use virtual technologies to accelerate the learning process and create high-impact teams. Edmondson (Chapter 2, Crossing Boundaries to Investigate Problems in the Field) describes how her research team's combination of management and economics knowledge yielded a rich theoretical and practical set of findings about the learning curves in surgery settings.

A number of authors describe the usefulness of having interventionists on the research team in order to develop methodologies for introducing the resulting knowledge into organizational practice. As Mirvis and Lawler (Chapter 6, Rigor and Relevance in Organizational Research) point out, the organization of a complex research team requires researchers to become good team leaders, and, we might add, good team members.

The Importance of Rigor and Expertise

Doing research that is useful for theory and practice does not free a researcher from the tenets of good research—in fact, in our view it requires a more nuanced view of rigor. Research expertise matters and is the sine qua non of doing useful research. As Van de Ven (2007) made clear in his book *Engaged Scholarship*, and the researchers in this book have reiterated, crafting and executing research that is actionable and that addresses important practice issues requires a strong base of research skills and knowledge of the literature. These are the competencies that academics must bring to knowledge-producing collaborations. Doing research that influences practice should never be done by anyone who does not have the right skills; it is too important; it impacts people's lives and well-being! The importance of expertise is why it is critical that academics find ways to be important players in the organizational effectiveness knowledge generation landscape.

Wageman (Chapter 10, Academic-Consultant Collaboration) points out that even though the consultants who were members of the collaborative research team investigating top leadership team effectiveness were academically trained, they relied on the academic researchers to provide deep and current knowledge of the literature so that the research team was not redis-covering the wheel. Edmondson (Chapter 2, Crossing Boundaries to Investi-gate Problems in the Field) also sees knowledge of the literature as a source of hypotheses and a check on the interpretation of data and results. Van de Ven (2007) clearly sees academic researchers as being responsible for ensur-ing that appropriate methodologies are used to investigate the questions at hand and to apply and develop useful theory in the course of investigating important issues.

Doing research that is designed to contribute to practice and theory is particularly demanding because it must yield knowledge that speaks to two very different constituencies. The researcher must find the overlap between interesting theory and the challenge of practice. It is clear that researchers who make a difference to practice operate effectively across boundaries and have the creativity to craft and execute research that addresses the complex-ity of the real world in a valid manner. As pointed out by Mirvis and Lawler in Chapter 6, Rigor and Relevance in Organizational Research, addressing real world problems may require backing off some of the elements of "rigor" as traditionally defined in positivistic research, but it should not be nonrigor-ous or oblivious to the areas where rigor is lacking.

Conclusion

In this book we chose not to deal with paradigm wars and with conflicting, strongly held views concerning what constitutes rigorous research. The focus of this book is on providing insight about how research can be con-ducted in a manner that connects with and generates knowledge useful to practice while advancing the fundamental understanding of organizations.

Young scholars who aspire to do research that makes a difference to prac-tice must purposefully craft their educations and experiences toward this end. This means pushing back on pressures to continually narrow their focus to the self-referential world of academic disciplines. It means connecting to practice and practitioners and crafting research that takes into account the contexts in which organizations and their employees operate. It requires be-ing aware of the pressures and challenges facing organizations, understand-ing them as dynamic phenomena that are continually being shaped through the practices within them, and anticipating how knowledge may be applied by them. It means crossing boundaries, working collaboratively, and contin-ually learning new aspects of the world of organizations and of the disci-plines that are required to comprehend the full complexity of organizations. It requires developing the skills to operate effectively as part of a complex network of actors in the value stream.

Many of the capabilities needed to do useful research are best learned gradually and through experience. A number of the authors in this book entered academia after spending time working in other organizations, having developed an appreciation for practice. Others developed a deep sense of organizations through doing field research and working across organizational boundaries. In Chapter 21, Reflections on Research for Theory and Practice, Van de Ven offers sage advice to young scholars: Do not try to tackle all of the aspects of dealing with complex, ambiguous problems at once. Rather, he advises start by mastering research methodologies and learning to operate in the field through small projects. He also advises them to partner with colleagues who are experienced at working in the field. We might also advise them to consider crossing boundaries regularly, both in the course of doing research and in the course of disseminating and working with organizations in applying research findings.

New researchers who aspire to do useful research should develop a plan for their own development and gradually build a program of research that generates knowledge that is valued by the field. Experienced researchers who care about bridging the gap between theory and practice should pave the way for new scholars to do so, both by example and by creating opportunities for young scholars. Last but not least, they need to send the right messages by establishing reward criteria that speak loudly and clearly about the importance of doing useful research.

REFERENCES

Argyris, C. (1970). *Intervention theory and method.* Boston: Addison-Wesley.

Lawler, E., Mohrman, A., Mohrman, S., Cummings, T., & Ledford, G. (Eds.). (1985). *Doing research that is useful for theory and practice.* San Francisco: Jossey-Bass.

Lawler, E., Nadler, D., & Cammann, C. (Eds.) (1980). *Organizational assessment.* New York: Wiley.

Lewin, K. (1948). *Resolving social conflicts.* New York: HarperCollins.

Mohrman, S. A., Cohen, S. G., & Mohrman, A. M., Jr. (1995). *Designing team-based organizations.* San Francisco: Jossey-Bass.

Mohrman, S. A., & Mohrman, A. M. (1997). *Designing and leading team-based organizations: A workbook for organizational self-design.* San Francisco: Jossey-Bass.

Rynes, S. L., McNatt, D. B., & Bretz, R. D. (1999). Academic research inside organizations: Inputs, processes and outcomes. *Personnel Psychology, 52,* 869–898.

Van de Ven, A. H. (2007). *Engaged scholarship: A guide for organizational and social research.* Oxford: Oxford University Press.

Acknowledgments

PRODUCING A BOOK LIKE THIS ONE requires the help of many talented individuals. The production process began with a workshop attended by the authors. It was managed by the staff of the Center for Effective Organizations (CEO). Special thanks to Anjelica Wright for the excellent work she did on logistics. The production of the manuscript was managed by Anjelica Wright, with help from Arienne McCracken. With the large number of contributors to this book, this was a challenging task, and so we are particularly appreciative of their efforts.

The chapter authors were a great group to work with. Almost without exception, they met our deadlines and honored our editorial requests. It was obvious that they felt strongly about the topic and, as you will see, produced first-rate chapters. We especially appreciate the contributions of our practitioner colleagues. David Nadler and Ian Ziskin took time to look through the chapters, listen to the presentations, and share their thoughts about our ideas and about useful research.

We would also like to thank Steve Piersanti of Berrett-Koehler Publishers. He saw the promise of this book and provided guidance as to how to make it more than just a book of readings. He actively participated in the authors' workshop and helped to shape expectations for the contributions.

Special thanks go to James Ellis, Dean of the Marshall School of Business at University of Southern California. He provided the funding for the workshop and strongly supported holding it and producing the book. He, like us, believes that business schools should do research that is useful.

Special thanks are due to the family of C. K. Prahalad. C. K. died during the production of this book, and his chapter appears with the consent of his family. We appreciate the time and attention they gave to it during a very difficult time for their family. C. K. was a valued colleague and he will be long remembered and greatly missed.

Finally, we would like to acknowledge the many practitioners and companies who have been supporters and collaborators in the research carried out at the Center for Effective Organizations during the past 30 years. They continually share their knowledge with us, and remind us how important it is that our research is useful to them in addressing the challenges they face in building and managing effective organizations.

Index

Bartlett, Christopher, 293, 378

Bartunek, Jean, 233–47, 250, 401

Becton Dickinson (BD), 155–56, 159, 160, 161, 163, 164

Beer, Michael, 81, 84, 87–88, 147–68, 170, 324–25, 353, 378, 379, 399–400, 410

Belbin, R. Meredith, 293

Benedictine University, 211–12, 214, 222, 401

Bennis, Warren, 293, 298, 370, 372–73, 380

Benson, George, 125, 289–308, 401, 410

Berg, David, 121, 124

Berlin, Isaiah, 374

Berry, Leonard, 293

"best practices," 139, 142, 197, 263, 356, 408

The Black Swan (Taleb), 296, 297

Blanchard, Ken, 298

Blink (Gladwell), 292, 296, 297

Blue Ocean Strategy (Kim and Mauborgne), 297, 299

Blumenthal, Michael, 126

BOC, 175

Bohmer, Richard, 41

Bohr, Niels, 171, 172

Booz and Company, 133, 371, 378

Boston University, 125–26, 194, 198

Boudreau, John, 125, 269–83, 287, 397–98

boundaries, crossing, 47–49, 82, 84, 99, 164–65, 392–93

Bowers, Dave, 117

BP, 85, 86, 89, 90

Brandenburger, Adam, 293

bridging institutions, 244–46

British Sky Broadcasting, 99

Brown University, 114

Buchholz, Rogene, 382

Built to Last (Collins and Poras), 294, 297, 300, 304

Bullock, R. J., 121

Burruss, James, 189, 191

business schools
academic disciplines in, 339, 371, 373
barriers to useful research at, 333–40
changing reward system of, 152, 314, 316, 341–43, 380

competitive pressure on, 334–36, 354

criticisms of, 331, 355–56, 370

cross-disciplinary issues and, 381

enablers to useful research at, 340–47

faculty of, 338–39, 354–55, 379–80, 381–82

forces shaping research at, 333–34

government funding of, 337

impact of, 331

limitations of, 131

professionalizing, 380, 382

rankings of, 337–38, 354, 408

recruiters at, 336

relationship between universities and, 339–40

research centers at, 345–47

rigor and relevance at, 130–31, 172–73, 310–11, 340, 370, 376, 382

students at, 334, 336

trends in, 381–82

Business Week, 292, 297–98, 299, 301, 307

C

California, University of (Berkeley), 114–15

Cammann, Cortland, 121

Canon, 140, 142

Cascio, Wayne, 251–65, 267, 353, 356, 401, 411

Case Western Reserve, 212, 223, 401

Center for Creative Leadership, 131, 245

Center for Effective Organizations (CEO), 57–59, 69–71, 76, 124–25, 128, 133, 151, 245, 319, 421

Christensen, Clayton, 293, 299

Cialdini, Robert, 303

Circuit City, 133

CNN, 142

co-authors, 361–62

Cohen, Susan, 71, 125

Cole, Nina, 315–16

collaboration
between academics and consultants, 189–207
benefits of, 159–61
creating structure and processes for, 161–62, 226–27

The Innovator's Dilemma (Christensen), 294, 297, 298, 299, 305
In Search of Excellence (Peters and Waterman), 133, 290, 292, 293, 294, 296, 297, 298, 299–301, 304, 372
Institute for Scientific Information (ISI), 353, 355, 357
Institute for Social Research (ISR), 117, 121, 123, 127
Intellectual Capital (Stewart), 298, 305
International Association of Applied Psychology (IAAP), 312
Irving Oil, 175

J
James, William, 161
Japan Inc. (Ishinomori), 298, 306
Jenkins, Douglas, 121
Johns Hopkins University, 223
Journal of Applied Behavioral Science, 245
Journal of Applied Psychology, 254, 358, 359
Journal of Organizational Behavior, 358, 359
journals, 357–59. *See also individual journals*

K
Kahn, Bob, 117
Kanter, Rosabeth Moss, 293, 372
Kaplan, Robert, 293
Katz, Dan, 117
Katz, Ralph, 170
Kelman, Herb, 103
Khurana, Rakesh, 381
Klein, Jan, 72
knowing-doing relationships, 173–79, 180
knowledge
actionable vs. relevant, 148–49
boundaries, 47–49, 82, 392–93
co-creation of, 128–30
combining, from different communities, 16–17, 28, 69–71, 412–16
commercialization of, 10
distributed generation of, 10–11, 25
as linear value stream, 23–26
movement of, 16

as network, 26–27
principles for developing, 150–65
relevance of, 113
translating into tools, 323–24
The Knowledge-Creating Company (Nonaka and Takeuchi), 297, 298, 306
knowledge networks, 344
Knowledge Work Teams (KWT) research program, 62–71
Korn/Ferry, 133
Kotter, John, 293, 299
Kouzes, James, 293
Kram, Kathy, 198
Krishnan, M. S., 138, 139
Kuhn, Thomas, 222

L
Labor, U.S. Department of, 120
Labor and Employment Relations Association (LERA), 260–61, 264
Latham, Gary P., 12, 309–18, 353
Lawler, Edward E., III, 9–30, 57, 113–33, 135, 151, 323, 324, 353, 399, 402–3, 407–18
Lawrence, Paul, 151, 159, 170
leadership
business schools and, 375–79
teams, 189–90, 201–3
Leadership Pulse, 292
Leary, Timothy, 115
Ledford, Gerry, 121, 125
Lewin, Kurt, 37, 60, 104, 113, 123, 237, 243, 309, 391, 415
Likert, Rensis, 117, 132
Locke, Edwin, 313
London Business School, 82, 99
Lorsch, Jay, 151, 159, 369, 381

M
Macy, Barry, 121
Made to Stick (Heath and Heath), 270
management
communicating research to, 326–27
evidence-based, 108, 132
relationship of researchers and, 160–61
responsibilities and, 371, 375

high-commitment, high-
performance, 147
participation by, in research,
22–23, 28
research on behavior of, 106–7
understanding, 60
Organization Science, 358, 359
O'Toole, James, 125, 369–83
Ouchi, William, 293
Our Iceberg Is Melting (Kotter), 299
Out of the Crisis (Demming), 293, 294,
298, 304
Owens Corning, 170, 173

P
Pasteur, Louis, 171, 172, 401
Pasteur's Quadrant (Stokes), 171–72,
401
People & Strategy, 257
Pepperdine University, 212
performance management studies,
62–65
Perkins, Dennis, 121
Personnel Psychology, 254, 358, 359
Perspectives on Work, 260
Peters, Tom, 133, 295, 296, 298, 299–301,
372, 378
Peterson, Mark, 121
Pettigrew, Andrew, 104
Pfeffer, Jeffrey, 173, 293
phronesis, 213–14
Pink, Dan, 311, 316
Pisano, Gary, 41, 49
Planning for Quality (Juran), 294, 298,
304
Porter, Lyman, 115, 116
Porter, Michael, 293, 298
Posner, Barry, 293
practice
academics' attitude toward,
261–62
assessing effectiveness of existing,
205–6
bridging multiple communities of,
15–18
gap between research and, 9–15,
29–30, 171, 251–52, 402–3
impact of research on, 18–27
management books and, 295–96

organizations as artifacts shaped by,
14–15
university-based research programs
aimed at, 133
The Practice of Management (Drucker),
372
practitioners. *See also*
scholar-practitioners
collaboration between researchers
and, 311, 332, 343–47, 395–98
definition of, 251
perspectives of, 319–27
presenting research findings to,
240–42, 273–82, 410, 411
relationship between academics
and, 233–34, 235–46, 244–47,
262–63, 273, 322–23, 412
research evidence and, 264–65,
271–72, 309–16
Prahalad, C. K., 133, 137–45, 293, 400
problems
emphasis on solving, 324–25
relationships between fieldwork,
collaboration, and, 50–51
research motivated by, 39–42, 52,
61–62, 104, 109, 152, 332–33, 413
Procter & Gamble, 123
professional associations, 131, 251,
252–65, 312–13, 411. *See also*
individual associations
prospect theory, 270

Q
Quality of Employment study, 118
Quality of Worklife program, 14–15, 22,
118–23, 395, 414, 416

R
Ramaswamy, Venkat, 138, 139
Ram Dass, Baba, 115
recruiters, power of, 336
reductionism vs. holism, 122
Reengineering the Corporation (Hammer
and Champy), 293, 294, 304
Reflections, 245
relevance
business schools and, 172–73
dual, 206, 226
instrumental rationales for, 10–12

Schneider, Ben, 116
scholar-practitioners. *See also*
consultants
career path of, 149–52, 165–66
characteristics of, 165, 221
collaboration and, 161–62
definition of, 212–14, 234
depth of academic knowledge of,
236–39
education of, 211–12
effectiveness of, 221–23
focus of, 163–64
as independent operators, 224
learning from practice, 242–43
as research partners, 224–25
role of, 214–21
Schon, Donald, 293
scientist-practitioner model, 252
Seashore, Stan, 104, 117, 118, 123, 124
self-designing, 20
Senge, Donald, 293
Senior Leadership Teams (Wageman),
190
The 7 Habits of Highly Effective People
(Covey), 290, 292, 296, 297,
298
Siebel Systems, 175
Singapore Ministry of Manpower, 83,
85, 87, 88, 93–95, 97, 98, 99
Smith, Diana, 45, 49, 53
social psychology, 106–7
Social Science Research Network
(SSRN), 355
Society for Human Resource
Management (SHRM) Foundation,
131, 253–56, 264, 265, 312–13,
356
Society for Industrial and Organiza-
tional Psychology (SIOP), 252–53,
263, 264, 312–13, 315, 356
Society for Organizational Learning
(SoL), 245
Standard Chartered, 82
Steele, Fritz, 116
sticky findings
characteristics of, 270, 273–82
definition of, 269
implications of, 282–83
need for, 270–73

Stokes, Donald, 171–72
Strategic Fitness Process, 154, 156, 157,
160, 161–62, 163
strategic leadership forums (SLFs),
174–75
sustainability, 143
Sutton, Robert, 293, 299

T
Takeuchi, Hirotaka, 293
teams
assessing effectiveness of, 190
boosting performance of, 92–93
for conducting useful research,
415–16
cooperation within, 87
fault lines and, 91
healthy, 92
leadership, 189–90, 201–3
virtual learning signature of,
92–93
technological transitions, 169–70
Tenkasi, Ram, 72, 125, 211–28, 231, 401,
415
Theory Y management, 152
think tanks, 131
Thought Leaders Retreat, 255
Tichy, Noel, 129, 293
The Tipping Point (Gladwell), 270, 292,
296, 297
Toronto, University of, 315–16
total quality management (TQM), 174
Towers Watson, 133
Toyota, 142
TruePoint Partners, 150, 151, 156
TRW, 123, 124
Tucker, Anita, 49
turns, 219–20
Tushman, Mike, 82, 151, 169–82, 185,
378, 400, 401–2

U
United States Postal Service, 175
The Unseen Revolution (Drucker), 371
USC (University of Southern
California), 57, 69, 103, 124–25,
127, 401
Useem, Michael, 293
utility analysis, 271

About the Center for Effective Organizations (CEO)

CEO HAS A NATIONAL AND INTERNATIONAL reputation for research on a wide range of organizational effectiveness issues. It does research that actively involves corporations in researching and developing new knowledge about how organizations can be more effective and competitive. It is also widely recognized for its outstanding executive education programs in human resources management, organization design, and leadership. *Business Week* ranks them among the top three university programs.

Pioneering research in the areas of compensation, performance management, employee involvement, organization change and design, organizational learning, human resources management, and sustainable effectiveness has positioned CEO as a leading authority in these fields and given it the ability to inform and influence corporate practices.

CEO is regularly mentioned in published listings of university-based research centers as one of the top three organizational effectiveness research centers in the United States. *Fortune* magazine recently cited CEO as one of the major sources of research information on U.S. industrial competitiveness.

CEO research findings have been published in leading academic journals such as the *Academy of Management Journal*, *Academy of Management Review*, *Organizational Dynamics*, *Human Relations*, and the *Journal of Applied Psychology*. CEO research findings have been reported and quoted in many leading business and popular publications including *Business Week*, *Harvard Business Review*, *Fortune*, the *Financial Times*, the *Los Angeles Times*, the *New York Times*, the *Wall Street Journal*, and the *Washington Post*. They have also been featured on the *Today Show*, *CNN*, *MSNBC*, and *CNBC*.

CEO researchers have published over 30 books, including books that are targeted to an academic market and books that are written for practitioners.

CEO research scientists are thought leaders in their respective fields and have been honored by the Academy of Management, the American Compensation Association, the American Psychological Association, the Society for Human Resource Management, and other national and international professional associations.

About the Editors

Susan Albers Mohrman is senior research scientist at the Center for Effective Organizations (CEO) in the Marshall School of Business at the University of Southern California. Her research and publications focus on organizational design for lateral integration and flexibility, networks in basic science, design for sustainable effectiveness, organizational change and implementation, and research methodologies for bridging theory and practice. She is cofounder and a faculty director of CEO's certificate program in organization design. In the area of useful research, she is an editor and author of the *Handbook of Collaborative Management Research* (2007).

Edward E. Lawler III is Distinguished Professor of Business and Director of the Center for Effective Organizations in the Marshall School of Business at the University of Southern California. He has been honored as a top contributor to the fields of organizational development, human resources management, organizational behavior, and compensation. He is the author of over 350 articles and 43 books. His most recent books include *Achieving Strategic Excellence: An Assessment of Human Resource Organizations* (2006), *Built to Change* (2006), *The New American Workplace* (2006), *America at Work* (2006), *Talent: Making People Your Competitive Advantage* (2008), and *Achieving Excellence in Human Resource Management* (2009). For more information, visit http://www.edwardlawler.com and http://ceo.usc.edu.

Digital versions of individual chapters available

Individual *Useful Research* chapters are available for purchase as part of Berrett-Koehler's Fast Fundamentals digital whitepaper series. Quick and convenient, the PDF file will be downloaded instantly to your desktop.

You can purchase chapters by going to the Fast Fundamentals page on the Berrett-Koehler website, http://www.bkconnection.com/fastfundamentals, or by going to the *Useful Research* page on the Berrett-Koehler web site at, www.bkconnection.com/usefulresearch, and clicking on the "Purchase chapters of *Useful Research*" link.

BK Berrett–Koehler Publishers, Inc.
San Francisco, *www.bkconnection.com*   800.929.2929

Berrett–Koehler
Publishers

Berrett-Koehler is an independent publisher dedicated to an ambitious mission: *Creating a World That Works for All*.

We believe that to truly create a better world, action is needed at all levels—individual, organizational, and societal. At the individual level, our publications help people align their lives with their values and with their aspirations for a better world. At the organizational level, our publications promote progressive leadership and management practices, socially responsible approaches to business, and humane and effective organizations. At the societal level, our publications advance social and economic justice, shared prosperity, sustainability, and new solutions to national and global issues.

A major theme of our publications is "Opening Up New Space." Berrett-Koehler titles challenge conventional thinking, introduce new ideas, and foster positive change. Their common quest is changing the underlying beliefs, mindsets, institutions, and structures that keep generating the same cycles of problems, no matter who our leaders are or what improvement programs we adopt.

We strive to practice what we preach—to operate our publishing company in line with the ideas in our books. At the core of our approach is stewardship, which we define as a deep sense of responsibility to administer the company for the benefit of all of our "stakeholder" groups: authors, customers, employees, investors, service providers, and the communities and environment around us.

We are grateful to the thousands of readers, authors, and other friends of the company who consider themselves to be part of the "BK Community." We hope that you, too, will join us in our mission.

A BK Business Book

This book is part of our BK Business series. BK Business titles pioneer new and progressive leadership and management practices in all types of public, private, and nonprofit organizations. They promote socially responsible approaches to business, innovative organizational change methods, and more humane and effective organizations.

Berrett–Koehler
Publishers

A community dedicated to creating
a world that works for all

Visit Our Website: www.bkconnection.com

Read book excerpts, see author videos and Internet movies, read our authors'
blogs, join discussion groups, download book apps, find out about the BK
Affiliate Network, browse subject-area libraries of books, get special discounts, and more!

Subscribe to Our Free E-Newsletter, the *BK Communiqué*

Be the first to hear about new publications, special discount offers, exclusive articles, news about bestsellers, and more! Get on the list for our free
e-newsletter by going to **www.bkconnection.com**.

Get Quantity Discounts

Berrett-Koehler books are available at quantity discounts for orders of ten or
more copies. Please call us toll-free at (800) 929-2929 or email us at **bkp
.orders@aidcvt.com**.

Join the BK Community

BKcommunity.com is a virtual meeting place where people from around the
world can engage with kindred spirits to create a world that works for all.
BKcommunity.com members may create their own profiles, blog, start and
participate in forums and discussion groups, post photos and videos, answer
surveys, announce and register for upcoming events, and chat with others
online in real time. Please join the conversation!